Shari'a

Shari'a

ISLAMIC LAW IN THE CONTEMPORARY CONTEXT

Edited by Abbas Amanat and Frank Griffel

Stanford University Press
Stanford, California
2007

Stanford University Press
Stanford, California

Printed in the United States of America on acid-free, archival-quality paper

Library of Congress Cataloging-in-Publication Data

Shari'a : Islamic law in the contemporary context / edited by Abbas Amanat and Frank Griffel.
p. cm.
Includes bibliographical references and index.
ISBN 978-0-8047-5639-6 (cloth : alk. paper)
1. Islamic law—Interpretation and construction. I. Amanat, Abbas. II. Griffel, Frank.
KBP440.3.S53 2007
340.5'9—dc22 2007014097

Typeset by Binghamton Valley Composition in Minion, 10/14

CONTENTS

PREFACE

THE IDEA OF THIS BOOK first came to us in response to public debates in recent years about Islamic law and its relevance in our time, especially how the different positions in Islamic law respond to such issues as civil liberties, gender, ethnic and religious diversity, toleration and violence, freedom of expression, and the relationship between the sacred and the secular. The chapters in this volume address the role and the status of Islamic law (Shari'a) not only in Muslim societies, where it is partly incorporated into the civil and penal codes, but in a broader context of our time and in reference to issues of modernity. Despite its great importance for modern Muslim thought and for current international turmoil, contemporary Shari'a has rarely been covered in depth in the literature.

In recent years Western attention has turned to debates among Muslims on what Islam forbids, allows, or advocates. Moreover, it has brought into focus the problem of authority and representation: who is qualified to interpret the law, form opinions, and issue judgments. These discussions center largely on the content, applicability, and implementation of Islamic law. One can argue that the failure of many modern Muslim nation-states to live up to their initial promises led to a widespread debate on the need for a return to Shari'a as an idealized system whose application has yet to be fully realized. Muslim fundamentalists in particular claim that Shari'a and its sources, the Qur'an and the *ḥadīth*, constitute a divine law that regulates all aspects of Muslim life, as well as Muslim societies and Muslim states, in the most perfect and everlasting way. Muslim modernists, a far less audible voice these days, on the other hand, criticize the old approaches to Shari'a by traditional Muslim jurists as obsolete and instead advocate innovative approaches to Shari'a that accommodate more pluralist and relativist views within a democratic framework. Moreover, multiple sources of judicial authority in the Muslim world pose obstacles to the formulation of Shari'a as a normative system and contribute to ambiguities concerning the meaning and usage of Islamic law. *Shari'a: Islamic Law in the Contemporary Context* addresses these implications and ambiguities, the current application of Shari'a, and the potential of developing into a modern legal system and, alternatively, the obstacles it poses as a barrier to Muslim modernity.

As co-organizers of the workshop in February 2003 on the theme of this volume, sponsored by the Council on Middle East Studies at the Yale Center for International and Area Studies (now the Whitney and Betty MacMillan Center for International and Area Studies at Yale), and as coeditors of this volume, we would like to thank the center's staff and particularly its anonymous donor for making the workshop possible that led to this publication. We also thank the other participants in the workshop and our students and colleagues at Yale for their contributions during the workshop. Special thanks go to Tanya Wiedeking, Fiona Ford, and the editorial staff at Stanford University Press for their help in improving chapters of this book.

Abbas Amanat, Frank Griffel
New Haven, December 2006

Shari'a

1 INTRODUCTION

Frank Griffel

WHEN MUSLIMS DISCUSS the ethical imperatives of their faith regarding contemporary moral issues such as abortion, stem-cell research, or the treatment of racial or religious minorities, they will at one point consider what Shari'a says about these questions. All normative discussions within Islam, as well as between Muslims and members of other faiths, center on the content of Shari'a, a concept that can be roughly translated as Islamic religious law. What many Muslims regard as being determined by Shari'a, however, includes much that modern Westerners would not recognize as law. Handbooks on Shari'a have been in circulation since the ninth century and are still widely used by Muslim scholars today. A traditional handbook of Shari'a starts with acts of worship (Arabic *ʿibādāt*), for example, the five daily prayers and the ritual purity required to perform prayers, the month of fasting, or the alms tax. Next the manuals move to issues concerning human relationships (*muʿāmalāt*), such as marriage, divorce, inheritance, commerce, taxation, and war. These the modern Westerner might easily recognize as legal issues. However, Shari'a goes beyond what in the West would be considered legal discourse, for it extends to matters concerning proprieties of clothing, conduct between spouses, filial piety, behavior at funerals, and other questions that Westerners would treat not as legal, but as moral issues or mere etiquette. At the same time, Shari'a also provides answers to the most vital moral questions of the contemporary world, such as the legitimacy of violence or torture, just war, suicide and self-sacrifice, or the means of combating injustice.[1]

Over the centuries of Muslim history a vast amount of literature has been generated discussing these normative questions. The first impression one gets from looking at this library is that of continuity and congruency. Legal authorities from many different centuries of Muslim history are quoted to determine the response of Shari'a to today's moral questions. When asked about the notion of just war between nations and the rules for conducting warfare, for instance, contemporary Muslim scholars often refer to one of the earliest treatments of this matter, that of the jurist al-Shaybānī (d. 805).[2] On achieving a balance between combating injustice and not interfering in other people's affairs, the jurist and theologian al-Ghazālī (d. 1111) is still regarded as one of the most prolific experts.[3] Al-Ghazālī, who was also one of the foremost authorities on legal theory in Islam, understood Shari'a as human efforts to derive congruent rules and norms from divine sources. He stressed that although the sources of Shari'a are divine and go back to a revealed text, the establishment of Shari'a is a distinctly human enterprise that requires its own kind of scholarship. During the course of its development this understanding changed, and by the twentieth century the meaning of the term *Shari'a* had been subtly but fundamentally transformed. Contemporary Shari'a is in many ways different from what classical scholars such as al-Ghazālī had in mind. This collection of essays is devoted to a further understanding of what Shari'a means in the contemporary context.

SHARI'A IN THE CLASSICAL MUSLIM PERIOD

"Islamic religious law" is at best only an approximate translation of the term *Shari'a*. The origin of this word is Arabic, yet today it appears in all languages used by Muslims, including English.[4] It evolved as a technical term in the early period of Islam during the seventh and eighth centuries. Originally the Arabic word *sharīʿa* described the practical aspect of religion. This is how it is used in the Qur'an, for instance, where God is quoted as saying, "We have set you on a *sharīʿa* of command, so follow it" (Q 45.18). But the word *sharīʿa* does not play an important role in the Qur'an; this is, in fact, the only time it appears.[5] In the context of this Qur'anic chapter (*sūra*) the verse refers to the fact that Islam is a new religion that is distinct from, for instance, Judaism or Christianity. Its distinction comes with new kinds of worship and new ritual duties—the five daily prayers, for instance—and most interpreters translate *sharīʿa* in this verse as "rites," "the right way of practicing the religion," or simply as "the way." Muslim lexicographers give a wide range of explanations of how the Arabic word *sharīʿa*, which initially referred to the place around a well and whose original meaning may have also been connected to "path," "road," or "highway," came to refer to the correct way of practicing a religion.[6] These shifts of meaning are not always clear. What is important is that within Muslim discourse the word *Shari'a* came to designate the rules and regulations that govern the lives of Muslims.

Once it became clear that Islam had its own ritual duties and rules for human actions, these regulations needed to be identified. The academic discipline whereby Muslim scholars describe and explore Shari'a is called *fiqh*, Islamic jurisprudence. Doing *fiqh* is a human activity and cannot be ascribed to God or to His prophets, although revelation and prophetic insights are, in fact, the sources from which the Muslim scholar who does *fiqh*—the *faqīh* or Muslim jurisprudent—takes his clues. The discipline of *fiqh* arose in the early days of Islam, during the eighth century or probably even earlier.[7] By the early ninth century Muslim scholars had developed two or three different methodologies for how the norms of Shari'a can be determined. Most of them place the Qur'an and the practice of the Prophet Muhammad at the center of Muslim jurisprudence and differ only regarding the balance between these two sources and the weight of third sources such as commonly practiced law or legal analogies. These slightly different approaches to the sources of jurisprudence are reflected in four different schools (sing. *madhhab*) of law, each of which has its own authorities and teaching tradition.[8]

The centrality of the Qur'an for Shari'a stems more from theological considerations than from the ability to generate substantive legal rulings from its text. Although a number of the most central judgments in Islamic law are derived from the Qur'an, the majority of rulings in Shari'a derive from the practice of the Prophet Muhammad. Information about his actions and legal decisions was collected from oral reports. These reports were gathered as *ḥadīth*. Since the ninth century they have been available in six large collections that Sunni Muslims regard as canonical.[9] Muslim jurisprudence in the classical period aimed at reducing all new legal problems to existing rulings in the Qur'an and the corpus of collected *ḥadīth*s. Because there are only a few legal rulings in the Qur'an, and because even the great number of cases in the *ḥadīth* corpus cannot exhaust all future legal problems, Muslim jurists understood that the most important technique in Muslim jurisprudence is to reduce new cases to ones that are mentioned in these two sources. This was done by legal analogy (*qiyās*). Thus the Qur'an, *ḥadīth*, analogy with the rulings contained in these two, and a fourth source, the consensus of legal scholars (*ijmāʿ*), which has always been of limited relevance, make up the four sources of classical Muslim jurisprudence (*uṣūl al-fiqh*) for Sunni Islam, which has based most of its rulings in

Shari'a on the example given by the Prophet Muhammad's actions. In Shiite Islam the actions and sayings of the early imams, especially the first imam, ʿAlī ibn Abī Ṭālib (d. 661), and the sixth, Jaʿfar al-Ṣādiq (d. 765), are an important additional source.

The complexities of legal theory soon made Muslim jurisprudence into a professional discipline with its own experts, handbooks, and encyclopedias. Practitioners went through a long and thorough education in professional schools, *madrasa*s or seminars, such as the influential al-Azhar college in Cairo. If one had asked two hundred years ago what Shari'a was, the answer would not have been difficult. It was the norms studied by students at places such as al-Azhar from teachers who had gone through a long and rigorous education in *fiqh*. These authorities stood in a scholarly tradition with earlier ones and wrote books in the established genres of legal literature. After graduation the students of Shari'a became legal experts and collaborated in the implementation of Shari'a in Islamic countries. Two hundred years ago Shari'a was the law of Muslim lands.

But *law* is not the right word to describe Shari'a before the nineteenth century. There were no documents, no paragraphs, and no commentaries that one could refer to as "the law." Rather, Shari'a was a practice and a process of deriving law and of adjudicating disputes. These processes were associated with specific institutions and techniques of education and adjudication. The form of derivation and instruction of Shari'a cannot be separated from its content. "Law" was established not by issuing legal codes or by the decisions of principal authorities such as high courts or central administrations, but rather by the rules of its legal discourse. In traditional Sunni religious writing, texts always refer to previous texts; by discussing the rulings and decisions of previous generations, these texts set a standard of what is accepted by the community. This led Sunni jurisprudence to become a legal discourse whose first source of normativity was the variety of the views discussed and accepted by its scholars.[10] Before the nineteenth century Shari'a was never understood as an abstract code, but rather as a series of commentaries on particular practices and of commentaries upon those commentaries.[11]

It has already been said that in classical Arabic the word *Shari'a* refers to the law that God has ordained through revelation.[12] Shari'a is understood as divine law and practiced in a realm that connects religion and law. Historically, law and religion have always been close companions, not only in Islam but also in the Western tradition. Plato (427–347 BCE), for instance, requires that all citizens of a polis must accept three basic religious tenets, namely, that there are gods, that they care for humans, and that they cannot be easily bribed by sacrifices given on their altars.[13] People are to believe that the gods implement the laws and that they punish humans for transgressions. Most legal traditions of antiquity include the belief that the gods gave humans their laws. This is the case in the Mosaic law of Judaism that developed in the books of Exodus and Leviticus, believed to be composed around the seventh century BCE. The notion of a divine law that has its source in prophecy, that is, in the verbal pronunciation of divine norms, imperatives, and promises of rewards, as well as punishments, became fundamental for all three monotheistic religions of the Mediterranean basin, Judaism, Christianity, and Islam. Even when the societies shaped by these religions consider themselves thoroughly secularized, their practice of law often cannot hide the religious provenance of many of its procedures. Courthouses are designed to produce respect and awe and often resemble ancient temples. Judges and lawyers dress in robes, just as ancient priests did. People's behavior at court follows certain procedures that resemble a ceremony. They stand when an individual in a special robe—the judge—enters the room where the law is practiced and rise when this individual leaves the room. Lawyers begin their address with certain formulas, such as "May it please the court," and end it with a "pray" for relief. A higher authority than their own words must back everything they say in court. Indeed, they do best if they do not use their own words but quote from higher authorities.[14]

These similarities suggest that the practice of law and the practice of religion are not as far apart as they seem at first. There is a structural similarity between the two because both look at superior authorities.[15] Working with authority in both cases means that they work with authoritative texts. The meaning of these texts and the authority they convey are not within them but are established through the reading of these texts and their interpretation. A constitution, for instance, conveys authority not only from the words it contains but also through the context that is known to its reader, namely, that a political community adopted the text as a foundational document for the norms that govern political actions.

Islam's understanding of divine law arose from the same tradition as Judaism and Christianity. Muslim jurists accepted the validity of the Mosaic law, as well as the law practiced by Christians. The Muslim point of view on earlier laws that are based on revelation assumes that they are, like Islam, genuinely inspired by divine decree. They have, however, been abrogated by the clear message of the

Qur'an and the law that comes with it. Islamic revelation is considered a more fruitful and a more precise source of divine law than any earlier revelation. However, although there are many similarities in these three traditions, there is an important difference. Compared with the Old and the New Testaments, the character of the Muslim revelation is a much more literal address to its reader. In the Qur'an God speaks to Muhammad in the second person ("you") and through him to the whole of humanity. Often Muhammad is bypassed, and the "you" in the text is an address to humanity as a whole. The only parallel in the two earlier books of revelation would be the Ten Commandments of Exodus 20.2–17 and those passages in the four Gospels of the New Testament in which Jesus, who is regarded as part of the Holy Trinity, is quoted literally. These words can be understood as God's direct address to mankind. Other parts of the Old and the New Testaments are often considered equal in holiness and authority. Their textual manifestation, however, is that of a text written by humans to humans, even if the authors are considered prophets or evangelists and the words directly inspired by God. The narration in the Qur'an is a more straightforward imperative from God to humanity. The readers find themselves directly addressed—a powerful feature of the text that might be responsible for much of the success of Islam as a world religion.

The most important branch of Muslim jurisprudence, that of Sunni Islam, emerged in the ninth century CE from a dispute about the nature of Muslim revelation. Rationalist theologians of the now-defunct Muʿtazilite school of theology had suggested that the Qur'an is a document that God had created like any other of His creations. When this view was adopted by the caliph al-Ma'mūn (reg. 813–33), it prompted a vigorous reaction from a more conservative group of Muslim scholars. These scholars were the nucleus of what is today called Sunni Islam. They argued that the Qur'an represents God's speech, and as such, it is one of God's eternal attributes. Therefore, unlike any other of God's creations, the Qur'an cannot be created, but must be coeternal with God. The close connection between the text of the Qur'an and of God as its author almost led to an identification of the two. The dogma of the existence of the Qur'an from eternity was an undisputed cornerstone of Sunnism from the ninth century to the beginning of the twentieth. Even if this dogma plays almost no role within contemporary Muslim debates on the Qur'an, it has deeply shaped the Muslim understanding of its revelation. This is true not only for Sunni Muslims—who make up 80 percent of the contemporary Muslim community—but in a similar way also for Shiites and other smaller branches of Islam. For Muslims, the

Qur'an is the door between the manifest world of our experience and the transcendence of God. It is the bridge between the Creator and His creation. Some interpreters have coined the word *inliberation* for this process.[16] In Christianity the divine word (the *logos* of John 1.1) became flesh in Jesus Christ as its incarnation, but in Islam the divine word became a book.

This difference may lead one to the conclusion that Islam developed a unique understanding toward divine law and its sources that is different from that of Judaism or Christianity. The contemporary significance of Shari'a, one may argue, can only be explained out of the history of its central role within Islamic scholarship of the past. Shari'a is the *Wesenskern*, the essential core of Islam, the quintessence of the true Islamic spirit, and the decisive expression of Islamic thought.[17] This essentialist view leaves little room for Shari'a to change or to be understood differently by different generations of Muslims. In contrast, this book wants to explore how the contemporary understanding of Muslims is different from that of previous generations. An essentialist view, for instance, downplays the strength of the intellectual convulsion that has been caused by the confrontation with European thought and culture since the early nineteenth century. Modern Muslim theology, which is the ultimate home of jurisprudence of the divine law, is in many ways different from its predecessors during classical Islam and the Muslim Middle Ages. We have already said that the dogma of the uncreatedness of the Qur'an plays almost no role in contemporary debates. Having been taught and discussed for many centuries, it flew out of the textbooks of Muslim theology, so to speak, when Muhammad ʿAbduh (1849–1905), the most influential Muslim theologian of the period around 1900, published a book in which he said that the Qur'anic text and its recitation are created. This and his casual remark that he could not comprehend the historical dispute on the eternity of the Qur'an prompted harsh criticism from his peers at al-Azhar.[18] Later, when his student Muḥammad Rashīd Riḍā (1865–1935) reedited ʿAbduh's work on this subject, he omitted the controversial passage and added a long footnote that responds to the complaints.[19]

Rashīd Riḍā's reaction illustrates the ambiguity of modern Muslim thinkers toward the classical heritage of Muslim theology and jurisprudence. On the one hand, they wanted to avoid the impression of introducing innovations that prior generations of Muslim authorities considered heresy. On the other hand, they understood that some teachings had simply become obsolete. They recognized and often preached the necessity for widespread *ijtihād*, intellectual efforts that lead to new kinds of teachings. A widespread strategy in dealing with the dilemma between tradition and innovation was the silent omission of outdated teachings even if they had been of key significance in the past. Cornerstones of classical Sunni dogma, such as God's determination of all events in His creation, the "acquisition" (*kasb*) of human actions, or the incapacity of humans to develop sound moral judgments independent from revelation, are hardly mentioned in contemporary Muslim discourse.

SHARI'A IN THE ERA OF MODERNIZATION AND WESTERNIZATION

The nature of Shari'a, its practice, and its understanding changed most drastically during the nineteenth and twentieth centuries. The crushing defeat of the Egyptian-Ottoman army by Napoleon's expeditionary force and the short-lived French occupation of Egypt (1798–1802) led in the subsequent decades to several circles of modernization in Egypt and the Ottoman Empire. Other Muslim nations followed suit. Although the reform programs and the results were not the same and did not happen at the same time, each was guided by the perception that traditional Islamic law, the Shari'a practiced in the seminaries and implemented as the law of the land, was an obstacle to progress and antithetical to modernization.[20] The reforms affected the educational as well as the legal system and led to a decline of the traditional *faqīh*'s significance, status, and self-confidence. The government opened secular schools inspired by the European polytechnics, first for the military and bureaucracy elites and later for all higher education. In the Ottoman Empire the government took control over the schools away from Muslim scholars and opened its own secondary schools during the Tanzimat era (1839–79). The new elites of the increasingly modernizing Muslim countries were educated outside the curriculum of Shari'a studies. They challenged the belief that an education in Shari'a was sufficient—or even helpful—to administer the Muslim countries and their judicial system.

Most important, the state expanded its new ideas of jurisdiction into areas previously reserved for Shari'a. It introduced legal codes that were influenced—sometimes copied wholesale—from European prototypes. During the Tanzimat era the Ottoman Empire formed legislative councils that were beyond the control of Shari'a-trained jurists. They drew up the Penal Code (1840 and 1859), the Commercial Code (1850), and the Imperial Land Code (1858), all influenced by French law. With the new codes came a system of secular courts that replaced Shari'a courts and restricted their activities to the laws of personal statutes such as marriage and some transactions such as inheritance. This created an institutional differentiation between "religious" and "worldly" (secular) law. Finally, even the practice of Shari'a law became the subject of government regulation. In 1877 the Ottoman government issued the Mejelle, intended as a civil code based on Shari'a. It codified large areas of Islamic law, mainly concerning transactions (*muʿāmalāt*), in order to apply it in secular courts and make it binding on all subjects, regardless of religion.[21]

Most Muslim governments followed the example of the Ottoman Empire and marginalized the Shari'a that was studied in the seminaries and applied in courts at the beginning of the nineteenth century. Those countries that came under direct European control, such as Algeria in 1830, India in 1858, Tunisia in 1881, or Egypt in 1882, often adopted the legal system of the colonial power. In hindsight, it is astonishing that this process met with little resistance from traditionalist legal scholars.[22] This may be explained by the fact that changes, which were ordered from above, were slow to reach the populace. The reforms came step by step over a long period of time. Nowhere did they lead to an outright abandonment of Shari'a. Throughout the Middle East the decision was made to maintain two separate legal systems, one based on Shari'a and the other on Western codes and procedures.[23] In Egypt Shari'a courts were reorganized during the 1880s in a hierarchical system of tribunals. This system has been adopted in most other Islamic countries, including Saudi Arabia.[24] Traditionalist Muslim scholars—the *ʿulamā'* who had been educated at colleges such as al-Azhar—continued to play an important role in society, particularly in education. At the turn of the twentieth century the majority of Egyptian Muslims were still receiving their education from religious schools.[25] Traditional Shari'a still mattered a great deal for them. Although it had lost much of its significance in the courts, it still dominated expectations of moral conduct and virtuous behavior. Stripped from the practice of actual law, Shari'a jurists still dominated the moral discourse of Muslim countries. They continued to be asked for their guidance, and they issued their views in the form of *fatwā*s, nonbinding legal opinions that carried a moral weight equivalent to the authority of their authors. In principle, at least, traditional Shari'a always made a distinction between law and morality. Unlike European jurisprudence, however, where the law is taught in its own faculty and where morality is a branch of philosophy and the humanities, the practice of Shari'a includes all branches of normative human behavior.

A new era of the meaning of Shari'a began during the 1930s to the 1950s and coincided with the full implementation of the legal reforms started in the nineteenth century. During this time Egypt gradually abolished Shari'a courts—and with them the system of parallel legislation—by amalgamating them with the civil courts.[26] This provoked opposition from the Muslim Brotherhood, a religious, philanthropic, and political movement founded in 1928 by Ḥasan al-Bannā (1906–49). By now Egyptian publishing houses had started to issue literature on classical Islamic jurisprudence. The textbooks of traditionalist education became accessible to all, and Shari'a could be studied as a discrete subject, like all others.[27] No particular training was necessary to participate in debates regarding the content and proper role of Shari'a. Subsequently the word *Shari'a* assumed a new set of meanings.

In the 1920s reformers such as Muḥammad Rashīd Riḍā and ʿAbd al-Razzāq al-Sanhūrī (1895–1971) argued that French law was culturally inappropriate for Egypt and that the legitimacy of laws should be judged against Shari'a.[28] In the late 1940s and early 1950s leaders of the Muslim Brotherhood such as ʿAbd al-Qādir ʿAwda (d. 1955), a civil-court judge educated in French law, turned this argument in a radical direction. ʿAwda claimed that a Muslim's first commitment has to be toward the implementation of Shari'a. Muslims were obligated, he said, not only to ignore but even to combat those laws that contradict Shari'a.[29] The publication of Sayyid Quṭb's (1906–66) programmatic pamphlet *Milestones* in 1964 moved the call for the application of Shari'a to the center of the new Islamist movement.[30] Sayyid Quṭb is typical of this new kind of contemporary Shari'a theorist. He was self-taught and had no formal training in the Islamic sciences. The formative period of his religious thinking fell into a time when the works of the conservative Muslim theologian Ibn Taymiyya (d. 1328) were rediscovered and reintroduced into Muslim discourse. During the 1920s Muḥammad Rashīd Riḍā chose a number of short programmatic texts by Ibn Taymiyya to be serialized in his widely read journal *al-Manār*.[31] Ibn Taymiyya had lived at a time of religious confrontation between Islam and other religions, when the Crusaders' occupation of Muslim lands had just ended and the effects of the Mongol invasion were very present. His sharp distinction between Islam and non-Islam seemed to provide applicable answers for Egyptians of the 1920s and 1930s. Although nominally independent since 1923, Egypt still hosted British troops and depended greatly on decisions made in London or by the British high commissioner in Cairo. Ibn Taymiyya, who in the thirteenth century had preached the virtues of Islamic identity and *jihād* against infidel rule and domination, appeared like a neglected voice that inspired the newly formed Islamist movement with his uncompromising stand against any kind of non-Shari'a rule.

In the law-finding processes of traditional Muslim jurisprudence, Ibn Taymiyya was one of the many voices in the concert of Shari'a. Sayyid Quṭb and others in his generation, however, were looking for a set of identifiable rules that make up *the* Shari'a. This quest is most evident in Quṭb's influential commentary on the Qur'an.[32] Once those monolithic rules had been identified, any law that did not conform to them was branded a violation of Islam. For Islamists such as Sayyid Quṭb, divine law was understood as a law of absolute validity—the one single law that God has given to His creation and that all lower law has to conform to. Sayyid Quṭb's understanding of Shari'a is significantly different from that of classical Islam. His usage of *Shari'a* must be studied with other parameters in mind than those that have been developed for the study of classical Muslim jurisprudence. The Muslim Brotherhood's view of Shari'a never included the four classical schools of law as its manifestations.[33] But no inquiry into contemporary Shari'a can do without the results of the study of classical Islam and its jurisprudence. The example of the intellectual connection between Sayyid Quṭb and Ibn Taymiyya shows that the dynamic of contemporary Muslim thinking is such that it always connects itself to a context in classical Islam.

Normative practices, as well as the legal education according to traditional processes of Shari'a, are still alive in many Muslim countries. Modernized versions of a traditional *madrasa* education in the legal theory of Shari'a (*uṣūl al-fiqh*) can still be found in such places as al-Azhar in Cairo or the Qarawiyyīn mosque and university in Fès, Morocco. Many of the modern universities in the Middle East offer courses of study that focus solely on Islamic law. Their graduates often have no chance of being integrated into the modern Western-oriented legal apparatus. The educational goal of these courses of study is, in fact, not very different from that of the classical *madrasa* education. All these places use modern textbooks that aim at enabling the student to read, understand, and do active research on the classical body of literature on Shari'a, most important, the works on its methodology (*uṣūl al-fiqh*).[34] Yet the perspective on Shari'a that these new textbooks take is often a distinctly modern one in the sense that Shari'a is approached from the perspective of a codified law. Today's students of Shari'a often encounter it in the form of articles embedded in Western-inspired codes. Modern professors sometimes clothe the Islamic legal tradition in Western garb in order to convince law professionals at the Western-inspired law schools that Shari'a is as modern and universal as the Western tradition is perceived to be. The diverse tradition offered in the classical literature on Shari'a and its theory has effectively become conflated with what in the Islamic context is called *qānūn*, the law practices in contemporary Muslim states, which are mostly imported from the West.[35]

Where the tradition of the classical approach to find legal judgments among the diverse opinions of a specific school of law survived, it often merged with the modernist understanding of Shari'a as the one and only eternal divine law, which can be expressed in simple articles. This is also true for Shiite Islam, where the tradition of premodern Shari'a scholarship managed to survive more substantially than in Sunni Islam. The Shiite community continuously upheld a system of institutionalized learning in the *madrasa*s and *ḥawza*s of Najaf in Iraq or Qom and Mashhad in Iran. When their graduates were excluded from the modern legal system, the schools were nonetheless able to generate their own financial resources from among the Shiite community. Before 1979 they had never come under the control of the expanding modern nation-state. Unlike key Sunni institutions such as al-Azhar, the Shiite *madrasa*s and *ḥawza*s did not become subject to several waves of modernization of their curricula and an effective bureaucratization of their teaching activities. The Shiite schools, on the other hand, lost much of their social base to state bureaucrats, populist dictators, liberal modernists, and Muslim activists, none of them trained in Islamic law. What was left of the elaborate *madrasa*-based system of Shiite jurisprudence in the 1960s was of little legal consequence for Iranian and Iraqi society.

From the dwindling normative relevance of the study of Shari'a—both Shiite and Sunni—emerged during the second part of the twentieth century a Shari'a that often had little to do with the law that was taught at the *madrasa*s of old and practiced at the premodern Shari'a courts. This new type of Shari'a was advocated by Islamic activists who were unified by their opposition to the secularizing state and its law. During the twentieth century intellectuals such as Ḥasan al-Bannā, Sayyid Quṭb, and Abū l-Aʿlā Mawdūdī (1904–79), who were self-trained in their competence of Islamic law, led the call for the implementation of a Shari'a that in this form had never existed in premodern times.

SHARI'A IN THE CONTEMPORARY CONTEXT

Shari'a today means different things to different Muslims. This volume brings together contributions that look closely at the various meanings of Shari'a for Muslims today. Some of them connect more closely to the classical period of Islam, when Shari'a was the law of the land, others to the modernist period, when Islamist thinkers revived the concept of Shari'a and made attempts to establish a unified vision of what Shari'a entails. Each of these contributions focuses on a small facet of what Shari'a can mean to contemporary Muslims.

The process of canonization of law during the nineteenth and twentieth centuries has shaped the understanding of Shari'a probably more than anything else. Many Muslims today understand Shari'a as a canonized code of law that can be easily compared with the European codes, which were introduced during this period. In the 1940s ʿAbd al-Qādir ʿAwda wrote a detailed comparison of the criminal justice legislation of Shari'a and the French legal tradition that was and still is practiced in Egypt. The book is still an influential bestseller.[36] It promotes the idea that the content of Shari'a is methodologically on an equal footing with European law, and the two can thus be easily compared with one another. ʿAwda stood at the beginning of the movement that rediscovered Shari'a as a source for contemporary Muslim law. Because he was a judge active in the Egyptian judicial system, his legal thinking was deeply rooted in European-style codes of law. His generation of Muslim thinkers—and this includes such influential authors as Sayyid Quṭb, as well as Mawdūdī—shaped the contemporary understanding of Shari'a as a law where the individual sayings of the Prophet Muhammad collected in the books of *ḥadīth*, as well as the individual verses of the Qur'an, are viewed almost as if they were paragraphs in a Muslim civil code.

This understanding has profound consequences. In the premodern period, when Shari'a law was practiced by Muslim jurists, these verses and sayings of the Prophet were contextualized in the process of law. Legal literature of a secondary nature, namely, procedural law and its commentaries, played an important role in this process. Almost every legally important *ḥadīth* was surrounded by interpretations that suggested or demanded how the law that derived from it was to be practiced. In the case of apostasy from Islam, for instance, Muslim jurists developed a certain legal institution that almost entirely circumvented the harsh ruling that can be found in the *ḥadīth* corpus. There Muhammad is quoted as having said, "Whoever changes his religion, kill him!"[37] In the early period of Muslim law, jurists agreed that before this imperative is to be applied, an accused apostate must be given a chance to repent and return to Islam. This "invitation to repent" (*istiṭāba*) soon became a legal loophole that prevented the application of the harsh law of apostasy in all but the most manifest cases, namely, when someone was intentionally provoking the Muslim community and its judges. When Islamist activists managed to apply the law of apostasy in the 1980s in the Sudan and in the 1990s in Egypt, they disregarded all premodern injunctions and did not adress any invitation to repent (*istiṭāba*) to their victims. They rather pointed to the prophetical *ḥadīth* and demanded that its literal contents be put into practice.[38]

Similar observations can be made in applications of the law of adultery. Again, there is a seemingly clear injunction in the Qur'an that demands the harsh punishment of one hundred lashes for those involved in extramarital sexual relations (Q 24.2). In the premodern period, however, the procedural law set huge obstacles before a public flogging could take place—some of them prompted by ambiguities in the text of the Qur'an (cf. Q 4.15–16). In recent cases in Nigeria, for instance, the Muslim jurists neglected the textual ambiguities, as well as the traditional procedural law of Shari'a, and focused entirely on the injunction in verse 24.2, as if it were a paragraph in a code of law. Hence codification has often limited the flexibility of premodern Shari'a law. In the premodern period individual circumstances were highly important and often influenced the ruling more than abstract legal reasoning. In a codified law, a defined case simply needs to be matched with an established ruling, and this often leaves little room for flexibility.

In contemporary Shari'a one also comes across what is effectively a pick-and-choose mentality with regard to the rulings that were practiced in the premodern period. Authors such as ʿAwda, Sayyid Quṭb, and Mawdūdī meant to take the norms they identified as being Shari'a not from the classical and premodern periods of Islam—that is, the period between 700 and 1800—but rather from the earliest period, before 661. They believed that after 661, when the era of the "four rightly guided caliphs" ended, corruption set in and created a distance from the original spirit of Shari'a that increased with time. Hence these twentieth-century thinkers focused even more on the Qur'an and the *ḥadīth* corpus than classical Shari'a does, and they neglected the procedural law that was developed in the centuries after 661. This is a thoroughly "modern" understanding of the earliest Muslim sources.

Pick-and-choose also applies to the contents of the law. Both the earliest sources of Shari'a and its practice in premodern Muslim societies set few limitations on the possession of slaves, for instance. Yet no contemporary advocate of Shari'a would argue that today's Muslims should apply these rules and become slaveholders.[39] In cases where the direct comparison between Shari'a and the tradition of Western law is too much in favor of the latter, proponents of Shari'a often abandon it. In fact, when contemporary Muslims call for a revival of Shari'a, they can mean a range of different options. For some, revival may include only the adaptation of selected rulings that go back to the Prophet Muhammad.

For others, it means the establishment of an allegedly pure Shari'a legislation in which the whole Western tradition of law is replaced with a code of law that is based on one of the many types of premodern Shari'a scholarship. However, as the example of slavery shows, every contemporary call for Shari'a, even the purest, is in practice a call for a mixed judicial system in which premodern Shari'a legislation is to some degree enriched or replaced by the Western legal tradition in addition to the replacement of the discursive nature of premodern Shari'a scholarship by an understanding of Shari'a as a code of law.

Language is another aspect where the contemporary call for premodern Shari'a legislation reveals its distinctly modern character. The earliest sources of Islam, including the Qur'an and the *ḥadīth* corpus, are in Arabic, the same language that is used by many interpreters today. The meaning of certain words in that language, however, changed over the centuries. Shahrough Akhavi discusses in Chapter 8 a contemporary debate among Iranian intellectuals about what the Arabic word *ḥukūma* really means. This debate is just one of many reflections of the Islamist concept of God's sovereignty of earth—God's *ḥākimiyya*—as it first appears in the works of Mawdūdī and Sayyid Quṭb in the mid-twentieth century. This idea has become a key element of most Islamist political practice today. The Qur'an contains numerous verses where it is said that God is the one who judges human affairs. He is the only one whose judgment humans should heed. Hence they should adopt these judgments as their own. Qur'an 5.44–45 says, "Those who do not judge by what God has revealed, they are the unbelievers . . . and the wrongdoers."

The Qur'an expresses this judgment with the Arabic verb *ḥakama*, which may simply be translated as "to judge, to pass judgment." For Sayyid Quṭb and Mawdūdī, who read these verses with a contemporary understanding of the Arabic vocabulary, the verb *ḥakama* means not only "to judge" but also "to rule." It is, in fact, among the many small changes in the Arabic language over the past centuries that the verb *ḥakama* also assumed the meaning "to rule." The active participle "he who passes judgment" or "a judge," *ḥākim* in classical Arabic, may in modern standard Arabic also mean "he who rules" or "a ruler." Yet this meaning is not known to have applied to the Arabic of the Qur'an, and none of the classical commentators of the Qur'an reads it that way. For them, the verses that use *ḥakama* refer to God's judgment about human deeds, and not to God's rule on earth.[40] Verses such as the quoted Q 5.44–45, however, are, for Sayyid Quṭb, Mawdūdī, and many Islamist thinkers who have been inspired by them, key revelatory witnesses that God claims to exert a political rule (*ḥukm*) over humans. If humans heed only His rule, then they must apply His rules—Shari'a—in their communities. The Qur'an says in Q 5.44–45, they argue, that those who do not rule by what God has revealed are unbelievers and wrongdoers. This Qur'anic verse means, according to Sayyid Quṭb, that the governments of contemporary Muslim states that do not apply Shari'a legislation are unbelieving (*kāfir*), and their rulers are not real Muslims. For Islamists who do not historically contextualize the language of the Qur'an, the call for Shari'a legislation has always been the most important imperative of the divine revelation. Sayyid Quṭb's and Mawdūdī's concept of *ḥākimiyya*, God's political rule in this world, reflects a distinctly modern understanding of the Qur'an's language.[41]

There is no question that Shari'a plays a more important role in the minds of Muslims today than during the early part of the twentieth century, the nineteenth century, and probably also the period before.[42] The contributions in this volume address the implications and ambiguities of Shari'a in the contemporary context. They analyze the current applications of Shari'a and the potentials and obstacles for its development into a modern legal system. These studies challenge the view that during the centuries of Muslim history, Shari'a has been an unchanged entity, and that contemporary Shari'a is the mere extension of its classical notion into our times, but they also point out the connections between classical Muslim scholarship and the positions on contemporary Shari'a.

Several contributions deal with the Islamist call for the implementation of Shari'a. In the second chapter Gudrun Krämer examines the place of values in contemporary Muslim debates. Classical Islamic scholars identified a set of five essential goods in society that Shari'a serves to uphold and to advance. Krämer asks which are the moral values most emphasized in the writings of contemporary Islamist authors from Egypt and from other Muslim countries such as Nigeria. Her inquiry leads to an investigation into the role and the understanding of justice in these debates. Islamist authors claim that justice is the key moral value of Shari'a, and that its implementation leads to a more just society than the ones that follow the Western legal tradition. Krämer asks critically whether the understanding of justice in these works relates to equality among all legal subjects or rather to a situation of *suum cuique*, where the legal subjects receive a certain share of rights according to their role or function in society and according to their gender.

In Chapter 3 Frank Griffel also looks into the writings of Islamist authors and explores the relationship between natural law and Shari'a in the thought of their most influential writers in the twentieth century. Their position that Shari'a is identical to natural law is today widely used to legitimize the application of Shari'a in Muslim countries. These authors develop their position from Qur'anic verses that mention a divinely created universal human nature (*fiṭra*) to which the revelation of the Qur'an responds. This concept of Shari'a as a divine law that corresponds to human nature is sometimes regarded as a strong point of Islamist ideology. Griffel argues that the claim of Shari'a to be part of or identical to natural law remains exactly that—a declaration that is not verified. There is only a very vague idea of natural law in Islamist literature and no real inquiry into its contents. In Islamist literature natural law is defined as being identical to Shari'a, and that makes the process of verifying the claim circular. This circular approach has diminished the intellectual appeal of Islamist theology, particularly among the academic elite of contemporary Muslim societies, whose impression of natural law may differ from what they know about Shari'a.

In Chapter 4 Felicitas Opwis gives an overview of the development of what has become the most important legal concept for the contemporary practice of Shari'a: *maṣlaḥa*. The Arabic word *maṣlaḥa* means the well-being, welfare, and social wealth of a person or a community. It is not one of the traditional four sources of Shari'a. At some time during the eleventh century, however, Muslim jurists made the case that it should be considered as an extension of those sources. Opwis looks at Islamic legal theory both in the classical and in the contemporary period and analyzes how *maṣlaḥa* gained an increasingly prominent position. For contemporary jurisprudents, *maṣlaḥa* has become the most important vehicle for legal change.

This innovative use of *maṣlaḥa* in contemporary Shari'a is illustrated in the fifth and the sixth chapters. In Chapter 5 David L. Johnston contributes a case study of the Moroccan thinker and politician Muḥammad ʿAllāl al-Fāsī (1910–74). In addition to being one of the most important figures in the Moroccan independence movement, ʿAllāl al-Fāsī was also an influential writer on the methods of Shari'a. Johnston explains the innovative elements in his legal thinking. The concept of *maṣlaḥa* plays a key role. Similarly, ʿAllāl al-Fāsī connects his thinking to the idea of a divinely created human nature (*fiṭra*) and to Sayyid Quṭb's concept of Shari'a as natural law. The result is a most interesting concept in which Islam is viewed as a religion that can easily connect to all humans.

Noah Feldman presents in Chapter 6 a vivid portrait of Yūsuf al-Qaraḍāwī, one of the most influential Sunni jurisprudents today. Al-Qaraḍāwī grew up in

Egypt but chose exile in Qatar, where the popular satellite channel al-Jazeera is based. His frequent appearances on the most widely watched Arabic television channel made him one of the most recognized Muslim scholars today. Feldman takes a close look at al-Qaraḍāwī's discussion of the compatibility between Shari'a and democracy. Al-Qaraḍāwī develops the somewhat surprising argument that in today's world Shari'a demands democratic rule in Muslim countries. The key legal category that makes al-Qaraḍāwī come to this conclusion is again *maṣlaḥa*, the common benefit of the Muslim community.

Three chapters in this collection are devoted to Iran and developments in Shiite religious law and leadership. In Shiite Islam the contemporary discourse about Shari'a is shaped by Rūḥallāh Khomeini's (1902–89) demand that the legislative and the judicative branches of a Muslim Shiite state should be overseen by a council of experts in Shari'a legislation, headed by a very distinguished Muslim jurisprudent. Khomeini's concept of the "guardianship of the jurist" (*wilāyat-i faqīh* in Persian, *wilāyat al-faqīh* in Arabic) puts enormous political power into the hands of Muslim jurisprudents, who thus far had not seen themselves as part of the executive branch of the state.

In Chapter 7 Abbas Amanat examines the emergence of the doctrine of "guardianship of the jurist" out of the organization of Shiite scholarship. After having successfully parried the challenges of *akhbārī* criticism during the eighteenth century, the Shiite *ʿulamā'* of the remaining *uṣūlī* branch developed a hierarchy in which a single scholar, called the *marjaʿ-i taqlīd* (the source of emulation), became accepted as the highest authority in Shiite jurisprudence. The principle of *taqlīd*, in which lower-ranking jurists "emulate" the decision of higher-ranking ones, became a hallmark of Shiite scholarship. This structure had a significant influence on the development of the doctrine of the "guardianship of the jurist" and facilitated its implementation after the Islamic revolution of 1979. Amanat looks into the dynamics between the *wilāyat-i faqīh* and the acceptance of a single *marjaʿ-i taqlīd* in the past and surveys the arguments of contemporary Iranian defenders and critics of the principle.

In the eighth chapter Shahrough Akhavi evaluates how notions of social contract affect the contemporary understanding of Shari'a in Shiite Iran. Akhavi takes a broad view of social contract theories in Islam and concludes that they never had much impact before the twentieth century. Once they were introduced into contemporary debates about Shari'a, they questioned the special role of the clergy and led to disputes about the *wilāyat-i faqīh*. They also questioned the claim that the divine law of Shari'a is identical to natural law. Akhavi analyzes these tensions by looking into the publications of some contemporary proponents of social contract theory in Iran and the reactions they prompt.

In Chapter 9 Saïd Amir Arjomand also takes a closer look at the relationship between Shiite jurisprudence and the state. In his perspective he focuses on the state's side. He examines the tradition of constitutionalism in Iran and asks to what extent Shari'a plays a role in this tradition. Constitutionalism began in Iran during the early twentieth century, when Muslim jurists took an active part in its first parliamentarian movement. Arjomand examines whether this early involvement of Muslim scholars facilitated the development of such ideas as the "guardianship of the jurist" and the realities it creates.

Anna Würth has looked into the practical application of what can be called a codified version of Shari'a in today's Yemen. She studied the practice of Shari'a law at a family court in Yemen's capital Sanaa. In Chapter 10 she describes the contemporary practice of Shari'a in a Muslim country. Würth challenges the Western view that codification has negatively affected the highly flexible and often-accommodating nature of premodern family law rulings. Her study shows that judges have a significant amount of flexibility that they often use in order to create some neutralizing social justice to the often-unequal realities in a highly patriarchal society.

In his Afterword Roy P. Mottahedeh sums up the debates and provides a context for the study of contemporary Shari'a. He reminds us that the study of contemporary Islamic law must not define its subject in a way that would exclude normative practices and ideas that describe themselves as "Islamic" by their practitioners but are not regarded as distinctly Islamic by other Muslims. Mottahedeh also observes that today considerations about the rulings of Shari'a are increasingly driven by the spirit of the law—even if this concern is not always plainly expressed. This should be viewed as an encouraging sign and offers a way for contemporary Shari'a to move—as Mottahedeh puts it—toward a "strong positive expression of citizenship."

2 JUSTICE IN MODERN ISLAMIC THOUGHT

Gudrun Krämer

IN A THOUGHTFUL ESSAY titled "Much Ado About Wuḍū'," Ze'ev Maghen has argued that most religions are essentially about ritual. Ritual, he argued, functions both as a "temporal and spatial glue" and as a barrier separating one religious community from others, thereby "essentially *creating* that community on a continuous basis":

> While it may be true for certain small elites during various periods in Islamic and Jewish history that ethical and theological pursuits formed the most significant element of their religiosity, for the masses at all times religious experience has consisted first and foremost of ritual. . . .
>
> Logically, psychologically and sociologically speaking, then, for most of his waking life, it is the *ʿibādāt* which make a Muslim specifically Muslim, the *mitzvot bayn adam lamakom* which make a Jew specifically Jewish.[1]

As Maghen pointed out, elaboration of the minutest detail of ritual practice (and, it might be added, proper behavior more generally) has taken up much of the time and energy of Muslim legal and religious scholars, including the most eminent ones.[2] It is therefore quite possible that the current interest in Islamic thought, and more particularly in certain principles and values that Muslims today claim to be specifically Islamic, reflects a distinctly modern understanding of religion in which religion appears primarily as a set of beliefs, ethical principles, and general rules of conduct rather than of ritual observances, even though the latter may, as Maghen suggested, provide a stronger sense of community and continuity to the ordinary believer. Yet this is an understanding of religion shared by many contemporary Muslims.

"Islamic thought" is a problematic concept that possibly suggests more coherence and continuity and at the same time more power over the minds and behavior of Muslims than it actually holds. Like any other intellectual tradition, the Islamic one is plural and filled with discordant voices. As in most other cases, it is difficult to place specific elements of "Islamic thought" within a given sociocultural and political context and to assess their capacity to shape the thought and conduct of Muslims in their own time and place and beyond. For present purposes, it may be best to think of Islamic thought as a repertory of references that Muslims draw upon without being restricted to it. They are also not confined to the readings of past generations. As a rule, Muslims do not dispute the binding character of the normative texts (that is, the Qur'an and Sunna) and the authoritative tradition more generally, but they do make their own selection of references, and what is more, they define their scope of normativity.

What has been said is particularly pertinent to modern Islamic thought. The religious field is becoming increasingly crowded, with more and more actors entering the stage to speak on Islam and very often in the name of Islam. Islamists constitute only one segment of a large number of speakers, although during the last few decades they have come to set the tone of public debate and to define some of its most salient features. They can be usefully labeled as Islamists because of their conviction that Islam provides a distinct, coherent, and comprehensive set of norms and values that makes it into a unique system competing with other religious, cultural, and political systems,[3] and that to establish an "Islamic order" on any given territory, Shari'a has to be "implemented" in its entirety (Islam as a system requiring the so-called application of Shari'a). These assumptions pose many problems (how novel is the conception of Islam as a system, what is the relation between "divine" Shari'a and human *fiqh*, who is to have the power of definition in the process of "applying" Shari'a, and so on), but the identification of Islam with Shari'a as an all-embracing moral and legal code has proved powerful enough, appealing to many and provoking others, to dominate public debates in most Muslim communities—and not just the debates, but also private conduct and public order, including legal, social, and cultural policies at various levels of society. My use of the term, then, defines Islamists as a discursive community sharing a common theme or concern, rather than as members of any specific group or movement. The following will be based on writings in Arabic and English of the period since 1945, representing an educated Sunni middle class, whose authors, except for the debate on gender, are almost exclusively male.

BASIC VALUES: THE GOLDEN FIVE

Under the impact of Islamism, contemporary Islamic thought concerning economics, politics, and the social order more generally appears largely as a moral discourse that uses the language of Islamic jurisprudence, *fiqh* (without necessarily upholding its logic, let alone its substance). Discussions of justice serve to illustrate this tendency. What interests me here is not so much the Islamist contention that Islam represents a distinct, coherent, and comprehensive set of norms and values regulating individual and communal life that is divine in origin and solely accessible through the Qur'an and Sunna at the expense of all other sources of morality and normativity.[4] It is the claim made by certain Islamists, as well as most Muslim liberals (and the categories must, of course, be used with care),[5] that Islam or, as they often put it, Shari'a is primarily concerned with general principles or values rather than with the detailed rules and regulations derived from the Qur'an and Sunna according to the conventions of Islamic jurisprudence. In more technical language, it is the finality or spirit of the law (*maqāṣid al-sharīʿa*) that matters rather than its specific provisions, and it is therefore incumbent upon Muslims to "discover" the objectives (*maqāṣid*), principles (*mabādi'*), and "values" (*qiyam*) embodied in the normative texts so as to be true to the spirit of the law rather than blindly following its letter. What they mean by "objectives," "principles," and "values" is not just the effective cause (*ratio legis*, *ʿilla*) or purpose (*ḥikma*) of a particular injunction that traditional *fiqh* seeks to establish with a reasonable degree of certainty, especially in the context of analogical deduction (*qiyās*). Nor is it the legal rules or principles (*qawāʿid*) derived from examining particular injunctions.[6] They aim at a different level of abstraction that is not so much concerned with the epistemology and hermeneutics of Islamic legal reasoning as with the moral economy enshrined in revelation.[7]

"Classical" Islamic legal thought was, of course, not devoid of abstraction, though the bulk of scholarship followed a casuistic approach. Two concepts are proof of this spirit of abstraction that seeks to go beyond the text without losing a firm grounding in formal legal rationality: first, the concept of the "common good" or "welfare" (in modern usage *maṣlaḥa ʿāmma*, which is to be distinguished from the classical concept of *maṣlaḥa mursala*, "unattached" benefit or utility that is not explicitly defined in the Qur'an or Sunna, but accepted as valid on the basis of consensus, *ijmāʿ*), and second, closely related to the first, the doctrine of the so-called five essential goods, benefits, or interests (*maṣāliḥ*/*ḍarūriyyāt*: the protection of religion or the Islamic way of life, *dīn*; life or soul, *nafs*; lineage or offspring, *nasl*; property, *māl*; and either intellect/reason, *ʿaql*, or honor, *ʿirḍ*) as it was elaborated, with different emphases, by al-Ghazālī (d. 1111), Fakhr al-Dīn al-Rāzī (d. 1210), al-Qarāfī (d. 1285), al-Ṭūfī (d. 1316), and al-Shāṭibī (d. 1388).[8]

Modern authors frequently refer to these doctrines when they are trying to link their value-oriented approach to the grand tradition and so win respectability for an idea, practice, or institution that might otherwise be seen as novel and hence of questionable status.[9] Yet as often as not, they go well beyond the ancient masters, arguing that what Islam essentially is all about, and what Shari'a represents, are basic values, such as justice, freedom and equality, consultation/participation (*shūrā*), and accountability/responsibility (*mas'ūliyya/musā'ala*),[10] a list of items that I have somewhat irreverently called the Golden Five. Indeed, it would be possible to further reduce the list and make it a Golden Three, consisting of justice, equality, and responsibility, under which both *shūrā* and accountability would be subsumed. This is clearly something quite different from what al-Ghazālī, al-Shāṭibī, and even al-Ṭūfī had in mind when they discussed the common good and the five essential benefits or interests to be protected under Islam. The difference primarily concerns the status accorded to reason in determining the objectives (*maqāṣid*) of divine law, the status of these objectives as weighed against explicit scriptural injunctions in formulating legal rules and rulings, and the frame of reference chosen to determine the hierarchy of norms, values, and objectives attributed to the divine lawgiver.[11]

ISLAMIC NOTIONS OF JUSTICE

Justice regularly appears first on the list of values, and not only in the writings of committed Muslims. Non-Muslim scholars equally consider justice to be the most basic and characteristic value, or virtue, of Islam, even though they may differ in their interpretation of its scope and meaning. According to legal anthropologist Lawrence Rosen, "Justice is the most essential, if indeterminate, of virtues for Muslims, because it keeps open the quest for equivalence, a quest seen as central to both human nature and revealed orderliness in the world of reason and passion."[12] But if justice is so basic to the Muslim *imaginaire social*, why do we have so few studies of the subject, be they theoretical, empirical, or comparative?[13] The dearth of critical work may well have something to do with the very elusiveness of the concept that Rosen alluded to when he speaks about its "indeterminate" character. What he says about injustice, namely, that it is most often "felt rather than articulated,"[14] seems to apply equally to justice. It may also have something to do with the fact that with few exceptions, such as Miskawayh, Muslim theologians, jurists, and philosophers did not systematically reflect on justice.[15] In the following, I, too, will make no attempt to capture the spirit of Islam (in the singular and with a capital "I") by defining an Islamic concept of justice. Muslim understandings of justice have varied significantly over time and space, and different groups and strata within society have often held quite different opinions of what justice meant and implied.[16] The fact is largely undisputed among the scholarly community, but as yet is not really reflected in systematic analysis. What we are getting, though, is a growing number of empirical studies that cast light on notions of justice and equity as reflected in gender relations.[17]

A DELICATE BALANCE: ON JUSTICE AND ORDER

Premodern notions of justice may not have been "indeterminate," as Rosen put it, but they certainly covered a wide semantic field.[18] Islam (which in this particular instance is meant to include both the normative textual references and Muslim interpretation) is no exception: "justice" could be understood to refer to a wide range of ideas and ideals, from straightness and evenness to fairness, equity, and impartiality, from the reciprocity of rights and duties to balance and harmony, the golden mean, and, quite simply, abiding by the law. What they have in common is a concern with order or orderliness, which could, however, be defined in various ways. Justice could be inextricably linked to God's will, but it was not necessarily or exclusively so.[19] The same is true with regard to the role of the ruler. No matter how exactly it was defined, justice still was part of a larger scheme, reflecting ideals of the well-ordered universe and a balanced society, or body politic. The various possibilities are richly reflected in the classical, early modern, and modern literature on the subject.

Qur'anic references are indispensable to Islamic discourse past and present, as is Arabic philology to the critical scholar. The Qur'an offers a number of terms to describe just and righteous behavior (rather than justice in the abstract), which were subsequently used to create, or "construct," more systematic conceptions of "Islamic justice."[20] These include, first and foremost, two terms that involve dealing fairly with others, as applied to both God and human beings: *qisṭ*, which is derived from the verb "to distribute," and which is used to designate equity and fairness as, for example, in Q 3.18 (where God is described as *qāʾiman bi-l-qisṭ*) or Q 55.9 (where the reference is to giving the correct measure: *wa-aqīmū l-wazna bi-l-qisṭi wa-lā-tukhsirū l-mīzāna*); and *iḥsān*, which equally designates fair and righteous behavior toward others. The term most frequently translated as "justice," *ʿadl*, has a somewhat broader meaning in that it also refers to what has been called personal justice: the verbal root signifies "to be" or "to make straight, even, or equal," which can imply following the straight path (*al-sirāṭ al-mustaqīm*, as mentioned in the opening sura of the Qur'an and Q 11.56), as well as acting impartially to all. Several verses give *ʿadl* a clear legal meaning. As a technical term of *fiqh* and *ḥadīth* transmission, *ʿadl* or *ʿadāla* denotes moral integrity, probity, and uprightness, and more specifically a person with an honorable record.[21] In post-Qur'anic usage *inṣāf*, as well as its derivatives *naṣaf, naṣafa*, or *niṣfa*, was added to the repertory defining the fair and equitable treatment of others.[22]

All the terms mentioned here refer to fairness and moral probity that translate into action: it is the righteous act that reflects the pious mind. In Q 16.90 God orders humankind "to act with justice and equity and to give to one's kin [what is their due]" ("*inna Llāha ya'muru bi-l-ʿadli wa-l-iḥsāni wa-ītā'i dhī l-qurbā*"). According to Q 60.8, God "loves those who act with equity" ("*inna Llāha yuḥibbu l-muqsiṭīna*"). Believers are enjoined to do right (*iḥsānan*) by their parents, other kin, orphans, and the poor (see, for example, Q 2.83). The obligation to give alms (*zakāt, ṣadaqa*) testifies to the high religious value attached to charity and social solidarity (primarily among Muslims, but not exclusively so), which also served as the moral basis for the post-Qur'anic and initially disputed legal institution of the pious foundation, or charitable endowment (*waqf, ḥubs/habous*; for the Shiites, see also the *khums*).[23] Balance, temperance, and moderation (*iʿtidāl*, which is, of course, derived from the same verbal root as *ʿadl*) were seen as part of the divinely ordained way of life (*dīn*). This in turn was best expressed in the ideal of *al-wasaṭ*, the golden mean as the very epitome of this sense of good and proper measure, or proportion (the prime reference here is Q 2.143, "*wa-kadhālika jaʿalnākum ummatan wasaṭan li-takūnū shuhadā'a ʿalā l-nāsi*"). By the same token, exaggeration (*ifrāṭ*) or "extremism" (*ghulūw*) in faith, as well as in behavior, including religious devotion, was denounced as contrary to the Islamic way of doing things.[24]

For the *ʿulamā'* (but not all premodern Muslims), justice was equivalent to behavior conforming to God's law. Conformity with God's law made both the act and its performer "just" and "right(eous)." This becomes particularly clear if one looks at some of the terms that are commonly understood to denote opposites of justice: depending on the context, these include wickedness, sinfulness, sacrilege, oppression, sedition, and lawlessness (*fisq*, *jawr*, *ṭughyān/ṭāghūt*, *baghy*, and, most of all, *ẓulm* and *fasād*).[25] What they have in common is the link between injustice and the violation of, or disregard for, God's law and the divinely ordained order at large. They constitute a transgression of the bounds set by God. The issue of taxation could serve as an excellent illustration of this perceived link, with non-Qur'anic dues and taxes (*ḍarība*, *mukūs*, *maẓālim*) being widely considered to be unjust and illegitimate and their imposition a justification for rightful resistance to established authority.[26]

The link between justice and Shari'a is crucial, but it is not always unequivocal. There are instances when for the classical authors, including eminent *ʿulamā'*, it was no longer a matter of preserving the divinely ordained order, but simply of maintaining order in the most basic sense, that is, the absence of violence, civil strife, and anarchy. Most revealing are statements following the well-known pattern of "better *x* years of *a* than *y* days of *b*," such as "better one hundred years of unjust rule than one day of anarchy," attributed to al-Ghazālī and others.[27] If justice was identified with Islamic rule and law, the statement sounded outright defeatist. It was certainly ambiguous: the term *fitna* that at least in post-Qur'anic discourse is commonly used to designate disorder, disturbances, anarchy, or civil war carries a strong religious connotation, denoting an (external) temptation or trial sent by God to test the faith of the believer(s).[28] Disorder was thus depicted as a menace not only to the existing sociopolitical order, or the unity of the believers (*jamāʿa*), but also to the divinely ordained moral universe: it challenged and jeopardized "revealed orderliness." What remained was the marked concern with order, or more precisely law and order, with the tacit assumption that in extremis the latter might be better served by an unjust ruler.[29]

The concern with order is most clearly expressed in what are essentially elite presentations of a "just society." Deeply influenced by Hellenistic and Indo-Persian concepts of monarchy and the body politic, they focus on the need to establish and maintain a harmonious interplay of unequal parts that are kept in balance by the conscious intervention of the ruler—be it within the framework of divine law, as in Islam, or combined with different notions of law and morality, as in the Hellenistic and the Indo-Persian traditions.[30] This reflects a static conception of society that is not concerned with equality, but with equity and stability—or order *tout court*.[31] Justice here means essentially "to put everything in its place without [doing] too much or too little," a formula attributed to Ibn Ḥajar al-ʿAsqalānī (d. 1449) and amounting to the perfect expression of the golden mean.[32] Putting everything in its place also means keeping it there: people had their assigned place in society, and life ran smoothly precisely because they knew their place and kept it. The classic formula from late Roman antiquity puts it perfectly: *suum cuique*, to everyone his or her due, which need not be an equal share of rights and duties, but an appropriate one.[33] For this to happen, justice must not be blindfolded. On the contrary, it has to take the station and social relations of the individual(s) or group(s) involved into account in order to render justice, thereby reestablishing a social balance and harmony that had been threatened by a transgression of boundaries, be it a crime, misdemeanor, discord, or violence.[34]

The emphasis on equity and equilibrium, resting on differing understandings of what they imply, allowed for considerable variation in definition and application. Different configurations of religious, ethnic, and status groups, all internally stratified according to age and gender, could thus be seen and portrayed as just, equitable, and Islamic. By the same token, they could be contested as unjust and un-Islamic, and here reference to Shari'a as the supreme set of norms and values to which even the ruler had to submit was of special relevance.[35] Justice and equity were thus determined by what was thought to be desirable, or even "thinkable," not only at specific times, as is often said, but also in specific social milieus.

MODERN VOICES: JUSTICE AND THE ISLAMIC ORDER

In modern writings justice appears as the supreme and quintessential Islamic value, and the emphasis is usually on its legal, political, and social dimensions, with gender relations very prominently on the agenda. Notions of divine justice as advocated by thinkers of the Muʿtazila and certain Shiite theologians, or of royal justice as defined by court poets and numerous other Muslim writers since the times of the Umayyads, if not the rightly guided caliphs, are of more limited relevance to contemporary Muslims. Not that they have become entirely obsolete: it is precisely the selective use of references of diverse origins, from the Qur'an and Sunna to the *salaf ṣāliḥ*, scholars, poets, and bureaucrats of the early, classical, and middle periods, that characterizes modern discourses on all things Islamic, including justice. For this reason, the selection itself merits as much attention as the shifts in meaning and emphasis given to it. Two aspects call for closer scrutiny: the connection between justice and Shari'a, on the one hand, and between justice and equality, on the other.

JUSTICE AND SHARI'A

The English language does not allow for a distinction that is easily made in, say, Latin or German between justice as a value, virtue, or principle (*iustitia*, *Gerechtigkeit*) and as the adjudication of legal disputes (*ius*, *Recht/Justiz*). Attempts made by certain modern authors to differentiate between *ʿadl* and *ʿadāla* have failed to influence common usage or the scholarly literature.[36] For most contemporary Islamists, the distinction is largely irrelevant because Shari'a equals justice in the twofold sense: it comprises both *ius* and *iustitia*, *Recht* and *Gerechtigkeit*. To identify justice with Shari'a is, of course, nothing new, but this is not the point. What matters is the perception of justice as the supreme and overarching value of Islam, integrating all spheres of life within one coherent moral and legal framework, or system, in which, at least according to the Islamists, ethics, morals, and the law are no longer differentiated (as they are convinced that they were under the influence of non-Islamic and hence alien legal concepts, practices, and institutions).[37]

A study of Islamic political doctrine (*fiqh siyāsī Islāmī*) by the Egyptian author Farīd ʿAbd al-Khāliq exemplifies this approach, in which political ideas are typically expressed with reference to the vocabulary of *fiqh*. According to ʿAbd al-Khāliq, justice (*al-ʿadl*) is the supreme value of Islam, embracing all aspects of life. Not only does it serve as a constitutional principle to the Islamic state, it also enjoys special status within the Islamic legal system: as one of the "claims of God," or "public rights" ("*ḥaqq min ḥuqūq Allāh*"), or at least part of that mixed sphere in which the claims of God predominate over the "claims of individuals/humans" ("mā yakūn fīhi ḥaqq Allāh ghālib"), justice belongs to the inviolate sphere of law that is beyond human intervention:

> God the Highest made justice (*al-ʿadl*)—and equity (*qisṭ*), which here also means justice—the essence of what is right (*aʿraf al-maʿrūf*) because it is the foundation of all the comprehensive principles and general rules the lawgiver has defined in his divine law. It truly represents God's order and law (*niẓām Allāh wa-sharʿuhu*), preparing a straight path for humankind in this world and the hereafter (*wa-ʿalā asāsihi tastaqīm li-l-nās dunyāhum wa-ākhiratuhum*).[38]

This short passage is rich in meaning, managing to compress most of the traditional connotations of justice and at the same time integrating them into a decidedly modern framework: there are comprehensive principles and general rules established by the divine lawgiver (God); Islam is a system (*niẓām*) that is inextricably linked to divine law (*al-sharʿ*); God's law makes a straight path for humankind, guiding them in this world and to the hereafter. Similar statements will be found in many contemporary treatises on Islam, Shari'a, and the ideal Islamic order. Less conventional is ʿAbd al-Khāliq's characterization of justice as the epitome of what is good and right (*al-maʿrūf*), which evidently refers to the duty of all Muslims, or at least the qualified among them, to "command right and prohibit wrong" ("*al-amr bi-l-maʿrūf wa-l-nahy ʿan al-munkar*"), which plays a very prominent role in contemporary Islamist discourse (and practice).[39]

ʿAbd al-Khāliq goes on to subsume the essentials of the faith and politics under the principle of justice: just as the doctrine of the unicity of God (*tawḥīd*) is built on justice, so are the principles of consultation (*shūrā*), accountability (*musā'alat al-ḥākim*), equality, freedom, and human rights, because, he concludes, quoting Ibn Taymiyya's treatise on *ḥisba* (but neither Miskawayh or any of the Muʿtazilite thinkers), justice is "the framework of everything" ("*niẓām kull shay'*"). Therefore, he continues, it can be rightly said that justice is "the essence of what is good and right" and "the spiritual pivot of legitimate politics conforming to divine law" ("*al-quṭb al-rūḥī fī l-siyāsa al-sharʿiyya*") (*Fī l-fiqh*, 196–97). What is true for politics also applies to law: as times and circumstances are forever changing, justice can be realized by various means, provided they aim at the common good (*maṣlaḥa*) and do not conflict with the immutable elements of divine law. (The distinction between changeable and unchangeable elements of Islam and Shari'a is fundamental to most modern authors who write on Islamic law and politics, but is hardly ever clearly defined.)[40] Any means that results in justice and equity is part of religion and does not contradict it (here ʿAbd al-Khāliq relies on Ibn Taymiyya's disciple, Ibn Qayyim al-Jawziyya [d. 1350]; both are great favorites with contemporary Islamists).[41]

Again quoting Ibn Taymiyya, ʿAbd al-Khāliq finally defines justice as the supreme value that ultimately ranks even above Islam (which here seems to refer to the Islamic identity of state and society): God upholds just rule even if it is not Muslim/Islamic (the term *kāfir* is ambiguous), but does not sustain unjust rule even though it be Muslim, for the world can live with justice and unbelief, but not with injustice and Islam (*Fī l-fiqh*, 205). ʿAbd al-Khāliq offers no further comment on the possible differentiation between, or even dissociation of, Islam and justice, which is difficult to reconcile with his identification of Islam with Shari'a, and of Shari'a with justice. Maybe he conceives of Muslims acting unjustly or of a state inhabited by a majority of Muslims doing so, but not of Shari'a allowing for injustice. In the hierarchy of values (*al-sullam al-qīmī*), justice ranks even higher than order: it is the ultimate purpose of Islamic government and at the same time the ultimate justification of resistance to a ruler who violates human rights (which ʿAbd al-Khāliq equates with the inviolate claims of God, *ḥuqūq Allāh*) (203–4). This argument can be interpreted in various ways: as a tacit condemnation of violent action against a government that is un-Islamic or non-Muslim but just, or as not-so-tacit support for resistance to unjust and oppressive rule even though it is "Islamic" or Muslim. Nothing of this is spelled out in any detail, and neither do we get a clear idea of exactly what justice is.

ʿAbd al-Khāliq's vision may be contrasted with a different and more conventional exposition of justice "in Islam." In a textbook on Shari'a published in London in 1984, the Nigerian legal scholar Abdur Rahman Doi also made justice the highest value within Islam and declared Islamic justice to be superior to any other kind of justice (a topos of much contemporary writing on Islam and the West, reflecting the spirit of competition that is characteristic of mutual relations, past and present):

> Justice is a comprehensive term, and may include all the virtues of good behaviour. But the religion of Islam asks for something warmer and more human, the doing of good deeds even where perhaps they are not strictly demanded by justice, such as returning good for ill, or obliging those who in worldly language "have no claim" on you; and of course the fulfilling of the claims of those whose claims are recognised in social life. Similarly the opposites are to be avoided: everything that is recognised as shameful, and everything *that is really unjust*, and any inward rebellion against Allah's Law *or our own conscience* in its most sensitive form. . . .
>
> Islamic justice is something higher than the formal justice of Roman law or any other human law. It is even more penetrative than the subtler justice in the speculations of Greek philosophers. It searches out the innermost motives, because we are to act as in the presence of Allah, to whom all things, acts, and motives are known.[42]

All overt references to politics are absent here (although Doi does speak about Islamic democracy and the just ruler later in the book). He is concerned with the spiritual, legal, and social dimensions of Islamic justice, which he, not surprisingly, declares to be simply the best.

JUDGING WITH DISCRIMINATION: THE ISSUE OF EQUALITY

If justice ranks at the top, equality (*al-musāwāt*) is rarely ever missing from the list of cardinal values of Islam and Shari'a.[43] What most authors seem to have in mind, though, is still the classic notion of *suum cuique* (to everyone his or her due), which does not aim at achieving strict equality of rights and duties among all human beings irrespective of status, gender, ethnicity, or religion, but searches for equity or, in certain contexts, equivalence. It is rare to read as blunt a statement as the one made by Doi. Quoting Q 57.25 (*"laqad arsalnā rusulanā bi-l-bayyināti wa-anzalnā maʿahumu l-kitāba wa-l-mīzāna li-yaqūma l-nāsu bi-l-qisṭi wa-anzalnā l-ḥadīda fīhi ba'sun shadīdun"*), he writes: "Three things are mentioned as gifts of Allah. They are the Book, the Balance, and the Iron, which stand as emblems of three things which hold society together, *viz.*—Revelation, which commands Good and forbids Evil; *Justice, which gives to each person his due*; and the strong arm of the Law, which maintains sanctions for evil-doers."[44] Discussions on the status of women and of non-Muslims serve to illustrate this point.[45] Here I will limit myself to some remarks concerning gender, and more specifically the legal rights and duties of women, that strongly bear out Rosen's comment on Muslim concern with justice and equivalence. Incidentally, this is about the only topic where female voices, who make a major contribution to the public debate, are being heard. The argument centers around a number of distinctions: first and foremost, equivalence or "ontological equality," implying equal spiritual and moral worth of men and women, which is derived from the fact that according to the Qur'an (Q 4.1; 16.72 is less clear), both were created from the same soul (*nafs*) and have the same obligations toward God. This is contrasted with social differentiation responding to the different physical and emotional qualities of men and women that find expression in different social roles and functions and in certain circumscribed domains, and that also translate into differential legal rights and obligations. To be equal, then, does not mean to be identical. Difference must not be denied but must be accommodated with justice and discrimination.

The ambiguity of the term *ʿadl* is demonstrated particularly well in the heated debate about polygyny, which usually involves interpretations of Q 4.3, especially the cautionary note "and if you fear that you will not be just then [take only] one" (*"fa-in khiftum allā taʿdilū fa-wāḥidatan"*), and of Q 4.129, which states that even with the best of intentions, men will not be able to do this (*"wa-lan tastaṭīʿū an taʿdilū bayna l-nisā'i"*).[46] The verses can be taken as a warning against polygyny or even its prohibition, as some contemporary authors would have it, only if *ʿadl* here is interpreted to mean strictly equal rather than (merely) fair and equitable treatment of legal wives. The majority of Muslim readers, male and female, see no contradiction between polygyny and equality provided all wives receive a fair and equitable share of space, property, and attention from their husband. Equality is accepted as valid and desirable within a given social category (women, and more specifically legal wives), not across social categories (men and women, husbands and wives). Once again, the relevant question is how these categories are defined, or "constructed."[47]

Discussions of *qiwāma* (precedence, dominance, maintenance, protection?) that focus on Q 4.34 ("*al-rijālu qawwāmūna ʿalā l-nisāʾi bimā faḍḍala Llāhu baʿḍahum ʿalā baʿḍin wa-bimā anfaqū min amwālihim*") point in a similar direction: with its calm and clear statement that God gave preference to (some?) men over (some?) women, combined with reference to men's (unspecified) financial responsibilities, the verse acts as a major irritant to all advocates of gender equality, the more so since it goes on to allow men/husbands to deal with disobedient women/wives by admonishing them, keeping away from them, and, ultimately and most provocatively to modern sensibilities, beating them until they obey them (*aṭaʿnakum*). No wonder interpretations of *qiwāma*, *nushūz* (disobedience, but in what?), and *ḍaraba* (to beat, to bash, to warn?) differ widely. To begin with *qiwāma* and its social consequences, principally the conception of family as male dominated (patriarchal), trying to get around so explicit a statement by recourse to some higher principle in order to diminish or completely obliterate its import seems problematic. A number of contemporary authors interpret *qiwāma* in the sense of (physical) protection and (material) maintenance granted to women by men, rather than of male dominance to which women have to submit, negating their status of ontological equality.[48] The discussion on what precisely is meant by *ḍaraba* should women/wives show themselves disobedient (toward their husbands, as the majority of exegetes have it, or solely toward God, as a minority, including Amina Wadud, argue) illustrates the lengths to which defenders of human equality and dignity are prepared to go when faced with problematic parts of scripture.[49] In classical as well as modern standard Arabic, *ḍaraba* means "to beat," which in the given context would entail physical punishment. There is no way that the relevant verse could be interpreted to condone, let alone encourage, wife battering, that, is to inflict bodily injury, which *fiqh* clearly prohibits. But even less than outright violence tends to hurt modern sensibilities. The prevalent tendency is, therefore, either to deny the physical aspect by translating *ḍaraba* in different ways (to hold in confinement, to admonish) or to carefully circumscribe the amount of admissible force: "beating her softly with a folded handkerchief" is a practice recommended by some scholars, but is not very promising as a strategy for conflict resolution in real life, not to mention the fact that it does not do away with male agency.[50]

What we are essentially getting, then, is the notion of equivalence, emphasizing the equal (moral and religious) worth of men and women, who, however, fulfill complementary roles and functions in society, entailing differential legal rights and obligations that in this view lose their character of being discriminatory. Justice consists precisely of recognizing essential (moral) equality and at the same time acknowledging (social) difference, which renders an indiscriminate application of the principle of equal rights and duties fundamentally unjust.[51]

In a booklet titled *Milestones* (*Maʿālim al-ṭarīq*, not *Maʿālim fī l-ṭarīq*, like Sayyid Quṭb's famous treatise), Saʿīd Ramaḍān, son-in-law of Ḥasan al-Bannā, the founder of the Egyptian Muslim Brotherhood and a lawyer by training, presented an idiosyncratic version of this view:

> Just as Islam declared the basic relationship between man and woman to be one of partnership, it defined their relationship within the family by basing it on equality of rights and duties (Q 2.228: *wa-lahunna mithlu lladhī ʿalayhinna bi-l-maʿrūfi wa-lil-rijāli ʿalayhinna darajatun*). This degree[52] is [like] an administrative ranking that no business company can do without. In this way the company of life has been created that produces the new generations for the community of believers.[53]

The Qur'anic verse quoted by Ramaḍān deals with divorce. In this context it does not explicitly refer to (social) equality between men and women, but to an equal or equitable share of rights and duties granted to (married) women within the limits of what is socially and morally accepted as just and right (*al-maʿrūf*), with men being placed one degree above women.[54] His notion of family as a partnership, or companionship, between husband and wife merits attention: although it is true that partnership does not necessarily imply equality of status, it does require some kind of consultation between husband and wife and a certain measure of shared responsibilities. It is at any rate far removed from traditional role models according to which husband and wife (or wives) lead largely separate lives that do not require or even allow for a sense of shared interest and responsibility.[55]

By and large, one gets the impression that in spite of the tribute paid to the prestige term *equality*, most contemporary Muslim authors, male and female, consider equality to be consistent with considerable differentiation, if not discrimination, on the basis of gender and religion. By contrast, equality is strongly asserted with regard to social rank and status: all Muslims are equal regardless of descent, color, wealth, or power. Many would not hesitate to claim that all citizens of a given Islamic state are equal without, however, resolving the issue of how to reconcile equality, differentiation, and discrimination in a way acceptable to all.[56] Legal and fiscal privileges formerly attached to noble lineage (applying especially to the descendants of the Prophet, *ashrāf, sāda*), residence and culture (urban versus rural/tribal), or status vis-à-vis the ruler (for example, the Ottoman distinction between *ʿaskerī* and *reʿāya*) have either become obsolete or are no longer discussed. The same applies to slavery, which has been universally abolished, though it has not completely disappeared as a social fact in certain parts of the Muslim (as well as the non-Muslim) world. The concept of *kafāʾa* (equality of the spouses, or suitability of the match, involving social, legal, and moral criteria), which used to be of major importance in arranging and contesting marriages and served as an excellent indication of how equivalence and/or equality were defined within a given society or community, is of special interest here: despite the fact that *kafāʾa* continues to play a role in contemporary social and legal practice, it does not seem to be raised in theoretical discussions of justice, equality, and gender relations.[57]

A VERY MORAL ECONOMY: REFLECTIONS ON SOCIAL JUSTICE

Justice is, for obvious reasons, extensively discussed in the equally extensive literature on Islamic economics in general and *zakāt* in particular.[58] Contributions range from Sayyid Quṭb's seminal treatise *Social Justice in Islam* (*al-ʿAdāla al-ijtimāʿiyya fī l-Islām*) and Muḥammad Bāqir al-Ṣadr's equally influential *Our Economics* (*Iqtiṣādunā*) to more technical studies on what are thought to be Qur'anic instruments of profit sharing and loss (*muḍāraba*, and so on) that replace "non-Qur'anic" interest and usury (*ribā*), as well as equally non-Qur'anic insurance policies. Added to them are attempts at creating institutions of Islamic charity at a private level and at institutionalizing *zakāt* as a sort of Islamic income tax at the level of the modern territorial state.[59] The sensitive issue of land reform has been empirically studied with regard to the Islamic Republic of Iran,[60] but, individual contributions notwithstanding (Muṣṭafā al-Sibāʿī, Umar Chapra, Syed Naqvi), does not seem to have been systematically integrated into theories of Islamic ethics and economics, and (distributive) justice more particularly. There is little to be added to the existing critical literature on the subject, which has explored the main themes of what is largely an effort to define an ethics of Islamic economics with a heavy emphasis on the moral obligations attached to wealth and property, the imperatives of social solidarity, and distributive justice in the framework of an Islamic welfare economy resting on free enterprise and the protection of private property.[61]

Conventional views have not gone unchallenged, and there are interesting new approaches that explored the possibilities of reconciling Islamic morality with economic efficiency and economic growth with justice and equality (not just of opportunity, but of condition). They are theoretical rather than practical in nature and as a rule are not based on systematic recourse to the language of *fiqh*, though their authors liberally quote from the Qur'an and Sunna and refer to *maṣlaḥa* and the five essential goods, benefits, or utilities as defined by al-Ghazālī, al-Shāṭibī, and others.[62] One of the most articulate voices is the Pakistani economist Syed Nawab Haider Naqvi, who searches for a model of Islamic economics that is open to non-Islamic debates on justice, fairness, and efficiency.[63] To him, *ʿadl* comprises the two core elements of Islamic ethics and the Islamic way of life (*dīn*): justice and equilibrium. He defines justice as a condition in which human spiritual and material needs are in a state of balance or equilibrium. This, in turn, he assimilates to the Islamic doctrine of divine unity/unicity (*tawḥīd*). In contrast to most other exponents of Islamic economics, Naqvi insists on the need to define equality not just in terms of opportunities, allowing for wide discrepancies in wealth and social status, but of conditions, with the aim of narrowing social disparities without blocking economic efficiency, growth, and creativity. What marks him out even further is his impatience with seemingly Qur'anic instruments of profit sharing and loss as a substitute for interest and insurance policies, which, according to his view, fail to secure the core Islamic values of justice and fairness. It is for this very reason that in his foreword to Naqvi's book, Khurshid Ahmad saw fit to sound a note of caution. After castigating both liberal and conservative approaches to Islamic economics, law, and society, Ahmad continued: "The middle path then is the right option. Faith, fortitude and loyalty to Divine Principles should go hand in hand with creativity, flexibility and the ability to face the ever-changing intellectual, economic, technological and civilisational challenges. Perhaps what is needed is faith with fortitude, confidence with humility, loyalty with openness, and innovations rooted in tradition. This should be the defining character of the contemporary Islamic debate."[64]

JUSTICE AND THE MORAL ECONOMY OF ISLAM

The quest for justice, deeply felt but as a rule vaguely defined, continues to preoccupy Muslim thinkers, writers, and activists just as it preoccupies non-Muslim thinkers, writers, and activists—as well as most ordinary men and women. It occupies a prominent place in modern Islamic thought, and contemporary Islamist thought more particularly. In contrast to certain other values such as political freedom, *shūrā* in the sense of participation, or even parliamentary democracy, justice did not have to be "invented" as a basic value of Islamic law and ethics or an Islamic moral economy. The much-used term *invented traditions* is easily misunderstood, but justice has obviously been defined in new ways that tend to identify Islam with Shari'a as an all-embracing moral and legal code and to interpret both in the light of general values or principles that are thought to be rooted in the normative textual tradition.

This approach involves methodological risks, and modern discussions of justice and equality illustrate them very well. They are predicated on an attempt, first, to "discover" justice as the prime value underlying divine legislation (following Muʿtazilite doctrines without as a rule acknowledging them) and, by the same token, guiding all human "application" of divine law; second, to identify justice with equality, defining equality in the sense of either equivalence or equity; and third, to contextualize explicit references to inequality in the Qur'an and Sunna by placing them in a specific context (which is established on the basis of conventional Muslim accounts, largely unaffected by critical scholarship, no matter whether it is carried out by Muslims or non-Muslims) with the aim of limiting their scope of normativity, and to redefine the relation of general and specific rules and injunctions to make ("unwanted") specific ones subordinate to general ("wanted") ones.[65] The last step consists of "applying" the fundamental principles or values (justice, equality, freedom, consultation, accountability, and so on) thus discovered at the expense of some, but not all, specific injunctions contained in the Qur'an or Sunna to a contemporary context, claiming that this (human and hence subjective) enactment of Qur'anic principles embodies God's (absolute) will and law. The potential of this rationalist approach to Shari'a, and to Islam more generally, for developing a radical critique of convention is obvious: it underlies most efforts to legitimize legal innovation (*ijtihād*) as opposed to conformist imitation (*taqlīd*); the former, at least since the eighteenth century, have been of paramount concern to Muslim reformers.[66] The systematic use of reason within the parameters of established belief, and the utilitarian logic employed in the process, could allow a complete reevaluation of past assumptions concerning not only the letter of the law but also its spirit. In spite of the obvious risks, this approach seems to open the way to new and creative thinking about law, culture, and society that has a chance of being accepted by devout Muslims as legitimate, or "authentic." In the shadow of globalization, the quest for "authenticity," spurious as it may be, appears to loom ever larger.

3 THE HARMONY OF NATURAL LAW AND SHARI'A IN ISLAMIST THEOLOGY

Frank Griffel

IN A PAPER PRESENTED at a congress of European scholars in Arabic and Islamic studies in 1996, Emilio Platti pointed toward what he perceived as a contradiction in the Muslim fundamentalist concept of Shari'a.[1] Platti analyzed the writings of one of the most influential Muslim fundamentalist theologians of the twentieth century, the Indian writer Abū l-Aʿlā Mawdūdī (1904–79), and concluded that he held two conflicting views on the relationship between Shari'a and what can be understood as natural law. Although in one of his major works Mawdūdī praises the perfect compatibility of the Islamic moral code with the universal moral values that humans are able to detect in their search for knowledge,[2] he rejects elsewhere any congruency between the positive law of Shari'a and any kind of "natural law."[3] On the one hand, Mawdūdī claims that the moral obligations of Islam are in harmony with the normative rules and values that humans discover through their study of nature and society. On the other hand, Mawdūdī characterizes Islam as absolute submission to God's revealed Shari'a, a submission that rejects any other kind of law—including what some people call "natural law."[4] For Platti, this contradiction is not just an academic matter that would earn Mawdūdī the disrespect of more systematic thinkers and fellow intellectuals. It limits the political and ideological impact of Mawdūdī's thinking. For Platti, this incongruity prevented Mawdūdī's followers in Pakistan from rallying the necessary support to create an Islamic revolution. In consequence, Mawdūdī was unable to carry out his initial project of a revival of Muslim society. According to Platti, this is, in fact, the major obstacle of Mawdūdī's thinking that barred him from becoming an effective and innovative theologian and that limited him to being the source of a fundamentalism gone astray.[5]

This chapter takes a fresh look at the problem that Platti brought up. It analyzes the relationship between Shari'a and natural law in Islamist theology. After a brief introduction to the notion of the law of nature and its general relation to divine law such as Shari'a, the chapter discusses how the tension between divine law and natural law has been treated in classical Muslim theology up to the nineteenth century. The main focus, however, is on contemporary Muslim theology and the writings of Sayyid Quṭb (1906–66). Next to Mawdūdī, Quṭb is the most influential theologian of Islamist thought. In the Arab world his influence undoubtedly surpasses that of Mawdūdī. Quṭb read the works of Mawdūdī in the Arabic translations of his follower Abū l-Ḥasan Nadwī (1914–99), whom he met in 1951. Quṭb was profoundly influenced by Mawdūdī's interpretation of Islam as a way of life (*dīn, manhaj,* or *niẓām*),[6] and from it he developed a distinct position on the relationship between Shari'a and natural law that is in many ways more refined than that of his predecessor.[7] Analysis of Quṭb's position allows a better understanding of Mawdūdī's view and leads to the conclusion that there is no contradiction in this matter, but rather a vicious circle.

NATURAL LAW AND THE LAW OF NATURE

Natural law as a source of moral and legal judgments has been on a steady rise in the Western tradition since the early Renaissance. It spread widely during the Enlightenment and came to prominence during the nineteenth and twentieth centuries, when more traditional sources of law, based on custom or the authority of the state or of religion, for instance, became more and more contested. The concept of a set of guaranteed rights of every human is rooted in natural law. The American Declaration of Independence of 1776, which was drafted by Thomas Jefferson (1743–1826), refers to certain natural rights of humans—among them the pursuit of happiness—that all are endowed with by virtue of being human.[8] The French Declaration of the Rights of Man and of the Citizen (Declaration des droits de l'homme et du citoyen), drafted by the Marquis de Lafayette (1757–1834) and adopted by the French National Assembly in 1789, presents itself as "a solemn declaration of the natural, unalienable, and sacred rights of man." The concept of natural law is openly acknowledged in such legal codes as the French Code Civil (1794) or the Prussian and Austrian General Codes of Laws (1804 and 1811), documents that were influential for many other nations. During the twentieth century a series of political and constitutional crises in Europe led to a further rise of natural law, which now became an accepted source of international legislation. The General Declaration of Human Rights that was ratified in 1948 by the General Assembly of the United Nations, for instance, stands firmly within this tradition of natural law.

Normative discussions about a law of nature and its place in human ethics and jurisprudence have a much longer tradition in philosophy and theology that goes back to antiquity. "Natural law," however, is not the same as the "law of nature." While the former describes a set of normative rules and consequent imperatives, the latter may refer to any kind of regulation or law that governs the world, including physical laws or laws of human behavior. Natural law is, however, legitimized by the existence of laws of nature. Natural law is understood as precepts for ethical behavior that are derived from the study of nature. The concept of natural law assumes that there are ethical constants in human behavior that determine which actions are right or wrong in a given situation. Humans are able to detect and determine these judgments in an endeavor that is similar to an investigation of the physical laws of nature or of logics or mathematics. Natural law may be determined in two ways that are not mutually exclusive: first, from determining innate notions in our minds about what must be right and wrong, and second, from an inquiry into nature or, generally, the world that is outside our minds. The sources of natural law are thus (1) the notions about right or wrong that humans find "naturally" within their minds and/or (2) the rules that govern nature.[9]

The understanding of what natural law contains varies widely and often depends on a prior understanding of what "nature" is. For those who understand nature as the original and untouched state of affairs, natural law is the original order or *Ur-Order* of human practice. Others understand nature as the realm of rationality, and for them, natural law is simply rational law that can be deduced from rational principles. Both these notions of natural law rely on an understanding of "nature" as efficient causality. Nature is determined by a set of rules that make a particular effect necessary if a given set of causes is fulfilled. The rules of physics provide the simplest understanding of the law of nature—they are the physical laws of causes and effects. In these laws the relationship of causes and effects is often understood as necessary. Necessity, however, is not a required condition in order to speak of laws. Laws might be perceived to exist even where the relationship between cause and effect is considered only habitual and not necessary. Also, for a legal theory based on natural law, it makes no difference whether one assumes that nature is God's creation or not. Natural law may or may not be rooted within a religious understanding of God's creative activity.

The apparent orderliness of nature in physical matters gives rise to the idea that nature includes a normative order that follows a set of necessary or habitual laws in a way that parallels the physical order. Aristotle (384–322 BCE), for instance, argued that the political law (*politikon dikaion*) of a state is divided into a natural law (*dikaion physikon*) and one that depends on rules that its citizens have agreed upon (*dikaion nomikon*).[10] Natural law has in each and every city or state the same authority and does not depend on the opinions and accords of its citizens. Its opposite is positive law, that is, the law that is set in the way human artwork is created (*non natura, sed positione, arte constitutum*).[11] For Aristotle, the source of natural law was not nature itself, which is mute with respect to legislation, but rather human intellect (*nous*), where these laws are "naturally" inscribed, and rational concepts (*logos*), from which they can be derived.[12] Identifying the difference between natural law and positive law, however, has always been a problem. Aristotle, for instance, regarded the subordination of slaves to their masters as one of the laws of nature[13] and argued against people who claimed that slavery contradicts nature (*physis*).[14] The most frequently quoted normative law of nature is the so-called Golden Rule: Do unto others as you would have others do unto you.

In the context of this debate, divine law falls into the category of positive law. Since it is considered to be revealed by God, divine law is not created, as human artwork is. But the revealed law is often understood as a divine imperative that needs to be implemented by humanity. As such, it is "set" (*positivum*) either by God or by humans, who aim to implement it, and thus it stands in a possible tension with natural law.

Hellenistic Jewish philosophers were the first to realize the potential difference between divine law and natural law. Since God is considered the creator of both natural law and the divine law of the Torah, this tension is difficult to sustain. Philo of Alexandria (d. ca. 50 CE), for instance, argued that the laws revealed to Moses are included in the law of nature (*nomos physeôs*). The law of nature is the eternal law of God's creation and is identical with the written laws in the Pentateuch.[15] Philo considered the divinely revealed law a replica of natural law.[16] The early Christian community had a similar understanding. The Epistle to the Romans, written by the apostle Paul around 56 CE, refers to the fact that the non-Jewish Gentiles (*ta ethne*) do by nature things contained in the Mosaic divine law (*nomos*). "These, having not the law, are a law unto themselves. Which shows the work of the law written in their hearts."[17] God's revealed law—or at least a part of it—is present even to those who have never heard of it, because they naturally find it within themselves. Early Christian authors, such as Tertullian (ca. 150–230), read this passage as a reference to a "natural law" (*lex naturalis*) that guides humans just as the Torah guides toward what is ethical and just. This guidance is independent of scripture.[18]

To claim that the law God created in order to govern nature is the same that God revealed as a divine lawgiver is plausible. Any other position seems rather inconsistent and would lead to the assumption that God as creator has different motives from God as lawgiver. Jewish, Christian, and Muslim theologians implicitly acknowledged this principle and claimed the identity of divine and natural law, at least on some level. In Christianity the twelfth-century Italian jurist Gratian defined the most basic relationship between natural law and the Christian revelation. Natural law (*ius naturae*) is the law that is (1) contained in the Old and New Testaments and that is (2) in accord with the Golden Rule as outlined in Matthew 7.12.[19] All laws are divided into a divine and a human part. Divine laws are those laws that are based on nature—that is, God's immediate creation—while human laws are based on custom.[20] Natural law is present in every human, and it is common to all people.[21] Human law, however, varies between people. Gratian thus formulated the most general parameters of the relationship between divine law and natural law in Western, mostly Christian, literature: Natural laws are those ordinances of the Old and New Testaments that command one to do to others what one wants done to oneself.

NATURAL LAW IN CLASSICAL ISLAMIC THEOLOGY

The idea of a divine law—Shari'a—in Islam developed within the tradition of Christian, Jewish, and other late antique notions on this issue and is therefore not radically different in its relationship to natural law. The terminology used by Muslim theologians when discussing these issues is, however, quite different. In the West the language comes from Greek philosophy and Roman law,[22] but in Islam the issue of natural law is discussed in notions that stem from the Qur'an. Verse 30 of sura 30 of the Qur'an mentions the way in which God has created mankind. It uses the Arabic word *fiṭra* in order to refer to the natural disposition of humans:[23]

> So set your face toward the religion just like a *ḥanīf* does,
> the disposition (*fiṭra*) of God
> according to which He created humankind.
> There is no changing (*tabdīl*) for God's creation.
> That is the right religion, but most people don't know.

The syntax of this verse is not altogether clear, a fact reflected in the English translation. Read in the way translated, the verse suggests that the *fiṭra* is the original disposition of humankind and that being a *ḥanīf* means to follow this original disposition. In the Qur'an a *ḥanīf* is a monotheist who is neither Jew nor Christian. Abraham, for instance, who is not considered a Jew in the Qur'an (Q 2.135, 2.140), is a *ḥanīf*. He abandoned the polytheist religion of his fathers and inclined to a monotheist religion of his own. He is described as someone who has reached monotheism by means of logical reflection and the empirical observation of nature (Q 6.75–79). Finally, the quoted verse expresses the idea that the monotheism of a *ḥanīf* is part of the natural constitution (*fiṭra*) with which humans have been created.[24]

Although the Qur'an is not explicit about what exactly the original constitution of humans is, Muslim theologians understood verse Q 30.30 to mean that being a *ḥanīf* is the original religion of humans and that polytheists, as well as Jews and Christians, have distorted this natural religion, a religion that is preserved in Islam. Being a *ḥanīf* was initially understood as being a Muslim *avant la lettre*.[25] This notion was reinforced by a passage in the Qur'an where Abraham is called "a Muslim *ḥanīf*" (Q 3.67). Islam is therefore the revealed expression of the disposition according to which humans—and by implication the world as such—are created. The religion of Islam is in accord with what in Western literature has been called the law of nature.

The concept of the *ḥanīf* is an important part of the anthropology of the Qur'an. God originally created humans as just and right. Humans are thus able to attain salvation even without the privilege of being granted a revelation. There is no original sin in Islam that is punished with expulsion from paradise. Humans, however, have always been subject to the temptations of evil, injustice, and wrongdoing. These temptations lead to polytheism, decadence, and vices. Prophets and warners are God's way of reminding humans of what they can naturally find within themselves, that is, the ability to follow monotheism and to do good. Temptation led the Jews and Christians to tamper with the revelation they had received and to change it according to their desires. This process is described as *taḥrīf*, literally meaning "to change the letter" and "to tamper with the meaning" of a text. In the Qur'an deviation and divergence (the *tabdīl*, "changing," verse Q 30.30 talks about) from the Straight Path shown by God is the reason for evil and vices in this world. The tendency to follow such deviations is inherent in humans and tempts them constantly. The Straight Path (*al-ṣirāṭ al-mustaqīm*, cf. Q 1.6–7, 2.142, and other verses) that leads to salvation is present in humans within their original disposition (*fiṭra*). It is also reaffirmed in the revelations that God sent to humankind in order to keep them from deviating from what is right. This understanding is expressed in a famous *ḥadīth*: "Every child is born according to the *fiṭra*. Only his parents make him a Jew, a Christian, or a Zoroastrian."[26] God created humanity according to a single *fiṭra*[27] that would lead every child—if left unchanged by its parents—to become a Muslim.

The general claim that Islam is in accord with the original constitution of humans is present in early Muslim literature in almost the same way that Gratian's claim that the natural law is part of the Christian revelation and part of canon law runs through Christian writings.[28] Muslim theologians, however, saw a number of problems associated with this claim. Those theologians who accepted the identification of Islam with *fiṭra* had to address the issue of the exclusiveness of revelation. If Islam is just a preservation or a repetition of what is contained in human *fiṭra*, then there is no need for the detailed imperatives and injunctions of revealed divine law, since all these rules can also be deduced by means of human reflection. Although a number of early Muslim theologians from among the Muʿtazilites and the early Shiites accepted this implication and considered *fiṭra* to contain the same rulings and laws that have been revealed by the divine law of Islam,[29] others vigorously objected to this as a devaluation of revelation. The original *fiṭra* of humankind is distinct from Islam, they argued, because Islam contains more than what can be known through intuition, logical deduction, or empirical observation of nature. When these arguments gained ground, they developed into the understanding that monotheism is part of the original *fiṭra*, while the detailed injunctions of divine law cannot be part of it.[30] This view tallied with the Qur'an's identification of *fiṭra* as the monotheism of a *ḥanīf*.

The influential theologian al-Ashʿarī (d. 935) argued against the Muʿtazilites that moral imperatives and injunctions are not known through any source other than revelation. Human reflection and human arguments cannot determine what is good or bad in human behavior. An action is good or bad not because it is so by its nature, but rather because it is recommended or condemned in the revealed law.[31] Theologians of the influential Ashʿarite school of Sunni Muslim theology, which was founded by al-Ashʿarī, argued that good is what God commands and bad is what He forbids.[32] They conceded that humans may have vague notions of what is good and bad in matters of moral judgments, but these notions are always overshadowed by considerations of our self-interest.[33] Equally, the moral quality of an action or a person's character cannot be assessed through rational judgment (*ʿaql*) independent from revelation. Ashʿarite theologians believed that human normative judgments are intrinsically affected by considerations of their own benefits and therefore cannot recognize the real moral value of an act.[34] There is no reliable faculty that is able to distinguish good from bad within the original disposition (*fiṭra*). Therefore Shari'a cannot be part of *fiṭra*, nor can it be the result of reflections that rely exclusively on a priori judgments or on the observation of nature. All normative judgments must be learned from revelation.

Although monotheism is indeed part of *fiṭra* or of what might be considered the law of nature, Islam and its divine law are not. Shari'a, on the other hand, does not violate anything that humans consider true through rational reflections of what they find inside themselves or through empirical observation of nature.[35] The influential Ashʿarite theologian al-Ghazālī (d. 1111) brought together several traditions of Muslim thought, among them Aristotelian philosophy in Islam (*falsafa*).[36] He agreed that monotheism is part of the content (*muḍammana*) of the original *fiṭra*.[37] Although the belief in one God is rooted within the soul, some people turn away from it and forget it, mainly by uncritically following what has been said to them during their education.[38]

Classical Muslim theologians acknowledged the existence of laws of nature. The rational sciences discover and describe these laws. These laws are also mentioned in the Muslim revelation. Rationalist theologians such as al-Ghazālī considered the character of God's being, His unity, and His attributes legitimate subjects of human understanding that are independent of revelation. In physics and metaphysics, for instance, laws can be deduced from self-evident principles and observations of nature. Rational arguments lead to the conclusion that there is only one God and that He is radically different from humans.[39] This is, according to al-Ghazālī, precisely what the Qur'an teaches. The inquiry into God's creation proves the truth of revelation, and vice versa. Thus, within the realm of the physical and metaphysical, revelation and the laws deduced from the observation of nature and the human mind must be identical. This, however, does not apply to normative judgments on human behavior and thus not to Shari'a.[40] The laws that determine which actions are good and which are bad cannot be drawn from nature nor the human mind.[41] Ethics and jurisprudence are sciences that must be based on the revealed texts. For Ashʿarites such as al-Ghazālī, there is no natural law that Shari'a could be compared with.[42]

Although most Sunni theologians and jurists denied the existence of natural law, some developed the view that Shari'a responds to the requirements of a natural order. This direction of thought proved to be influential for the development of the contemporary Islamists' position and should be examined closely. Traditionalist theologians, who developed their teachings within a literalist reading of the text of the Qur'an and the prophetic *ḥadith*, advanced this view alongside the prophetic saying that the children of the Jews and Christians do not follow their *fiṭra*. The Ḥanbalī theologian Ibn Taymiyya (d. 1328) taught that humans have a natural tendency to become Muslims—and not to become Christians, Jews, or even polytheists.[43] Although humans are born "empty," without any prior knowledge of any religion or law, "the human *fiṭra* requires (*yaqtaḍī*) the religion of Islam. It requires knowledge of Islam and the love of Islam."[44] These needs and "necessary requirements" (*mūjibāt*) of *fiṭra* develop one by one with increasing age. This development is similar to the need for milk and for solid food that are acquired one after the other. In adults the requirements become more developed and go beyond bodily needs.[45] If left intact, their *fiṭra* will make humans choose Islam because this is what satisfies their need for moral guidance. As for the children of the Jews and Christians, the "requirement" for Islam and its Shari'a is not satisfied, and these people have abandoned what their *fiṭra* calls for:

> The children are born with an intact *fiṭra*, and if left intact and sound, the *fiṭra* will make them choose knowledge over denial and belief over unbelief. But if this [development] is obstructed by corruption and immorality (*fasād*) then the soul abandons the *fiṭra*. . . . Within the *fiṭra* is a faculty (*quwwa*) that has a tendency toward knowledge and belief, just as there is a faculty in the intact body that makes it prefer the most beneficial food.[46]

This tendency of humans to follow Islam rather than any other religion does not mean that humans could do without revelation. Islam can only be established by revelation. Only after its establishment does Islam become the preferred choice of humans. Islam is thus not "included" in *fiṭra*, and its law could not be created from it. Rather, Islam answers to the natural needs of humans in a most perfect way. Only after people were given Islam did they come to recognize it as the most perfect law with which to govern the world. No other law is more "natural" than Shari'a. Although Ibn Taymiyya has no concept of a natural law that follows by itself from the normative requirements of nature, he considered Shari'a to fulfill the same function that in Western literature is ascribed to natural law: it responds perfectly to the normative requirements of God's creation.

NATURAL LAW IN MODERN ISLAMIC THEOLOGY

Ashʿarite theologians maintained their rejection of the notion of a natural law until the middle of the nineteenth century. Jurisprudence (*fiqh*) and the establishment of ethical and judicial judgments must be pursued from the basis of divine revelation. Al-Bājūrī (1783–1860), for instance, the most influential theologian of his generation at al-Azhar seminary of Sunni theology in Cairo, presents the Ashʿarite position on normative judgments very clearly: "According to the Sunnis, good (*ḥasan*) is what revelation (*al-sharʿ*) calls good and bad (*qabīḥ*) is what revelation calls bad. . . . The Ashʿarites hold that all normative judgments are determined by revelation, but in a way that does not violate reason."[47]

Beginning with the second half of the nineteenth century and particularly during the first half of the twentieth century, the traditional study of theology as it was pursued under teachers such as al-Bājūrī lost much of its credibility. Muslim theology went through a number of radical changes that led to the development of new genres of theological texts. The authors of these new texts were no longer connected to the teaching tradition of earlier Muslim theologians. Often these new theologians had only a superficial knowledge of how issues had been dealt with in classical Muslim theology. Muslim theology became a much more open business where the diploma and reader certificates that were the basis of a traditional career in theology at colleges such as al-Azhar were replaced by the success of books or journals on newsstands and in bookshops. The most influential Sunni theologians of the twentieth century were not trained at theological seminaries. Often they were distinctly modern intellectuals, having acquired a secular education in one of the European-style academies in Muslim countries that did not focus on Islamic scholarship.

Sayyid Quṭb is a prime example of this kind of modern intellectual. He grew up in a small village in Upper Egypt, where he was among the first generation of children who were not sent to a traditional *kuttāb*, a so-called Qur'an school, where pupils acquired the basic religious education that would enable them to continue at places such as al-Azhar. When a primary school with a mostly secular curriculum appeared in his village, Sayyid Quṭb demanded to be sent there.[48] He went through all the stages of the nascent modern educational system in Egypt, culminating in a diploma in 1934 from one of the European-style teacher-training colleges (Dār al-ʿUlūm). During his professional career his connection with the modern educational system became even closer. He worked in the Egyptian Ministry of Education, where he was one of the increasing numbers of state officials who administered the rapid expansion of the new, secular-based education system.

During the 1930s Sayyid Quṭb became affiliated with the Muslim Brotherhood (al-Ikhwān al-muslimūn) of Ḥasan al-Bannā (1906–49). From 1948 to 1950 the Egyptian government sent Sayyid Quṭb to the United States to study its higher-education structure. Quṭb wrote articles about his sojourn and returned an even more radical supporter of the Muslim Brotherhood.[49] After al-Bannā's assassination in 1949, Sayyid Quṭb assumed the intellectual leadership of Muslim fundamentalism in Egypt, and his books became its most influential mouthpiece. The new Egyptian republican government acknowledged this position and imprisoned him between 1954 and 1964 and in 1965 until his execution for treason in August 1966. Sayyid Quṭb's most influential works were written in a prison cell.[50]

Sayyid Quṭb's basic interpretation of *fiṭra* follows more the lines of Ibn Taymiyya's thinking than those of the classical Ashʿarite school of, for instance, al-Bājūrī. The most fundamental tenet of Ashʿarite legal thought, namely, that all normative judgments about human behavior must be based on divinely revealed principles, had already been rejected by Muḥammad ʿAbduh (1849–1905). ʿAbduh, who was the most influential Muslim theologian at the turn of the twentieth century, was educated in Ashʿarite theology but showed a remarkable independence in his own teachings. He held that the moral characteristics of human actions are absolute and can be known through reason.[51] His leaning toward moral objectivism has sometimes been explained as an influence from Muʿtazilite thought.[52] In reality, he had been influenced by the rationalism of the Aristotelian tradition in Islam (*falsafa*), which he became acquainted with at al-Azhar and through his intellectual mentor Jamāl al-Dīn al-Afghānī (1838–97).

ʿAbduh's rejection of classical Ashʿarism allowed him to develop a notion of natural law. Since humans can achieve proper knowledge of whether an act is good or bad without recourse to revelation, they can deduce from this a moral law that is known independently from God's revealed law. This natural law, however, is not accessible to all humans. The faculty of reason (*quwwat al-ʿaql*) enables some individuals to lay down the "rules of justice" (*qawāʿid al-ʿadl*) and to distinguish the "foundations of virtue" (*uṣūl al-faḍīla*) from the "manifestations of vices" (*wujūh al-radhīl*). Although people "who are trained in the use of reason" (*ʿuqalāʾ*), as ʿAbduh calls them, know the natural law through their rational capacity (*quwwat al-ʿaql*), a society as a whole will not develop the knowledge that enables it to follow natural law. A community will simply not listen to its "intelligent ones" (*ʿuqalā'*), and it will not obey the moral rules they devise from reason. A society will, however, be willing to submit to a higher authority than reason, and this is prophecy. Legislation, therefore, to be effective, cannot come from humans. The only effective legislation is by divine law. Divine law spells out the link between human actions in this life and rewards or punishments in the afterlife and thus gives a clearer incentive to do good and avoid wrong than is given by natural law.[53] The tendency of every community not to submit to rules made by itself makes Shari'a a necessity.[54] Muḥammad ʿAbduh's argument for the need of divine prophecy echoes the one that Muslim philosophers developed in the tenth and eleventh centuries: the unequal distribution of the faculty of reason among humans requires human societies to accept divine law rather than natural law.[55]

Sayyid Quṭb wrote in an environment in which the two main intellectual movements that had earlier opposed Ashʿarism were much more influential than Ashʿarism itself. The first was the traditionalism and antirationalism of the Ḥanbalī school as it appeared in Ibn Taymiyya's writings. The second was the rationalism and antitraditionalism of the Muslim Aristotelian tradition (*falsafa*). It is remarkable that both these directions of thought, inherently opposed to each other, enjoyed high intellectual standing among Muslim intellectuals of the first half of the twentieth century. Both movements influenced Sayyid Quṭb's thought. Thus his theology contains both more traditionalist and more rationalist elements than the Ashʿarism of classical Azhar teachers such as al-Bājūrī.

In his commentary on Q 30.30 Sayyid Quṭb repeats the traditionalist claim that the religion of Islam is in harmony with human *fiṭra* and—by implication—with the law of nature. In his commentary on the Qur'anic words that "being a *ḥanīf* is the disposition (*fiṭra*) of God, according to which he created humankind," he writes:

> These words bring the *fiṭra* of the human soul together with the nature (*ṭabīʿa*) of this religion (*dīn*). God created both of them, and both of them are in agreement with the law that governs existence (*nāmūs al-wujūd*). Both of them are in harmony with one another regarding the nature of this law and its direction. And God, who has created the human heart, is also the one who has sent humans this religion in order for them to be judged by it, to be turned towards it, to be healed [by it] from diseases, and to be rectified from transgressions. God knows more than we about what He has created. He is the Kind One and the Knowledgeable. Both the human *fiṭra* and this religion are firmly established: "There is

> no changing for God's creation" [Q 30.30]. And when the souls have deviated from the *fiṭra*, only this religion will be able to bring them back to it. This religion is in harmony with the *fiṭra*—the *fiṭra* of humanity as well as the *fiṭra* of existence.[56]

The religion of Islam is in harmony with (*mutanāsiq maʿā*) the nature of the human soul, that is, the way God created it, according to *fiṭra*. *Fiṭra* is itself in line with the law (*nāmūs*) that governs God's creation.[57] Since God has created all three, Islam, human *fiṭra*, and nature, there can be no contradiction or even inconsistency between the laws that govern these three. Both the way humans are created and the religion of Islam are firmly established (*thābit*), and neither can be changed. In fact, only Islam can bring a human soul back to its original state, its *fiṭra*, after it has deviated from it. Islam is the only religion that responds to the particular way the human soul is created. Islam is the right religion for all humans.

Sayyid Quṭb claims a harmonic relationship of the divine law and the way God created this world. He claims that Muslim Shari'a does not violate or conflict with anything that God has created. In fact, it is the only religious law that is in harmony with God's creation and that responds to its needs. For Sayyid Quṭb, humans are created with a dual nature (*muzdawij al-ṭabīʿa*). They are made of clay into which God breathes a part of His spirit (*rūḥ*). Both steps are mentioned in the Qur'an, where verses refer to how God formed humans from clay (for example, Q 23.12–15, 38.76) and how He gave them hearing, seeing, and "heart" (*fu'ād*) by breathing a part of His spirit (*min rūḥihi*) into the material form (Q 32.9). In another place the spirit (*rūḥ*) is singled out as one of the things that belong to the Lord's domain (Q 17.75). These Qur'anic passages are central for Sayyid Quṭb's understanding of human nature.[58] The two elements of human nature make it equally disposed to two kinds of actions, good and bad ones. There is no stronger inclination to do good deeds than to do bad ones. Thus a natural human tendency to do good and to become a pious Muslim is balanced, or rather limited, by an equally strong tendency to do wrong and to become an unbeliever (*kāfir*). Left to themselves and without divine revelation, humans are, however, capable of choosing good over bad.

> Humans are capable of distinguishing between what is good and what is bad just as they are capable of directing their souls equally toward the good and the bad. This faculty [to distinguish good from bad] is concealed within the nature of the individual. The Qur'an sometimes talks about this faculty as "inspiration" (*ilhām*), as in the following verse:

> "By the soul and the one who has formed it; He, who has inspired it to become either wrong-doing or god-fearing." [Q 91.7–8]
>
> Sometimes, the Qur'an expresses this notion as "guidance" (*hidāya*), as in the verse where it says that "We have guided him toward (*hadaynāhu*) the two highways." [Q 90.10][59]

The "two highways," or rather the "two high pastures" (*najdān*), are the good and the bad that human souls can incline to. They are part of the human natural condition and thus part of *fiṭra*: "The dual nature of the human is concealed within his inner core. It is within the form of a disposition (*istiʿdād*). . . . These [two] dispositions are created according to the *fiṭra*, formed according to nature, and concealed as inspiration."[60] Inspiration (*ilhām*) or instinct refers to the human ability to distinguish right from wrong and good from evil. Sayyid Quṭb teaches that in the state of their original *fiṭra*, humans have the ability to know the moral value of their actions.[61] They know moral judgments instinctively. Sayyid Quṭb calls this instinctive ability to know right from wrong the "faculty of moral awareness" (*al-quwwa al-wāʿiyya*):

> There is within the human essence alongside these innate and concealed capacities a faculty that is heedful, perceptive, and refining. The responsibility of humans depends on this faculty. Whoever employs this faculty for the refinement of his soul, for its purification and the further advancement of the disposition to do good that is within the soul—in order that it gets the upper hand over the disposition to do wrong—he will be prosperous. Whoever suppresses this faculty, who hides it, and who makes it weaker, will fail miserably: "Prosperous is he who purifies it, and failed has he who seduces it." [Q 90.10][62]

Being good and believing are therefore not limited to humans who have received divine revelation and a divine law. Humans know "by their nature" what is right and what is wrong. This, however, creates a responsibility to act according to what is good: "Therefore, as a result of the fact that humanity is bestowed with this innate faculty that is able to choose and to guide, there comes a responsibility (*tabiʿa*). The faculty [to know right from wrong] guides the dual disposition that is part of the *fiṭra* and that has the potential to grow within the field of goodness, as well as in the field of evil."[63] The imperative for humans to do good exists from the very moment of humanity's creation. Humans are obliged to answer this call. Human nature responds to it with the "faculty of moral awareness." Revelation is not necessary to act adequately in response to this responsibility. Revelation does, however, help humans master this task:

> In his mercy toward humans God did not make them rely entirely on the dual disposition of man's instinctive *fiṭra*. Nor did He make them entirely dependent on the faculty of moral awareness that enables them to turn [towards good]. Rather, He helps them through revelations that lay down the scales [of moral judgment] in a firm and precise manner. [Through revelations] God discloses to humans what their inspiration had told them about what to believe. He exposes the signs of right-guidance that were [already] in the human soul and on the horizons around them. He reveals to them the disasters of human caprice and makes them see the truth in its right form. Through this the right becomes clear, and a light is given that discloses and that has no dark spot in it and no uncertainty.[64]

To sum up, human nature includes the freedom (*ḥurriyya*) to choose one's actions. At the same time, humans are held responsible (*tabiʿa*) for their actions and put under the obligation to do good. In order to cope with these two key conditions of their existence (*wujūd*) and createdness (*khalīqa*), God breathed into humanity "from His spirit" (*min rūḥihi*) and provided humanity with a faculty to distinguish good actions from bad ones. For Sayyid Quṭb, this faculty is not reason but rather "inspiration" (*ilḥām*). The basis of human judgments on the moral characteristics of their actions lies hidden within their souls. In principle these judgments can also be deduced from God's creation because they are "in the signs on the horizons around them" (*dalāʾil . . . fī al-āfāq min ḥawlahu*). In addition, God confirmed these judgments in clear and precise revelations. God's last and most precise revelation, the Qur'an, addresses the challenge of human existence and createdness most appropriately and provides humans with the moral judgments most suited to the world and the nature they live in.[65]

Moral guidance has three possible sources: the "faculty of moral awareness," the signs of nature, and divine revelation. All three bear witness to the same moral judgments. The "faculty of moral awareness" is part of what God has breathed into the clay that was the material kernel of humanity. The dual nature of humanity—that is, its inclination to follow Islam and its equally strong inclination toward wrongdoing—is determined by humanity's dual source of creation through matter (clay) and the spirit. The spiritual side of humanity includes its moral awareness. Its content is confirmed in God's revelations, in particular in the revelation of Islam.[66] This dual condition of matter and spirit is humanity's *fiṭra*. Shari'a, understood as the moral rules contained in the last revelation, responds most perfectly to the dual condition of *fiṭra*. Moral laws that differ from Shari'a violate the balance between matter and spirit within *fiṭra*. These laws are not in accord with moral instincts or with the human experience (*tajriba*) of the world.[67]

One example where the divine law of Shari'a responds most adequately to the particular nature of God's creation is the division of labor between the sexes.[68] Quṭb claims that there is a set of "simple realities in the *fiṭra*" (*ḥaqā'iq fiṭriyya basīṭa*) that are fundamental for human life and by which all human communities have to abide. One of these realities is that all human communities are based on the family and the protection it offers to the individual.[69] According to the rules of Shari'a, a family may consist of one husband and more than one wife. The Qur'an allows men to take more than one wife but limits the number of wives to four (Q 3.4). "Why," asks Sayyid Quṭb, "has this license been permitted?" His answer lies in an interpretation of *fiṭra*:

> Islam is an order (*niẓām*) for humanity, a realistic and a positive order that befits the *fiṭra* of man and the way he has been created. Islam is suitable to man's reality and the things that are necessary for him. . . . It is a realistic, positive order that takes man from his reality that he is in and from his place that he has and elevates him to an advanced position until he reaches the very top. This happens without rejection of man's *fiṭra* and without denying it.[70]

Looking at the different human societies that have been established through the course of history, one finds many with laws that permit more than one woman for one man. These laws may not always legitimize these kind of relationships as marriages. They do, however, acknowledge that the ratio between men and women with regard to sexual relations is not one to one. In fact, laws that allow men to marry only one woman lead to a situation where not all women find a husband and where, in addition to this, men develop illicit relationships with the women who are left unmarried. This situation violates *fiṭra*; it does not adequately regulate the reproductive capacity of the two sexes, nor does it protect the honor of women. According to Quṭb, Islam has chosen a solution that is most equitable to men and women and that organizes human reproductive abilities in a most productive way. These abilities are different in men and women, a fact reflected by the divine law's injunction to have one man marry a maximum of four women.[71]

> The authorization [for men to marry a maximum of four women] reflects the reality of the human *fiṭra* and the reality of life. It defends the community from its tendency—under the pressure of the necessities in the diverse reality of human *fiṭra*—toward disintegration or restlessness on the one hand. On the other hand, the limitation defends marital life from chaos and disorder, and it defends the wife from tyranny and oppression.[72]

The destructive tendencies that lead human communities either to become unproductive or to become licentious are part of *fiṭra*. They are part of the material aspect of humanity that leads it to act unjustly and immorally. Divine law addresses these tendencies in *fiṭra*. It strengthens the positive dispositions that enable humanity to act in a just and good manner. The legislation of Shari'a is in perfect harmony with nature and with natural law. In fact, all other legislation that would restrict men to marry fewer than four women or that would allow them to marry more than four would violate the "realities of the human *fiṭra*."

Polygamy is one of a number of instances where Shari'a limits the rights of women in comparison with the rights of men. Fundamentalist literature that follows Sayyid Quṭb's line of reasoning in these cases recognizes the restricted role of women in a Muslim society and legitimizes it with similar arguments. Muḥammad Quṭb, Sayyid's younger brother and the ideological caretaker of his oeuvre, wrote a long chapter on women's rights in one of his most influential books, published as early as 1954.[73] Muḥammad addresses what he calls a licentious lifestyle of women in European societies and criticizes it as a violation of both natural and divine law. The situation of women in Europe is mainly the result of the Industrial Revolution, which overburdens women with the care of children and with factory work. The tendency of humans to exploit their weaker peers led men to exploit the female workforce of their own societies. The natural role of women is, according to Muḥammad Quṭb, to raise children. It is a violation of *fiṭra* if women who raise children take on tasks outside the family household. This does not mean that women play a secondary role in human society. Bringing up children is in no way secondary to any other work. Also, there is still the opportunity to take up political responsibilities before children are born or once the children have left the home. Shari'a decrees, according to Muḥammad Quṭb, that women may seek leadership (*siyāsa*) in life only so long as they have no children to care for. "After having children she can ill afford to shoulder extra responsibilities, for her function as a mother is already far too great a burden upon her."[74]

For Sayyid Quṭb and his brother Muḥammad, there is no tension between divine law and natural law. Divine law as encoded in Shari'a is in perfect harmony with the way God has created humans and nature. In fact, Shari'a and the laws of God's creation are one and the same. In his most influential book, *Milestones*, published in 1964 shortly before his final imprisonment and execution, Sayyid Quṭb expresses the view that Shari'a is part of the laws that govern nature. In a chapter titled "A Universal Shari'a" ("Sharīʿa kawniyya"), Quṭb presents Shari'a as the foundation of a holistic normative order that mirrors the order of the natural world.[75] It is evident that in the natural world God has created an order that is in perfect harmony with itself. The rules of this order determine that in nature all things dovetail with one another. Sayyid Quṭb calls this state of harmony "the truth" (*al-ḥaqq*) and says that it is created by "the law" (*al-nāmūs*), meaning the law of nature. Humans are able to know this law:

> The *fiṭra* of humans has in its depths a perception of this truth. The nature of man's creation and the nature of the universe around him reveal to his *fiṭra* that what is existent is based on truth and that truth is the authentic core in it. It reveals that what is existent stands firmly upon the law (*al-nāmūs*). There is no turmoil, there are no overlapping ways, no conflicting purposes, and no disagreement between its parts. It does not move at random, nor does it depend on chance. . . . It advances according to a detailed order that is determined and ordained.[76]

The whole universe is subject to God's rule, which is exercised in the law (*al-nāmūs*) that governs His creation. Humans know about this law from their study of nature. Human knowledge of this law, however, will never be more than an imperfect approximation of the perfect law. The normative law of moral values is part of this universal law of nature. Humans know about this law intuitively. God has created a universal law that governs all aspects of His creation—including human actions—such that people are able to know the universal law in all its aspects, albeit not in its perfection. Those aspects of the law that govern nature are known from scientific inquiry, while those aspects that govern the normative values of human actions are known through the study of the signs of God's creation.[77]

Humans are part of universal existence (*al-wujūd al-kawnī*), and the rules that govern *fiṭra* are not separated from the law that governs universal existence. Because God has created humans with a dual nature from matter and from the spirit of their Lord, humans, through the material aspect of their nature, are bound to the laws that govern the material world. They have no choice in these actions. Breathing, eating, drinking, feeling pain, having feelings, and having understanding are involuntary actions governed by the universal law of nature.[78] Regarding voluntary actions of humans, however, God has prescribed Shari'a "in order to regulate the voluntary human life in a way that is in harmony with man's natural [involuntary] life. On account of this, Shari'a is nothing else than one section (*qiṭāʿ*) of the divine general law that governs human *fiṭra* and the general *fiṭra* of existence, and all parts are well coordinated with one another."[79] Because of its divinely created character, Shari'a is part of the universal law that God has ordained for the totality of His creation. Shari'a is therefore a universal law and valid for all of humanity.

> The Shari'a that God has ordained for the life of humanity is a universal Shari'a in the sense that it is connected to (*mutaṣṣil bi*) and in harmony with (*mutanāsiq maʿā*) the general law of the universe. Obedience to Shari'a is necessary for humans in order to bring their lives into harmony with the movements of the universe that they live in. Furthermore, this is necessary in order to achieve harmony between the rules that govern the inner human *fiṭra* and the rules that govern the outer human life. Thirdly, it is necessary in order to achieve a perfect harmony between the inner personality and the outer personality of man.[80]

A moral law that achieves this kind of harmonious relationship between the different sections of God's creation will lead to universal peace among all elements of creation. If humanity applies Shari'a, it will be at peace with itself, and all conflicts between men will end. Similarly, it will be at peace with nature and with the whole universe.[81] A moral system that achieves this universal harmony can only be legislated by God Himself. Since humans have only incomplete knowledge about God's creation and the laws that govern it, they will never succeed in formulating a law that creates harmony between the different parts of God's creation.[82] Shari'a is the only legislative system that is in accordance with the normative rules of the universal law. The divine law of Islam is, in fact, a return (*rajʿ*) to this universal law. "When Islam builds its structure in this manner as a unique order that is singled out from all the other orders that humanity has known, it returns to the most universal foundations in the rules that govern all existence—not only human existence. And it returns to the ways most appropriate for all existence—not only to the ways most appropriate for human life."[83] Islam is submission to God's law—the universal law of existence of which Shari'a is one branch.

SAYYID QUṬB AND MAWDŪDĪ: HOW NATURAL LAW IS TO BE DETERMINED

The claim that Shari'a is an integral part of natural law is eloquently expressed in Sayyid Quṭb's writing. Many authors of the Islamist movement share this claim.[84] Abū l-Aʿlā Mawdūdī, who published his first works in the 1930s in Urdu and whose books became available in Arabic in the 1950s, expresses a similar notion. Although moral values of human actions are absolute, they are also laid down in Shari'a as *maʿrūfāt*, "allowed actions," and *munkarāt*, "disallowed actions":

> The term *maʿrūfāt* denotes all the qualities that have always been accepted as "good" by human conscience. Conversely, the word *munkarāt* denotes all those qualities that have always been condemned by human nature as "evil". In short, the *maʿrūfāt* are in harmony with human nature and the *munkarāt* are against nature. The Shari'a gives precise definitions of *maʿrūfāt* and *munkarāt*, clearly indicating the standards of goodness to which individuals and society should aspire.[85]

This passage reveals a slightly different view of human nature than Sayyid Quṭb's. Mawdūdī says that only those actions that Shari'a describes as morally good are in harmony with human nature. Mawdūdī's view of human nature is that of an entirely good person who fights the evil that is outside his nature. Shari'a is in harmony with natural law because both Shari'a and nature aim "to make sure that good flourishes and evils do not destroy or harm human life."[86]

Compared with Mawdūdī's position, Sayyid Quṭb's view of human nature is more developed. For him, *fiṭra* includes the disposition both to do good and to do evil. In addition to this, it includes an innate and instinctive faculty that knows what is good and bad in human actions. Predecessors of Sayyid Quṭb such as Mawdūdī and Ibn Taymiyya had acknowledged such a faculty as a central part of *fiṭra*.[87] But these thinkers did not distinguish between the dispositions (*istiʿdādāt*) of the *fiṭra* and the "faculty of moral awareness" (*al-quwwa al-wāʿiyya*). Only the combination of the ability to do good and bad with the faculty to know what is good explains why humans so often fall into unbelief and evil. Human *fiṭra* makes people become unbelievers and follow their inclination to do evil. It is "natural" for humans to do wrong. Were it not for the "faculty of moral awareness," the inner struggle between good and bad actions would be without direction. This natural faculty leads humanity to follow the good and true path that their nature also provides. Quṭb writes: "Distortions (*shiqāq*) of the natural way of things appear when mankind—under the influence of his whims and desires (*ahwā'*)—sways from the truth that is hidden in the depths of his *fiṭra*. This happens when he accepts a moral law for his life that is based on his whims and desires rather than on God's Shari'a."[88] Thus Sayyid Quṭb and Mawdūdī explain humanity's deviation from God's law differently. For Sayyid Quṭb, the struggle between good and bad is within human nature because both are part of it. For Mawdūdī, human nature struggles with the bad temptations that come from outside it.

Contrary to Sayyid Quṭb, the natural law that humans find within themselves is for Mawdūdī not identical to Shari'a. In Sayyid Quṭb the notion of an identity between natural law and Shari'a can hardly be more complete. There is nothing in Shari'a that is not also within natural law. For Mawdūdī, however, there is simply more moral guidance in Shari'a than in natural law. This is particularly evident in the constitution of human communities:

> The Qur'an leaves no room for the impression that the divine law may mean merely the law of nature and nothing more. On the contrary, it raises the entire edifice of its ideology on the basis that humankind should order the affairs of its ethical and social life in accordance with the law, i.e. the Shari'a, that God has communicated through his Prophets. . . . It denies in the clearest terms the right of humans to exercise any discretion in such matters as have been decided by God and His Prophet.[89]

Mawdūdī clearly rejects the idea that humans may be able to determine their own communities according to what they believe is natural law. For Mawdūdī, there are two key elements in the relationship between divine and natural law: first, the fact that Shari'a contains a more extensive and more precise set of normative judgments not included in natural law, and second, the resulting fact that natural law cannot be identified independently from Shari'a.

For Mawdūdī, Shari'a responds to moral questions that are more complex if they are compared with natural law. Thus God revealed normative knowledge in the Qur'an that humans are unable to obtain by other means. Mawdūdī follows theological notions of the Ashʿarite school that were widespread in premodern Muslim theology and that still resound in modern Muslim thinking:

> Even if this world and its natural laws (*qāwānīn ṭabīʿiyya*) are sufficient and adequate for what is within the human essence of mineral, organic, and animal elements, they cease to be sufficient for his creational element (*al-ʿunṣur al-khalqī*). This needs a different order for the universe, an order in which the only governing law is the creational law (*al-qānūn al-khalqī*) and in which the natural law is only auxiliary to it.[90]

Still, Mawdūdī shares the general claim that Shari'a is in harmony with natural law. Crucially, he leaves open how the harmonious or identical moral judgments that both contain are to be determined. One might suppose that Mawdūdī, as well as Sayyid Quṭb, assumes that moral judgment can be established from two sources, (1) a reading of Shari'a or (2) an inquiry into the moral judgment of natural law, and that both methods come to the same result where these fields overlap. This, however, is not the case. Although Muslim scholarship has developed a relatively clear method to determine the first source, that is, Shari'a, no clear method is available to determine the moral judgments of natural law. Neither Mawdūdī nor Sayyid Quṭb is able to name such a method. Both agree that human inquiries into nature can produce only incomplete knowledge of the laws that govern it and thus give only incomplete information of natural law. God's revelation, on the other hand, has given decisive knowledge of the law that is both divine and natural. Thus for both thinkers, the moral laws of nature are those of Shari'a. This identity makes an inquiry into the exact laws of nature obsolete. Shari'a is the clear and unambiguous spokesperson of natural law. Sayyid Quṭb's treatment of polygamy, for instance, starts at the injunction of Shari'a and develops from there what is natural in humans. The ratio of a maximum of four women for one man is, according to Sayyid Quṭb, equitable because it reflects the natural dispositions of men and women most perfectly. These dispositions and the equitable solution of the one-to-four ratio are known not from a detailed study of human nature, but simply from Shari'a.

Islamist theologians make no attempts to establish the harmony of Shari'a and natural law from a detailed comparison of the two. When faced with the question, what is the normative law of nature? Islamists answer that it is represented by the rulings of Shari'a. This response is not descriptive but normative. It is based on the prior claim of the harmony between Shari'a and natural law. It does not establish this harmony from a comparison of the two. For Sayyid Quṭb, the laws of nature are the injunctions and judgments of Shari'a. Shari'a is the only point of reference for knowledge of what natural law is. Therefore, obedience to Shari'a is obedience to natural law. In fact, obedience to Shari'a establishes natural law:

> Obedience to God's Shari'a is imperative in order to completely harmonize human life and the life of the universe and to harmonize the law (*nāmūs*) that governs the human *fiṭra* and that governs the universe. Obedience to God's Shari'a is necessary in order to bring the law that governs the social life of humans in

> accordance with the general law. Only if humanity obeys God does it make sure that it submits to God alone—just as this universe submits to God alone.[91]

The assumed natural imperative to obey natural law simply becomes the imperative to obey Shari'a. Since the believer is unable to establish natural law from any source other than Shari'a, he must obey Shari'a and not what he may think natural law is. Any perceived conflict between the two must not be referred to Shari'a. Whoever notices a conflict between Shari'a and natural law must correct his idea of what natural law is. Westernized intellectuals, for instance, who claim to have knowledge of natural law that is in conflict with Shari'a follow their whims and their desires (*ahwā'*).

Here lies the explanation of Emilio Platti's observation that Mawdūdī held a contradictory position regarding the relationship between Shari'a and natural law. Although Islamists such as Mawdūdī and Sayyid Quṭb energetically claim that Shari'a is in harmony with natural law, they reject efforts to establish natural law from anything other than Shari'a. Ethical discourses based on rational arguments or scholarly inquiries into nature can only establish crude approximations of the perfect harmony established by the laws that really govern God's creation. These investigations often lead to wrong conclusions about natural law. Islam is submission to God's revealed Shari'a, and this includes the rejection of other kinds of law—including what some people often falsely believe is "natural law."

CONCLUSION

Sayyid Quṭb and Mawdūdī respond to the scientific and modernist claim that nature is the realm of reason with an alternative concept that equates Shari'a with the moral laws established in "nature." In their alternative concept "nature" is not determined by reason or by a study of the world around us, but rather by Shari'a. Sayyid Quṭb accepts the results of the rationalist sciences and of philosophy only if their conclusions tally with Shari'a. Although humans know intuitively and through reflection what is right or wrong, their faculty of reason is unable to grasp the full meaning of these judgments if it is unassisted by revelation. Reason can never be the judge (*ḥākim*) of the truths of revelation. Rather, reason should "meet with" (*yaltaqī ʿan*) revelation, meaning that it should receive and embrace Shari'a's claim for truth. Reason, Quṭb says, should make efforts to understand revelation and to align itself toward it.[92]

The implication that Shari'a dictates what human reason should produce within the field of moral judgments makes it particularly difficult for educated modernist intellectuals to accept Quṭb's theology. The points of conflict between Shari'a and moral judgments based on the contemporary notion of what reason dictates are clear to many intellectuals educated in philosophical ethics. Islamists' apologetic attempts to prove that all judgments of Shari'a are reasonable and represent natural law struggle to be convincing.[93] This is why Islamists went on the offensive and embraced the equation between Shari'a and reason from both sides. If Shari'a is truly rational, then rationality must follow Shari'a. Once accepted, this concept offered a positive counterpart to the Islamist rejection of the established categories of rationalism and of contemporary science as "Western" and contrary to Islam. For those who consciously choose retreat from Westernized societies, Shari'a offers an "Islamic reason" that is regarded as the true reason that governs God's creation. Or, as Emmanuel Sivan put it in 1985, analyzing the writings of Arab Islamists of the 1960s and 1970s: "The Maudoodi dictum, often quoted by Arab fundamentalists, sums up well this rejection: instead of claiming that Islam is truly reasonable, one should hold that reason is Islamic."[94] This is not a contradiction—as Emilio Platti claims—but rather a vicious circle. The claim that Shari'a is in harmony with natural law is verified with the assertion that natural law follows Shari'a. Although Shari'a and natural law correspond to one another, what should be obeyed is Shari'a, not what humanity may establish as natural law.

4 ISLAMIC LAW AND LEGAL CHANGE: THE CONCEPT OF *MAṢLAḤA* IN CLASSICAL AND CONTEMPORARY ISLAMIC LEGAL THEORY

Felicitas Opwis

SINCE THE LATE NINETEENTH CENTURY discussions of *maṣlaḥa* have become ubiquitous in Islamic jurisprudence and not uncommon in Islamic writings of various types, ranging from *ḥadīth* studies[1] to policy recommendations.[2] *Maṣlaḥa* literally means a cause or source of something good and beneficial; in English it is frequently translated as "public interest," although it is much closer in meaning to well-being, welfare, and social weal.[3] Why has the concept of *maṣlaḥa* become so pervasive in contemporary Islamic legal discourse? The answer to this question has many facets. One factor contributing to its importance is that Muslims think of *maṣlaḥa* as the embodiment of the spirit of Islamic law. Another factor is its long history; it is thus seen as an authentic Islamic concept, unrelated to Western intellectual traditions. In addition, the concept of *maṣlaḥa* can be used as a vehicle for legal change, and that capacity is the main focus of my chapter. How much legal change can be brought about by means of this concept depends on the purpose *maṣlaḥa* serves within a jurist's overall concept of Islamic law. In this chapter I first address the question of legal change in Islamic law. Then I summarize the teachings of those Islamic legal theorists from the eleventh to the fourteenth century CE whose concepts of *maṣlaḥa* influenced jurists in the modern period. Finally, I analyze how the concept of *maṣlaḥa* was understood by some prominent figures of Islamic jurisprudence in the modern period. I restrict myself to a number of key authors of the Arab world who wrote from the end of the nineteenth century to the 1960s. Furthermore, I attempt to explain how the historical and personal context influenced jurists' interpretations of *maṣlaḥa* and the way in which they integrated it into the framework of legal theory.[4]

ISLAMIC LAW AND LEGAL CHANGE

Social change poses important questions for any legal system that is based on a finite text, be it a constitution or a religious scripture. The main issue jurisprudents have to come to terms with is how the limited material foundation of the law can be brought to bear on everyday life in an ever-changing environment. In a legal system that is based on a man-made constitution, legislators have the possibility to address social change by means of enacting laws or constitutional amendments.[5] In Islamic law, God is conceived to be the sole legislator. With the death of the Prophet Muhammad in 632 CE the possibility of enlarging or changing the material sources of the law, namely, the Qur'an and Sunna,[6] by means of revelation came to an end.

As in other legal systems, Islamic jurists resort to interpretation in order to apply the material sources of the law to the actual legal cases that need to be ruled upon. This interpretive activity includes extending the existing law to new situations that are not immediately addressed in the scripture and adapting or setting aside rulings established in the material sources of the law according to changed circumstances.

Extending and adapting the revealed law raise the question of how to derive the correct ruling for instances in which the law does not regulate the believer's conduct explicitly. That the ruling be correct is important for several reasons. One is that only a correct ruling will be considered legitimate and will be followed (barring brute force). When jurists extend or adapt the law, they risk destabilizing their own and the law's legitimacy unless they can demonstrate with considerable certainty that the new ruling remains true to the divine will. Theoretically, jurists can achieve legal certainty in two ways. First, they can adopt a formal legal rationality in which the validity of the derived ruling depends on the application of strict procedural rules that are logically sound; the correctness of the procedures guarantees legal certainty and minimizes subjectivity and arbitrariness. Second, jurists can follow a substantive legal rationality that evaluates whether the derived ruling accords with the ethical purpose of the law; the more the ruling corresponds to the purpose of the law, the higher its degree of certainty and the closer its approximation to the divine legislation.

Another reason why a ruling that extends or adapts the Qur'an or Sunna needs to be correct results from the religious character of the law. Obedience and disobedience to God's laws affect the believer not only in this world but in the afterlife in the form of divine reward and punishment. A jurist's pronouncement that the believer is prohibited from performing or obligated to perform a particular action involves consequences beyond the material world. Only a correct ruling can guarantee that the believer's conduct is correct in the eyes of God.

Historically, Islamic jurists and theologians developed two different answers to the question of why or when a ruling is correct. Their inquiry was connected more generally to the question of how to attain knowledge about the ethical value of an act. One position, which is characterized by rationalistic objectivism and associated with the Muʿtazilite school of theology, holds that acts are inherently good or bad and that the human intellect is able to know their value without the aid of revelation.[7] The goodness or badness of an act is tied primarily to its beneficence or harm, which the human intellect can assess.[8] A correct legal ruling thus would be one that permits a beneficial act or prohibits something harmful. The other position, characterized by theistic subjectivism, is that of the Ashʿarite school of theology.[9] Adherents of this position hold that something is good only because God commands it and bad only because He prohibits it. If God imposed lying or idolatry on the believer, then lying and idolatry would be good by definition. This school of thought emphasizes that the human intellect is incapable of arriving at moral knowledge independent from the divine revelation. The ethical and legal value of an act is knowable exclusively through an evaluation of God's will as revealed in scripture. A correct ruling can be derived only from the revealed law.[10]

Both positions are problematic. Although the adherents of the position of rationalistic objectivism accept revelation as a supplementary source of moral knowledge,[11] their view that the intellect is able to determine what is good leads ultimately to the irrelevance of the revealed law. When any legal issue that is not directly addressed in scripture can be decided by recourse to rational inquiry unaided by revelation, then with the passing of time and social change the applied body of law based on revelation will continuously decrease. With the exception, perhaps, of the area of ritual worship (*ʿibādāt*), God's law as pronounced in the Qur'an and Sunna will lose its importance for people. This position also raises questions about identity: what makes an individual a Muslim or a society Islamic? Is it only the performance of different religious rituals that distinguishes Muslims from Christians and Jews? What is the role of the Qur'an and Sunna in society?

If rationalism has difficulties with slipping into secularism, subjectivism has problems remaining relevant. The position that right and wrong are whatever

God commands, although it affirms the importance of revelatory knowledge to make moral statements, leaves unanswered the question of how to know God's judgment when it is not unequivocally expressed in the scriptural sources of the law. If the revealed law cannot address new and changed circumstances, it will become in time less useful to the people it is supposed to serve.

Neither of these two positions in unadulterated form was historically viable.[12] Although by the middle of the eleventh century the school of theistic subjectivism established itself as the orthodox view of Sunni Islam, one factor that helped its ascendance to mainstream Islam was its rapprochement with the rationalistic position in the field of legal theory.[13] Islamic jurisprudents of both camps, wishing to strengthen their positions, developed procedures that aimed at curbing the unchecked use of human reasoning in the area of religious law and at making the law-finding process less arbitrary and more objective. These efforts to formalize legal reasoning produced a systematized and coherent legal theory. Both Ashʿarites and Muʿtazilites accepted that the sources of the law are the Qur'an, Sunna, consensus (*ijmāʿ*), and legal analogy (*qiyās*).[14]

The four sources of Islamic law are explained in Chapter 1 of this book. Of these four sources of law, consensus and legal analogy primarily work to extend existing rulings of the Qur'an and Sunna to new situations. They are procedural sources of law and cannot, in theory, be used to set aside Qur'anic or Sunnaic rulings. In practice, when existing rulings were revised, reference to subsidiary legal principles, such as juristic preference (*istiḥsān*) and custom (*ʿurf*), were made. For jurists who adhered to the Ashʿarite school of theology, both of these principles had drawbacks: juristic preference was associated with arbitrary opinion, while custom could not claim to be part of the revealed law. Perhaps as a result of efforts to resolve these dilemmas, later Ashʿarite jurists, in particular al-Ghazālī, developed the concept of *maṣlaḥa* as a method not only to extend the divine law but also to adapt it to changed circumstances.

Our knowledge about the development of the concept of *maṣlaḥa* in Islamic legal theory before the eleventh century is still vague.[15] Although rulings based on some kind of consideration of the social good are found in legal writings that go back to the eighth or ninth century,[16] the first discussions in legal theory that used *maṣlaḥa* (or *istiṣlāḥ*) as a technical term are found in the late tenth century.[17] Toward the end of the eleventh century al-Ghazālī (d. 1111) first defined *maṣlaḥa* in a tangible manner.

Al-Ghazālī argued that *maṣlaḥa* was God's purpose (*maqṣad*, pl. *maqāṣid*) in revealing the divine law, and, more concretely, that this intention was to preserve for humankind the five essential elements for their well-being, namely, their religion, life, intellect, offspring, and property. (These elements became known in legal writings as *al-ḍarūrāt* or *al-ḍarūriyyāt al-khamsa.*) Whatever protects these elements and averts harm from them is a *maṣlaḥa*, and whatever fails to do so is its opposite, namely, *mafsada.*[18]

Al-Ghazālī's understanding of *maṣlaḥa* set the parameters for the interpretation of this concept by later scholars. Jurists generally accepted that the believers' *maṣlaḥa* is the lawgiver's purpose in laying down the law. The point that remained controversial is to what extent this *maṣlaḥa* is discernible by the human intellect without the revealed texts indicating it. Technically the debate is about the unattested *maṣlaḥa* (*maṣlaḥa mursala*), one for which there is no concrete indication (*dalāla*) in the Qur'an, in Sunna, or by consensus (*ijmāʿ*). Despite the controversies over the unattested *maṣlaḥa*, the concept of *maṣlaḥa* gained acceptance among jurisprudents. It became an important, if not the most important, vehicle for legal change in Islamic legal theory. However, the capacity of *maṣlaḥa* to extend or adapt the law to new cases or changed circumstances depends on the way jurists incorporate it into the law-finding process. It is crucial whether jurists emphasize a formal or a substantive legal rationality. How jurists integrated *maṣlaḥa* into procedures to derive new rulings is the focus of what follows.

THE CONCEPT OF *MAṢLAḤA* IN CLASSICAL ISLAMIC LEGAL THEORY

In the discourse on *maṣlaḥa* from the eleventh to the fourteenth century one can identify four models of *maṣlaḥa*. The first model is that of the Shāfiʿī jurists al-Ghazālī and Fakhr al-Dīn al-Rāzī (d. 1210). Despite differences in their understanding and scope of application of the unattested *maṣlaḥa*, the thought of these two jurists is representative of a model that primarily follows a formal rationality and applies considerations of *maṣlaḥa* in the procedure of legal analogy. One may object that al-Ghazālī himself did not consider the unattested *maṣlaḥa* to fall under the rubric of legal analogy.[19] Nevertheless, one is justified in including it in this legal method because in the Ghazālī/Rāzī model the unattested *maṣlaḥa* conceptually takes the place of the *ratio legis* in legal analogy. This was accomplished by defining suitability (*munāsaba*), which is one of the criteria jurists use to establish the correctness of the *ratio legis* (*ʿilla*) of a scriptural ruling, in terms of *maṣlaḥa*. Something is suitable (*munāsib*) when it leads to *maṣlaḥa.*[20] For example, jurists generally identify as the *ratio legis* for the prohibition of consuming wine (*khamr*) its inebriating nature and not its color or the fact that it is liquid. Wine's quality of inebriation is a suitable characteristic for its prohibition because it thus leads to *maṣlaḥa* by protecting the believer's intellect from harm. By analogy, other substances can be subsumed under this prohibition when they share the same *ratio legis*, that is, when they too are inebriating. By identifying *maṣlaḥa* with suitability, al-Ghazālī and al-Rāzī integrated this concept into legal analogy; the unattested *maṣlaḥa* was considered one type of suitable characteristic that indicates the *ratio legis*.[21]

Al-Ghazālī defined attaining *maṣlaḥa* as the purpose of the law that was known with certainty.[22] He envisioned *maṣlaḥa* as a method to extend the law in those cases to which no textual evidence directly applies by using *maṣlaḥa* as their *ratio legis* following specific criteria and categories.[23] However, al-Ghazālī assigned the unattested *maṣlaḥa* a very limited role in the actual derivation of laws. He stipulated that the *maṣlaḥa* had to be known with certainty (*qaṭʿī*), refer universally (*kullī*) to all believers, and be a necessity (*ḍarūra*) for securing one of the essential elements of human existence (religion, life, intellect, offspring, and property). Whatever constituted merely a need (*ḥāja*) or improvement (*taḥsīn*) with respect to these elements was inadmissible in deriving laws without concrete reference to it in the Qur'an or the *ḥadīth*.[24]

Al-Rāzī, in contrast, argued that on the basis of God's habitual custom one obtained high probability that a suitable characteristic that entails *maṣlaḥa*, be it attested or not, was the *ratio legis* of the ruling. He further maintained that in legal matters probability had to be acted upon.[25] In keeping with this argument, al-Rāzī reasoned that not only a *maṣlaḥa* that is necessary (*ḍarūrī*) to secure one of the five essential elements of human existence could serve as a valid *ratio legis* in legal analogy, but also one that pertains to a need (*ḥāja*) or improvement (*taḥsīn*) for these elements. In addition, he accepted as *rationes legis* *maṣlaḥa*s that are known with less than certainty and that do not apply to all believers universally.[26] In his theory of law a pure unattested *maṣlaḥa* did not exist. All valid *maṣlaḥa*s were—at least on the level of their genus (*jins*)—expressed in the texts of the Qur'an and Sunna. Al-Rāzī's legal theory thus enables an extensive application of *maṣlaḥa* within the procedure of legal analogy.

One should keep in mind that legal analogy is a procedure that serves to extend the law to new situations; in theory, it cannot be used to adapt existing textual injunctions to changed circumstances. I say "in theory" because jurists may use an unattested *maṣlaḥa* as *ratio legis* to validate a new ruling and give it priority over a conflicting established ruling. The standard example, supplied by al-Ghazālī, is that of unbelievers shielding themselves with a group of Muslim prisoners against Muslim armies. Although the Qur'an (6.151) prohibits the killing of innocent believers, al-Ghazālī argued that it is permissible to disregard this ruling in order to save the Islamic community. The extent to which considerations of *maṣlaḥa* may set aside scriptural laws depends on the way jurists define what a valid *maṣlaḥa* is. Al-Ghazālī, in this example, permitted that the Qur'anic ruling be set aside only when not killing the Muslim prisoners would certainly threaten the necessary elements of the Muslim community universally.[27] With less stringent conditions for the validity of unattested *maṣlaḥas*, al-Rāzī and other jurists assigned it greater potential to extend and adapt the law than al-Ghazālī.

A second model of *maṣlaḥa* was articulated by the Mālikī jurist Shihāb al-Dīn al-Qarāfī (d. 1285). Al-Qarāfī integrated the concept of *maṣlaḥa* into legal theory in two ways. First, he used it to extend the law through the procedure of legal analogy. Here he adopted al-Rāzī's formal categories for identifying suitable characteristics that may validly serve as *rationes legis*, including the unattested *maṣlaḥa*.[28] Second, al-Qarāfī employed the concept of *maṣlaḥa* in the area of legal precepts (*qawāʿid*). He rationalized precepts such as eliminating pretexts to illegal ends (*sadd al-dharāʾiʿ*) and granting exceptive license to commit something ordinarily prohibited (*rukhṣa*, pl. *rukhaṣ*) on account of *maṣlaḥa*.[29] Scriptural laws could be set aside and changed when they did not bring about *maṣlaḥa* for the case under investigation. Applied in legal precepts, *maṣlaḥa* functions as an independent standard to which a ruling has to conform to be valid; the jurist does not have to take recourse to the sources of the law directly, as in the procedure of legal analogy. Al-Qarāfī's model of *maṣlaḥa* combined both formal and substantive legal reasoning by applying it in legal analogy, as well as in legal precepts. Although this did not alter the extendability of the law, it increased the potential to adapt existing laws to new circumstances over the Ghazālī/Rāzī model.

A third model of *maṣlaḥa* was formulated by the Ḥanbalī jurist Najm al-Dīn al-Ṭūfī (d. 1316). Al-Ṭūfī rejected integrating *maṣlaḥa* into formal procedures and adopted almost exclusively a substantive rationality. He understood *maṣlaḥa* to be the purpose of the law, and an independent criterion for deriving rulings. It constituted for him the most important legal indicant (*dalīl*)—one that was known with certainty, based on inductive reading of the scriptures, and that was discernible by the human intellect.[30] In effect, al-Ṭūfī's theory meant that anything that brought about *maṣlaḥa* or averted harm was commensurate with the purposes of the law. Any unprecedented situation on which the textual sources of the law remained silent could be easily integrated into the fold of Shari'a. In order to adapt the law according to circumstances, al-Ṭūfī argued that a ruling entailing *maṣlaḥa* should receive priority over a contradictory ruling, even one supported by scriptural authority.[31] He limited the supremacy of *maṣlaḥa* in the law-finding process by excluding acts of worship (*ʿibādāt*) from its purview and by stipulating that *maṣlaḥa* could override neither fixed textual injunctions (*muqaddarāt*) nor a specific indicant (*dalīl khāṣṣ*) from the Qur'an, Sunna, or consensus.[32] With those exceptions, al-Ṭūfī's model provided jurists with easily applicable means to extend and adapt the law by using *maṣlaḥa* as a legal indicant in its own right.

The thought of the Mālikī jurist Abū Isḥāq al-Shāṭibī (d. 1388) represents a fourth model of *maṣlaḥa*—the last to be presented in this chapter. Al-Shāṭibī emphasized in his theory of law the early part of Qur'anic revelation. The Meccan suras, he argued, embody the general message of Islam in which the universal sources of the law were laid down. The Medinan suras, as well as Sunna, constitute the particulars of the law that elucidate, specify, qualify, or complement the Meccan revelation.[33] He considered the universal sources of the law to be certain, whereas the particulars of the Qur'an and Sunna were probable, though Qur'anic verses and recurrent *ḥadīth*s were certain in their validity. Whatever was certain was immutable, and whatever pertained to probability was subject to change.[34]

For al-Shāṭibī, attaining *maṣlaḥa* and averting *mafsada* at the level of necessities, needs, and improvements were universal sources of the law and the purpose of the lawgiver.[35] Any situation that lacked textual evidence could be judged using considerations of *maṣlaḥa*.[36] Whether or not an act was commensurate with the law depended in al-Shāṭibī's theory on the actual outcome. As long as an act entailed *maṣlaḥa* and no harm resulted from it that was equal to or greater than the attained *maṣlaḥa*, it was legal.[37] Al-Shāṭibī's concept of *maṣlaḥa* as a universal source of the law also enabled him to use it in adapting the law. In case a particular ruling from the Qur'an or Sunna stood in opposition to a universal source, that is, *maṣlaḥa*, he gave preponderance to the universal source. Likewise, a general ruling should receive priority over a specific ruling that contradicted it. Al-Shāṭibī, however, did not consider *maṣlaḥa* to be weightier in every case. Exempted were those particular rulings that constituted a legal license (*rukhṣa*) or specification (*takhṣīṣ*); here the particular textual ruling could not be set aside on grounds of a general *maṣlaḥa*.[38] In addition, considerations of *maṣlaḥa* had no bearing on acts of worship (*ʿibādāt*), acts that happened or could have happened during the lifetime of the Prophet,[39] and the continuous practice of the early Islamic community.[40] Any other act could be judged according to the *maṣlaḥa* it entailed under particular circumstances, which, of course, varied by place, time, and person.[41] Al-Shāṭibī's model of *maṣlaḥa* provided jurists with a comprehensive system to extend and adapt the law to new circumstances.[42]

These four models of *maṣlaḥa* were developed over the course of four centuries. Although the constituent elements of the concept of *maṣlaḥa* did not actually change after al-Ghazālī defined them, the application of this legal concept was transformed during this time period. In al-Ghazālī and al-Rāzī's interpretation *maṣlaḥa* was a subsidiary legal principle within the rubric of legal analogy. By elaborating strict formal criteria that a jurist had to consider when validating a ruling, al-Ghazālī and al-Rāzī sought to ensure that decisions based on unattested *maṣlaḥa*s did not stray far from the textual sources. Later jurists were less constrained. Over time they increasingly accepted the epistemological certainty of *maṣlaḥa* and interpreted it to mean that *maṣlaḥa* could be used as an independent standard by which to judge the conformity of rulings to the purposes of the law. Although al-Qarāfī applied the *maṣlaḥa* standard only in some areas of legal precepts (*qawāʿid*), al-Ṭūfī elevated it to the dominant criterion of the law-finding process. Finally, in al-Shāṭibī's model *maṣlaḥa* became the element upon which his whole interpretation of Islamic law was based and by which he integrated and harmonized all its areas.

The transformation of the concept of *maṣlaḥa* from a subsidiary principle to the foundation of the law was facilitated by changes in legal logic and epistemology.[43] The most important was the change from relying on formal rationality in the law-finding process, primarily legal analogy, toward using substantive reasoning to attain legal certainty. Attributing legal certainty to the results of substantive reasoning enabled Islamic jurists to justify *maṣlaḥa* as a criterion to derive rulings outside the procedure of legal analogy. *Maṣlaḥa* was understood as an independent standard that was derived from the revealed law and knowable by the human intellect on account of concrete objective criteria. In this interpretation the concept of *maṣlaḥa* incorporates both the Muʿtazilite and Ashʿarite positions on how to attain moral knowledge.

The shift in legal rationality from formal to substantive reasoning structured the capacity of *maṣlaḥa* to extend and adapt the law to new circumstances. The Ghazālī/Rāzī model permits a modicum of legal change and emphasizes the continuous validity and applicability of the revealed scripture. Al-Qarāfī's model has greater potential for adapting the existing law when undesired results would follow its application, without making many changes to the body of Islamic law. Al-Ṭūfī's model allows for legal change in all areas except worship but has the propensity to disregard much of the edifice of Islamic law under changed circumstances. Al-Shāṭibī's model enables jurists to extend and adapt the law in a comprehensive manner, but requires a rethinking of legal hermeneutics. These four models represent the heritage of Islamic thinking on *maṣlaḥa*. Historically the Ghazālī/Rāzī model was the most widely accepted among Islamic jurisprudents. Al-Ṭūfī and al-Shāṭibī's models failed to gain followers for reasons that are not yet known.[44] Only in the modern period, to which we now turn, did Islamic jurists embrace al-Ṭūfī and al-Shāṭibī's models of *maṣlaḥa*.

THE CONCEPT OF *MAṢLAḤA* IN THE MODERN PERIOD

When in the late nineteenth century jurisprudents looked for ways to reform Islamic law, many advocated the practice of *ijtihād*. Because the concept of *maṣlaḥa* falls under the rubric of *ijtihād*, turning toward it was a logical consequence of the reformers' insistence that the gate of *ijtihād* was open. Naturally, jurists built upon the models of *maṣlaḥa* that already existed in Islamic legal theory. Most jurists of the modern period chose aspects of different models, combining them eclectically or reinterpreting them in a manner that fit their own understanding of the law. In the following I present three avenues taken by modern jurists to address, on the one hand, extending and adapting Islamic law in light of social change and, on the other hand, determining the place of Islamic law in the modern state.

The Reformers of the Late Nineteenth and Early Twentieth Centuries: Jamāl al-Dīn al-Qāsimī and Muḥammad Rashīd Riḍā

In the late nineteenth and early twentieth centuries the reform-oriented jurists Jamāl al-Dīn al-Qāsimī (1866–1914)[45] and Muḥammad Rashīd Riḍā (1865–1935)[46] espoused al-Ṭūfī's model of *maṣlaḥa*.[47] Why did these figures herald al-Ṭūfī's model of *maṣlaḥa*? The short answer is that this model best suited the aims of these modern reformers.

Rashīd Riḍā and al-Qāsimī propagated al-Ṭūfī's model of *maṣlaḥa* at a time when the social position of traditionally educated religious scholars was beginning to erode. Within the context of state-initiated modernization programs of the Ottoman Empire and Egypt, secular reformers saw the religious law and its exponents as a factor that slowed progress and hindered administrative and educational reform programs.[48] To retain or even enlarge the relevance of Islamic law, and thereby their own influence, jurists had to prove that Islamic law was able to address the contemporary needs of society and was compatible with the aims of a modern state.[49] Al-Ṭūfī's emphasis that *maṣlaḥa* was rationally discernible supported Rashīd Riḍā and al-Qāsimī's claim that the laws derived on the basis of revelation do not contradict those required by reason.[50]

Furthermore, al-Ṭūfī's concept of *maṣlaḥa* fit into the reformers' idea that Islam could be invigorated by returning to the true, purified Islam based on its scriptural sources.[51] Taking the believer's *maṣlaḥa* as the foremost criterion in deciding rulings was seen to correspond to the spirit of the law.[52] Rashīd Riḍā's desire to facilitate the derivation of rulings could be accomplished by using *maṣlaḥa* as a preponderant standard in law-finding.[53] In addition, al-Ṭūfī's departure from traditional legal methodology constituted the liberation al-Qāsimī and Rashīd Riḍā sought from the fetters of *madhhab* discipline and of adhering to the legal decisions pronounced by earlier jurists (*taqlīd*).[54] At the same time, al-Ṭūfī's model neither questioned Islamic legal hermeneutics per se nor overturned the traditional interpretation of the scripture. Adopting it challenged neither the Islamic character of the law nor the religious education of the *ʿulamāʾ*. Both Rashīd Riḍā and al-Qāsimī were traditionally educated scholars with little exposure to a Western curriculum;[55] and both were part of and identified with the *ʿulamāʾ* as a social group. They aimed at reforming Islamic law from within to strengthen its relevance and enhance the position of the *ʿulamāʾ* in society.

That Rashīd Riḍā saw the concept of *maṣlaḥa* as a way to strengthen the religious scholars' participation in the affairs of the state is manifest in his statements favoring *maṣlaḥa* as a legislative tool. He envisioned mundane legislation to be a type of consultative forum (*shūrā*), consisting of the *ʿulamāʾ* and the political leader (*imām*), that establishes laws on the basis of considering people's *maṣlaḥa*.[56] Similarly, al-Qāsimī saw the reform of Islamic law within its larger social context. The *ʿulamāʾ*, he maintained, need to interpret rulings according to temporal circumstances to make Islamic law relevant to the affairs of society and enable the *ʿulamāʾ* to be its leaders.[57]

Another factor that may have attracted al-Qāsimī and Rashīd Riḍā to al-Ṭūfī's model was that the latter saw his interpretation of *maṣlaḥa* as a means toward bridging differences between schools of law and toward unity of all believers.[58] The reformers of the late nineteenth and early twentieth centuries had the same concern.[59] Although the era of nation-states had not yet come to the Middle East, the region nevertheless experienced centrifugal forces and saw the rise of nationalist sentiments. In addition, increasing European imperialist activities made Muslim societies appear weak. Rashīd Riḍā blamed the differences (*ikhtilāf*) among the legal schools for the weakness of the Islamic community.[60] Al-Qāsimī called on Muslims to unite behind the universally accepted features of religion.[61] Proposing *maṣlaḥa* as a generally accepted legal and ethical standard was intended to overcome sectarian strife between Muslims, unify them, and strengthen them against the onslaught of European domination.[62] In short, al-Qāsimī and Rashīd Riḍā saw in the concept of *maṣlaḥa* as interpreted by al-Ṭūfī the answer to their quest for a pure and simple Islam that invigorates Islamic societies and makes them strong and unified, progressive and innovative, while at the same time enabling the *ʿulamā'* to assume a prominent leadership role in society.

The Concept of *Maṣlaḥa* After the Early Reformers

Jurisprudents who wrote after the early reformist movement represented by Rashīd Riḍā and like-minded *ʿulamā'* were drawn toward interpretations of *maṣlaḥa* other than al-Ṭūfī's. The main reason to turn away from al-Ṭūfī's model was that it was discredited as a type of utilitarianism, like the theories of Jeremy Bentham and John Stuart Mill. Critics accused al-Ṭūfī of limiting God's injunctions based on fallible human reason and of changing the divine law arbitrarily.[63]

Another reason for turning away from al-Ṭūfī's model of *maṣlaḥa* was the continuous marginalization of Islamic law in the countries of the Middle East and North Africa. Although at the beginning of the twentieth century Islamic law and its exponents still exercised a considerable influence, that influence decreased with the breakup of the Ottoman Empire after World War I and the creation of nation-states in its wake. In Chapter 1 it has been explained that most countries established legal codes based in full or part on Western law. The growth in secular legislation, issued frequently by governments that did not identify with Islam, diminished the societal importance of Islamic law. Egypt and Tunisia, for instance, abolished their Shari'a courts in the mid-1950s.[64] Proving that Islamic law was able to function in the legal system of a modern state and preventing it from being reduced to personal-status law interpreted by secular-educated jurists became pressing issues for Islamic jurists over the course of the twentieth century.

Two general trends can be discerned among jurisprudents who addressed the concept of *maṣlaḥa* after the early reformers. Jurists who belonged to the traditional religious establishment, by which I mean that they were educated and/or employed in an institution such as al-Azhar and were *muftīs* or professors of Islamic law, leaned more toward the Ghazālī/Rāzī and al-Qarāfī models, whereas jurists who received some substantial part of their education in Western-style schools and/or were closely involved with the nonreligious state sector, especially as lawyers or politicians, were more attracted to al-Shāṭibī's theory of law.

Proponents of al-Shāṭibī's Model of *Maṣlaḥa*

Ṣubḥī Maḥmaṣānī One proponent of al-Shāṭibī's model of *maṣlaḥa* was the Lebanese jurist and politician Ṣubḥī Rajab Maḥmaṣānī (1909–86).[65] With a doctorate in law from the University of Lyon and an LL.B. diploma from the University of London, Maḥmaṣānī was a scholar of both Western and Islamic law.[66] In his work *The Philosophy of Legislation in Islam* (*Falsafat al-tashrīʿ fī l-Islām*), published in 1946, he laid out an understanding of Islamic legal theory that was closely modeled after al-Shāṭibī.

Maḥmaṣānī built his theory of Islamic legislation on the premise that *maṣlaḥa* and the purposes (*maqāṣid*) of the law were the *rationes legis* for all rulings.[67] These *rationes legis*, he emphasized, were rationally discernible—with the exception of rulings concerning ritual worship (*ʿibādāt*), which he excluded from his investigation.[68] Hence in the area of social transactions (*muʿāmalāt*) humans could extend the law to new situations by using an unattested *maṣlaḥa* of the rank of necessity or need as the *ratio legis* in the procedure of legal analogy.[69] In order to address the issue of adapting existing laws to changed circumstances, Maḥmaṣānī embraced al-Shāṭibī's theory of immutable universals and changeable particulars in the law.[70] In Maḥmaṣānī's view, legal revisions could extend to textual rulings when they no longer brought about the intended *maṣlaḥa*, when necessity (*ḍarūra*) required it, or when the ruling was based on a custom that people had stopped practicing.[71] In this manner jurists could address those laws of the Qur'an and Sunna that were perceived to be incompatible with modern needs and attitudes, while the religious and ethical message of Islam as embodied in the sacred texts would be left intact.

Adopting al-Shāṭibī's theory of universal and particular rulings served yet another purpose that, I believe, represents the primary motive for Maḥmaṣānī's discussion of Islamic legislation. He emphasized that Islamic law was in fact very similar to other, nonreligious legal systems.[72] Maḥmaṣānī claimed that the universal rulings of Islamic law were the same laws that the ancient Greek philosophers had called natural laws, including principles such as justice, truth, and *maṣlaḥa*.[73] This interpretation implies that adopting particular rulings from another legal system did not introduce foreign laws because those particular laws were based on a universal precept, which was substantively the same in all legal traditions. Thus Western law was compatible with Islamic law as long as the people's *maṣlaḥa*, that is, the intention of the lawgiver, was preserved. Al-Shāṭibī's model enabled Maḥmaṣānī to present the current legal systems in the Middle East in general and in Lebanon in particular, which were heavily based on Western legal codes, as truly Islamic. He was writing at a time when the application of traditional Islamic law within the nation-states of the Middle East had been reduced mainly to matters concerning family law. In addition, Lebanon had a large non-Muslim population; as a lawyer and judge he had to apply Lebanese law to all citizens of the state.[74] Al-Shāṭibī's model of *maṣlaḥa* provided the framework for a legal system that in Maḥmaṣānī's interpretation could accommodate all these aspects.

ʿAllāl al-Fāsī The Moroccan jurist Muḥammad ʿAllāl al-Fāsī (1910–74) also adopted al-Shāṭibī's concept of law, although in a less comprehensive fashion.[75] Al-Fāsī was a leader of the Moroccan independence movement. He came from a prominent religious family and studied Islamic law at al-Qarawiyyīn college in Fès. After graduating in 1930, he taught Islamic history at al-Qarawiyyīn and later became a professor of law at the new University of Rabat. He is a complex figure among those who thought about Shari'a and its modern applications and will also be dealt with in a more detailed study by David Johnston in the next chapter. Al-Fāsī's fame derives from his role as the ideologue and leader of the Moroccan independence movement.[76]

Like Maḥmaṣānī, al-Fāsī wanted to demonstrate the ability of Islamic law to provide a legal system for a modern state.[77] His desire to adapt Islamic law to the ever-evolving environment led him to selectively draw upon al-Shāṭibī's adaptive concept of immutable universal and changeable particular rulings.[78] At the same time, he attempted to preserve the traditional structure of Islamic law as much as possible. When he discussed the procedures to derive rulings, he relied heavily on the Ghazālī/Rāzī model of *maṣlaḥa*.[79] As a result of the tension between al-Fāsī's aims to present a modern yet traditional interpretation of Islamic law, his legal theory lacks the internal cohesion that Maḥmaṣānī's thought displays.[80]

Proponents of the Ghazālī/Rāzī and al-Qarāfī Models of *Maṣlaḥa*

Although al-Shāṭibī's legal theory provides a coherent system to extend and adapt the law, implementing his model of *maṣlaḥa* in totality has the potential to challenge not only a large part of the applied law but also elements of Islamic theology, exegesis, and *ḥadīth*. Adopting it without qualification could precipitate a radical departure from the historical body of Islamic law. The desire to avoid dramatic discontinuities led jurists such as ʿAbd al-Wahhāb Khallāf and Muḥammad Saʿīd Ramaḍān al-Būṭī, who were educated in a traditional environment and connected closely with the religious establishment, to be more inclined toward models that followed a formal legal rationality. In light of the continuous marginalization of Islamic law by modern nation-states, they aimed at retaining as much as possible of its traditional character; at the same time, they sought ways to address the extension and adaptation of the law by using the Ghazālī/Rāzī model of *maṣlaḥa* with or without elements of al-Qarāfī's model.

ʿAbd al-Wahhāb Khallāf The Egyptian scholar ʿAbd al-Wahhāb Khallāf (1888–1956) studied at al-Azhar and the School of Law (Madrasa al-qaḍāʾ al-sharʿī) in Cairo, where he later taught for several years.[81] In 1920 he became a judge serving in the Shari'a courts in Egypt and in 1931 was appointed supervisor (*mufattish*) of these courts. His most lasting influence was probably as a professor of Islamic law at Cairo University from 1934 until his death in 1956.[82] During Khallāf's lifetime Islamic law became increasingly replaced in the Egyptian judiciary with Western-inspired legal codes. Khallāf attempted to counter the pressures against Islamic law by promoting a legal principle that was acceptable to various groups within Islam. He considered the concept of *maṣlaḥa* a way to achieve unity, and thus strength, in Islamic legislation.[83] But instead of giving predominance to considerations of *maṣlaḥa* in the way Rashīd Riḍā or al-Qāsimī had done,[84] he sought to preserve the sacredness of the texts and the edifice of Islamic law by turning to the Ghazālī/Rāzī model.

In his 1954 book *Maṣādir al-tashrīʿ al-Islāmī fīmā lā naṣṣa fīhi* (Sources of Islamic Legislation in Cases Where No Text Applies) Khallāf laid out his interpretation of *maṣlaḥa*. He wanted to demonstrate that the legislative sources of Islam were not limited texts or rulings that applied only to a specific historical environment, and that the practice of *ijtihād* guaranteed legislative progress and lawmaking (*taqnīn*) according to the needs of Islamic nations.[85]

Like al-Ghazālī and al-Rāzī, Khallāf integrated considerations of *maṣlaḥa* within the framework of legal analogy (*qiyās*), following predominantly al-Rāzī's criteria to identify a valid *maṣlaḥa*.[86] Deriving rulings on the grounds that thereby an unattested *maṣlaḥa* was safeguarded constituted for Khallāf the most fertile legislative method on matters on which the scripture was silent.[87] Khallāf increased the potential of the unattested *maṣlaḥa* to extend the law to new situations by accepting as valid even those instances in which it was doubtful or illusory that the unattested suitable characteristic indicating the *ratio legis* of the ruling would lead to *maṣlaḥa*.[88]

Although Khallāf's interpretation of *maṣlaḥa* seems at first sight to deny the possibility for an unattested *maṣlaḥa* to set aside textual rulings, he left room for adapting the law by limiting the applicability of the texts.[89] In the area of social transactions Khallāf allowed considerations of unattested *maṣlaḥas* to be employed in deriving laws for those instances when no certain text (*naṣṣ qaṭʿī*) or explicit consensus applied and when recourse to direct legal analogy was not possible.[90] This means that an unattested *maṣlaḥa* may constitute a stronger indicant than an equivocal Qur'anic or Sunnaic text. Khallāf's presentation of the concept of *maṣlaḥa* and the way he integrated it into legal theory reflect his self-perception as a traditional interpreter of previous generations. He nevertheless did not just reiterate their conceptions or the Ghazālī/Rāzī model of *maṣlaḥa* but reinterpreted them in a manner that achieved a twofold aim. First, he enlarged the area of valid rulings based on an unattested *maṣlaḥa* by giving less scope to the texts and more scope to a jurist's independent reasoning. Second, he was careful to preserve the law's divine and Islamic character by excluding from the purview of *maṣlaḥa* those matters in the scriptures that pertained to religious worship, were unequivocally stated, or that differentiated Islamic society from other societies, such as the prescribed punishments (*ḥudūd*) and the regulations about inheritance and divorce.[91] This allowed expanding and adapting Islamic law within the environment of a modern nation-state without losing its traditional character.

Muḥammad Saʿīd Ramaḍān al-Būṭī One of the most interesting exponents of the more restrictive stand on *maṣlaḥa* is the Syrian scholar Muḥammad Saʿīd Ramaḍān al-Būṭī (b. 1929). He graduated from al-Azhar in 1956 with a diploma in teaching Shari'a and taught at several Syrian institutions of learning. After completing his doctorate at al-Azhar in 1965, he joined the faculty of Damascus University as a lecturer in comparative law and religious studies and served as dean of its Shari'a Faculty.[92] Apart from his academic influence, al-Būṭī is well known as a preacher and interpreter of the Qur'an and Sunna through his regular appearance on Syrian television, where he "walks the tightrope to verify *shar'i* rules in the light of secular law and society."[93]

In his work *Ḍawābiṭ al-maṣlaḥa fī l-sharīʿa al-Islāmiyya* (The Precise Determinants of Maṣlaḥa in the Islamic Sharīʿa), which was first published in 1965, al-Būṭī criticized the liberal interpretation of *maṣlaḥa*. He expressly wanted to turn away from using *maṣlaḥa* as a means to legislate and to change textual rulings and the existing legal edifice without proper recourse to the sources of the law.[94] Al-Būṭī emphasized that the intellect alone is incapable of grasping the rulings laid down in Shari'a; neither can it comprehend the order of importance of the essential necessities (*ḍarūrāt*).[95] Mundane *maṣlaḥas*, he maintained, can be determined only on account of Qur'anic or Sunnaic statements and correct legal analogy to these texts.[96] *Maṣlaḥa*, in short, is not an independent legal indicant, as al-Ṭūfī thought it to be.[97] Al-Būṭī rejected the formulation often repeated by Khallāf that "wherever one finds *maṣlaḥa*, there lies God's legislation."[98]

Despite the fact that al-Būṭī adopted the Ghazālī/Rāzī model of *maṣlaḥa* and elements of al-Qarāfī's thought, he couched his elaboration in the language used by al-Shāṭibī. He considered the realization of the believers' *maṣlaḥa* to be the universal meaning of the law; the particulars to this universal meaning were the concrete rulings that hinged upon criteria indicating their *maṣlaḥa*. In order to prevent the use of considerations of *maṣlaḥa* to disregard scriptural rulings, al-Būṭī restricted the universal meaning of *maṣlaḥa* by precise determinants (*ḍawābiṭ*). The two most important determinants are, first, that a legally valid *maṣlaḥa* ought to pertain to the preservation of religion, life, intellect, progeny, and property at the level of necessity, need, or improvement.[99] In this area of legal expansion al-Būṭī followed closely the Ghazālī/Rāzī model of *maṣlaḥa* and incorporated the unattested *maṣlaḥa* under the rubric of legal analogy in the form of the suitable characteristic.[100] Second, a valid *maṣlaḥa* could not contradict a ruling from the Qur'an, Sunna, or a correct legal analogy (*qiyās*).[101] The only way al-Būṭī allowed for adapting existing laws from the Qur'an or Sunna to new circumstances was by specification (*takhṣīṣ*), a method that included, in his interpretation, legal precepts such as averting hardship (*mashaqqa*), necessity (*ḍarūra*), or facilitation (*taysīr*).[102] Specification meant for al-Būṭī that the specifying ruling had its basis in the texts of the Qur'an and Sunna. An unattested *maṣlaḥa* could not specify and thus set aside a textual ruling or one based on legal analogy.[103]

To give jurists guidelines to determine the correct ruling when two unattested *maṣlaḥa*s or two attested *maṣlaḥa*s call for contradictory rulings,[104] al-Būṭī developed an elaborate scale of preponderance that weighed the *maṣlaḥa*, as well as the *mafsada*, entailed in a ruling.[105] He wanted to demonstrate with this scale—which ironically resembles al-Ṭūfī's procedure of determining rulings[106]—that using the criterion of suitability was a better method to determine rulings than basing them on considerations of *maṣlaḥa*.[107]

In al-Būṭī's concept of legal theory *maṣlaḥa* in the form of the criterion of suitability functioned only to extend the law within the framework of legal analogy when the texts were silent. To prevent rigidity in addressing social change, al-Būṭī employed two interpretive strategies. First, he defined the unattested *maṣlaḥa* narrowly as one for which no textual evidence exists regarding the specific class (*jins qarīb*) to which the ruling belongs. The narrow definition of the unattested *maṣlaḥa* enlarged the scope of the attested *maṣlaḥa*. By means of attested *maṣlaḥa*s, mainly in the form of the precepts of necessity and facilitation, al-Būṭī was able to justify disregarding particular scriptural rulings.[108] Al-Būṭī's second strategy was to increase the area of changeable Sunnaic rulings. Only those Sunnaic rulings that concern religious duties or regulations for contracts, sales, gifts, and the like are immutable. The remaining laws derived from the Prophetic Sunna fall under the legislative authority of the imam. In this area he proclaimed that Sunna must be followed only in its universal regulations, that is, attaining *maṣlaḥa*, but its particulars are changeable according to person, place, and time.[109] By adopting the Ghazālī/Rāzī model of *maṣlaḥa* and interpreting the unattested *maṣlaḥa* in a manner that precludes its use in adapting the law, al-Būṭī was able to preserve the particular laws laid down in the Qur'an and much of Sunna.

CONCLUSION

Achieving legal change without forsaking the divine origin of Islamic law has been a persistent challenge for Islamic jurists. At its heart lies the task of finding a balance between reason and revelation. A certain amount of human reasoning is needed to extend and adapt the revealed law to changed circumstances and to retain its relevance to Islamic society. One successful approach has been the concept of *maṣlaḥa*, which entered Islamic legal theory as a mature concept in the eleventh century. Since then, *maṣlaḥa* has been interpreted in various ways. In the premodern period we can distinguish four different models of *maṣlaḥa*, namely, those of al-Ghazālī and al-Rāzī, al-Qarāfī, al-Ṭūfī, and al-Shāṭibī. The models differ primarily in the dominance of formal or substantive legal reasoning used to integrate *maṣlaḥa* into the law-finding process. Employing a formal legal rationality, al-Ghazālī and al-Rāzī incorporated the concept of *maṣlaḥa* into legal analogy (*qiyās*) to extend the law, giving it only minor scope to adapt the law. Al-Qarāfī, leaning more toward substantive reasoning, added to this the use of *maṣlaḥa* in legal precepts (*qawāʿid*). In al-Ṭūfī and al-Shāṭibī's legal thought substantive rationality was predominant. Although al-Ṭūfī applied considerations of *maṣlaḥa* widely in the area of extending and adapting the law, al-Shāṭibī conceived all of Islamic law to be based on this concept.

The degree to which a jurist employs formal or substantive legal rationality not only determines the capacity of *maṣlaḥa* to bring about legal change but also reflects his stand toward the use of reason in the law-finding process. As a rule of thumb, one can say that the more a jurist leans toward substantive rationality in deciding legal matters, the more confidence he has that the human intellect is capable of determining whether or not a concrete situation entails *maṣlaḥa* even without evidence from the material sources of the law.[110] The extent to which *maṣlaḥa* can be used to achieve legal change thus depends on a jurist's worldview concerning the role of reason and revelation in interpreting the law.

That these general attitudes toward law and the human intellect are not completely random is demonstrated by the interpretations of *maṣlaḥa* in the modern period. The jurists presented in this chapter shared a common concern to show that Islamic law was capable of functioning in a modern state. Differences in historical setting and personal position, however, influenced whether a jurist tended to integrate *maṣlaḥa* in a formal or substantive manner into the law-finding process. The intellectual environment at the turn of the twentieth century was such that Rashīd Riḍā and al-Qāsimī felt compelled to prove the compatibility of Islamic law and the rational sciences. Al-Ṭūfī's interpretation of *maṣlaḥa* served their claim that Islamic law was rational and easily applicable to the modern environment. In addition, it provided an agreed-upon standard that they hoped would achieve unity among Muslims and strengthen them against all kinds of foreign intrusion.

Jurists who wrote on *maṣlaḥa* in the 1940s to the 1960s had different concerns. The continuous marginalization of Islamic law diminished the influence of religious jurists in society. With the takeover of socialist, Arab nationalist regimes in many countries of the Middle East and North Africa, the role of the Islamic jurist was frequently reduced to not much more than giving legal opinions (*fatwās*) and sanctioning the state's secular legislation.[111] Jurists who wrote after the early reformers had a more pressing need than their predecessors to prove the relevance of Islamic law to the nation-state and to demonstrate that it was able to provide answers to new questions arising from scientific, social, and political developments. Their interpretations of *maṣlaḥa* as a means to address these issues mainly took two forms. One group presented Islamic law as a comprehensive legal system by focusing on the ethical message of Islam. They drew upon al-Shāṭibī's model of *maṣlaḥa* with its coherent system of immutable universal and changeable particular rulings to achieve the desired extendability and adaptability of Islamic law. They advocated, to varying degrees, changing the methodology and hermeneutics of Islamic law to make it a functioning legal system for the modern nation-state. In this group we find scholars who were involved in the secular legal system and in the state-building process, such as Ṣubḥī Maḥmaṣānī and ʿAllāl al-Fāsī.

The other group aimed at preserving the traditional structure of Islamic law as much as possible. These jurists, such as ʿAbd al-Wahhāb Khallāf and Muḥammad Saʿīd Ramaḍān al-Būṭī, were closely associated with the religious establishment through their education and/or employment. In their interpretation of *maṣlaḥa* they focused on the traditional areas of extending and adapting the law. They were drawn to the Ghazālī/Rāzī model, which integrated considerations of *maṣlaḥa* into the formal procedure of legal analogy. Khallāf and al-Būṭī applied different interpretive strategies to extend and adapt Islamic law to the needs of modern society. Khallāf's interpretation limited the applicability of the texts and enlarged the scope of the unattested *maṣlaḥa* for extending the law. Al-Būṭī, in contrast, enlarged the scope of the texts, and thereby the attested *maṣlaḥa*, and reduced the derivation of new laws on account of unattested *maṣlaḥa*s. Conceptually, however, both scholars limited the adaptation of the law to comparing textual rulings and giving one prevalence over another. Despite the novel points that they contributed to the concept of *maṣlaḥa*, Khallāf and al-Būṭī stayed within the mainstream.

This presentation of different interpretations of the concept of *maṣlaḥa* has intended to show that *maṣlaḥa* as a means for legal change has many facets and may be used for different purposes. It is necessary for scholars of Islam and Islamic law to look closely at the way a jurist integrates this concept into the legal system as a whole to understand its potential to extend and adapt the law. Furthermore, this chapter has shown that a jurist's interpretation of *maṣlaḥa* is not random. A jurist's attitude toward the use of reason in deriving religious laws, his tendency to focus on formal or substantive legal rationality in the law-finding process, and the scope he assigns to the concept of *maṣlaḥa* in shaping the legal sphere are influenced by the nexus of education, occupation, and historical environment.

5 ʿALLĀL AL-FĀSĪ: SHARI'A AS BLUEPRINT FOR RIGHTEOUS GLOBAL CITIZENSHIP?

David L. Johnston

MORE THAN IN NEIGHBORING ALGERIA OR TUNISIA, Islam in Morocco played a central part in the politics of independence.[1] The 1920s peasant revolts and the armed struggle staged by Abdelkrim al-Khattabi[2] that led to the very brief Islamic Republic in the Berber Rif area were the first initiatives to fire the imagination of Morocco's youth.[3] But more lasting in impact was the movement that grew out of a spontaneous student protest against the French Protectorate's new decree (*ẓahīr*) authorizing the Berber regions to follow their customary rules rather than the Islamic law (Shari'a) that applied to the rest of Morocco. The urban student elite that for the previous three years had not been able to forge a common nationalist political program was suddenly galvanized into action, and this time the masses took notice.[4] For them, to touch the integrity of Shari'a was to denigrate Islam. For a colonial power to cunningly sow the seeds of division between Moroccans—all united under the banner of Islam—was to defame the honor of their country.

The three main leaders were, not surprisingly, from the chief families of Fès, the religious capital of Morocco. One of them, Muḥammad ʿAllāl al-Fāsī (1910–74), was to emerge as the leading figure of the Moroccan independence movement.[5] Besides his immense charisma and eloquence, his appeal also stemmed from an impeccable Islamic pedigree: a family tree going back to the Prophet's own Quraysh tribe, with four centuries in al-Andalus and settlement in Fès around 1466.[6] From then on this clan produced some of the best-known Islamic jurists and *ʿulamāʾ* of the venerable Islamic university al-Qarawiyyīn, founded as a mosque in 859. Surprisingly, little research in Western languages has been done on this pivotal figure.[7] After some biographical remarks, this chapter will seek to lay bare the essentials of his legal theory and then show how he weaves them into a theological whole that promotes the universal dignity of humanity.

AL-FĀSĪ'S KEY ROLE IN MOROCCO'S INDEPENDENCE MOVEMENT

ʿAllāl al-Fāsī's father, ʿAbd al-Waḥīd, was a professor and top administrator at al-Qarawiyyīn and a close friend of several of the king's highest dignitaries.[8] This explains not only al-Fāsī's entry into a Qur'anic school at the age of five but also his early immersion into the political effervescence of the elite families who, while protesting the military presence of the French and Spanish on Moroccan soil, had already presented the outlines of a constitution to the monarch. Moreover, since the *ʿulamāʾ* had already in the nineteenth century acquired a popular edge over the monarchy because of their anticolonial positions,[9] it was natural for the young al-Fāsī, who was admitted to al-Qarawiyyīn at age fourteen, to associate with some of the older students who had begun to launch their nationalist activities in 1919.[10] Two years later he was among those who protested the colonial plan to divert some of Fès's water reserve for the use of agricultural lands cultivated by French colonists.

Around that time he began to write poetry on patriotic themes and almost overnight became his generation's spokesperson.[11] But his poetry was only a sideline to two more absorbing activities: teaching Islam and political activism. In 1930 he began to lecture in mosques, Qur'anic schools, and even at al-Qarawiyyīn (he officially graduated in 1932) on the theme of the Prophet and the "rightly guided caliphs." Hundreds attended these religious talks, particularly the youth, because they were enthused about the obvious political implications of what he was saying. Because he kept the nationalist propaganda in a religious setting, the French authorities could not object or intervene. Meanwhile his influence grew rapidly.[12]

Both al-Fāsī's and his father's generations never questioned the wisdom or authority of the Moroccan sultanate, or monarchy. This fact remains central, even though al-Fāsī spent his last years in the opposition. In a real sense he helped mold the character and reinforce the legitimacy of the Moroccan monarchy as it is today. In 1934, together with a coalition of nationalist students and graduates he had helped start two years earlier (Comité d'Action Marocaine [CAM]), he stirred up popular support for the first royal visit of Sultan Muhammed V to Fès. The king, who was also from their generation, was overwhelmed by this show of enthusiasm, but so was the French governor, who, citing different official reasons, immediately closed down the CAM newspaper (*Action du Peuple*), which had the audacity to title its front page "Fès Acclaims the Moroccan Sovereign."[13] In December of that year the CAM became de facto the first Moroccan political party and simultaneously presented the sultan and the French administration with a reform plan. On top of its agenda was the demand for the civil liberties of association, speech, and a free press. The first name on the list of signatories was ʿAllāl al-Fāsī.

Though rebuffed by both the French and the palace, the CAM continued to consolidate its popular base, and by the time it was dissolved in 1937, al-Fāsī was considered its leader. He then created the underground National Party, which quickly became effective, especially in the north. However, as a result of a popular uprising in Meknes, he was arrested and exiled for nine years in the French African colony of Gabon. This only contributed to making him a national hero, and with the events of World War II as a political shield, his colleagues founded the Istiqlāl (Independence) Party in 1944.[14] Upon his return in 1946, he was named its head, which he remained until his death nearly thirty years later.

WRITINGS FROM EXILE: THE TRIUMPH OF SHARED HUMAN VALUES

To understand ʿAllāl al-Fāsī's thought on Shari'a and global citizenship, I propose to look at four of his major works. The first two were written in Egypt, the last two at home after independence.

Shortly after his return to Morocco, sparked by the hardening of French policies in Morocco, al-Fāsī decided to go into voluntary exile (1947–56), this time in Cairo, where he felt that he could do more for the cause of Moroccan independence. In that city he became a regular lecturer at al-Azhar University. These lectures were gathered in a volume published in 1956 under the title *From the West to the East* (*Min al-gharb ilā l-sharq*). During that same time his Cairo radio talks—mostly political sermons—were published in a book titled *The Call from Cairo* (*Nidā' al-Qāhira*). I begin with a few remarks taken from this book as a useful introduction to his work.

Not surprisingly, a good three-fourths of this work is devoted to political speeches and commentaries, but the last part is titled "Between Past and Present" ("Bayna l-māḍī wa-l-ḥāḍir"). Its subject matter is religious (several essays deal with fasting in Ramaḍān, and others treat Islamic virtues), connecting to his main purpose: to prepare Muslims for the task of shaking off the yoke of Western colonialism. In the first essay, "Islam Commands the Use of Power" ("al-Islām ya'muru bi-l-quwwa"), al-Fāsī announces that Islam is the "religion of human nature" (*dīn al-fiṭra*), distinguishing between animal nature, with its natural instincts in common with the animal kingdom, and the special calling of humans, sealed in the "ancient covenant" but which, in order to be fulfilled, requires them to live out their arduous call to freedom and responsibility.[15] Yet no one can succeed in this high calling without following God's directives: "Thus there had to be statutes (*sharā'iʿ*) that guide them and throw light on their path, and from this we see the need for the law (*al-nāmūs*), that is, religion."[16] As will be repeated later, except for two works, al-Fāsī downplays the role of Islamic law (Shari'a) in his political and cultural writings. The word *nāmūs* is a deliberate attempt to move the debate away from the traditional perimeters of *fiqh* (applied Islamic jurisprudence) and its methodological theory, *uṣūl al-fiqh*.[17]

In one of his longer essays, "The Muslim's Pride" ("ʿIzzat al-muslim"), al-Fāsī presents his listeners with his twin theological pillars: *tawḥīd* (God's oneness) and *khilāfa* (humankind's "caliphate," or trusteeship) with, undoubtedly, Shari'a in the background, because it is an extension of God's more general "laws in the universe":

> True assurance comes from the oneness of God (*al-tawḥīd*), from one's confessing it in all circumstances, one's relying on it in all one's affairs; for there is no power without it; and thus there is no fear that counts except the fear of contravening His ways in the universe (*sunanuhu fī l-kawn*) and of departing from doing His will as revealed for this life.
>
> Thus a deep sense of pride (*ʿizza*) wells up from the soul of the Muslim because of the responsibility imparted to him as a human being, so he strives and toils—glad of his striving and exulting in his toil—that he might be worthy of the deputyship (*al-khilāfa*) entrusted to him by God for the management of this earth (*fī ʿamārati hādhihī l-arḍ*), and because of the trust invested in him—and thereby challenging the angels who said, "Wilt thou place therein one who will make mischief therein and shed blood? Whilst we do celebrate Thy praises and glorify Thy holy [name]?" He said, "I know what ye know not." (Qur'an 2.30, transl. Yusuf Ali).[18]

This passage attributes the role of deputyship to the Muslim community only—not to humanity as a whole—which then is called to be a witness to the rest of humanity, but, after all, the context here is a sermon. Al-Fāsī shows us elsewhere that his vision is much grander. In his most famous work al-Fāsī develops what could aptly be called the most influential Salafiyya treatise of the second half of the twentieth century—certainly the most consistent application of its ideals to a particular state since the movement was initiated by Jamāl al-Dīn al-Afghānī (1838–1897).[19] From his adopted home in Cairo his *Self-Criticism* (*al-Naqd al-dhātī*) eloquently intones the themes of free thought, human liberation, and, on the surface at least, a global pluralistic civilization in which emerging national entities such as Morocco could bring their contributions to the table as equal partners.[20] As the title indicates, it also rings with often-stinging criticism of Morocco's rigid conservatism in its political and economic structures, as well as in its religious and traditional thought patterns.

But surprisingly for the scholar (*ʿalīm*) from the traditional Qarawiyyīn university that he is, the tone is more that of a moral reformer than that of a religious preacher. In his first chapter ("Selfishness") he calls his people to awaken from the slumber of human selfishness—which pits families, classes, ethnic groups, and regions one against another—and rise up together to rebuild the Moroccan nation.[21] To think of our country as one—giving all regions their due importance—we must "free ourselves from the relics of the recent past and their impact on our mentality and get used to thinking in a comprehensive way (*an nufakkira tafkīran shāmilan*), thus rejecting what the colonial powers want to impose on us—the new feudalism."[22] The renewal Morocco so urgently needs, argues al-Fāsī, must touch on every area of its lives: the spiritual, social, economic, political, and national realms. Constitutional democracies are popping up everywhere, and those of the Middle East do not compare unfavorably with those in Latin America and Eastern Europe. At the same time, there is much oppression, corruption, and blame to go around on all sides. Iraq is in sad shape with its armed tribes (*ʿashā'ir*) and warlords, but so is France with its elites, who monopolize its wealth with impunity.[23] Admittedly, Arabs love adventure, but they are poor thinkers and planners. They are too proud, al-Fāsī laments, to take stock of their sickness, find its causes, and remedy it. They are not motivated by a sense of duty, but they should be. This is the very thing that is eating away at the health of their families and corrupting the core of their society. The final and only essential question when one gets up in the morning should be this: "What should I do for my country (*ummatī*) today?"[24]

The striking feature of this moralistic discourse is its silence about Islam. In a chapter about "the aristocracy of thinking," al-Fāsī makes an impassioned plea for the adoption of the thinking of the enlightened class, not that of the street—"we live that one out on a daily basis!"[25] If they want to join the elite class, Moroccans must progressively liberate themselves from the logic of the streets. Nevertheless, he does not connect the dotted lines between the call to adopt the best in modernity and the theological vision of Islam until page 112, when he writes, "Our ideal as humans is to please the One in whose hands rest our destiny and our arrival into the sacred fold in the highest kingdom"—thus fulfilling the divine will in the civilizing and reforming of the earth. Al-Fāsī also declares that it was the Salafiyya movement that brought Morocco to the dawn of its renewal.

Al-Fāsī sees in the modern aspirations for freedom and independence of thought a new context in which the message of Islam can shine again in its pristine beauty: "The rational school has won a great victory in the world today," but Moroccans, he insists, are still reeling under the many shackles of which they are not even aware. The protection of oneself and one's family is a right deemed natural by all cultures, but freedom of thought is a "rational right," a step beyond.[26] The kind of revolutionary thinking that is now required, he argues, must be dynamic (*mutaḥarrik*) if it is to play the role of a democratic dynamic. Sadly, he muses, Morocco is still laboring under the weight of medieval structures. The truth is, "There can be no responsibility without freedom, and there can be no freedom without thinking!"[27] The main argument, then, in this first part of al-Fāsī's *Self-Criticism*, titled, "Issues of Thought," is that the Islamic *umma* must put on a new, progressive thinking (*al-fikr al-taqaddumī*).[28]

The second part ("Thinking by Ideal") is the section where Islam, nationalism, and internationalism are integrated.[29] In order to explain what Islam really is, al-Fāsī tells his readers, one first has to revisit Islamic history: "Islam in its origin did not deal as an enemy with any foreign nation nor attack them."[30] Islam in its essence was the intellectual, social, and spiritual revolution against all the idols, including the mercantile aristocracy of the Quraysh in Mecca. Thus the Arabian Peninsula came to be seen by those who had been persecuted and oppressed by political and religious tyrannies as a haven of human emancipation. He goes on to develop his Islamic liberation theology:

> And thus we can easily discern that Islamic thought worked to serve human values globally by calling to an all-embracing liberation and the refusal to recognize one person as being a supernatural mediator between God and His creatures. Our mission, therefore, is to continue the struggle so that this sacred liberation will be victorious and that these global human values (*insāniyya*) will fill all minds with a spirituality of serenity and all thoughts and actions with a faith in independence. This work of ours cannot be accomplished except as part of a continuous human struggle for the victory of freedom and the resisting of

> tyranny. It will also necessitate a permanent coalescing of human thought in its many forms and our sincere cooperation with all people of good will in the world, without regard to their backgrounds or orientations, as long as they hold to the belief in the true human nature (*fiṭra*) and the belief in free thought, independent reasoning, the dignity of the human person, the victory of justice, and the fight against tyranny, even if they do not become Muslims or acknowledge Islam as a religion revealed from heaven.[31]

Precious little, then, is said in *Self-Criticism* about how the traditional legal framework of Islam and inherited Shari'a would accommodate such a universal, democratic, and pluralistic program. What he does spell out is significant, however. Al-Fāsī had already established that a democratic (and Islamic) government was to achieve the common good of the people. The key word here—as it was with the reforming jurists Muḥammad ʿAbduh (1849–1905) and Muḥammad Rashīd Riḍā (1865–1935)—is *maṣlaḥa* (benefit, interest, well-being). In Chapter 4 of this book Felicitas Opwis explains the concept of *maṣlaḥa* and also analyzes the significant role it plays in al-Fāsī's concept of Shari'a. Al-Fāsī states that "[Islam] has left for Muslims the right to reflect and decide in all areas of everyday life and in that which Islam's experts called the areas of human benefit (*al-maṣlaḥiyyāt*), that is, the questions pertaining to the common good (*al-maṣlaḥa al-ʿāmma*), which evolves and changes sometimes radically."[32] This starts on the level of government, with people themselves choosing their own state: "Islam directs Muslims to a consultative life that leads them to reflect on their own destiny and the consequences of their methods, in the light of different human experiments, by getting rid of evil passions and by laying hold of truth, justice, and righteous living (*al-maʿrūf*) in religion."[33]

The mechanics of how this is to take place are not spelled out—al-Fāsī's main concern at this point is to elicit in his people the kind of mind-set that will carry them beyond independence and enable them to join and actively contribute to the new spirit of democracy and human rights that is blowing around the world.[34] Perhaps the most eloquent passage of this work compares human progress to a caravan:

> Time is ticking away, the human caravan is on its way and it waits for no one. . . . Islam is movement, and for that reason we must always keep moving forward, without cutting our ties with the past, but attempting to follow our new course, despite the fact that one thousand years is not enough for human society to pursue its emigration (*hijra*) toward the true and noble progress for which it strives.[35]

WRITINGS ON SHARI'A: A SALAFĪ CALL TO REFORM

After Morocco's independence in 1956 ʿAllāl al-Fāsī was offered a government portfolio, which he accepted for a short time, but most of his political activity was concentrated on leading the Istiqlāl Party in opposition to the palace-run government. This is also the period of his life when he paid the most attention to Islamic law, a dimension that is almost totally lacking in *Self-Criticism,* and that is spelled out in two later works.[36] Was it his vantage point as political leader that led ʿAllāl al-Fāsī to the conclusion that Islam was being jeopardized in postindependence Morocco, or did he simply postpone the task of spelling out his "progressive" Islam to a later date? More studies will certainly be needed to answer these questions, but this juxtaposition of mainstream politics and a call for the application of law reveals a point of tension in al-Fāsī's legacy, as we shall see again. The first work is a series of lectures delivered to law students, both at the Rabat Muhammad V University and at its branch in Fès, which he called *The Objectives and Ethics of Islamic Law* (*Maqāṣid al-sharīʿa al-Islāmiyya wā-makārimuha*), and in which he seeks to convince Morocco's *ʿulamā'* that his vision is profoundly Islamic and thus deserves their support.[37] The second book, *Defense of the Islamic Law* (*Difāʿ ʿan al-sharīʿa al-Islāmiyya*), was written as a follow-up to the first one and was published in 1966.[38] It is less apologetic than the first, aimed at persuading the Moroccan intellectual and political elite to adopt much more of the contents and spirit of Islamic Shari'a in every branch of Morocco's legislation. Practically, this meant a Mālikī form of *fiqh* (referring to Mālikism, the traditional school of Islamic law practiced in Morocco) mixed with the elements of contemporary Western legislation that are compatible with the spirit of Shari'a.[39] Perhaps the clearest way to elucidate al-Fāsī's Salafī thinking is to look at his approach in three steps: first, in terms of epistemology, what he sees as the connection between the human mind and Shari'a; second, in terms of hermeneutics, how he develops an interpretive process in which the objectives and ethical principles of Shari'a are emphasized over the specific injunctions; and finally, how his theology of humanity is pressed into the service of a global citizenship blessed by justice and peace.

THE EPISTEMOLOGICAL TURN TOWARD RATIONALISM

In a section titled "Islam, Religion of Reason (*al-ʿaql*) and of Justice" al-Fāsī considers the philosophical implications of his thesis that establishing justice between people on earth is at the core of Shari'a's objectives.[40] But how can we humans know what justice is? If this quality of relationships has no objective standing in people's minds (or is only known through revelation), how could people reach meaningful international agreements and cooperate in managing the earth's bounty? Also, how can Muslim jurists apply Shari'a to changing sociopolitical conditions if there is no objective standard for what justice might look like in human society? The classic *uṣūl al-fiqh* epistemological question, at least since al-Ghazālī's (d. 1111) fundamental work *The Choice Essentials of the Science of the Principles of Law* (*al-Mustaṣfā min ʿilm al-uṣūl*),[41] is the role of reason in both understanding God's law (its two primary sources being the Qur'an and Sunna) and applying it to changing circumstances (*ijtihād*).[42]

First, al-Fāsī dismisses the old Muslim debate about whether justice determines the nature of God's dealing with His creatures or not.[43] In ethical terms, is an act good because God says that it is good (ethical voluntarism, the Ashʿarite position), or because it is good in itself (ethical positivism, the Muʿtazilite position)? For him, both positions intersect a good deal on the related issues of God's will and justice. Interestingly, he seeks help from the Muslim philosopher (*faylasūf*) of al-Andalus, Ibn Rushd (Averroes, d. 1198), to find a reasonable middle way.[44] For Ibn Rushd, God wills evil only for the good it can accomplish for the world in the long run. Human beings, therefore, are created free, with the ability to choose good or evil.[45] As the angels put forward their objection to God placing Adam on earth as his trustee ("Wilt thou place therein one who will make mischief and shed blood?" Q 2.30), God answers, "I know what ye know not." Thus good always prevails over evil, even in this life.[46] Admittedly, adds al-Fāsī, there is an impasse (*ma'zaq*) here: if people choose by their own power, then God's power is diminished, and this contradicts the Muslim conviction that God's will creates everything. Conversely, if people are incapable of choosing between right and wrong, they cannot be held responsible before a just God for their choice. Yet this impasse itself is part of God's will, for in His wisdom He desires that all (including the *ʿulamā'*) pay attention to His revealed word. Having said this, it is equally obvious, continues al-Fāsī, that human will is not absolute (*muṭlaq*) and is limited by the external causes that God placed in the universe. It is plain to every thinking person that he or she is confronted in many cases with a clear choice. At that point that person is free. Therefore, concludes al-Fāsī, Ibn Rushd is correct when he argues that neither is God's power to predestine events in the future (*al-jabar*) all-determining, nor is human will absolute.[47]

Next al-Fāsī turns to a somewhat unlikely ally, the Ẓāhirī jurist and theologian Ibn Ḥazm (d. 1064) of al-Andalus. Ibn Ḥazm denied that reason plays a significant role in developing the divine law by means of analogy (*qiyās*).[48] Despite this, Ibn Ḥazm understood that reason (*ʿaql*) does play a significant role in the fulfillment of those obligations that are expressed by the Islamic notion that a human is a *mukallaf*. In Islamic law the term *mukallaf* describes an adult person who is in full possession of his or her mental faculties and—as a consequence of the process of revelation—is entrusted with the burden to fulfill the injunctions of Shari'a.[49] Ibn Ḥazm accepted that by virtue of divine endowment, human reason stands as the arbiter, discerning right actions from wrong ones. This capacity is valid for all matters coming to a person's attention by way of the senses or understanding (*fahm*). Al-Fāsī points to the fact, however, that human understanding has its limits, a fact illustrated within the sciences.[50] There are indeed areas where only revelation can inform and guide us. On the other hand, one might have expected al-Fāsī to explicitly connect the Creator's calling for a human *khilāfa* with the human accountability to obey the Creator's commands as a *mukallaf*. In fact, he does not. What gives him some flexibility in being able to dissociate the general human *khilāfa* from the specific rulings of Shari'a is his emphasis on human reason. Al-Fāsī forcefully stresses the fact that Shari'a never violates human reason. He falls short of claiming, however, that human reason and Shari'a are one and the same:

> There is no source (*aṣl*) of knowledge in Islam that is clearly set above human reason, that is, that cannot be understood by reason—in contrast to Christianity today. At the same time, there is no reason that is above revelation, as some Muʿtazilites declared. But here is a religion in harmony with reason, and a reason in support of religion. This [that is, Islam] is no religion in contradiction with science, but rather science enabling to discover the realities of the universe and its indications that point toward the Creator.[51]

In the next section, titled "Islam Is the Religion of Human Nature (*dīn al-fiṭra*)," al-Fāsī explains that the nature with which God endowed His human creatures is centered around the faculty of reason. Reason allows humankind to gain knowledge and extend civilization (*ʿāda*),[52] to establish social order, starting with the family and going up to the state, and to enforce obedience to authority, including that of God. In this sense, Islam is the religion of humanity's *fiṭra* because it covers both areas—people's relationship to God (*al-ʿibādāt*) and their mutual relationships (*al-muʿāmalāt*). In al-Fāsī's own words, "Islam is the religion of true civilization. It is what human nature (*al-fiṭra*) longs for, finding guidance in some of its manifestations, but also needing instruction and training to perfect itself in its most brilliant aspects and to discover its own signs and laws (*maʿālim wa-nawāmīs*), both in the universe and inside the human person."[53] While seeking to explicate the content of the human *fiṭra,* al-Fāsī calls the philosopher Ibn Sīnā (Avicenna, d. 1037) into the arena.[54] For him, *fiṭra* is "the power called reason (*ʿaql*), in the sense that when people are stripped of their knowledge, their eyesight, and their hearing," what is left in their minds—that which they cannot doubt—originates in the *fiṭra.* It is this pure creation-molded nature that leans on a sometimes-fallible intellect (*ʿaql*) and yet finds in it a guide complementary to revelation. Islam is, no doubt, in agreement with the Muslim philosophers, concludes al-Fāsī, who saw humankind as good from the beginning and able through reason to build the "virtuous cities."[55]

Echoing the thoughts of another of the great Muslim philosophers (*falāsifa*), al-Fārābī (d. ca. 950),[56] Ibn Sīnā taught that people are created with the need for social ties and mutual exchange, and that is what places humans above animals. They cannot attain the perfection intended by their creation, however, unless they gather in large cooperative groupings in which "each person provides sustenance for each other person and vice versa."[57] This fact proves to be the connecting link with Shari'a, which in response to this *fiṭra* is not content to bring comfort to the soul and the mind, but addresses directly the collective characteristics and needs of human nature.

What is especially noteworthy here is the rationalist strategy of connecting Shari'a to human experience and thus al-Fāsī's overt reliance on the writings of *falāsifa* who had been shunned for centuries by conservative Sunni theologians. Clearly al-Fāsī has decided to showcase human reason as the standard-bearer of Islam and the main criterion used in the urgent task of bringing Shari'a to bear on the concerns of humanity in the twentieth century. He explains, "In the Islamic Shari'a there is no imposing of obligation (*taklīf*), either in terms of doctrine or of behavior, that contradicts reason."[58] This is because in the words of the Qur'an, Islam is both proof or demonstration (*burhān*) from God and thus is akin to the light that casts knowledge and certainty into the human mind (Q 4.174). In his epistemology al-Fāsī follows Salafī writers such as Muḥammad ʿAbduh and Muḥammad Rashīd Riḍā. Malcolm Kerr has noted, for instance, that the theme most stressed in ʿAbduh's writings is "the essential harmony of reason, revelation, and individual moral temperament. When properly expressed and understood, there can be no conflict between them."[59] The next section illustrates how al-Fāsī transports the Salafīs' hermeneutic strategy into legal theory and practice.

THE HERMENEUTIC TURN FROM SPECIFIC RULINGS TO THE OBJECTIVES OF SHARI'A

On the first pages of his book *The Objectives of Shari'a* (*Maqāṣid al-sharīʿa al-Islāmiyya*), al-Fāsī explains that the title is a direct reference to the work of the Mālikī jurist Abū Isḥāq al-Shāṭibī (d. 1388) of al-Andalus:

> I am confident that this book will fill a void in the Arab libraries, because those who have successively written about the purposes of the Shari'a have not gone beyond the point at which al-Shāṭibī himself had arrived, or did not even reach that for which he was aiming. And some of them strayed from the subject, attempting to find causes (*taʿlīl*) for every specific ruling (*juz'*) of Islamic law (*fiqh*) and thus understanding the objectives (*maqāṣid*) in a literal fashion.

On the same pages al-Fāsī says that he has chosen to approach the sources (*uṣūl*) for rulings in Shari'a from the angle of Shari'a's objectives (*maqāṣid*) rather than relying entirely on the cause of the ruling (*ʿilla*, the *ratio legis*). At the beginning of the methodological thinking on the sources of Islamic law (*uṣūl al-fiqh*) in the eighth century, Muslim scholars agreed that the legal edifice of *fiqh* is built on four foundations: the Qur'an, Sunna, the consensus (*ijmāʿ*) of legal experts, and the analogy (*qiyās*) between a textually attested injunction and new situations not covered in the text. For the reformer al-Fāsī, the human mind's endeavor to reach behind the specific, textually attested injunction plays a very important epistemological role. Al-Fāsī chooses deliberately a hermeneutic strategy that aims behind the textually attested rulings. How does a jurist venture into the unknown areas not covered by the revealed text, keeping in mind that those areas are multiplying constantly as societies change and evolve? Al-Fāsī claims that the traditional, cautious consideration that affected the ground (*ʿilla*) of a specific injunction will not do. Following al-Ghazālī, he contends that from a close study of the Qur'an and Sunna one can discover that God's overall purpose in revealing Shari'a is to benefit humankind. The key term for al-Fāsī, as we have said, is *maṣlaḥa* (benefit, interest, welfare). Al-Fāsī is influenced by the fourteenth-century jurist al-Shāṭibī, who defined *maṣlaḥa* in the following way:

> I mean by benefits (*maṣāliḥ*) that which promotes human life and fulfills human existence, and the provision of all that is required by their emotional and intellectual makeup in an absolute sense, so that they might have a perfectly

> comfortable life. This is not meant to be merely on the level of people's customs, because the benefits I am speaking of are mixed with responsibilities and hardships, which, whether they be many or few, will always be tied to the benefits. The hardships may either precede or follow the benefits, which may be food, drink, clothing, housing, beasts to ride, marriage, and other things. For all these things cannot be acquired except by hard work and fatigue.[60]

The purpose of Shari'a is, according to al-Fāsī, the fulfillment of human existence along with its natural share of toil and hardships. Therefore, there is no difficulty for humans to find God's will in those areas God has not explicitly addressed in His revelation. Sometimes traditional *qiyās* will do, but in most cases seeking the common interest and avoiding harm for the greatest number of people will provide ample guidelines for drafting new legislation. All legislation of human societies, including that revealed to Moses, which Jesus modified only slightly, al-Fāsī claims, has justice as its goal, and the notion of the common good (*maṣlaḥa*) can easily be subsumed under the commanding rule of justice.[61] Therefore, the objectives of Shari'a are not just a secondary source in the jurists' toolbox but rather at the heart of Shari'a itself, on a par with the texts themselves because they are implicitly attested by them. The objectives (*maqāṣid*) are part of the original sources of Islamic law (*al-maṣādir al-aṣliyya*).[62] Any injunction that humans adduce from the *maqāṣid*, argues al-Fāsī, by way of the consideration of *maṣlaḥa*, *istiḥsān* (legal equity), or any other tool at their disposal is considered a *ḥukm sharʿī* (a Shari'a injunction) and thus valid and binding. The injunctions of Shari'a are "an address (*khiṭāb*) of God directed to those people who are called upon to fulfill God's law (*al-mukallafūn*)."[63]

Without losing sight of the particular injunctions in the revealed text, the jurist must increasingly focus on the objectives and purposes indicated by the collection of isolated texts. "The principle of justice in Islam [literally "the general Islamic justice"] admits no changes. As for the specific (*juz'iyya*) injunctions of Islam, however, they may change according to the circumstances and considerations of time and place, for they are not intended in themselves [to be changed or not] but rather intended to lead to the fulfillment of Shari'a justice."[64] Al-Fāsī's focus on the general principles (*kulliyyāt*) of Shari'a rather than the individual aspects (*juz'iyyāt*), that is, the individual judgments, is, as he stresses, not a recent invention in Islamic law. It is true, he concedes, that the focus on the general principles had not been an explicit part in the science of Shari'a's roots (*uṣūl*). If one looks into the historical facts, however, one finds that this was how the successors of Muhammad ran their affairs of state. When there was a food shortage, the second caliph ʿUmar ibn al-Khaṭṭāb (reg. 634–44) lightened the explicit punishment for theft that was commanded in the Qur'an. When laws were enacted, al-Fāsī points out, the Prophet's companions were interested in the preservation of the objectives of Shari'a amid changing circumstances.[65] Shari'a is divine, but in everyday life we experience it as *ijtihād*.[66]

In his general exposition of the sources (*uṣūl*) of Islamic law al-Fāsī follows a fairly common outline.[67] There are, however, two exceptions to what had been commonly written on this subject.[68] The first is that after his treatment of the consideration of *maṣlaḥa*, which is not indicated in the revealed text (*maṣlaḥa mursala*), he devotes four pages to what he calls "the school of al-Ṭūfī."[69] In her chapter in this volume Felicitas Opwis documents that the Ḥanbalī jurist Najm al-Dīn al-Ṭūfī (d. 1316) had always been considered excessive in his use of *maṣlaḥa*. He went so far as to assert that the principle of *maṣlaḥa* should take precedence over the sacred text even if no *maṣlaḥa* is indicated in the text. Al-Ṭūfī nevertheless became prominent among Muslim reformers.[70] Although al-Fāsī is more conservative than al-Ṭūfī and does not consider that *maṣlaḥa* has precedence over the source of law even where there is no indication in the divine text, al-Fāsī gives much credit to al-Ṭūfī and in the end says that he does agree with him. This agreement is confined to the outcome and does not extend to the way al-Ṭūfī argues his case. According to al-Fāsī, considerations of *maṣlaḥa* are included in all of Shari'a's injunctions, but he criticizes al-Ṭūfī for considering a *maṣlaḥa* even in rulings where he admits that the divine source does not indicate one. In contrast, al-Fāsī says that there is always a *maṣlaḥa* indicated in the divine text. Al-Fāsī recommends the consideration of *maṣlaḥa* because it has already been factored into the revelation as one of its general purposes. Al-Ṭūfī could have defended his position much better, al-Fāsī says, if he had only pointed out the fact that *maṣlaḥa* is always present in the divine text. He need not have sounded so radical because, as al-Fāsī puts it, "there is no contradiction between *maṣlaḥa* and the Shari'a texts."[71]

The second exception that distances al-Fāsī's treatment of the sources of Islamic law from a classical treatment in the *uṣūlī* tradition is the addition of a last section, titled "Human Rights" ("ḥuqūq al-insān"). The commands and prohibitions found in the Qur'an and Sunna are backed up by a host of indications that one might call an "order of advice" (*amr irshād*) or simply wise principles God intends us to apply in everyday life. These principles should be considered a source (*aṣl min al-uṣūl*) of Shari'a on the same rank as all the other sources devised by the jurists to establish rulings for the Muslim community.[72] Al-Fāsī, in fact, tries to establish the "order of advice," which lies behind the text of revelation, as an additional source of Shari'a: "What should hinder us from relying on this source, the order of advice, which is realized through the fulfillment of what the Legislator intends in any particular command: as the longing for freedom, the desire to establish justice and peace in the family, the realization of world peace and the banning of war, something he intends for every unit of humanity?"[73] The "order of advice" found in the Qur'an and Sunna, namely, the establishment of freedom, justice, and peace, should be considered an *ʿilla*, that is, an efficient cause of rulings that establishes their validity. Legal experts of today should widen their perspective about the rationale behind these commands and discern God's overall intentions as they relate to the well-being of individuals, families, societies, and nations. The perspective of legal experts must first and foremost be a moral one.

AN INTEGRATED THEOLOGY OF HUMANITY WITH A UNIVERSAL ETHIC

Al-Fāsī's chief innovation is his emphasis on the ethical implications of the law. This is expressed in the title of one chapter of his book, "The High Ethical Standards of Shari'a" ("Makārim al-sharīʿa").[74] In a section devoted to these high standards,[75] al-Fāsī presents a justification why Islam offers the best means to achieve the peaceful coexistence of all nations and why, therefore, Shari'a is superior to all other laws that aim to achieve this goal. Shari'a, al-Fāsī insists, aims to achieve the welfare (*maṣlaḥa*) and happiness of all people in this world and in the afterlife. But how, one might object, is one to distinguish between true well-being and other, debatable notions of well-being? Capitalism and socialism, for instance, both have very different conceptions of what the common good is. Yet people of all cultures agree on a basic ethical standard "emanating from how human nature (*fiṭra*) is created and based on an active cherishing of the high ideal the human person seeks to attain in life and in action."[76] The welfare of individuals and society that the laws of Shari'a seek to achieve is the common ethical standard approved by one and all humans. These are the "well-known and approved" (*al-maʿrūf*) standards, and therefore they are honorable and the opposite of what is detested (*al-munkar*) by all humans.[77] Among these common values that people agree on are the need for justice, truthfulness, loyalty in covenants, and compassion for the less fortunate. Among them are also the ideal that all humans should have an equal opportunity and basic equality before the law. All humans agree on these standards, and the only difference between various faiths and cultures arises in how these standards are to be applied.

Al-Fāsī teaches that these standards are best exemplified in the lives of the prophets and in the teaching of the Qur'an. "Islam calls all people to enter the abode of peace," following God's plan for the uniting of humanity under the banner of justice for all.[78] When various groups vie for preeminence, however, ethical values can sometimes become murky. To counter this development, Shari'a provides the surest guide for ethical values. These values are the general principle and the objectives (*maqāṣid*) behind Shari'a. In al-Fāsī's view humans are allowed to act upon them, for "the door of *ijtihād* is open in Islam on the basis of the Shari'a's objectives, the source of its laws, and in the circle of what is morally good (*al-maʿrūf*), that is, the circle encompassing the divine will that gives the *mujtahid* a criterion (*al-furqān*) for discerning good from evil."[79] Beyond the obvious apologetic tone of his arguments, one cannot help but notice al-Fāsī's desire to integrate the great ethical writings of the Islamic philosophers (*falāsifa*), with perhaps al-Fārābī in the forefront, especially because al-Fāsī concludes this section: "And this is, in any case, the foundation of the righteous nation that can overcome all of its human and social weak points by rooting its laws in the eternal principles that humans cannot change, even if at times they deny them in their behavior and thinking."[80]

It should be kept in mind that al-Fāsī is a political figure with a highly visible role in the launching of a newly independent nation. Mustering all the historical resources of his Islamic heritage, he skillfully weaves together themes of Islamic philosophy, *kalām* (rationalistic theology), and the theological themes related to humanity's answerability to God's divine address as debated by the great *uṣūlī* jurists of old times. In his final argument he connects the moral linchpin of the human person as a *mukallaf*—as someone who is called to act on God's divine law—with a theme that is prominent in many Salafī thinkers of the early twentieth century: humanity's trusteeship (*khilāfa*) of God's creation.[81] Here he parallels Sayyid Quṭb's stress on the human *fiṭra* and its correspondence to the divine laws (*nawāmīs* or *qawānīn*) woven into the universe, which humankind through reason can progressively discover.[82] Thus he is able to articulate an attractive reinterpretation of older themes in a way that promotes international cooperation, as well as the edification of individual Muslim nations on the basis of their own unique historical and cultural identities. In one passage he writes,

> Humanity must believe that there is a Lord over these worlds and that He is their originator and guide; that everything returns to Him; that people were created for Him and entrusted (*mukallaf*) beforehand [in the "primordial covenant," *al-mīthāq*] with the management of the earth[83] in conformity with the laws (*nawāmīs*) that He established in it. These are the laws that He taught him through His prophets and messengers, as well as through His reason (*ʿaql*). God did not create them and then give some humans the Book, sovereignty, and prophethood in order for them to say to their brethren, "Worship us instead of God." Rather [God has given humans this] as a call for them, together as equals, to fulfill what God has laid upon them (*taklīf*), that they should worship Him with sincerity, and make Him the highest ideal to which they reach and the one their actions seek to please. Furthermore, in order to come to Him, they must take on the qualities of God Himself, which He has planted in their true human nature (*fiṭra ḥaqīqiyya*).[84]

The crucial question here is what *taklīf*, the notion that humanity is called upon to fulfill the responsibility that God has laid upon its shoulders, means. To what extent can this obligation (*taklīf*) be fulfilled by Muslims or by non-Muslims? To be sure, there are passages in al-Fāsī's writings in which the trusteeship (*khilāfa*) of humans seems to be narrowed down to the Muslim community.[85] But al-Fasi's vision is larger. For him, the term *mukallaf* that describes the one who is called upon to fulfill what God has laid upon him cannot be applied only to Muslims but must also include humanity in general. For al-Fāsī, "the one who is called upon to fulfill what God has laid upon him" (*al-mukallaf*) is synonymous with "human citizen":

> The Legislator coined the term *mukallaf* for any Muslim or non-Muslim as a sign of the human citizenship in the universal nation (*al-muwāṭana al-insānīyya fī l-dawla al-kawniyya*). This citizenship empowers each one with the responsibility to establish justice, to apply natural law (*qānūn*),[86] and to guarantee the freedom and dignity of the human person. The person obligated to fulfill what God has laid upon him (*al-mukallaf*) in this nation is the citizen. Each one's conscience and behavior is his or her ethical code, and everyone's duty is to civilize the earth and to stand in God's stead as the manager of its wealth.[87]

There is a deliberate vagueness in al-Fāsī's writing about the term *mukallaf*. He avoids specifying what the *mukallaf* is actually called upon to fulfill. The classical position of Islamic scholars is that the *mukallaf* is called upon to fulfill the injunctions of the divine law, that is, Shari'a. For al-Fāsī and many Islamic thinkers of his generation, however, the divine law is in harmony with the law (*qānūn*) that God has created for all humans as part of the way He created humanity according to a *fiṭra*. This allows al-Fāsī to extend the meaning of *mukallaf*. Although traditionally the *mukallaf* is a Muslim, that is, the one who has accepted the responsibility to fulfill Shari'a as it is derived from divine revelation, for al-Fāsī, the *mukallaf* is every human who finds within himself the moral rules by which he has to abide. Humanity as such is under the obligation to fulfill the objectives of Shari'a and to establish freedom, justice, and peace.

One great fear that looms throughout al-Fāsī's writings is the danger of dictatorship—the menace of Hitler, Stalin, and Mao, as well as the neocolonial ambitions of the Western capitalist powers.[88] Quoting from Qur'an 49.13, he calls for the equality of all persons, regardless of creed, race, or nation. Wars have always existed, notes al-Fāsī, but "Islam came with a law that imposed peace as a duty and permitted in cases of necessity the use of defensive means."[89] The only two valid causes for war are military aggression and the robbing of religious freedom. Hence Muslims should join all others who seek a world of peace, freedom, and justice, calling for the respect of each person's dignity—rich or poor, Muslim or non-Muslim, male or female. The world will indeed be a better place when human dignity is recognized and legislated, contends al-Fāsī:

> True human dignity flourishes when people believe that they are held responsible (*mukallaf*), that is, when they experience the meaning of human citizenship. Once people believe that they are held responsible (*mukallaf*), they believe that they were created to be instruments for the realization of the high goals that surpass their own narrow desires and personal whims. Once they believe this, they do not return to the consideration of their own private existence without affirming that they are part of the human collectivity that God established on earth to manage it on His behalf. This impels them to act according to recognized ethical standards (*al-maʿrūf*) while making them mandatory for others, and to avoid what is base while forbidding it to others.[90]

The principles of human legislation are, in al-Fāsī's view, general ones that all humanity is called to fulfill. They are also the principles that are within the objectives (*maqāṣid*) of Shari'a. When it comes to the details of human legislative activity, however, legislation often proves to be more complex than these general principles. Al-Fāsī had not yet worked out the full implications of his broad vision. Although his views on the rights of women came close to the norms set out by the United Nations' Universal Declaration of Human Rights, for instance, his views on religious freedom did not.[91] Al-Fāsī adhered to the death penalty for cases of apostasy from Islam.[92] In 1962, as minister of state for Islamic affairs, he sought to restrict the activities of some Bahā'īs in the north of Morocco.[93] Al-Fāsī instigated the arrest and trial of fourteen Bahā'īs "on charges of corrupting youth, forming an illegal association, and seeking to destroy Islam and the Moroccan State."[94] Three of these Bahā'īs were given the death penalty and five of them life imprisonment. Although the Moroccan Supreme Court later overturned the local court's sentences, there was no doubt what al-Fāsī had wished. This incident also reveals the lack of clarity about what his definition of the "Islamic state" was—a distinctly Salafī predicament. Reinterpreting a medieval corpus of laws in the context of the modern nation-state was obviously a daunting task. By 1962 al-Fāsī had entered the postcolonial period, but he was still unsure how to define his Islamic framework.

In the section on international peace, for instance, al-Fāsī writes that "according to Islam, either one is a Muslim, or a person who has entered a covenant [with Muslims] (*muʿāhid*), or an enemy"—a clear reference to the tripartite vision of the world that developed in early Islam.[95] He justifies the introduction of these three categories by an emphasis on simplicity and a favoring of the more liberal interpretations of traditional *fiqh* on the issue. Al-Fāsī concludes that "the foundations on which Islam conceived its domestic and foreign relations were complete justice, brotherhood among believers, fighting on behalf of the establishment of religious freedom, good neighborliness with those who make war [presumably a title for non-Muslim states]." Then he adds, "The most important objective is the achieving of perfect peace inside and outside, and of human solidarity leading to fruitful cooperation for the sake of civilizing the earth (*li-ʿamārat al-arḍ*) and establishing complete justice in it."

Here humanity's divine call in relation to creation, namely, the human trusteeship (*khilāfa*) of earth, has superseded the Islamic mission (*daʿwa*). Put otherwise, al-Fāsī has reinterpreted the classical tripartite division of the world into Muslims, *dhimmi*s, and enemies, and he has put the caliphate of humanity above Shari'a by linking it to a notion of natural law. But did al-Fāsī devise a consistent interpretation of Shari'a as natural law that all humanity is endowed with? For instance, is all humanity endowed to fulfill Shari'a's rulings on apostasy from Islam? Considering the weight of the apologetic material in al-Fāsī's two works, *The Objectives and Ethics of Islamic Law* and *Defense of the Islamic*

Law, and especially considering his emphasis on the fact that only Islam can bring peace and justice to this world, one would have to answer that al-Fāsī was not entirely consistent. Perhaps al-Fāsī's greatest weakness was not to have discerned the implications of religious freedom—and therefore the concept of pluralism in the modern state—for his model of international relations. Rachid al-Ghannūshī, a contemporary Tunisian thinker who identifies himself with al-Fāsī's project, has taken these same ideas one step further with much greater consistency.[96]

CONCLUSION

Certainly one of the guiding lights of the Moroccan independence movement and one of Morocco's brightest politicians thereafter, ʿAllāl al-Fāsī believed strongly in his country's vocation on the African continent, in the Muslim world, and in the community of nations. He was a devout Muslim, trained in one of North Africa's most prestigious Islamic universities, and he firmly believed that Islam's "socialism" was the only reasonable way between the destructive extremes of communism and capitalism, for only Islam could gather and sublimate the aspirations of humankind for a global, democratic rule of justice and peace. In two postindependence writings he defended and advocated the reapplication of Islamic Shari'a. Al-Fāsī used a two-pronged approach. First, he advocated the use of Shari'a's objectives as an ethical key to adapt Islamic law to the present context, and second, he raised the doctrine of humanity's caliphate as the rationale for global cooperation among nations. The result is a passionate plea for a righteous global citizenship in which all nations and religious communities would cooperate to "civilize" the earth. The picture that emerges from al-Fāsī's career and writings—expecially if one puts his two books *Self-Criticism* (*al-Naqd al-dhātī*) and *The Objectives and Ethics of Islamic Law* (*Maqāṣid al-sharīʿa al-Islāmiyya wa-makārimuha*) side by side—is a clear and ringing affirmation of full Muslim participation in building a more peaceful global human civilization.

What is less convincing, perhaps, is al-Fāsī's reinterpretation of the traditional concept of humanity's *taklīf* and his theological use of humanity's *khilāfa* through the use of Shari'a's objectives as applied and directed by human reasoning. The central idea seeems to be that non-Muslims, by virtue of applying ethical principles that they find within themselves (in their *fiṭra*), are in a real sense living out their role as those entrusted to fulfill God's law and His obligations (*mukallifūn*). These laws and these obligations are the same as the objectives (*maqāṣid*) of God's revealed Shari'a. If this was al-Fāsī's position and if the objectives of Shari'a included universal human rights, why then did he insist on the death penalty for Moroccan Bahā'īs? The complete implications of the human person as both a *mukallaf* and the one who is charged with the *khilāfa* are not fully worked out in his scheme.

More research will be needed to determine to what extent al-Fāsī's work built on and surpassed earlier Salafī writings. Yet despite some inherent tensions, some contemporaries have used his work to further develop an Islamic theology of pluralism and democracy. Al-Fāsī's writing certainly deserves wider circulation, if only for his use of the *maqāṣid al-sharīʿa* methodology—a strategy of legal methodology now more and more favored.[97]

6 SHARI'A AND ISLAMIC DEMOCRACY IN THE AGE OF AL-JAZEERA

Noah Feldman

AS ONE GLANCE AT HIS OFFICIAL WEB SITE, www.Qaradawi.net, will reveal, Yūsuf al-Qaraḍāwī is a phenomenon.[1] On the site one can listen to Friday sermons (*khutba*), purchase a dozen of his books (far from his entire literary output), and retrieve transcripts of numerous interviews on a wide range of subjects. The site offers a useful guide to the number of visitors (75,000 in May 2002 alone) and to the costs of site maintenance ($5,000 a year by latest count). Via satellite, al-Jazeera beams Arabic-language programs featuring al-Qaraḍāwī into millions of homes. Whatever trepidations one might have about pinning down categories such as postmodernity, there is an overwhelming tendency when watching al-Qaraḍāwī on television to say something like, "I know it when I see it."

Dr. Yūsuf al-Qaraḍāwī matters, then, because he is popularly accessible. The Egyptian-born, Azhar-trained, Qatar-based, unofficial *shaykh* of al-Jazeera network television is not reputed to be an especially great scholar. He is not known to have an organized mass following, whether religious or political. Yet he is nonetheless influential, both as the author of dozens of often-reprinted, widely available books on Islamic law and contemporary issues and in his capacity as the most important media cleric in the Arabic-speaking world today. He is also the author of an interesting *fatwā* on the topic of Islam and democracy—a topic whose importance cannot be overstated for anyone interested in the relationship between Islamic law and contemporary politics. The *fatwā* is not among the most theoretically sophisticated Islamic writings on democracy. But sophistication is not the only mark of importance. The study of ideas also requires attention to popular manifestations of debates that have spread beyond the discourses of intellectuals and entered the public sphere more broadly.

This chapter takes up al-Qaraḍāwī's concept of Shari'a and the way it shapes his views on the question of the relationship between Islam and democracy. It offers a sketch of the way an actual theorist of Islamic democracy engages the concept of Shari'a in the context of his project of demonstrating the proper relationship between "democracy" and what he takes to be normative Islam. Elsewhere I have argued that the present intellectual engagement between Islam and democracy is best characterized not as the emergence of a creole of accidental juxtaposition nor as the liberated and deliberate picking and choosing of worldly cosmopolitanism, but as a self-conscious attempt to produce an intellectual synthesis out of disparate universalizing ideas.[2] Here I wish to develop my account of this attempted synthesis by focusing on the question of how transcendent value claims such as those associated with normative Islam are shaped when they are presented as compatible with the value claims of some version of democratic theory. The concept of Shari'a is, we shall see, at the heart of this engagement; both the boundaries of the concept and its capacity to generate particular, practical moral directives outside those boundaries make it a touchstone of the synthetic enterprise.

I do not claim novelty for al-Qaraḍāwī's views on the concept of Shari'a. I also make no claims here about the extent to which al-Qaraḍāwī's views match or differ from those of the politicians who have successfully run for office under the auspices of self-described democratic Islamic parties in Morocco, Jordan, Turkey, or Pakistan. I do want to suggest, however, that al-Qaraḍāwī's views provide some insight into a movement of remarkable intellectual vitality in the contemporary Muslim world, a movement that takes seriously the productive capacities of an encounter between Islamic political, constitutional, and legal theory, on the one hand, and democratic political theory, on the other.

Although al-Qaraḍāwī is in some sense a representative figure, his ideological approach resists easy classification. One aspect of al-Qaraḍāwī's thought and self-presentation that may have some explanatory power in accounting for his broad popularity is his remarkable ability to assume simultaneously the mantles of several different strands of contemporary Muslim thought. First, he is a classically trained Azharī *faqīh*, professionally qualified to give *fatwā*s as a *muftī* in an era in which the term *fatwā* has been co-opted to cover many nonlegal pronouncements by persons with no formal training. But unlike many other Azhar-trained scholars, whose expertise-derived legitimacy has been drastically undercut by popular Islamist ideology that systematically marginalizes classical Islamic legal texts and the scholars who study them, al-Qaraḍāwī almost effortlessly identifies himself as a figure within the movement of Islamism. He will refer in passing to his concerns as similar or identical to those of the *Islāmiyyūn*, that is, Islamists.[3] He has authored a book professing to state "the priorities of the Islamist movement," understood as an "organized, collective work, undertaken by the people, to restore Islam to the leadership of society, and to the helm of . . . all walks of life."[4] Furthermore, al-Qaraḍāwī can plausibly be presented as a follower of the modernist Islam of Muḥammad Rashīd Riḍā (1865–1935),[5] in which guise he even appears in Western anthologies, such as Charles Kurzman's *Liberal Islam*.[6] As we shall see, it is not unreasonable to associate al-Qaraḍāwī with the modernist Islamic tradition, but neither does he fit squarely within the broad category of liberal Islamic reformism that calls for fairly radical rereading of the Qur'an in pursuit of values associated with Western liberalism.

Yet instead of seeming idiosyncratic or iconoclastic, al-Qaraḍāwī somehow manages to fit into multiple niches that in the cases of others might well seem mutually exclusive. His publicly taken political positions buttress this impression. He spoke out on September 12, 2001, in condemnation of the attacks on the World Trade Center and has repeatedly condemned terrorism as a violation of Islamic law. On the other hand, like other Islamist public figures, he has endorsed the technique of suicide bombing in what he categorizes as "occupied Palestine," which presumably includes not only the occupied territories of the West Bank and Gaza but also Israel proper. Recurrent rumors associate al-Qaraḍāwī with Ḥamas in some advisory capacity, a connection rendered plausible by the association of each with the Muslim Brotherhood.[7] He has also held that *jihād* against the U.S. occupation in Iraq is a legal duty.[8]

. . .

Let us turn, then, to al-Qaraḍāwī's use of the concept of Shari'a and its relevance to his views on Islam and democracy. Al-Qaraḍāwī presents and qualifies Shari'a by way of a contrast with the term *fiqh*, a term for which he has developed a distinctive set of uses. Shari'a, says al-Qaraḍāwī in one place, consists in "the manifest laws (*aḥkām wāḍiḥa*) of God and his messenger, which come in the Book of God and the *sunna* of the messenger of God in manifest form (*bi-shakl wāḍiḥ*). That is the Shari'a; Shari'a is revelation; the laws of revelation (*aḥkām al-waḥy*)."[9] This is, in its general outline, a fairly conventional definition of Shari'a, distinctive perhaps only in its emphasis on the "manifest form" that Shari'a takes.

The reason for this emphasis on the "manifest form" of Shari'a becomes clear when one considers al-Qaraḍāwī's juxtaposed (and also roughly conventional) definition of *fiqh*. *Fiqh*, explains al-Qaraḍāwī, is "an undertaking (*ʿamal*), the undertaking of the Islamic intellect in discovery of laws (*istinbāṭ al-aḥkām*), and that undertaking is a human undertaking (*ʿamal basharī*), *fiqh* is a human undertaking."[10] The practitioner of *fiqh* is "a wise human (*insān ʿālim*)," which is to say that "his intellect works in the discovery of laws according to principles of Shari'a (*uṣūl sharʿiyya*) and an order that must be complied with (*ḍawābiṭ mar'iyya*)."[11] The actor, then, is human, but the action of discovering the law occurs within the context of divinely specified principles: the practitioner of *fiqh* "does not work in a vacuum, but rather works according to principles; because the Muslim is not an unrestrained man who does what he wishes or what is pleasant for him or follows his desire (*hawāhu*); rather, the most important aspect of Shari'a (*muhimmat al-sharīʿa*), as the eminent jurist al-Shāṭibī[12] specified, is removal of man from his desire."[13]

To this initial distinction between revealed, manifest Shari'a and the human work of *fiqh* by which the law is derived from divine principles, al-Qaraḍāwī adds a more concrete distinction based on the presence or absence of an explicitly laid-down text. "There are matters regarding which the legislator has laid down law (*naṣṣa ʿalayhā l-shāriʿ*) and matters regarding which he did not lay down law; many matters have no text laid down for them, the matters that differ with the changing of time and place and situation; there is no escape (*lā budda*) from such matters, that is, from texts that are summary (*mujmala*) or brief (*qalīla*) or [framed in] a general way (*bi-ṭarīqa kulliyya*)."[14] By contrast, there are matters regarding which texts specify particular, unchangeable rules, such as worship, the laws of marriage and divorce, or matters of faith. In these cases, al-Qaraḍāwī specifies, there is no escape from what the texts specify, even though various classical interpretive methods will still have to be applied in order to discover the correct rules that are embedded in the texts.

Although this interpretation of explicit ("manifest") texts comes under the general heading of *fiqh*, al-Qaraḍāwī makes it clear that the primary realm of the "Islamic intellect" is to work within the sphere of the matters on which there is no explicit text. He invokes a series of techniques associated with classical Islamic law to explain how this process proceeds. One may proceed according to analogical reasoning (*qiyās*); according to various principles of utility, such as *istiḥsān* and *maṣlaḥa mursila* (a concept that is fully explained in Chapter 4 of this book); or according to custom (*ʿurf*).[15] Rather than providing precise technical definitions of each of these methodologies—and the question of the relationship between, for example, *istiḥsān* and *maṣlaḥa* is highly complex—al-Qaraḍāwī is concerned to include them all within a generalized approach that he describes as seeking out the ends of Shari'a (*maqāṣid al-sharīʿa*).

In short, al-Qaraḍāwī is offering an account of the hotly contested grounds of human discretion within the context of Islamic law: the ends are to be identified and derived from revealed text, but it is to be understood that the content of the rules that are derived from those divine principles is mutable and malleable. It can and will change according to time, place, and condition. The work of deriving the general principles and applying them to particular cases is distinctively human and also inevitable.

For al-Qaraḍāwī, the issue of the human work of interpretation is further complicated by various methods of interpretation that are available. The difficulty of understanding the texts in any absolute sense produces the diversity of interpretations. Again, al-Qaraḍāwī is concerned to offer a very general typology of approaches. On one side are literalists (*ẓāhirī* or *ḥarfī*); on the other are all those who seek to interpret texts in light of their ends. These schools, he emphasizes, were present already in the lifetime of the Prophet and persist to this day.[16]

It emerges from this analysis that *fiqh*, performed with attention to the purposes of Shari'a, is the characteristic activity of the Islamic legal scholar. But al-Qaraḍāwī takes the concept of *fiqh* beyond the particular sphere of technical legal analysis, with which it is conventionally associated. In various works he describes a range of different sorts of *fiqh*, most notably "the *fiqh* of balances" and "the *fiqh* of priorities." The former has two components: "the *fiqh* of Shari'a" and "the *fiqh* of factual experience."[17] These consist in connecting propositions of revealed law with actual practical circumstances and in determining a correct course of action on the basis of their relation. The practical work of determining a proper course of action is the *fiqh* of "balances" because it requires one to balance long-term goals with short-term evils, to choose the lesser of two evils, or even to choose between competing goods. The *fiqh* of priorities similarly involves "putting everything into true perspective."[18] Matters of various degrees of importance must be properly arrayed with respect to framing a course of action. This is especially true with respect to choosing among various desirable or even religiously commanded courses of action; some are nonetheless more important than others. There is an important temporal dimension to the *fiqh* of priorities as well: today's work must not be put off until tomorrow.

What is significant about al-Qaraḍāwī's expansion of the concept of *fiqh* beyond technical legal matters and into what one might aptly describe as a more general model of practical reasoning is that through it the work of *fiqh* expands to cover essentially the entire field of human endeavor. Coupled with the view that Shari'a proper issues commands in only a narrow sphere of action, al-Qaraḍāwī's model of the broader reach of *fiqh* leads to the conclusion that to direct oneself to a proper course of action, one must engage in a fundamentally human undertaking of weighing, balancing, and prioritizing in light of relatively nonspecific general principles. Shari'a is therefore simultaneously a highly determinate set of revealed laws that govern only a narrow band of human existence and a profoundly indeterminate set of general values that ought to infuse the process of practical reasoning and that apply to essentially every area of human endeavor.

• • •

With this admittedly introductory sketch of the relation between Shari'a and al-Qaraḍāwī's expansive concept of *fiqh* in place, one can turn to al-Qaraḍāwī's account of the relationship between Islam and democracy. The topic is addressed most directly in a *fatwā* published in the book of al-Qaraḍāwī's that is most directly a work of political theory: *On the Fiqh of State in Islam* (*Min fiqh al-dawla fī-l-Islām*). As the exposition of the word *fiqh* that I have just presented suggests, *fiqh* has a special sense in this title. It is not, or not only, *On the Jurisprudence of State in Islam*, although this translation might be serviceable. Rather, the *fiqh* of state is the human undertaking of determining the right course of action with respect to the state in the light of general values and principles of guidance derived from divinely revealed Shari'a. The book, in other words, is not merely an account of Islamic legal doctrine related to government, but a work of Islamic practical reason on political matters.

Al-Qaraḍāwī's *fatwā* appears in the book under the heading "Islam and Democracy" and takes the form of a reply to an anonymous Algerian Muslim questioner, a context that has significance for both the form and the substance of its engagement with its subject. The *fatwā* genre assumes Islam, or Islamic law in particular, as the field against which the question is put and the answer given. There can be no question of beginning with some assumption of comparable epistemological status with potentially competing claims of "Islam" and "democracy" in this generic context. Rather, the key framing question is whether democracy is "unbelief" (*kufr*) or "prohibited" from the perspective of Islam.[19] The question whether Islam is the enemy of democracy is also put in this context, but the question of the fundamental relationship between Islam and democracy is to be considered from the perspective of the former and not the latter.

Providing an answer to the question turns out to be both an exercise in the application of Qaradawian *fiqh* and a kind of allegory of the method. First, of course, democracy must be defined. Al-Qaraḍāwī opts for a definition that is both procedural and substantive, and he begins with the former, procedural features: "the people choose who will govern them and organize their affairs"; they are not ruled by a ruler or regime whom they reject; the law limits the ruler; and the people are not governed according to economic, social, cultural, or political principles on which they have not agreed or which are preferred only by a minority.[20] Al-Qaraḍāwī recognizes that elections and referenda are institutional practices that correspond to these procedural aspects of democracy and embody the principle of majority rule.[21]

Al-Qaraḍāwī's definition of democracy then specifies several substantive liberal commitments. He insists upon the pluralism of political parties. He expressly names minority rights in opposition, freedom of the press, and an independent judiciary, and he implies that other unspecified rights are also included.[22] This is not a purely majoritarian concept of democracy framed to enable a dictatorship of the faithful. In essence, al-Qaraḍāwī's definition of democracy is meant to be a functional one: a definition of "true democracy" that can actually be found in the world and that operates through practical means.

Having provided a working definition of democracy, al-Qaraḍāwī sets out to frame his *fatwā* according to a twofold structure that corresponds to his distinction between Shari'a and *fiqh*. The first question al-Qaraḍāwī poses is whether democracy as a form of government is explicitly prohibited by any revealed texts, that is, by anything in Shari'a itself. Once it is determined that this is not the case, the second structuring question is whether democracy may be shown to be not merely consistent with but recommended by the ends of the revealed law as understood by human interpretive effort. That is, the question is whether the human undertaking of *fiqh* leads one to the conclusion that democracy is desirable.

What is especially striking about this methodology is that although the *fatwā* begins with a query as to the permissibility of democracy, the *fatwā* itself disposes of that question almost incidentally, then moves into a lengthy *fiqh*-based (in al-Qaraḍāwī's sense) justification of the desirability and (ultimately, by inference) necessity of democracy under Islamic law properly understood. I shall return to this point later in the chapter, but it is worthwhile to note now the difference between this approach, which enables al-Qaraḍāwī to reach the conclusion that Islam sanctions and even mandates democracy, and the largely discredited approach of the early (and occasionally recurrent) strand of liberal Islam that denied that Islam had a teaching regarding government at all.[23] Al-Qaraḍāwī's approach is emphatically not an argument about the separation of religious from political principles but, on the contrary, an ambitious attempt to show that democracy is complementary to Islamic political theory. Not only does al-Qaraḍāwī avoid defining democracy in such a way as to require secularism, but he also infuses political theory of a democratic variety into the archetypally religious work of *fiqh*.

The argument proceeds by way of a series of Qur'anic verses condemning the repressive and arbitrary rule of such figures as Pharaoh, Nimrod, Hāmān, and Qārūn. Each is made to correspond, rather pointedly, to a different type of oppressive rule: Pharaoh is the megalomaniacal autocrat who claims to be God; Nimrod enslaves the people; Hāmān is the self-interested politician who props up pharaonic rule; and Qārūn is the capitalist who exploits his own people in conspiratorial collusion with Pharaoh.[24] The Qur'an's general condemnation of corruption and promise of the destruction of corrupt regimes is added, as are *ḥadīth*s condemning corruption.[25]

Then Islam's positive concept of desirable governance is presented. Consultation (*shūrā*) is described, although not developed to the same extent in which it figures in the writings of other theorists of Islamic democracy.[26] The ruler is described as a delegate of the community (*wakīl ʿan al-umma*), from whom the people may withdraw their delegated power should they so choose. The ruler in Islam is not absolute, but is a human who may err and go astray. It is one of the "rights" of Muslims to replace him should he do so. This right was acknowledged by the earliest, rightly guided caliphs, whose words to that effect are invoked.[27]

Then comes al-Qaraḍāwī's crucial transition to the complementarity of Islam and democracy. He asserts that one of the bases of Shari'a is that a means that is necessary for the completion of an obligatory end is itself obligatory. Thus if the ends (*maqāṣid*) of the Shari'a require some particular means for their accomplishment, those means take on the legal force of that end (*akhadhat hādhihī l-waṣīla ḥukm dhālika l-maqṣad*).[28] We can recognize in this language al-Qaraḍāwī's characteristic formulation of *fiqh* as the determination of the ends of Shari'a; here he specifically ascribes legally obligatory force to the means necessary to achieve those ends.

Al-Qaraḍāwī goes on to say that the non-Islamic origin of a means to achieve some end or a solution to some problem is no disqualification of the means or the solution; the Prophet relied on non-Muslims when necessary to achieve his ends.[29]

What is more, says al-Qaraḍāwī, he has written elsewhere that it is one of the rights of Muslims to adopt means and techniques from non-Muslims to achieve lawful ends.[30] Such means and techniques may be amended and supplemented in an Islamic spirit. Thus from democracy—acknowledged as non-Islamic in origin—Muslims must take the methods, techniques, and guarantees, always preserving their own right to amend and improve them. On the other hand, Muslims are not to take those aspects of democracy's "philosophy" (*falsafa*) that might permit forbidden things, forbid permitted things, or lift religious duties.[31]

It emerges from this discussion as a matter of legal logic that those elements of democracy that are necessary to achieve a properly successful implementation of the ends of Islam in governance are not merely permissible to Muslims but are obligatory on them. By characterizing democracy's procedural and substantive requirements as necessary means to the Islamic end of just governance, al-Qaraḍāwī—without, however, explicitly saying so—makes democracy into a legal requirement of Islam itself. If one begins with the major premise that a means that is necessary for the completion of an obligatory end is itself obligatory, then provides the minor premise that democracy is necessary today for achieving the obligatory end of just governance, it follows that democracy is mandatory under today's conditions. The non-Islamic origin of democracy is irrelevant for these purposes because both the procedural mechanisms for governance and the substantive guarantees of democracy in fact serve the basic aims of Islam in preserving just government.[32]

Al-Qaraḍāwī then offers several creative suggestions regarding points of commonality between democratic and Islamic law and politics. The first is a suggestive analogy between voting in an election and the legal requirement of testimony (*shahāda*) in Islamic law. Both are conceptualized as a duty, so exercising them incorrectly would be a sin; anyone who has not lost his reputation as a result of criminal conviction is qualified to take part.[33] This intriguing analogy suggests that voting may be understood as a kind of quasi-sacred duty. This is especially true in light of the multifarious nature of the phenomenon of testimony in Islam: the word *shahāda* can mean not only testimony before a court but the primal Islamic act of testifying to the oneness of God and the messengerhood of the Prophet; and *shahāda* can also mean martyrdom, although this meaning seems absent from al-Qaraḍāwī's formulation.

The second creative suggestion arises in the context of al-Qaraḍāwī's direct confrontation of the familiar argument that Islam and democracy must necessarily be contradictory because the basis of democracy is rule of the people, whereas the basis of Islamic legislation must be the rule of God.[34] Al-Qaraḍāwī shapes his answer by identifying the essence of democracy with rejection of tyrannical or autocratic rule that is not responsive to the electorate; he thus eschews a definition that would entail any metaphysical or essential commitment to the absolute sovereignty of "the people." Democracy insists, al-Qaraḍāwī says, on the right of the people to repudiate their leaders "should they violate the constitution of the community" (*idha khālafū bi-dustūr al-umma*), which "in Islamic terms" would mean that the leaders "ordered rebellion [against God]" (*idha amarū bi-maʿṣiya*).[35] The binding force of the constitution on the democratic ruler is made parallel to the binding force of divine sanction on the Islamic ruler. For the democratic leader to violate the constitution is comparable with the Islamic ruler engaging in rebellion against God.

Thus, says al-Qaraḍāwī, the vernacular radical slogan "sovereignty is God's" (*al-ḥākimiyya li-Llāh*) requires clarification. Properly understood, it may appear to resemble the incorrect Khārijite position that the expression "no decision but God's" (*lā ḥukma illa li-Llāh*) requires the rejection of human governance altogether.[36] Rather, the notion of God's "sovereignty," he reasons, must be understood in two different senses. The first is God's existential sovereignty as creator and director of the universe; the second is the sovereignty of legislation in specifying the prohibited and the permitted. No proper Muslim denies either of these sorts of sovereignty; but each, argues al-Qaraḍāwī, is compatible with an Islamic commitment to democracy in selection of leaders and consultation.[37]

The constitution of Islamic democracy must specify Islam as a religion of the state and must make "Islamic Shari'a" into "a source of positive law" (*maṣdar al-qawānīn*)—or perhaps, given the imprecision of the Arabic, "*the* source of positive law."[38] Such a constitution would embody the sovereignty of God's Shari'a. It would also be possible to add to the constitution an explicit requirement that any law contradictory to the manifest, decisive requirements of revelation (*qaṭʿiyyāt al-sharʿ*) would be void.[39]

This passage and the constitutional theory it expounds must be understood against the backdrop of al-Qaraḍāwī's concept of the relationship between Shari'a and *fiqh*: very little possible positive human legislation will explicitly contradict the decisive requirements of revelation because the manifest commands of revelation, that is, revealed verses of the Qur'an, are relatively few. Al-Qaraḍāwī goes on to explain that there are a handful of matters that are not to be subjected to voting, namely, the "decisive requirements of revelation" (*qaṭʿiyyāt al-sharʿ*) and the fundamentals of religion (*asāsiyyāt al-dīn*).[40] On the other hand, matters subject to interpretation (*al-umūr al-ijtihādiyya*) may be subject to voting. These include selection of candidates, as well as questions of industrial or technological or health policy "or other matters that fall under the category that the scholars call 'public interest' " (*al-maṣāliḥ al-mursala*),[41] such as decisions of war and peace, declaring a state of emergency, the calling of new elections, or other similar matters.[42] On such matters there must be some sort of decision, and majority rule is the best option.[43]

Al-Qaraḍāwī is choosing his words very carefully here, associating the sphere of human democratic choice with the realm of the human undertaking of *fiqh*. Interpretation and public interest, invoked here by their technical *fiqh* names, are marked as suitable for human collective decision making. In other words, the structure of Shari'a and *fiqh* turns out to structure the relationship between those matters removed from democratic consideration because they are specified in revealed Shari'a and matters suitable for democratic liberation from and determination by majority rule, which are within the human realm of *fiqh*. *Fiqh* is not only the human work of interpreting divine law; it is the very stuff of democratic praxis. In this human context disagreement is natural and inevitable, and voting is the best way to deal with it.

Al-Qaraḍāwī is now building toward a rhetorical conclusion to his argument. Asserting that arbitrary government is the cause of the downfall of governance, he claims that political freedom is the first thing that is needed in the Muslim world. Political freedom is the priority for Islamic religion and Islamic politics because it is the condition under which Islamists may advance both theological and practical political claims and be able to convince an interested audience. His point is not to insist upon the use of the "foreign word" democracy, which in any case, he says, has been much misused by various Islamist writers. "Many Islamists" see democracy and its guarantees of freedom as a bulwark against military government and as the instantiation of the will of the people instead of the will of the arbitrary autocrat.[44]

He himself, says al-Qaraḍāwī, seeks democracy because he sees it as a means "to a realization of our aim in an honorable life" (*li-taḥqīq hadafinā fī-l-ḥayāt al-karīma*), in which one might call others to God and Islam according to his beliefs without suffering from oppression. This in turn might lead to the realization for "our people" of a life of freedom and honor (*ḥayāt al-ḥurriyya wa-l-karāma*) and the right to choose government, hold it responsible, and change it where appropriate without revolution.[45] This would truly be desirable (*manshūda*) democracy.[46]

The rousing conclusion accomplished, al-Qaraḍāwī closes on a legal note, refuting those scholars who suggest that under Islamic teaching consultation (*shūrā*) is optional for a leader, not mandatory. Consultation, he says, would be meaningless if the ruler could consult and then act however he might wish. Consultation with the persons who are denominated "people of binding and loosing" (*ahl al-ḥall wa-l-ʿaqd*) would be a mere charade if the persons who bound the community lacked the capacity also to loose the community from its legal bonds in case of the leader's malfeasance.[47]

The effect of concluding the *fatwā* with this argument is to complete the process whereby democracy is shifted from a suspect political system whose permissibility under Islam is being questioned to the instantiation of mandatory Islamic principles. In the end, consultation embodies the basic principles of democracy. "Thus," says al-Qaraḍāwī in his final line, "Islamic consultation approaches the spirit of democracy; and if I had wished to, I could have said: the essence of democracy approaches the spirit of Islamic consultation."[48] The incorporation of democracy into Islamic principles is complete; and indeed the interchangeability of Islamic and democratic political principles is the claim with which al-Qaraḍāwī ends his argument. In what follows, I shall take al-Qaraḍāwī's conclusion as my starting point and offer some reflections on the way in which the "foreign" concept of democracy is made to interact with the conception of Shari'a in the Islamic democrats' project.

. . .

What is the nature of the relation between Islam and democracy that Yūsuf al-Qaraḍāwī constructs in his writing on the subject? To begin with, al-Qaraḍāwī is fully prepared to acknowledge that democracy has "foreign" origins, that is, that it derives from a non-Islamic source.[49] He is dismissive of the notion that "democracy is Islam itself."[50] He does not propose a conflation of Islam and democracy, but maintains that the two are conceptually distinct. Indeed, at one juncture al-Qaraḍāwī refers to the "philosophy" of democracy in the course of noting that it must not be adopted by Islam to the extent that it might permit the forbidden or forbid the permitted[51] So in order to argue, as I have elsewhere, that Islamic democracy is best conceptualized as an exercise in synthesis between disparate ideas, it would seem necessary to explain how there might be a synthesis in which the ideas nonetheless remain different from one another.[52]

To advance this claim, I want to investigate how democracy and Islam interact in al-Qaraḍāwī's own account. Structurally, it is true, democracy is evaluated with respect to its usefulness for the requirements of Islam itself. This is, after all, a *fatwā* produced by a *muftī*, for whom Islam constitutes the unquestioned ground of values. Yet al-Qaraḍāwī makes it clear that whatever is necessary to accomplish the ends specified by Shari'a "is itself obligatory" under Shari'a.[53] The logical implication, then, is that "democracy" must be understood as obligatory under Islam—not necessarily all of democracy, for al-Qaraḍāwī recognizes that democracy may have some philosophical implications at odds with Islamic teaching, but that part of democracy that al-Qaraḍāwī determines to be essential, namely, procedures to give rise to free elections and basic substantive freedoms of speech, press, and minority protection.[54]

This is, on its face, a striking position, even if al-Qaraḍāwī stops short of formally stating the unavoidable conclusion of his argument. Not only is democracy permissible under Shari'a or compatible with Islam, but, properly construed, it is obligatory because of its necessity for achieving the ends of Shari'a. It is al-Qaraḍāwī's concept of Shari'a and its relation to *fiqh* that enables him to make this argument. Shari'a, construed as revealed law, is silent regarding democracy. In the work of some writers on liberal Islam, that silence creates an unlimited space for the development of principles of political governance separate from Islam's transcendent claims. The result is a secular politics alongside a religious Islam, an approach that sounds appealing to political theorists raised on the Protestant "two-realms" approach to church and state, but that has consistently lacked the kind of popular appeal that might give it a chance to succeed in the Muslim world, and that also deprives the political theorists of the capacity to draw on the rich moral language embedded in Islamic sources that touch on questions of politics.

For al-Qaraḍāwī, however, the silence of revealed Shari'a with respect to democracy triggers the human interpretive work of *fiqh* to find how governance ought to proceed within an Islamic framework. The method of Qaradawian *fiqh* is to determine the ends of Shari'a. In this interpretive process al-Qaraḍāwī exercises fairly wide latitude to conclude that political freedom and the rule of the majority are indeed the ends of Shari'a, and he is greatly aided in this process by distinguishing a handful of matters that must be governed by revealed law from the vast majority of "public policy" matters that can and should be governed by democratic means.

Al-Qaraḍāwī's passing analogy to constitutional governance, in which certain matters are specified constitutionally while others are committed to democratic decision making, does a great deal of implicit work here. It provides a framework in which democracy need not be construed as a political practice committed to the absolute power of the majority to achieve whatever outcomes it wants. It is intriguing, therefore, to note that the developments in democratic theory that build certain constitutional (generally liberal) restraints into the definition of democracy itself turn out to be of great use for al-Qaraḍāwī's project. If democracy were construed in purely procedural terms, it would be far more difficult for al-Qaraḍāwī to argue that Islam requires it. After all, in that case the "philosophical" component of democracy that might authorize violations of Islamic law by means of majoritarian choice would pose a major threat to the limitations in Shari'a on which al-Qaraḍāwī insists. But once democracy is understood as constitutional, limited democracy, al-Qaraḍāwī can explain that the constitution of the Islamic democracy will limit the democratic majority with respect to legislation that might violate Shari'a.

Al-Qaraḍāwī's Islamic democracy is a synthesis, then, in the sense that the concept of democracy becomes necessary for a proper account of Islam. The effect of this co-optation is to make "foreign" democracy a part of Islam itself. As a result, Islam becomes in some sense democratic, while the democracy that is "desirable" is in an important sense Islamic.

In the first step of this synthetic process, democracy is treated as necessary for the proper expression of Islamic political governance and hence as integrated into the structure of Islam, broadly understood. Once incorporated within the Islamic structure, democracy in turn exerts a gravitational pull on the structure of governance that Islam is said to demand. That is, constitutional governance in which free elections and some substantive liberal rights are guaranteed becomes a part of what Islam requires. In this first synthetic step, Islam becomes "democratic" in the limited sense that Islam, construed by *fiqh*, is understood to mandate democratic procedures and rights.

The second part of the synthetic process Islamizes democracy by virtue of the imposition of certain substantive constitutional constraints on the democratic processes and rights that are being integrated into the structure of Islamic political governance. Thus the constitution of the Islamic democracy, for al-Qaraḍāwī, must declare Islam the state religion and must make Islam a source or perhaps the source of the laws; and very possibly the constitution of the Islamic democracy will specify that no democratically enacted law may violate the explicit commands of revealed Shari'a. This is still recognizably democracy in al-Qaraḍāwī's usage because the limited scope of what revealed Shari'a requires leaves great swaths of legal and policy decision making open to the democratic process. The fact that not every legislative option is available to the demos is presented as a familiar feature of constitutional democracy. Nonetheless, it is obvious that this is not democracy in any pure or absolute sense; it is, rather, an Islamized democracy from which the danger of deviation from immutable principles of Shari'a has been expunged. As al-Qaraḍāwī repeatedly insists, the Islamic democrat retains the "right" to amend, alter, and improve on democratic theories and institutions.

The Islam of the Islamic democracy, then, is not identical to Islam before its encounter with democracy. It is an Islam that has reached out to non-Islamic means to achieve its ends and in the process has rendered those ends necessary to its own flourishing and to the living of an "honorable" Islamic life. The democracy of Islamic democracy is also not identical to democracy as such because it has taken on substantive commitments of Islam as a source of law. This engagement may actually be termed a synthesis—not a synthesis of the full-blown Hegelian type in which implicit possibilities lead to contradiction and resolution in an ineluctable historical process but rather a carefully wrought, self-conscious synthesis in which potential contradictions are neutralized by virtue of cautious modification of the underlying ideas.

Finally, it would be plainly impossible to achieve such a synthesis if one conceptualized Islam or Islamic law in its broadest sense as itself timeless, universal, and therefore not subject to change. It is al-Qaraḍāwī's concept of Shari'a and its relation to *fiqh* that allows him to postulate simultaneously the existence of a universal, unchangeable element of Islam (revealed Shari'a itself) and a sphere of human activity—*fiqh*—in which the inevitable necessity of interpretation allows for the deployment of practical reason that takes account of changes in time, place, and circumstance. The existence of a sphere of human interpretation provides the flexibility for the introduction of the foreign concept of democracy. At the same time, it would be impossible to make that foreign concept into an Islamic necessity without conceptualizing *fiqh* as a practice of discovering the ends of Shari'a, weighing them in the light of contemporary priorities, and applying them through an undertaking of practical reason. It is the sacral element of the activity of *fiqh* that enables al-Qaraḍāwī to suggest that democracy, being necessary to achieve the ends of Shari'a, is itself obligatory upon Muslims, not merely optional or permitted.

We have here a creative, distinctively legal approach to the engagement of ideas that are understood to be grounded in disparate theories of value. Al-Qaraḍāwī recognizes democracy as grounded in a non-Islamic origin and as connected to a philosophy that might contravene Islam. His crucial move is to treat democracy as a means that may be deployed within a system of value, namely, Islam, that depends on transcendent truth. Fully cognizant of the possibility that democracy could be grounded in a competing transcendent claim, namely, the absolute sovereignty of the demos, al-Qaraḍāwī rejects this reading of democracy as inconsistent with the desires of most democrats and the structure of constitutional guarantees of basic rights within the structure of actually existing democratic countries.

It would be far too simple to suggest that al-Qaraḍāwī simply domesticates democracy into Islam by stripping it of its potentially threatening attributes. If this were so, one might expect Islam to remain somehow unchanged. But al-Qaraḍāwī's *fiqh* of political governance overtly recognizes that change is desirable and inevitable within the framework of Islam. Al-Qaraḍāwī's Islam changes as a result of the integration of democracy into it. This process of mutual change, arrayed self-consciously to cohere in a new configuration, is the synthesis that Islamic democracy aspires to achieve.

7 FROM *IJTIHĀD* TO *WILĀYAT-I FAQĪH*: THE EVOLUTION OF THE SHIITE LEGAL AUTHORITY TO POLITICAL POWER

Abbas Amanat

IN NOVEMBER 2002 an Iranian professor of history, Hāshim Aghājārī, a veteran of the Iran-Iraq war, was sentenced to death by the Islamic revolutionary court in Hamadan for questioning the practice of blind "emulating/following" (*taqlīd*) of the *mujtahids* in matters of belief and practice. His sentencing led to several days of widespread university protests fueled by Aghājārī's refusal to appeal his death sentence. What incensed the Iranian court, which accused him of blasphemy, was that by implication Aghājārī was denying the "authority/guardianship of the jurist" (Persian *wilāyat-i faqīh*; Arabic *wilāyat al-faqīh*), the very founding principle of the Islamic Republic. Aghājārī's objection was aimed not merely at the practice of *taqlīd* but at the legitimacy of the "guardian jurist" (*wālī-yi faqīh*), the "supreme leader" of the Islamic Republic. For the ruling elite of Iran, *wilāyat-i faqīh* is the prime source of their political legitimacy. The idea of the "guardianship of the jurist" over the political processes in a Shiite Muslim society goes back to Ayatollah Rūhallāh Khomeini (1902–89), who first published about it in the late 1960s. Aghājārī's criticism thus was a new anticlerical quest for Islamic modernity that was bound to stir much interest among younger generations of Iranians.

Aghājārī's speech commemorated ʿAlī Sharīʿatī (1933–77), the Islamic revolutionary reformist. Invoking Sharīʿatī's notion of "Islamic Protestantism" as the only way to liberate society from the impasse of "traditional Islam," Aghājārī was striving to arrive at a historical understanding of the Shiite heritage. Though still grounded in the Qur'an and *ḥadīth*, this new reading appeared to be engaged more deeply with individual choice, human rights, and plurality of ideas. By calling for social justice, economic democracy, and openness in politics, though, he distanced himself from Sharīʿatī's firebrand rhetoric. He does not, of course, remain entirely untouched by Sharīʿatī's exhortations to be the prophet of Protestant Islam, a claim made by a number of Islamic reformers going back to the celebrated Jamāl al-Dīn "al-Afghānī" (1838–97) and earlier, but he goes so far as to criticize the Shiite establishment for its culture of condescension, especially in the exercise of *ijtihād*:

> The people are not monkeys who merely imitate. They understand and react, and they try to expand their own understanding, so someday they will not need the teacher. The relationship that the fundamentalists seek is one of master and the follower; the master must always remain master and the follower will always remain follower. This is like shackles around the neck. We must understand that the master is not a holy, divine being, and we cannot grant him that status. They [the Shiite authorities in positions of power], however, want to exercise total power. Sharīʿatī did something about it; he told the religious leaders: "You are not imams, you are not prophets, [you] cannot consider the people a subhuman species."[1]

This critique of the abiding authority of *ijtihād* and that of the so-called source of emulation (*marjaʿ-i taqlīd*) inevitably brings forward the much-debated issue of legal authority in Shiite Islam and, more specifically, the problem of institutionalization of *ijtihād*.

Aghājārī does not address openly the *wilāyat-i faqīh,* but his reference to the "imams" in the quoted passage, as well as other allusions sprinkled throughout his speech, signifies the obvious to his sensitive audience. He deliberately seems to have touched on a sore point because the doctrine of the "guardianship of the jurists," it can be argued, stands on shaky legal grounds. Shiism never historically or institutionally made the necessary leap from the loosely defined *ijtihād* to a centralized *marjaʿiyya*, let alone ever developing the theoretical ground for creating a universal judicial authority.

Before the time of Ayatollah Khomeini, Shiite legal thought never seriously engaged in the sphere of public law and consequently never articulated a coherent theory of government. Even in the safety of the *madrasa* Shiite law remained largely preoccupied with articulation of civil and private law as practiced in the *mujtahid*-run civil courts. The practice of *ijtihād* was never systematized or, one may venture to say, was never subjected to clear and universally accepted norms. The Shiite law on which the *mujtahids* relied remained a matter of interpretation and scholastic scrutiny largely within the *madrasa* environment rather than through the actual practice of the law. Throughout the Safavid and the early Qajar periods (sixteenth to nineteenth centuries) Shiite law acquired a remarkable level of sophistication, especially in the theoretical field of the so-called roots of jurisprudence (*uṣūl al-fiqh*). Yet both in the study of the individual rulings (*furūʿ*) and in the methodology of *uṣūl al-fiqh*, Shiite scholarship resisted systematic codification beyond what was determined by earlier jurists between the tenth and fourteenth centuries.

Even the emergence of the status of the "supreme exemplar" (*marjaʿ-i taqlīd*, literally "the source of emulation") in the nineteenth century remained largely an informal practice. No set of objective standards for designating such a leadership ever developed, and no specific legal privileges were arrogated to this office. The *marjaʿiyya* was largely meant to address the need for a communal leadership rather than a supreme legal authority. No *marjaʿ* ever claimed his legal opinions to be universally binding. Nor did any of the *marjaʿ*s claim to be standing at the apex of a judicial hierarchy or was accepted as such by the *mujtahid*s or by the community at large. Whenever they effectively exercised their legal power, as in the tobacco rebellion of 1890–91, during the Constitutional Revolution of 1906–11, or in the banning of the drinking of Pepsi Cola in the 1950s, the *marjaʿ*s relied on their popularity and prestige rather than any legal precept. The three preconditions for a *marjaʿ*, being the most learned (*aʿlam*), the most judicious (*aʿdal*), and the most pious (*atqā*), were qualities barely measurable by legal or academic standards. No institutional procedure was ever set to determine these preconditions. What in reality determined the success of a *marjaʿ* or, for that matter, any *mujtahid* was his popularity and the size of his follower constituency (or congregation).[2] The question thus remains what process, historical and legal, transformed this informal and democratically chaotic form of diffuse judicial leadership into a binding, all-embracing, and authoritative office of the *wilāyat-i faqīh* with a claim over judicial and political authority.

IJTIHĀD AND THE *UṢŪLĪ* INTERPRETATION OF JUDICIAL AUTHORITY

As early as the tenth century the so-called Twelver Shiite (*Ithnā ʿAsharī*) jurists recognized the occultation (*ghayba*) of the Twelfth Imam, the state of his invisible (and directly ineffective) existence in the physical world, as the chief postulate for denouncing any form of temporal power in the absence of the Imam as inherently unjust and therefore illegitimate. Only the return of the Imam at an undetermined moment in the future, it was believed, could establish on earth the ultimate values of justice and legitimate rule. This absolutist messianic belief in the imam's eventual establishing of a utopian perfect order has often been viewed as the chief obstacle in the way of articulating a legal public space in Shiism. The same rationale also barred in theory any legitimate collaboration between the jurists and the state. Every government was in theory seen as inherently oppressive. The same principle of avoiding political collaboration was conducive to the flourishing of the Shiite study of *ḥadīth* as a means of emulating the models of the Prophet and the imams and to the early development of jurisprudence (*fiqh*) focusing on civil and contractual law, as well as on devotional acts and obligations.[3]

In practice, however, the quietist tendency among the Shiite jurists, as opposed to powerful messianic trends throughout the Shiite past, encouraged compliance and even collaboration with the "unjust" and "tyrannical" (*jā'ir*) state, especially if and when the state was accommodating the Shiites. This de facto acceptance of the temporal power, needless to say, was in full agreement with the ancient Persian notion of the "sisterhood" of the religious and the state institutions, an interdependency perceived to be essential for the endurance of both institutions and the stability of the social order against the corrupting influence of "bad religion." While the state maintained peace and order, upheld Shari'a, defended the domain, and guarded the jurists' vested interests, the jurists were in turn expected to maintain good relations with the state and even serve in the state-controlled judiciary.[4]

Already by the fourteenth century the Shiite jurists developed an elaborate legal system of private law based on *ijtihād*, the exercise of logical reasoning by using the sources of the law to form qualified legal opinions within a specific time frame. The exercise of *ijtihād* in turn led to the development of an elaborate methodology of jurisprudence, the science of *uṣūl al-fiqh*. Some of the best legal minds articulated complex linguistic debates on legal semantics and phenomenological discussions on the authority of the text. But oddly enough *uṣūl al-fiqh* avoided the practical dimensions of *ijtihād*, such as the *mujtahids*' qualifications and hierarchy, and failed to discuss such seemingly mundane issues as the *madrasa* curriculum. It also did not address the inconsistencies and ambiguities of Islamic law or question the rationale behind its archaic classification.[5]

Even the establishment of the Safavid state (1501–1736) and the declaration of Shiism as its official creed (in obvious contrast to the rival Ottoman Empire's expressed upholding of "orthodox" Sunni Islam) did not substantially alter the *mujtahids*' resistance to the development of institutions, despite the state's active sponsorship of the clerical establishment and heavy patronage of the teaching circles. The immigrant jurists from the Arab Shiite communities of Jabal Amil (in today's Syria and Lebanon), Qatif and Bahrain in northern Arabia, and Najaf in southern Iraq were incorporated into the judiciary of the Safavid Empire. These *mujtahid*s and their Iranian counterparts, many of whom were converts from Sunnism, considered the Safavid shahs legitimate defenders of the faith, and their empire the guarded Shiite domain. For the "learned" (*ʿulamāʾ*) community, it was therefore permissible to assume judicial offices, as a majority did, collect alms and the so-called share of the imam, and even to lead the congregational Friday prayer.[6]

The jurists' failure in this period to solidify their gains and to implement a judicial leadership independent from the state is not surprising. They were reluctant to better define the boundaries of *ijtihād* in part because the Safavid rulers successfully recruited the *mujtahid*s as state functionaries. Although the office of *shaykh al-Islām* was held by a high-ranking jurist, this was not understood to be a legal supervision over the entire judicial community. Nor did it mean administrative or financial control, a task that the Safavid state consistently conferred on a nonclerical bureaucrat with the title of *ṣadr*. Moreover, the Safavids did not hesitate in the late seventeenth century to patronize the alternative *akhbārī* school, which rejected *ijtihād* and its logical rationalization, in contradistinction to the *uṣūlī* school.

The debate between the two schools of *akhbārī*s and *uṣūlī*s in the late seventeenth and throughout the eighteenth centuries weakened the development of *uṣūl al-fiqh* as a discretionary methodology in favor of the wholesale validity of all the *ḥadīth*. More specifically, the *akhbārī* school held that all reports (*akhbār*) from diverse Shiite *ḥadīth* sources that are attributed to the Prophet and to the imams are valid, with little respect for their historical authenticity. The *akhbārī* resistance to independent reasoning was congruent with the Safavid state's aversion to allowing the emergence of an independent *mujtahid*-dominated judiciary.[7]

After the collapse of the Safavid Empire in 1722 and the ensuing political instability, the *uṣūlī* school reemerged as the predominant legal school during the late eighteenth and throughout the nineteenth centuries. In contrast to most scholars of the rival *akhbārī* camp, the *uṣūlī* jurists practiced *ijtihād* by employing analogical deduction (*qiyās*) in order to infer opinions from the text of the Qur'an and the *ḥadīth*. The analogical method no doubt was a far more effective strategy than Akhbarism in dealing with judicial issues of Shiite society at a time when the *mujtahid*s often found themselves leaders of their communities. In the early decades of the nineteenth century they made evident gains in the socioeconomic and educational areas, laying the foundation of a clerical establishment that has continued to the present with little interruption. They monopolized the *madrasa*s and the pulpits of the mosques, controlled vast charitable endowments (*awqāf*), and collected religious taxes. The latter included the so-called portion of the imam (*sahm-i imām*), paid by pious followers to the *mujtahid*s, who received it as legitimate deputies (*nā'ib*) to the Hidden Imam. They developed amicable, though somewhat distant, relations with the early rulers of the Qajar dynasty (1785–1925), an arrangement that was mutually beneficial to both sides and hence brought about the apex of *uṣūlī ijtihād*. The growth of religious circles, first in Najaf, where the *akhbārī* school was soundly defeated, and later in the Iranian cities, was supported by a large student body and by a closely knit network of teacher-pupil patronage.[8] An impressive number of legal works were produced both on the specifics of the law (*furūʿ*) and on the methodology of *uṣūl al-fiqh* with implicit emphasis on the role of the *mujtahid*s not only as legal scholars but also as judges and social mediators. The growth of congregations in mosques also strengthened jurists' ties with other social groups in search of their legal support, most noticeably the merchants of the bazaar, who backed the *mujtahid*s and financed their teaching circles.

Yet with all the success in developing a semi-independent legal network and a solid lay constituency, the jurists of the Qajar period did not seek to reconstruct the theory of *ijtihād* and its application to public law. Despite occasional "turf wars" with the state over privilege and sphere of influence or later in defiance of the state's Westernizing policies, they continued to honor the dichotomy of the religious law (Shari'a) as it concerned the jurists versus the customary law (*ʿurf*) as exercised by the state. The customary law generally covered penal law, such as punishing criminals, public order, land use and agrarian arrangements (*nasaq*), military, civic, and government affairs, taxation, and even family and business practices. Customary laws were based on historical precedent, and though some were universal across the land, most varied from region to region and even from town to town. They ran parallel with Shari'a law but operated in a more fluid environment and were seldom documented. Moreover, frequently the jurists drew on *ʿurf* as an important source to argue legal points or to determine actual cases in Shari'a courts.

Neither the jurists nor the state (at least before the rise of the European-inspired reforms) attempted to define each of these two spheres, Shari'a and

ʿurf, or demarcate their boundaries through codification, let alone to breach the informal boundaries between them. The *uṣūl al-fiqh* remained essentially concerned with its theoretical debates on the fine points of legal methodology. Voluminous works, commentaries, and glosses on commentaries were produced by the *uṣūlī* scholars on intricate details of semantics and epistemology. But the jurists simply did not see the need for a centralized corporate identity or for disturbing the delicate balance with the state upon which they continuously negotiated their power. The state in turn preferred ambiguity whereby through consent and coercion it hoped to persuade the jurists to comply with the state's otherwise waning power and prestige. By the end of the century, although the *mujtahid*s were more present than ever in the public space, they were intellectually stagnant within the world of the *madrasa* and the arcane judicial practices of Shari'a courts. Accordingly, the curriculum of the seminaries was substantially truncated to focus solely on the roots of jurisprudence and the *furūʿ* at the expense of nonreligious and especially nonlegal topics. Even such traditional fields as mathematics, astronomy, and philosophy were no longer part of the jurists' general education.[9]

Voices of protest against the jurists' monopolies and their intellectual petrifaction further moved the *mujtahid*s toward conservatism and distaste for new approaches. Most significantly, the messianic Bābī movement in the middle decades of the nineteenth century questioned the very legitimacy of the clerical community and its theoretical premises, educational methods, and legal practices. The Bābī religion (later transformed into the Bahā'ī faith) denied the long-held jurist position that they collectively represent the Imam of the Age in Occultation. With growing popularity, the apocalyptic Bābī movement not only sought leadership in the new "Imam of the Age," but declared the end of the historical cycle of Islamic Shari'a by ushering in a new cycle of prophetic manifestations. In response to the Bābī challenge, the jurist community closed ranks and came closer to full collaboration with the state in crushing the Bābī revolution. The *uṣūlī* jurists in no way heeded the Bābī call for fundamental reform, though in the long run the clerical community did produce a new form of communal leadership. The status of the *marjaʿ* was first recognized for Shaykh Murtazā Anṣārī (1799–1864) in the late 1850s and coincided with the growth of Bābī clandestine anticlerical subversion. His emergence as the "supreme exemplar" no doubt mirrored the public desire for a clerical leadership committed to higher standards of morality, learning, and social justice. Anṣārī came to represent these values for a growing constituency of seminarians in the *madrasa*s and among the lay followers.

The idea of *marjaʿiyya* continued in the second half of the nineteenth century and during the Constitutional Revolution (1906–11) as a communal leadership with an increasing claim over the political process. Perhaps the height of this politicized *marjaʿiyya* came with Mīrzā Ḥasan Shīrāzī (1815–95), an influential jurist and teacher whose access to funds and his ever-growing teaching circle placed him ahead of his competitors as the most widely recognized *marjaʿ*. His general ban on the use of tobacco during the Regie protest of 1890–91 for the first time demonstrated the *marjaʿ*'s power against the state and his potential for channeling public discontent into a political course. This came to be particularly true during the Constitutional Revolution. Several *mujtahid*s simultaneously recognized as *marjaʿ*s in this turbulent period appealed to diverse constituencies with contrasting political agendas and tendencies. This breakdown of a singular leadership more than ever demonstrated the crucial role of the jurists' constituencies in promoting the cause of one leader and demoting the other. Greater political polarization of the clerical community during the Constitutional Revolution vouched for this multiplicity of leadership.

FROM *MARJAʿIYYA* TO *WILĀYAT-I FAQĪH*

Only in the latter part of the twentieth century, however, do we witness the gradual shift back to a centralized *marjaʿiyya* under Ayatollah Muḥammad Ḥusayn Burūjirdī (1875–1962). He should be viewed as the first to hold a united leadership not only in the management of the Qom seminaries, collection and distribution of the religious taxes, and orchestrating a rigorous anti-Bahāʾī campaign but also in a certain degree of legal authority over the clerical community that came as a result of these measures. It goes without saying that the emergence of this form of centralized *marjaʿiyya* was a belated, albeit inevitable, response to the state's intrusion into the judiciary. The rise of the Pahlavi secular autocracy from the middle of the 1920s and the growth of modern educational institutions, the abolishment of the *mujtahids*' civil courts and replacement of them with a state-controlled judiciary, state regulation of the use of charitable endowments, and other measures were intended to undermine the social status of the *ʿulamāʾ*.

The growth of the secularized or semisecularized middle classes and the popularity of a variety of religious and ideological challenges, from the Bahāʾī faith to Marxism, Western-style modernity, and religious modernists and Islamic radicals of various sorts, persuaded the demoralized and shrunken clerical community to reorganize the *madrasa*s and solidify their network at the national level. Most important, they gradually moved away from the state-*ʿulamāʾ*

alliance that had been founded on the ancient principle of preserving social equilibrium through guarded collaboration. In due course the new *marjaʿiyya* reconstituted its base not only in the bazaar community, where it was traditionally strong, but among a new class of urban and urbanized poor. They offered a pool for clerical recruitment and an enthusiastic mosque congregation.[10]

Greater solidarity and group identity, however, did not result in reconsideration of Shiite legal thought or any serious attempt to institutionalize the informal *marjaʿiyya* leadership. The study of *fiqh* in the seminaries of Najaf and Qom and elsewhere remained almost entirely loyal to the traditional precepts and practices of Shiite law and its obsessive preoccupation with devotional acts (*ʿibādāt*) and contracts (*ʿuqūd*). The striking persistence of legal archaism among the Shiite jurists can be explained in part by the inherent conservatism of the legal curriculum and in part by isolation from society's secular discourse. Left out of the new state-run judiciary, the Shiite teaching circles in Najaf and Qom made almost no attempt to address new issues of public law or even to offer a modern reading of the old legal texts. The reconstituted Qom *ḥawza* continued to operate with informal teacher-pupil patronage and produced a growing number of jurists and/or preachers in need of new congregations.[11]

A number of *marjaʿ*s who emerged after the death of Burūjirdī in 1962, including Ayatollah Khomeini, were no doubt more organized in their teaching and charitable operations, but there was no attempt in clerical circles to revisit the nature and conditions of *marjaʿiyya,* let alone arrive at a consensus about criteria for such leadership or the hierarchy. As much as the lay constituency of the *marjaʿ*s grew and the funding sources improved, no equivalent of an ecclesiastical hierarchy emerged, even though there was a fairly coherent network of the *ʿulamāʾ* throughout Iran, southern Iraq, and Lebanon.

The diffuse *marjaʿiyya* leadership of this period relied heavily on both the lay and the clerical "followers." To mark their place in a complex game of prestige and popularity, the *marjaʿ*s depended on their followers for higher standing. At times they were naturally bound by their whims and wishes. In this popularity contest no *marjaʿ* could survive without his constituency's financial and moral backing, as Murtazā Mutahharī (1920–79), a prominent follower of Khomeini and a leader of the future Islamic revolution, pointed out in the early 1960s. In a conference organized by some religious modernists on the theme of *marjaʿiyya,* the largely modernist lay, among them Mahdī Bazargān (1907–95), joined hands with a new generation of activist clerics, such as Mutahharī, to urge the *marjaʿ*s to bring some order into the notoriously chaotic world of Shiite clerical leadership.[12]

The greater politicization of the clerical community, especially the clerical clique around Khomeini from the mid-1960s, responded positively to this call. Among the *marjaʿ*s of Qom and Najaf, Khomeini represented the most radical political position. His open anti-Pahlavi platform caused as much trouble for him as it gained him popularity, especially among the lower and middle-rank *ʿulamāʾ* disillusioned with other *marjaʿ*s and their collaboration with the shah's regime. Modernity thus came to the clerical establishment with political radicalization rather than a fundamental revision of the Shiite legal system and reconsideration of its curriculum and judicial premises. Even prominent students of Khomeini, such as Ḥusayn ʿAlī Muntaẓirī and Murtazā Mutahharī, seldom called for reconsideration of the Islamic legal tradition or new teaching methods or adopting a modern legal philosophy. For them legal reform equaled succumbing to an alien secular modernity.[13] A few *mujtahids* in Pahlavi times that attempted to reinterpret Shiite theology and exegesis, among them Muḥammad Ḥasan Sharīʿat Sangilajī (d. 1944) and ʿAlī Akbar Ḥakamzādah, were marginalized or soundly defeated by the jurists of Qom.[14]

The majority of the new seminarians and clerical followers of Khomeini came from among the underprivileged in small towns and villages. Increasingly they were drawn into political dissent and political activism in the late 1960s and 1970s because, among other reasons, they resented the wealth and privilege of the secularized urban middle classes. They were critical of the legal system that replaced the old *ʿulamāʾ*-dominated judiciary with lay judges. Moreover, they also resented the subservience of the higher clerical ranks to the wishes of the state. Khomeini and his prominent students capitalized on these factors to promote his leadership as superior to that of other leaders, not necessarily because of Khomeini's juristic qualifications, which were meager, but because of his uncompromising political stance.

In the tense environment of confrontation with the shah and his secret police, this message of political dissent was better transmitted to the lay population by recalling Shiite narratives of defiance and self-sacrifice, as in the commemoration of the martyrdom of ʿAlī ibn Abī Ṭālib (d. 661) and that of his son Ḥusayn (d. 680). Laboring over the obscure and mostly redundant details of Shiite law and the theoretical intricacies of *uṣūl al-fiqh* appeared secondary, if not entirely obsolete. Even Mutahharī, the most promising intellectual product of Qom in the 1970s, preferred to delve into Western philosophy or Islamic reformism and revolutionary rhetoric rather than adopting a novel approach to *fiqh* and *uṣūl*.[15]

In a climate of state-driven secular modernity versus the legal redundancy of the *ʿulamā'*, Khomeini's gradual tilt in the late 1960s toward the doctrine of juridical sovereignty was the solution to the prolonged problem of unregulated leadership. He borrowed from the Sunni reformist milieu the notion of the Islamic government, long debated by the likes of Muḥammad Rashīd Riḍā (1865–1935) and later Abū l-Aʿlā Mawdūdī (1904–79) in order to set the legal ground for what he defined as the "authority of the jurist" (*wilāyat-i faqīh* [also rendered as guardianship or governance of the jurist]). More of a teacher of Greco-Islamic philosophy than a teacher of jurisprudence, Khomeini was the right candidate to break through the inhibiting cobweb of juristic tedium. His theory no doubt had an unmistakable mystico-philosophical core that was colored on the outside by Shiite legal trappings. On a personal level it was the work of a reluctant jurist who was anxious to overcome his rivals for the status of *marjaʿ* through the philosophical back door, namely, the charismatic leadership of the *wālī*, long debated among mystics and Shiite theosophists.

The concept of *wilāya* upon which Khomeini propounded his theory is a complex and theologically charged term. Variably read as *wilāya* (authority, guardianship) and *walāya* (bond of friendship), for Shiites it was the hereditary status primarily arrogated to ʿAlī and his imam descendants as true successors to the Prophet Muhammad: a status of sovereignty over his true believers. In Sufism *wilāya* implied friendship with God, a saintly status of proximity to Truth, even, according to some, almost on a par with prophethood. For the Shiite jurists, however, *wilāya* was a purely legal term denoting the state of guardianship often assumed by the jurist over the legal minor (*ṣaghīr*) and mentally retarded (*maḥjūr*), hence *wilāyat al-faqīh*, the "guardianship of the jurist." Although in theory this guardianship could be extended to the public sphere, in reality no jurist of any substance did consider as viable the jurist's "authority to rule" (*wilāyat al-ḥukm*). In the absence of the Hidden Imam, who is the just and legitimate enforcer of the *wilāya*, few jurists even condoned the "authority to judge" (*wilāyat al-qaḍā*) beyond mere issuance of opinions (*fatwās*), but without the necessary power to enforce them. The notion of "general deputyship" (*niyāba ʿāmma*) on behalf of the imam, as claimed by some jurists in the Safavid and early Qajar periods, was never extended to the authority to govern, though it did reserve for the jurist certain prerogatives, such as declaring *jihād* under the auspices of the state.

In the latter part of the twentieth century, however, the prevalence of the idea of *marjaʿiyya* seldom allowed the doctrine of collective deputyship of the *mujtahids* to attract attention. The semantic shift in referring to the jurists also indicates a change in focus. Khomeini's use of *faqīh* (jurist) rather than *mujtahid* or *marjaʿ* in his own articulation of "guardianship" underlined sheer proficiency in *fiqh* rather than any acquired clerical status based on vague qualifications. His *wilāya*, in theory at least, could be extended to any jurist, not just the one who is publicly recognized as the most important *marjaʿ*, and he need not even be a *mujtahid*. This definition no doubt served Khomeini well while he languished in the exile of Najaf away from his Iranian constituency.

As defined by Khomeini, the doctrine of the "guardianship of the jurist" was applicable to public law, as well as civil law. In the absence of the Hidden Imam, he argued, the jurist presents the least oppressive form of authority, compared with temporal rule, because it is founded on Islamic principles. The jurist is the most qualified in matters of law, which according to Khomeini is inherently superior to any secular body of law, and he is obliged by the same Islamic legal principles to uphold and enforce it. It is therefore incumbent upon the jurist as an "individual duty" (*farḍ ʿayn*) to strive for acquiring political authority in order to form the Islamic government. Khomeini's doctrine was a revolutionary interpretation of the authority of the jurist even though he tried hard in his *wilāyat-i faqīh* (later *ḥukūmat-i Islāmī*) to fortify his theory with precedent from classical legal texts and citations from such *uṣūlī* jurists as the nineteenth-century Mullā Aḥmad Naraqī (d. 1829). No Shiite jurist before him ever extended the very limited application of legal *wilāya* to include public affairs, let alone the assumption of political power.[16]

Legal articulations aside, Khomeini's doctrine was driven by the requirements of his constituency not only to defy the legitimacy of the Pahlavi state and whatever it stood for but also to bring coherence and unanimity to clerical leadership. The *wilāyat-i faqīh* promised not only the ascendancy of the jurists to positions of political power but a virtual end to clerical resistance to institutionalization. The rise of the *wilāyat-i faqīh* as an institution harbingered the eclipse of the *marjaʿiyya* and all the ambiguity that was inherent in qualities of the *mujtahid*.

Moreover, throughout his Najaf lectures Khomeini remained critical of the clerical establishment for its narrow understanding of *ijtihād* as mere preoccupation with devotional acts and other conventional categories of Shiite jurisprudence:

> In order to demonstrate to some degree how great the difference is between Islam and what is presented as Islam, I would like to draw your attention to the

> difference between the Qur'an and the books of *ḥadīth*, on the one hand, and the practical treatises of jurisprudence (*risālah-yi ʿilmiyya*), on the other. The Qur'an and the books of *ḥadīth*, which are the sources of commands and ordinances of Islam, are completely different from the treatises written by the *mujtahids* of the present age both in breadth of scope and in the effect they are capable of exerting on the life of the society.[17]

Khomeini goes on to say that issues related to society, including the political affairs of Muslims, occupy the greatest portion of Islamic teachings in the Qur'an and the *ḥadīth*, in comparison with a very small section dedicated to ritual acts (*ʿibādāt*) and duties of man toward his creator. The thrust of *ḥukūmat-i Islāmī* thus was to shift the emphasis back to Islam as a social agency and as a political power and to the responsibility of the Shiite jurist to restore this vitality. This view was in direct contrast to the traditional understanding of the role of the jurists as legal experts who were solely concerned with the pragmatic aspects of Shari'a (*furūʿ*) and was thus received as such by the conservative jurists in Najaf and Qom.[18]

The assumption of political power by Khomeini and his *ʿulamā'* backers, which came with the revolution of 1979, however, imposed a bureaucratic regime on the Shiite *ʿulamā'* more rigid than the chaotic *madrasa* system of Najaf and Qom ever was. Even the honorary clerical titles, inflated over time, gained new hierarchical connotations. While Ayatollah (*ayāt-Allāh*, "the sign of God") applied to the higher clerical figures, *ḥujjat al-Islām* ("proof of Islam") signified the rank below. The highest status, however, was Khomeini's own. As the "guardian jurist" (*wālī-yi faqīh*), he assumed the title "imam," used for the first time ever in the history of Shiism in a context other than that of the twelve imams. Although the office of guardian jurist was considered one and the same as the "deputy of the imam" (*nā'ib-i imām*), more in vogue in the nineteenth century, in practice a consensus was reached on the universal and sole reference of the term *imam* to the founder of the Islamic Republic, hence Imam Khomeini.

The application of this honorific first appeared in Arabic works by Khomeini and about him published by a younger generation of his students in Najaf in the early 1970s. It is possible that the honorific was inspired by the Sunni notion of imam in the Arabic-speaking world. There an imam is a leader of prayer and, more commonly, a clerical figure of a certain prestige. With the rise of Khomeini's popularity in radical circles in the early 1970s, the term *imam* gained wide usage in Persian. The first known reference in Persian appears in a panegyric (*qaṣīda*) dated 10 Tīrmāh 1349 / July 1, 1970, by an unidentified poet:

O, the true designated imam (*imām-i bi-ḥaqq-i bar-guzīdah*)
You, the light of Islam's eye . . .
You are the great imam that after the [Shiite] imams.
Islam has never witnessed a leader (*rahbar*) like you.

Later, with the emergence of the Islamic revolution, the *imam* honorific was promoted by Khomeini's students and supporters (often intermittently with the more accepted notion of *nā'ib-i imām*) to denote not only his superior authority over the Pahlavi monarchy but also that over the authority of the Shiite *marja*ʿs in Qom and Najaf. Because he was the founder of the Islamic Republic, a certain semiprophetic sanctity also was attached to the title that was largely the work of propagandists in the revolutionary press but nevertheless was reminiscent of the recurring messianic tradition deeply embedded in Iranian Shiism.[19]

The constitutional authority and popular aura that Khomeini acquired as the guardian jurist and the imam indicated not only a desire for rationalization of the clerical community but also a drive toward clerical absolutism. The legitimacy and the mandate of the guardian jurist do not derive from his constituency of followers, as in the case of the *marja*ʿ, but from a sublime source. Despite the seemingly democratic trappings of the constitution of the Islamic Republic, the guardian jurist is answerable to no source but God, even though he is appointed by the Council of Experts (Majlis-i Khubragān), a select body of high-ranking *ʿulamā'* (and is impeachable by the same body). The range of the guardian's institutional authority is vast and universally abiding even though the Islamic Consultative Council (Majlis-i Shūrā-yi Islāmī), which is the Iranian parliament, tends to modify his ultimate power. Similarly, articles of the Iranian Constitution guaranteeing the inalienable rights and freedoms of the individual contradict the authoritarian power of the guardian jurist. Khomeini's charismatic aura in the early years of the revolution glossed over the obvious contradiction in the constitution between democratic freedoms and the totalitarian power of the guardian jurist. In the post-Khomeini era, twenty-eight years after the revolution, the contrast is glaring. The "supreme leader" (*rahbar*) of today's Islamic Republic, Khomeini's successor Ayatollah ʿAlī Khamenei, insists on these constitutional prerogatives to control, and if necessary to quell, the legislative, the executive, and the judicial branches of the government and to remain unaccountable to any elected body.

The authoritarian nature of *wilāyat-i faqīh* is no doubt indebted to the persistent culture of autocracy that the revolution denounced in theory but perpetuated in practice. But it also was reflective of the Shiite judicial community's failure to rethink the precepts of Shiite law and their applicability to pluralist values. The doctrine of the "guardianship of the jurist" was informed above all by a Shiite legal mind-set that essentially was alien to the modern notions of plurality and democratic leadership even though, ironically, Shiite *ijtihād* and *marjaʿiyya* operated on some form of popular representation. It was also colored, no doubt, by Khomeini's own mystical propensity for classical Sufism and specifically Ibn ʿArabī's (d. 1240) theory of *wilāya*. Moreover, the historical "guardianship" as it was evoked in the rhetoric of the Islamic revolution was an imagined narrative of Islam's golden age. These representations particularly promoted ʿAlī's pristine (though ultimately doomed) caliphate with great moral emphasis on the leadership qualities of compassion (*walāya*) and self-denial (*īthār*), qualities that were considered essential for creating a "classless" society. Added to the admixture that shaped the "guardianship of the jurist" was the modern revolutionary urgency for assertive leadership harking back to the French age of "terror" and the Soviet "dictatorship of the proletariat." These presuppositions were hardly conducive to a progressive legal framework that separates legal authority from political power and religion from the state. Missing from this politicolegal vision of absolute leadership was a desire to reexamine the long-held precepts of Islamic law in a new light of historical relativity.

As for the clerical community, in the more than two decades after the Islamic revolution, it largely came to constitute the backbone of the Islamic regime and actively sought to monopolize positions of power. A minority of the jurists remained critical of the theory and the implementation of total authority of the jurist and faced the consequences of their criticisms. But opposition to *wilāyat-i faqīh* further solidified the clerical hierarchy to an unprecedented degree. The Shiite establishment now more than ever appears as an equivalent to a state-sponsored church with its ecclesiastical hierarchy, perhaps, as Saïd A. Arjomand observed, comparable to a Weberian "cesaro-papist" model of the state. The concentration of power in the hand of an oligarchy consisting of the guardian jurist and his top echelons of clerical allies inevitably triggered much resentment. The laymen and laywomen of the younger generation with revolutionary credentials now feel that they have been left out by a clerical establishment that resorts to doctrinal repression to preserve its privileges and monopolies.

A whole body of literature on the doctrine of *wilāyat-i faqīh* that has appeared since the revolution, ranging from moderates such as Muḥsin Kadīwar to influential conservatives such as Muḥammad Taqī Miṣbāḥ Yazdī, discusses the still-undetermined parameters of the office of the guardian jurist in the Islamic Republic. In at least two of his works Kadīwar examines *wilāya* within its conceptual and historical bounds. In *Hukāmat-i wilā'ī* (The Governance of Guardianship) he offers a framework of inquiry that relies on the Qu'ran and the Shiite *ḥadīth*, as well as works of theologians, jurists, and mystics, to define *wilāyat-i sharʿī* as a theocratic office irreconcilable with democratic values and essentially opposed to the modern idea of social contract.[20] "Guardianship over people is incompatible with deputation on their behalf," he concludes.[21] In his *Naẓariyyahhā-yi dawlat dar fiqh-i Shīʿah* (Theories of Government in the Shiite Jurisprudence) he traces the roots and the development of the notion of government in the works of the Shiite *uṣūlī* writers of the nineteenth and twentieth centuries. Shiite jurists, he argues, avoided a universal theory of government but went through four stages in accepting or denying the temporal authority of the state and its legitimacy. Though never explicitly, Kadīwar demonstrates conceptual contradictions within the Islamic regime and its constitution.[22]

On the other end of the spectrum Miṣbāḥ Yazdī in his *Nigāhi guzarā bih naẓariyyah-yi wilāyat-i faqīh* (Brief Survey of the Theory of Guardianship of the Jurist) and a number of other works and collections of speeches argues that the guardian jurist is solely designated by the Mahdī—the Hidden Imam—rather than by the people and that his command (*ḥukm*) is obligatory to all.[23] The people's only prerogative is to "discover" (*kashf*) the guardian from among qualified jurists, but they have no say in accepting or rejecting his decisions and have no right to participate in decision making regarding affairs of state. The guardian jurist only consults with experts in various fields to better govern, but he has no obligation to comply with their opinions. Miṣbāḥ Yazdī thus offers the most absolutist interpretation of *wilāya*, even beyond Khomeini's earlier recognition of the parliament as a legislative body and the constitutional right of the people to elect the guardian jurist through the Council of Experts (Majlis-i Khubragān). In effect (and at times explicitly) Miṣbāḥ Yazdī thus questions the very idea of an Islamic Republic as an eclectic innovation that is incompatible with the doctrine of the divinely guided guardian jurist and his rule on behalf of the Mahdī. Therefore, he too, like Kadīwar, acknowledges a fundamental contradiction in the foundation of the Islamic state.

The anticlerical content of Aghājārī's speech and his call for an Islamic reformation originates in this very contradiction. The younger generation of Iranians who are frustrated with the monopoly of power, the heavy-handed treatment of dissident voices, and the obscurantist legal outlook of the clergy are implicitly critical of the very existence of the office of the guardian jurist. Their disillusionment is even more evident after repeated setbacks of the seemingly pro-reform wing of the clerical establishment as represented by the former president, Muḥammad Khātamī (reg. 1997–2005), and his supporters. Such dissenting calls for reforming Islam are by no means rare in the history of antinomian Islam. What distinguishes this postrevolutionary episode from earlier examples is that these voices of protest, especially since Khomeini's death in 1989, have been aimed at a consolidated clerical hierarchy that claims infallible and comprehensive authority. The guardianship of the jurist is far more explicit a claim over religious hegemony in the public sphere and on behalf of the imams than the old *marjaʿiyya* ever was. This is what makes the new criticism especially potent and enduring.

As for Aghājārī's fate, he seems to have been the involuntary beneficiary of the inconsistencies that are typical of Shiite legal practice. The same ruling of the Hamadan court that sentenced him to death for blasphemy also sentenced him to a total of eight years of imprisonment for three other related counts and after that to a ban on teaching in any university for ten years. The seemingly ludicrous verdict of the court points to the ambiguities of a legal culture built on negotiations and compromise, a culture that still seems to be thriving two and a half decades after the Islamic Revolution.[24]

8 SHIITE THEORIES OF SOCIAL CONTRACT

Shahrough Akhavi

PRELIMINARY CONSIDERATIONS

Social contract theory holds that human beings choose to form associations to promote their interests. It acknowledges that tension exists between the individual's inherent independence and the authority to which he or she must submit. As far as God is considered, the conception of social contract theory is deistic, meaning that God created the world but does not otherwise interfere. The theory privileges natural law and natural rights, whereby the individual is seen as fully rational, free, and autonomous. It holds that three steps are taken in the process of promoting humans' interests through contracts: (1) creating society; (2) creating the sovereign state; (3) discharging obligations and enjoying benefits.

Because Ashʿarite Sunni Islam views God as immanent and continuously intervening in the world and insists on the person's "acquisition" (*kasb*) of his action from God at the instant of acting, it did not generate a theory of social contract. The theory was introduced to the Muslim world in the nineteenth century as a convention when reformers became interested in contractarian theorists.[1] Muslim traditions do include concepts that are important for the elaboration of a theory of social contract, such as justice, obligation, mutuality, and interests.[2] But before the nineteenth century Sunni jurists would not have referred to people leaving the state of nature and creating a society that would be the trustee of their interests. Twelver Shiism, unlike Sunni Ashʿarism, has been influenced, on the one hand, by Qadarite and Muʿtazilite cosmological doctrines regarding God and free will and, on the other hand, by the doctrine of the imamate, that is, the leadership of Muhammad's descendants. Unlike Ashʿarism's thesis of the human's "acquisition" of one's action from God at the instant of acting, Qadarite and Muʿtazilite thought stresses a more robust notion of human responsibility for actions. On this argument, one is self-conscious about one's actions and chooses to act. But God mandates that believers be ruled by the Prophet and the imams because only they possess the knowledge of God. This being so, individual Shiites may be responsible for their specific individual moral acts, but otherwise they must accept the commands of the Prophet and the imams to form a religious community. They may not rationally vest their collective interests in the Prophet and imams and then reappropriate them should they decide that their leaders have not represented them well.

Thus the problem for both Sunnis and Shiites is that they equate natural law with divine law, an issue that is discussed in Chapter 3 by Frank Griffel in this book. Because natural law makes the human being, by virtue of reason, the agent of his own present and future, Muslim thought cannot readily accord this law an independent sphere. This results in ad hoc, not systematically integrated, incorporation of propositions about interests, representation, and justice to generate a would-be theory of social contract by Muslims.

CLASSICAL SOURCES AND SUNNI AND SHIITE INTERPRETATIONS

The Qur'an has several words that connote contract, including *ʿahd*, *ʿaqd*, *bayʿ*, *mawthiq*, and *mīthāq*. Early Muslims must have understood them in the linguistic contexts that were then current. Although it is impossible to know for certain what constituted the contemporary understandings of these terms, it is unlikely that they were understood as betokening social contract.

Ashʿarism holds that God had sent prophets with covenants to various peoples who broke them. He chose Muhammad in a final effort and rewarded believers who accepted the covenant with revelational knowledge. The Prophet's role was to articulate the message and call people to it. But the compact was not a social contract, which is formed when "each man, by right of nature, that is, by right of his human character . . . possess[es] the quality of freedom."[3] Tribalism's collectivist ethos precluded this sort of individualism. God ordained the Prophet's mission, but those who submitted were not seen as unrestrictedly and freely creating a society to protect their interests. They may accept or reject revelation but cannot negotiate or renegotiate the covenant with God.

Hence neither the Qur'an nor Sunna provides a warrant for social contract. As for consensus, a third source of Islamic law, it holds that (1) jurists regard contracts as core matters in the law; (2) they cover marriage, inheritance, divorce, guardianship, transactions to buy and sell, partnerships, leases on property, torts, and political pacts (for example, when an Arab Muslim tribe provided the status of "client" [*mawlā*] to non-Arab converts); (3) natural law is equated with God's law; (4) the interests of the believer qua believer are paramount, and requirements of community morality are best served when the believer's devotion to God is secured; (5) it is alien to Muslim thought to conceive the idea of an autonomous individual freely and rationally entering into a civil union that would act as temporary custodian of those rights; (6) God initiates all contracts with the believers, as seen in Qur'an 4.58: "God commands you to return trusts to their owners." God, not society, is the owner or truster in this tradition. Should believers fail to render up these trusts (the Holy Law itself and the earth's resources) to God, He may take them back, as stated in Qur'an 3.26: "You give whom it pleases You the kingdom and You take away the power from whomsoever You will"; and (7) constitutional theorists in the eleventh to thirteenth centuries elaborated the qualifications of leaders and discussed the relationship between these leaders and Muslims in the context of fulfilling religious, not worldly, obligations and rights.

Both Sunnism and Shiism share these ideas, though Shiites repudiate the writings of the constitutional theorists. Sunnis hold that with the death of the Prophet Muhammad a "double contract" came into force.[4] In addition to the original contract between God and the believers came a second contract whereby the leaders of the community identified one of themselves as best qualified to administer the law. Much later, as contact with the West deepened, they came to view the second contract as founded on popular choice. Shiites, however, reject this entire process of selection and stress the rule of imams, descendants of the Prophet.

As for "popular election," the early caliphs were chosen not by the people but by the elite, and shortly thereafter succession became dynastic. Meanwhile, although some jurists implied or stated the right to replace an unjust caliph, their greater concern was over possible chaos that disobedience to a ruler might unleash, making it impossible to fulfill the devotional obligations. Hence their writings had a strongly apologetic cast that overrode their weakly stated arguments that sinning rulers need not be obeyed. At any rate, they established neither a threshold of oppression nor a procedure to oust an unjust leader.

Although Shiites agree with Sunnis on three primary principles of the faith (God's unicity, the necessity of Muhammad's prophecy, and the Day of Judgment), they go beyond Sunnis in adding a fourth, the doctrine of the imamate.

Shiites hold that the Prophet vested his succession in his cousin and son-in-law ʿAlī ibn Abī Ṭālib (d. 661). This investiture included the inheritance of this office by ʿAlī's male heirs through his wife Fāṭima, Muhammad's daughter. These heirs, together with ʿAlī, were called imams and were considered to be exemplars of perfect (and prescient) knowledge, perfect virtue, and perfect justice. God's light, symbolizing truth, was incarnated in these imams, who were deemed the proofs of God's existence. According to Twelver Shiite belief, the twelfth of these imams disappeared miraculously upon God's command in the year 873–74 (260 AH).

These elitist Shiite ideas are even further removed from Sunni notions in regard to contractarian thought. Only the imams are entitled to rule, and believers may not question them. Although the commandment to obey the imams was suspended at the time of Imam Jaʿfar al-Ṣādiq (d. 765) on grounds of religious persecution that made it unsafe for Shiites openly to profess their faith, it was never eliminated in theory. Eventually, in the medieval Islamic era the Shiite clergy argued that they had become the general agents of the imams. They took these developments even further at the end of the eighteenth century, when their power was dramatically enhanced as a result of an intellectual dispute that vindicated their right to exercise independent judgment (*ijtihād*). This reinforced the elitist quality of Shiite thought and further vitiates claims that Shiite doctrines uphold contractually secured rights. It is true that some Shiite clerics in the early twentieth century justified restricting the power of the monarch in Iran. Even here, though, as will be seen, the clergy were not vanguards for social contract ideas.

Hence in both Sunnism and Shiism revelation trumps natural law, undermining any development of social contract concepts. Natural law, after all, arose from the belief that, as Cicero declared, "there is in fact a true law, namely right reason, which is in accordance with nature, applies to all men and is unchangeable and eternal."[5] If there is such a natural law, then there must be natural rights associated with such a law. As Ernest Barker puts it, "If there were any limitations imposed on natural rights, these limitations must be due to a voluntary contract made by the possessors of such rights."[6] This concept of natural law is that the universe operates according to the will of God, but this will is eternal and unchanging, and therefore God will not interfere in the laws created by Him. Although this position acknowledges God's creation of the universe and the laws that govern it, He is nevertheless understood as being either incapable of or refraining from interfering in it, a fact that makes the laws that govern creation necessary and unchangeable. This is quite different from Muslim perspectives—whether Ashʿarite or Twelver Shiite—that stress, besides God's transcendent nature, also His immanence and activism in this world.

MODERNIST MOVEMENTS IN SUNNISM AND SHIISM

In the Sunni world reformers launched a movement in the late nineteenth century that they called the Salafiyya, which meant returning contemporary Islam to the model of its believed original conditions, revivifying the Arabic language, and reconciling reason and science with revelation. Among its leaders were the grand *muftī* of Egypt, Muḥammad ʿAbduh (1849–1905), and his student Muḥammad Rashīd Riḍā (1865–1935). Attacking blind imitation and the pedantry of the formalistic theologians, the Salafī reformers advanced the cause of independent judgment to achieve a new consensus that rested on authentic Islamic principles and that could address the modern problems faced by Muslims. ʿAbduh and Rashīd Riḍā raised the general good and public interest (*maṣlaḥa mursala*) to the level of an important juristic principle, rescuing it from centuries of marginalization in Islamic jurisprudence dating back to the days of al-Juwaynī (d. 1085), al-Ghazālī (d. 1111), and al-Ṭūfī (d. 1316). (A deeper analysis of the rediscovery of *maṣlaḥa* in modern Muslim ideas of Shari'a is provided by Felicitas Opwis in Chapter 4 of this volume.)

ʿAbduh believed that education was the basis for reconciling Islamic belief and the requirements of a modern social order. He tried to counter the division of Egyptian society into two parts—one "always diminishing, in which the laws and moral principles of Islam ruled, and the other, always growing, in which principles derived by human reason from considerations of worldly utility hold sway."[7] Because ʿAbduh's own intellectual roots lay in Islamic tradition, he was not an advocate of democracy or constitutional rule in themselves, but he strongly criticized the jejune scholasticism of the traditional seminaries as being wholly irrelevant for solving the problems of modern society.

Malcolm Kerr notes that "consistency, clarity, depth, and sustained intellectual commitment . . . were not the qualities for which ʿAbduh was noted."[8] But in fairness, had he chosen to persevere in these qualities, he would likely have alienated the conservative Islamic establishment in Egypt. Despite his prudence, ʿAbduh implied that rationalism, long suppressed in Islamic thought, deserved to be resuscitated.

Among European authors, ʿAbduh was most influenced by Auguste Comte (1798–1857). Although he was a positivist, Comte warned against attempts to impose a secular rational order, which he felt threatened society because it abetted "the restless spirit of individual reason, always questioning, always doubting."[9] Comte advocated tying this spirit to the moral truths of revelation. ʿAbduh endorsed this perspective, but what was the correct interpretation of Islam?

Rashīd Riḍā paid more attention than his mentor had to matters relevant to social contract. He argued that the Islamic community's sovereignty is manifested in the elite, which the sources term "the people of loosing and binding." Although he failed clearly to specify who these people are, Rashīd Riḍā generally identified them as those of prominent rank whom the believers trust. He held that Muslims, having accepted God's covenant, have vested the people of loosing and binding, usually identified with the *ʿulamāʾ*, with the authority to nominate the leader. Kerr notes that Rashīd Riḍā identifies the people of loosing and binding with the whole Muslim community, seeing the *ʿulamāʾ* as its representatives.[10] Hence Rashīd Riḍā bestowed community sovereignty on a poorly identified elite, which Kerr rightly maintains is unacceptable for two reasons. First, Rashīd Riḍā seemed to be saying tautologically that authority devolves on those who have it or are able to exercise it, "which is another way of saying that might makes right."[11] Second, the people of loosing and binding seem to be a semiclosed elite to whom ordinary Muslims must submit—they are not delegates of the Muslims but "seemingly enjoy their status by virtue of what is assumed to be an undeniable and absolute capacity. . . . Their authority then appears to be in the nature of an oligarchy rather than a kind of publicly exercised sovereignty."[12]

Accordingly, one cannot consider Rashīd Riḍā an advocate of Muslim popular participation and choice, with people putatively exercising contractarian rights. Of the reformists, it is ʿAlī ʿAbd al-Rāziq (1888–1966) who came closest to contractarian thought. He held that God offered His covenant to the believers, and they joined the community to implement their religious obligations. But to him, the Prophet's successors established the caliphate not as a result of doctrinal necessity or divine ordainment but in response to historical contingencies. Muslims, he argued, like any people, possess natural rights and reason, which permit them to act in accordance with their own calculus of utility. Hence they do not have to model their government on the historical caliphate but may establish any form of government they wish. The Prophet himself was solely a religious leader who left it up to each new generation of Muslims to decide this matter.

However, opposition to these ideas overwhelmed ʿAbd al-Rāziq's thesis that Islam is religion but not politics, and his book was censured by the religious establishment. Such Sunni modernists as the contemporaries Muḥammad ʿAmāra[13] and Tāriq al-Bishrī have led the effort against it.[14]

As for developments in Shiite Islam since the late eighteenth and early nineteenth centuries, the clergy's self-confidence grew immeasurably. Although it was to be another century before they would demand formal rights to represent the Iranian people, they secured full consultation of the rulers with them in the 1800s. Eventually, largely because of the monarchs' growing tendency to grant economic concessions and commercial privileges to foreigners and cede territories to them, many clergymen joined the Constitutional Revolution of 1906 to restrict royal autocracy.

The theoretical tools that they used for this purpose included the principle of *ẓulm*, or oppression of the rights of God, the Prophet, and the imams; the categorical imperative in Shari'a to "command the good and forbid evil" (Qur'an 3.104, 3.110, 3.114, 7.157, 9.71); the Qur'anic injunctions to the Prophet to consult people in their affairs (3.159, 42.38); and the legal stipulation of accountability in conduct (*ḥisba*). However, their discourse was not oriented to national sovereignty and the rights of the people but rather to the impiety of the ruler. And it was revelation and not natural law that provided the litmus test for assessing the rule of secular leaders. The *ʿulamā'* remained content with their status as the general agents of the imams and were clearly sensitive to the accusation that they were trying to replace Islamic law with Western constitutionalism. Hence their discourse was one of *mashrūṭah-yi mashrūʿah* (literally, making [rule] contingent on the requirements of Shari'a). There was no Iranian equivalent (at this time) of the Sunni ʿAlī ʿAbd al-Rāziq, who might announce that it was up to every generation of Shiites to establish their own model of state and government and to declare that in Islam religion and politics were separable. So concerned were the "constitutionalist *ʿulamā'*" about the accusation that they were stalking horses for outright republicanism that they eventually abandoned the Constitutionalist cause by 1909.

Indeed, the Iranian clergy supported the claims of Reza Khān to be the new shah of Iran in the mid-1920s. The fact that he later turned upon them in pursuing Westernizing reforms does not alter this fact. Indeed, in 1941, the year the Allies forced the shah's abdication, Ayatollah Rūḥallāh Khomeini (1902–89) published a book, *Revealing the Secrets* (*Kashf al-asrār*), in which he condemned secular rulers for failing to consult the clergy. The broad implication was that the Islamic order could easily coexist with secular rule provided the rulers regularly sought the advice of the *ʿulamā'*. In the 1950s, during the oil crisis, the clergy essentially supported the pro-British monarch in his conflict with the nationalist prime minister. Even in 1963, when Khomeini condemned the policies of Reza Shah's son, he did not articulate a position founded on contractarian themes. At most, he upbraided the government for its failure to consult with the clergy on such issues as eligibility requirements to hold office and female enfranchisement. In short, both the people and the government were to heed the advice of the clergy.

CONTEMPORARY SHIITE MODERNIST WRITINGS RELEVANT FOR SOCIAL CONTRACT

In a 2003 article I compared and contrasted three contemporary Sunni Egyptian modernist theorists of social contract.[15] They endorse *ijtihād* and the exegetical doctrine of *al-nāsikh wa-l-mansūkh* (abrogation of a Qur'anic verse by another), as well as insist on contextualizing such verses (*asbāb al-nuzūl*) rather than taking them out of context. Public interest, historicization, and pluralism are major themes associated with their work, though lacunae in their thought make their arguments less convincing. They believe that they have vindicated a theory of social contract in the scriptural texts and in the actual practice of the early Muslim community (622–61), as well as in the modern era. Despite their efforts to materialize such a theory in Islam, however, they have not shown how believers did or could consciously decide to associate with one another to form a moral community that would be the guardian of their individual interests. Instead, they have inferred that this must have happened because God loves the Muslims and guarantees their welfare and prosperity, so the people could not but accept this bargain. They write about consultation, justice, interests, and freedom and discover these as motivating forces that joined the early Muslims in the *umma*, but in their writings the actual onset of the people's political consciousness and then its evolution are taken for granted rather than problematized.

In this context, what have contemporary Shiite thinkers been saying? I shall focus on three individuals who I believe have contributed to the discussion that is relevant for social contract: Ayatollah Rūḥallāh Khomeini, Ayatollah Niʿmatallāh Ṣāliḥī Najafābādī, and Ayatollah Dr. Mahdī Ḥā'irī. The rationale for including Khomeini is that his book *Islamic Government* (*Ḥukūmat-i Islamī*) of 1971 bears centrally—though negatively—on social contract ideas. Najafābādī is Khomeini's faithful disciple and a firm advocate of his elitist doctrine of the "guardianship of the jurist" (*wilāyat-i faqīh*). (The concept of *wilāyat-i faqīh* is explained by Abbas Amanat in Chapter 7 of this volume.)

Najafābādī's book *Mandate of the Jurist: Government by the Righteous* (*Wilāyat-i faqīh: Ḥukūmat-i ṣāliḥān*) was published in 1984 and goes well beyond Khomeini's position, converting it into a model of rule based on popular sovereignty. This breathtaking conversion of an elitist doctrine into a principle of popular democracy ends by reversing the words of the famous adage *vox populi vox Dei*, "the voice of the people is the voice of God," to read instead "the voice of God is the voice of the people." Mahdī Ḥā'irī, by contrast, rejects the doctrine of *wilāyat-i faqīh* by maintaining that government is totally outside the purview of religion. This indeed is the Shiite version of ʿAlī ʿAbd al-Rāziq, and it is revealing that his emergence into the public discourse on the clergy and politics came from a book he had to publish in the West. Ḥā'irī is a son of the founder of the modern seminary at Qom, Shaykh ʿAbd al-Karīm Ḥā'irī Yazdī (d. 1937). A graduate of the Qom seminary with the degree of *ijtihād*, he also received his Ph.D. in philosophy from the University of Toronto. Like Khomeini, he was a student of the eminent Muḥammad Ḥusayn Burūjirdī (d. 1962).

Khomeini maintained that the imams had vested their substantive authority (*wilāya*) in the jurists, pending the return of the Hidden Imam. In this scenario of rule the ordinary believer, whether as an individual or collectively, has no role to play, since the decisive events are taking place "over his head." Khomeini's approach first is to show logically that Islam, since it mandates a community of believers, necessitates a state and government. He appeals to the authority of Mullā Aḥmad Narāqī (d. 1829), who established nineteen arguments to confirm the validity of the concept of the *wilāyat-i faqīh*. In Narāqī's view, according to Khomeini, this mandate of the jurist was substantive and not just residual in nature. In short, it amounted to authority to be an executive ruler and could not be restricted to narrow, technical matters, such as the legal authority to represent the interests of minors or widows or to arbitrate legal disputes involving legacies or debts.

Khomeini finds the doctrinal proof for this robust interpretation of the authority of jurists in Qur'an 4.58–59 and in a *ḥadīth* (oral tradition) called *maqbūlat ʿUmar ibn Ḥanẓala*—"the accepted [tradition] of ʿUmar ibn Ḥanẓala"—which involves a set of questions and replies posed by this ʿUmar and answered by the sixth imam of Twelver Shiism, Jaʿfar al-Ṣādiq. The verses of Qur'an 4.58–59 are as follows: "God commands you to return trusts to their owners, and when you judge among the people to do so equitably. Noble are the counsels of God, and God hears all and sees everything. O ye who believe, obey God, obey the Prophet, and those in authority among you."

The tradition of ʿUmar ibn Ḥanẓala has ʿUmar asking about a situation. Two Shiites are arguing about a matter of debt or inheritance. May they have recourse to the courts of the Sunni caliphate for a ruling? Imam Jaʿfar al-Ṣādiq forbids this recourse and, when asked for instructions as to what they should do, replies that they must identify a Shiite believer who is well versed in imamite law and abide by his ruling, "for I appointed him a judge over you" (*laqad jaʿal-tuhu ʿalaykum ḥākiman*).

Khomeini translates the second verb in line 1 of verse 4.58 in the Qur'an as "rule" instead of "judge"; the latter had been the standard interpretation of Shiite exegetes from the earliest times. Furthermore, he translates the noun in the quoted passage of the tradition of ʿUmar ibn Ḥanẓala as "ruler" rather than "judge." Just to make sure that his reader knows what he means, he inserts the pre-Islamic Persian word *farmānrawā* (sovereign ruler) in brackets after the Arabic word in the accusative case, *ḥākiman*.[16] He justifies this innovative rendering of these words in the following way. First, the Qur'anic verses and the tradition of ʿUmar ibn Ḥanẓala must be read in tandem. The verb in verse 4.58 is "modifying secular princes."[17] These princes are being put on notice that they must return trusts loaned to them by God back to Him and must rule justly. In the tradition the imam is being asked whether the disputants could seek judgment from the Sunni authorities, and the imam replies that he who does so is in effect asking illegitimate governmental authorities. Khomeini then says that it is clear that there are legitimate and illegitimate government authorities and their judges to whom one might possibly have recourse for a decision. The imam tells ʿUmar that the disputants must find a knowledgeable and fair-minded person, and that that individual is not just a judge, but represents legitimate governmental authorities and their judges. The imam says, "I appointed a person who has these qualifications to be a ruler (*farmānrawā*) over you, and he who has such qualifications has been appointed by me for the governmental and judicial affairs of the Muslims, and the Muslims do not have the right to refer to anyone else."[18] Elsewhere Khomeini had maintained that the caliphs in the period of the sixth imam carefully avoided interfering in the jurisdiction of judges, and judges took the same care not to intrude into the bailiwicks of the caliphs. From this he concludes that the sixth imam was clearly making a distinction between the jurisdictions of rulers and those of judges, and in his operative phrase, "*laqad jaʿal-tuhu ʿalaykum ḥākiman,*" he is referring to a person whom he has appointed to be both ruler (*wālī*) and judge (*qāḍī*), as captured by the word *ḥākim*. This word can mean both ruler and judge. If, Khomeini adds, the imam wanted to restrict his appointment merely to judges rather than rulers and judges, he would have used the phrase *"laqad jaʿaltuhu ʿalaykum qāḍiyan"*—the word *qāḍī*, here in the accusative case, cannot mean ruler and can only mean judge.[19]

As for verse 4.59, Khomeini innovatively asserts that "those in authority among you" are the clergy. This represents a sharp departure from the traditional interpretation among Shiite commentators on the Qur'an, that the phrase referred to the imams. For example, the author of the most authoritative Shiite commentary on the Qur'an in the twentieth century, Muḥammad Ḥusayn Ṭabāṭabā'ī (1892–1981), explicitly rejected the contention that the referent was the clergy.[20]

No warrant exists for interpreting this argument for the entitlement of the clergy to be rulers in the absence of the Hidden Imam as grounds to endorse social contract notions, but this is what the cleric Niʿmatullāh Ṣāliḥī Najafābādī maintains. Borrowing terminology from rhetoric, he holds that the doctrine of *wilāyat-i faqīh* may be considered from two perspectives: its "originative" meaning (*mafhūm inshā'ī*) and its "notificatory" meaning (*mafhūm khabarī*). He claims that the doctrine was classically understood only in its restrictive sense, as something indicative and notificatory. He then seeks to "restore" the originative and creative meaning, which renders the doctrine into "one of the firmest and clearest rational, social, and political principles," and one in which the voice of the people is the key defining element.[21] In his opinion the jurist in whom the *wilāya* of the imam is vested has no independent authority to rule over the people. Rather, the relationship is reversed. In his construction it is the *vox populi* that is the driving force for the operationalization of the doctrine. On what basis does he maintain this? Reason tells us that popular sovereignty is the linchpin of *wilāyat-i faqīh*.

He who has *wilāya* may have it as a result of three modalities: (1) God grants it; (2) it is soundly acquired by the use of power—all clergymen have *wilāya* in this sense, but in order to prevent chaos, only one of them is the final authority in its implementation; (3) it is rule "in fact," as occurs when others persuade an individual to assume and exercise it, which happened with Imam ʿAlī in 656. This vesting of the *wilāya* according to the third modality occurs in an allegedly free environment, with the majority of the people taking the oath of allegiance (*bayʿa*) to the designee.[22] This passage is remarkable for more than one reason. First, Khomeini would adamantly maintain that the jurists have the imam's authority as a consequence of the first modality pure and simple. Second, Najafābādī appears to be eroding the forcefulness of the concept by suggesting that

Imam ʿAlī, no less, had the *wilāya* of God and the Prophet because ordinary human beings gave it to him. On this argument the designation of Imam ʿAlī resulted from a mass election in the modern sense of the term, and the Prophet's investiture of him fades into the background. Najafābādī applies the same pattern to Khomeini's status—mass election through majority vote.

Najafābādī appears to be arguing in the direction of social contract notions. The jurist thus "elected" is endowed with exemplary knowledge, justice, political consciousness, administrative skills, planning abilities, farsightedness, courage, and decisiveness. Once he is chosen, all must support his rule as an incumbent duty akin to the obligation to undertake the secondary principles of the faith: prayer, almsgiving, fasting during Ramaḍān, and making the pilgrimage. Whatever happened to the classical interpretation that *wilāya* was bestowed from above? He maintains that to hold this limiting view of the process would be a "contravention of divine law, the interest of society, and the glory, nobility, and freedom of the people."[23]

How can he uphold this view? His reply is through the principle of reason. Since government is a "social necessity," it would be wrong to dispense with it.[24] The way to establish a government is not by imposing a system on the people, because this violates the principle of reason. It is innate reason that is the dynamic force in all discussions of *wilāyat-i faqīh*.[25] The people, animated by rational understandings of their interests, play the key role in the devolution of authority to the *faqīh*,[26] and Najafābādī anchors his interpretation upon majority rule.[27]

To clinch matters, Najafābādī claims that the *wilāya* of the jurist is built upon the foundations of a contract between the people and the *faqīh*.[28] He uses the expressions *'aqd wa-qarardād-i ijtimāʿī* (social contract) and *mīthāq-i ijtimāʿī* (social compact) and offers "Islamic" grounds to support this view. Thus he cites Qur'an 5.1 ("O, ye who believe, fulfill your contracts"), blithely ignoring the fact that this verse is devoid of the connotation of members of a community making a contract with "society" and ceding their rights to that entity, which then becomes the trustee of such interests in the classic seventeenth- and eighteenth-century theories of social contract. The *faqīh* can be dismissed by the Council of Experts, he notes, but he fails to add that the Council of Experts is an oligarchic body whose members are themselves vetted for candidacy to that body by the *faqīh* and his appointees, not by the masses. In short, the Council of Experts is not a constituent assembly of the people but a narrowly based commission of aides.

Ayatollah Mahdī Ḥā'irī rejects these ideas out of hand. He totally opposes Khomeini's doctrine of the jurist's mandate by specifically denying that Islam has anything to do with politics. Politics is a human contrivance and convention in his view. In the first half of his book *Philosophical Wisdom and Government*, Ḥā'irī sets forth a dense discussion of being and existence that leads to a later discussion of government and politics.[29]

Ḥukūma (government) and *ḥukm* (rule) come from the Arabic verb *ḥakama* and connote judging, arbitrating. They indicate stability, firmness, certitude, and decisiveness. In contemporary politics and political science the Arabic word *ḥukūma* means statecraft, administration, and managing a country's affairs. In logic *ḥukm* and *ḥukūma* mean submission to arbitration based on sure and certifiable knowledge, and *ḥikma* (wisdom) comes from *ḥukm*, signifying not command but judgment.[30] In other words, *ḥukm* and *ḥukūma* mean decisive knowledge and, by extension, awareness of reality.[31]

Accordingly, says Ḥā'irī, government and statecraft refer to wisdom and not command, power, dominion, *wilāya* (authority), or *qayyimūma* (mandate, guardianship).[32] Ḥā'irī invokes Aristotle to show that statesmanship is the highest virtue because it centers on the interests of society as a whole. Therefore, it has nothing to do with ordering and commanding a people.[33]

Ḥā'irī asserts that societies before the modern era were either dictatorships with some role for religious groups or simple tribal systems. In neither did the people have the chance to express themselves to their rulers, and the individual counted for little. Modern democracy, however, is founded on individual rights and freedoms. These qualities emanate from the rights and privileges that individuals have to their own property.[34]

In the modern period thinkers have maintained that for a society to establish government, a social contract must exist, and the citizens and individuals, no matter how unaware, enter such a contract, transferring to an individual or a body the right of defending some of their own rights.[35] Ḥā'irī is unconvinced and posits that government and politics are not complex phenomena that must be conveyed through the rational processes of the theoretical mind. On the contrary, they are natural and empirical concepts that have arisen from the most basic and elemental needs of the natural life of the people. Government is not a metaphysical reality in the manner of Plato's theory of forms nor a superior, rational manifestation for which theoretical reason is a guide by means of axioms and rational proofs. Instead, it is a product of the humdrum experience of people who face daily, transient, and contingent needs in living as neighbors.

It is simply an artifact and cannot come under the rubric of the immutable divine laws.[36] Because government and administration from ancient times have been seen as derivations of practical reason, there can be no doubt that the administration of towns is completely outside the orbit of the universal divine laws.[37]

In short, government is not in any way a mental construct that, as Hegel saw it, represented the Spirit of History. Nor is it, as Rousseau maintained, a mere possibility (*padida-yi iʿtibārī*) that results from a transactional contract between citizens and rulers. Neither is it a logical necessity that, in Kant's view, embraces analytical judgments, nor is it a mathematical necessity. Instead, government is a natural necessity and is always epiphenomenal.

Ḥā'irī criticizes those who believe that government is rooted in the foundations and universals of rational or religious thought. Philosophy and jurisprudence are theories in the abstract, whereas politics is in the realm of the immediate. If, somehow, philosophers or jurists take political office, the exigencies of practical reason will mandate their dismissal, because they would be totally unqualified to rule. The holding of political office by philosophers or jurists would in itself constitute an injustice and provoke disorder and corruption in society, dangers that would be magnified should religious leaders take charge of government because of the passions religious motivations stir. Making religious credentials a prerequisite for officeholding is a logical error because religious deference and leadership are not grounds for qualifying one to be a political leader. The logical place for the religious leader is the realm of theoretical reason and not that of the personal affairs of the citizens and the governments of countries.

Ḥā'irī then invokes scripture to argue that practical reason is not the realm of the religious leader, the jurist, or the philosopher. He claims that the Qur'an vests politics completely in the hands of the people, citing Qur'an 42.38: "Their [the people's] affairs are a matter of counsel." He interprets this verse categorically by maintaining that the people themselves determine their affairs without any recourse to revelation.[38]

Thus the human being is a rational creature for whom "a natural-rational" existence is secured through the workings of practical reason on the empirical environmental conditions surrounding him, and decidedly not by any higher order of thinking. Rousseau mistakenly believes that humans enter into society through a deliberate, discursive process of reflection in which they solve the basic problem of surrendering their independence to the public person (legislator) while retaining their individual freedom as private persons. Ḥā'irī denies this and attributes their coming together to the obvious and unmediated requirements of security for their lives and their livelihoods. As he puts it, "The counsels and guidance of practical reason concerning the need for an arrangement and management of the affairs of the country are so obvious and necessary that they are decisively accepted by every person without the slightest awareness or rational comprehension, without the slightest need for being educated about any factors outside themselves."[39]

This is the essence of Ḥā'irī's argument: every person is an individual who crystallizes in himself all the traits of the universal type called the human being and is naturally independent and free of reliance upon others. Hence he must be endowed with all the rights that have been supposed and confirmed for the individual, among which is freedom to decide matters for himself. Accordingly, he has no need for society and social contract in the use of these natural rights. The reason for this is that these rights stem from the nature and essence of his being human, irrespective of time and/or place. It is impossible to violate this principle of his existence. Since his freedom is a natural rather than a positive or contractual right, this right inheres for him for all time and anywhere. If an individual gets together with other individuals, they form an aggregate. But if he decides to leave this aggregate, he takes all his natural rights with him.

The problem with Rousseau is that he cannot resolve the contradiction that arises when he says that people voluntarily cede their independence to the legislator, but in doing so they are as free as before because everyone has an interest in cooperating and hence willingly does so. There is nothing free about that choice, according to Ḥā'irī. As he puts it, "No human being . . . can really change his . . . true person into an unreal or public personality and escape from himself and change himself into an involuntary positive public personality and deprive himself of an independent and free existence."[40] He then investigates another model, proposed by Hugo Grotius, that is based on servitude to the state. Grotius maintains that people contractually agree to their submission and servitude to a masterful state, a process akin to a mercantile exchange between seller and buyer. Rousseau rejects the analogy by noting that the transaction is coerced because often the masterful state turns out to be despotic and corrupt. But Ḥā'irī believes that Rousseau's rebuttal itself is faulty because whether the state does behave corruptly or despotically does not vitiate the idea that a bargain is struck in the first place between insecure sellers and reassuring buyer. It merely shows that the terms of the contract have been violated. "Do not forget," says Ḥā'irī, "that violations occur also in normal contracts between sellers and buyers."[41]

Instead, the criticism of Grotius must be both empirical and theoretical. Empirically, no government historically has "owned" its people. If a herder buys a cow from another, he owns that cow as his property. But the relationship between government and citizens is one of guardianship, not ownership. It is true that some governments have behaved tyrannically, as though they regarded themselves as slave masters, but that does not validate the argument that Grotius is making that the people in actual societies have voluntarily enslaved themselves in some contractual way.

The theoretical rebuttal to Grotius's doctrine of state servitude goes as follows. In the Islamic law of contracts the buyer and seller must always be identified in advance, whether one is speaking of material goods, marriages, or leases. Failing this, the contract cannot be considered valid. In a contract of personal servitude, which is the standard of Grotius's doctrine, one of the parties is indigent and offers himself as a slave, while the other is the masterful state as purchaser of the slave. Once they have been identified as the parties, the process of the transaction can begin and be concluded. Note that before they have been identified, the concluding or nonconcluding of the transaction is inconceivable. Yet Grotius, without acknowledging this logical impossibility, presents his doctrine simply on the basis of a verbal analogy (*tashābuh-i lafẓī*). Grotius and, indeed, social contract theorists more generally ignore the fact that before the contract all citizens are equal in their privileges and rights.[42] Accordingly, no individual can alienate his inherent equality in rights and privileges to another, even if he wills to do so.

If both Rousseau and Grotius are wrong, then what is the correct interpretation? Ḥā'irī declares that it is a law of nature that human beings require a location on which to live, from which derives a second law that holds that anyone who has acquired territory that has not been otherwise claimed may rightly possess it. In the beginning the human being individualistically chooses his plot, which is for him alone and for his family. But in a later, second stage he acquires ownership of adjacent land, over which others, however, also exercise some ownership rights. In both stages the human being is making the choice of where to live on the basis of existential exigency, and so property ownership in both stages has been achieved as a matter of natural necessity. The difference is that in the first stage the property is a "private natural possession" (*taʿalluq wa-mālikiyyat-i khuṣūṣī wa-ṭabīʿī*), whereas in the second stage it becomes diffused and conflated with the properties of others. In the first stage the requirement was for monopolization of the location by the individual, whereas in the second stage the erstwhile private ownership (*malikiyyat-i khuṣūṣi*) is transformed into private joint ownership (*mālikiyyat-i khuṣūṣī-yi mushāʿ*). The property continues to remain private in the second stage, but no longer monopolistically or exclusively so in the hands of a lone individual. Under both individual and joint ownership the principle of private possession is retained in the sense that every person independently possesses these two kinds of locales—places that have been allocated to him to live on by his nature. The lone individual has moved from the small location in the first stage to the larger space in the second stage because of the natural requirements of finding food and making a living. He has thus responded to purely physiological needs. And there is nothing in all this that has anything to do with legislation, a collective will, or even the will and rational understanding of the human mind. In both stages the location where he lives is the human being's as a result of natural right and cannot in the first instance be legally established for nor alienated from him by some external power. Positive, legal, and nominal ownership are established only later and would not be possible without the prior establishment of natural ownership.[43]

Ḥā'irī maintains that in the second stage society has not yet appeared because there is as yet no need for it, given that each individual's right of exclusive private and joint private ownership accrues to him from his natural need for subsistence. Joint private ownership does not equal collective ownership in the modern sense. In this presociety phase ownership of the larger space is individual for every human being—which means that he has the unfettered right of access to the larger space, just as his neighbors do. He has no need to cooperate with others. When they do encounter one another, it is a product of their natural interaction, not of a contract between them. Moreover, just as he can bequeath his smaller space to his heirs, he can pass on the larger space to those heirs.[44]

But this is a situation that cannot last because, as each individual uses his practical reason to improve his life chances, eventually this brings him into contact with outsiders, who could make competing claims on his larger living space. At this point the individuals who are neighbors, still guided by their practical reason, deputize some person or some entity, compensate that person or entity, and task him or it with the mandate of ensuring the good life and peaceful coexistence for them all in the face of outsider pretensions to their living spaces. In case of disagreement among the individuals as to the identity of the deputy, the opinion of the majority is followed. Ḥā'irī insists that they are still acting as equal individuals endowed with equal natural inherent rights. He cites the *ḥadīth* "the people are masters of their wealth" (*al-nās musallaṭun ʿalā amwālihim*) to maintain his identification of this process as a natural one that has nothing to do with the workings of an Islamic society and its law of contracts.[45]

The contract that is effected between the individuals and the deputy is purely private in nature, not social, collective, or public. This deputy is totally dependent upon the individuals. He or it is not a deputy for a collective unit. There is no public legal body in which, as Rousseau would have it, each citizen would have membership, bound in a net of unity, and in which the citizens have lost their identity and independence. Consequently, this model of private joint property, with its deputy, is in the sense of all the individual citizens, not in the sense of a collective entity. The title Ḥā'irī gives to this model is the deputyship of private joint property (*wikālat-i mālikiyyat-i shakhṣī-yi mushāʿ*).[46]

CONCLUSION

The society of the contractarian theorists is a civil society. Such a society transforms individuals who, in a state of nature, were amoral, lawless, atomized units into moral beings. Khomeini would deny contractarian theses, though under his aegis the Islamic Republic possessed secular institutions such as a parliament and cabinet government. It would not occur to him to consider the people as a source of their own trusts, which they putatively would have deposited in civil institutions as expressive mechanisms of their collective will. Najafābādī, however, boldly asserts, though he fails to demonstrate, that Khomeini's constitution and Shiite thought both vest sovereignty in the nation, and people fully enjoy civil rights, freedom, justice, and equality. Yet it is clear that his assertions derive not from social contract premises but from his assumptions about the malleability of religious texts and inferences about the Prophet's and the early Muslims' behavior in response to those texts. In the end, these are religious texts that were introduced at a time when concepts such as popular sovereignty and civil rights were not known.

At bottom, the problem for anyone who wants to convert Khomeini's doctrine of the mandate of the jurist into a theory of social contract is that under the revelation it is the "rights of God" that dominate, and these rights are vouchsafed to human beings merely as revocable trusts to advance God's purposes. The individual's dependence on God supposedly does not vitiate his autonomy or freedom because God has the human being's interests at heart. But exactly how people can remain ultimately free if there is no natural law outside Shari'a is left unexamined. Consequently, there is an ad hoc quality to the claim that humans are absolutely free, independent, and rational in their actions in worldly matters. If natural law coincides with the divine law in Islam, this means that human beings cannot understand natural law (and hence the operation of the world) through reason alone.[47] If reason cannot be sovereign, then room exists for mandates, which of course are not self-evident but interpreted and imposed on behalf of God by not-always-benevolent human beings.

By contrast to Khomeini and Najafābādī, Ḥā'irī establishes an independent domain for natural law and, in the process, suggests that politics and government have nothing to do with Islam. This leads to two observations. First, if the argument about natural law necessarily establishes the irrelevance of revelation for forming a government, can there be a concept of social contract in a Muslim society? In other words, Ḥā'irī seems to be saying that an Islamic society is Islamic by dint of the private beliefs of its members in respect to the primary and secondary ordinances of pietistic faith (God's unicity, Muhammad's prophecy, the Day of Judgment, prayer, *zakāt*, fasting during Ramaḍān, and pilgrimage). Everything else is in the realm of secular affairs and is totally independent of religion. He may be right, but if so, he seems to be implying that there cannot be an Islamic theory of social contract. Is this necessarily so?

Second, Ḥā'irī has embraced the concept of natural law as separate from revealed law. This is precisely what Hobbes, Locke, and other classical social contract doctrine theorists have done, but they have gone on to anchor natural law's independence to a robust concept of social contract. Ḥā'irī, by contrast, seems to imply that this independence of natural law from religious law is a guarantee that social contract doctrines cannot be maintained. Ḥā'irī's arguments about joint private property are not convincing because he claims that people are acting out of their intrinsic and inherent individual rights to live and to own. But when they appoint someone or some body to arbitrate their disputes and protect them from the claims of outsiders, Ḥā'irī assumes that they are acting as individual, atomized units and are not fusing into a larger collectivity. This begs the question. It would appear that they have indeed constituted themselves as a public, legal, corporate personality.

9 SHARI'A AND CONSTITUTION IN IRAN: A HISTORICAL PERSPECTIVE

Saïd Amir Arjomand

AN ASTONISHING LACK OF HISTORICAL, institutional perspective has allowed discussions of Islam and constitutionalism to be wrapped in thick ideological clouds. This lack also accounts for a curious textualist convergence between Orientalism and fundamentalism, with the result that what was written by Harvard professor Hamilton Gibb in 1970 could easily have been written by Abū l-Aʿlā Mawdūdī (1904–79) or Rūḥallāh Khomeini (1902–89) at about the same time: "The community exists to bear witness to God amid the darkness of this world, and the function of its government is essentially to act as the executive of the Law [that is, Shari'a]."[1] To combat this widely accepted cliché, it is necessary to point out that the idea of monarchy, together with its norms as elaborated in the statecraft literature, was fully integrated into Islam by the time of the development of the legal order based on Shari'a in the tenth century. From the twelfth century onward the idea that God had chosen two classes of mankind above the rest, the prophets to guide mankind to salvation and the kings to preserve order as the prerequisite for the pursuit of salvation, was firmly established, certainly in the Persian-speaking world. I have called this a theory of the two powers.[2] The Safavid monarchs, who established Shiism in Iran, claimed to be the descendants and lieutenants of the holy imams, and this deviated somewhat from the Shiite tradition. Their deviation, however, was corrected, and the theory of the two powers was reconciled with Shiism, with the Shiite *mujtahids*, the qualified jurisprudents, assuming the mantle of the prophets.[3] The theory, however, was more typically stated without any reference to Shiism.[4]

With the advent of constitutionalism from the West during the second half of the nineteenth century, the two traditional powers were challenged in the name of modernity. Islamic modernists, notably the Young Ottoman Mehmet Namık Kemal (d. 1888) and the Iranian Yusūf Khān Mustashār al-Dawla (d. 1895), challenged the theory of the two powers in the name of Islam as well, arguing that representative, constitutional government captured the spirit of Islam. These Islamic modernists, however, were laymen and did not belong to the *ʿulamā'*, the official representatives of Shari'a. A distinctive feature of the Constitutional Revolution in Iran is the prominence of the Shiite *mujtahid*s. Despite their leading role in the popular protest movement that forced the shah to grant Iran a constitution in 1905–6, references to Islam and Shari'a during this period were incidental. The key concepts were rather the rule of law, justice, and the removal of oppression. The leading *ʿulamā'* tended to draw their notion of justice from the traditional theory of kingship rather than Islamic law.[5] As the revolution proceeded, however, the continued involvement of the Shiite religious leaders assured the first broad public discussion of the relation between Shari'a and constitutional government in the Muslim world. I have covered this debate in a paper I presented at a conference at Harvard a few years ago.[6] The important analytical conclusion is that if one begins with the traditional theory of the two powers and replaces autocracy by constitutional government, Shari'a is bound to appear as a limitation to constitutional government and not the basis of it.

For the constitution makers of 1907, the transfer of legislative power—the right to make public laws (sing. *qānūn*)—from the monarch to the people was conceptually nonproblematic, and it did not involve Islam because the latter was not an abstract ideology but an institutionally embedded order. Islam did enter the public debate surrounding the Supplement to the Fundamental Law in 1907—and it did so quite dramatically. The clash of Shari'a and constitutionalism in this phase, however, had little to do with the allegedly monolithic and political essence of Islam. The constitution makers of 1907 and their constituencies, in fact, recognized the fundamental dualism of temporal and religious laws in Islam as institutionally embedded in Iran. Article 27 of the Supplement acknowledged this dualism and made provisions for secular and religious courts, as did some of its other articles. The problem was not one of a fundamental conceptual order but one of delimitation. Legal dualism cannot exist without the possibility of conflict between the laws and their heterogeneous principles. The seriousness of the problem of delimiting the respective jurisdictions of the secular and religious law, the *qānūn* and Shari'a, became evident in connection with judiciary organization.[7] The Supplement to the Fundamental Law of 1907 purports to solve the problem of mutual delimitation and thus to bring the constitution into full congruence with Shiite Islam. Its Article 2 referred to the monarch as the "*shāhanshāh* of Islam" and declared: "At no time must any legal enactments of the National Consultative Assembly . . . be at variance with the sacred principles of Islam." Furthermore, a committee of no fewer than five religious jurists (*mujtahids*) was given the power to "reject, repudiate, wholly or in part, any proposal that is at variance with the sacred laws of Islam."[8]

We know that in practice this solution did not work. What is not generally known, however, is that the committee of five was never formed because the great majority of Shiite jurists selected by the Second Parliament (Majlis) in 1909–11 in several rounds considered it beneath their dignity to accept the supervising assignment. For a while two politically ambitious clerics in the Majlis, Sayyid Ḥasan Mudarris (d. 1936) and the Ḥājj Mīrzā Yaḥyā, Imam Jumʿah of Khoi, informally performed the supervisory role of ensuring consistency of legislation with Shari'a.[9]

The clerical ideologues of the Islamic revolution of 1979 found an important source of inspiration in Shaykh Faḍlallāh Nūrī (d. 1909), the high-ranking *mujtahid* who fell out with the constitutionalists after a year and led the Islamic traditionalist opposition to the Majlis. They have also since dug up the writings of some of Nūrī's followers as forerunners of a Shari'a-based constitution. Nūrī organized massive demonstrations with the slogan "We want the religion of the Prophet; we do not want constitutional government!" and eventually advocated a traditional autocracy on the basis of the theory of the two powers.[10] Nevertheless, his intermediate 1907 idea of "Shari'a constitutionalism" (*mashrūṭah-yi mashrūʿah*) gained considerable currency because it accurately described the position of a large number of pro-Majlis *ʿulamā'* as well. The latter followed him in insisting on the observance of Shari'a as a limitation on popular legislation. Thus Mīrzā Muḥammad Ḥusayn Nā'īnī's (d. 1936) book *The Admonition and Refinement of the People* (*Tanbīh al-umma wa-tanzīh al-milla*), published in Baghdad in 1909 and still the best work on constitutionalism in Shiite jurisprudence, accommodates the substance of the idea of Shari'a constitutionalism as regards the restriction of parliamentary legislation to customary affairs and explicitly restricts equality before the law to man-made or positive laws (*qawānīn mawḍūʿa*) on the assumption that they cannot override Shari'a. Another essay, written by a pro-Majlis cleric in 1909, similarly observes Shari'a's limitations on constitutional law and considers "Shari'a constitutionality" fully accommodated in Article 2 of the Supplement.[11]

Like those who had drafted the Ottoman Fundamental Law of 1876, the makers of the Iranian Fundamental Laws of 1906 and 1907 recognized the underlying dualism of temporal and religious law in the politicolegal system they were living under. Both groups used the term *qānūn* for the fundamental law and identified the legislative power as *muqannina* from the same root—that is, the power to make public law. For them, the transfer of the legislative power—the right to make public laws—from the monarch to the people was conceptually nonproblematic and did not involve Shari'a. It took the arrogance of Kemal Atatürk's militant secularists to use the Turkish word *teshri'iyye* (derived from Arabic *sharīʿa*) for the legislative power, thereby confusing, by appropriation, the people's newly acquired right to make public laws with the divine inspiration of the sacred law. The first generation of constitutionalists had no conceptual difficulty in recognizing that what was being transferred to the people was not any divine prerogative but the ruler's right, be he sultan or shah, to make public laws. The same cannot be said about the constitution makers of Pakistan a century after the replacement of the Mughul Empire by the British Raj in 1858. Only in the absence of an actual Muslim monarch could the notion of national sovereignty evoke the superiority of God over the nation and result in the declaration of God's sovereignty. And only thereafter would Gibb's ahistorical model of an Islamic state that exists primarily for the implementation of Shari'a become a social force in the Muslim world.

In Iran, as we know, this happened with the Islamic revolution in 1979, and it happened at the end of the era of ideological constitutions, which had begun with the Mexican Constitution of 1917 and the Soviet Constitution of 1918.[12] Islam was simply put in the place of the dominant ideology in the constitutional documents and was conceived as such. Shari'a came back with a vengeance and swallowed the modernized state and its constitution. An appendix consisting of a number of *ḥadīths* pertaining to its most important articles demonstrates that the 1979 Constitution of the Islamic Republic of Iran is partially derived from Shari'a; and its Article 4 declares all laws found inconsistent with Shari'a null and void, including the constitution itself. The critical function of nullification of all proposed and existing laws found inconsistent with Shari'a is given to the six clerical jurists of the Council of Guardians.

. . .

We next need to turn to Shari'a and the constitution under the Islamic Republic of Iran. Not only is its most important constitutional principle, the *wilāyat-i faqīh* as leadership principle, based on Shari'a as interpreted by Khomeini, but the judiciary has been fully Islamicized by abolishing the hierarchy of appellate courts and collapsing the functions of the judge and the prosecutor into that of the *qāḍī*. Even the atavistic punishments of Shari'a, which were never implemented in Safavid or Qajar Iran or earlier, are now fully enforced in a state whose primary function is the execution of Shari'a, as in Gibb's model. Let us look at this Islamic constitutional state closely with the following twin questions in mind: What are the contradictions between Shari'a, on the one hand, and other constitutional principles and ordinary laws of the Islamic Republic of Iran? And what are the mechanisms for resolving these contradictions? We can then decide whether or not the experience of the Islamic Republic of Iran suggests the possibility of resolving the contradictions between legislation and Islamic jurisprudence.

Regarding the first question, there is a three-way contradiction among three principles of legitimate authority—namely, the constitutional authority of the legislature, the new Shari'a-based constitutional authority of the supreme jurist (*wālī-yi faqīh*), and the old Shari'a-based authority of the highest rank of *mujtahids* (the *marājiʿ-i taqlīd* or "sources of emulation"). The mechanism devised by the constitution makers of 1979 for overcoming the first set of contradictions was the inclusion of six clerical jurists in the Council of Guardians to veto any item of legislation passed by the Majlis that was inconsistent with Shari'a. The council thus incorporated the 1907 idea of a committee of *mujtahids* into the model of a Conseil Constitutionnel adopted in Mahdī Bazargān's draft constitution from the 1958 Constitution of the French Fifth Republic. Khomeini himself intervened in the constitutional crisis that resulted from the clashes between the Majlis and the Council of Guardians, and his solution, which was duly incorporated into the constitutional amendments of 1989, consisted in the reception of the long-rejected Sunni principle of *maṣlaḥa* or public interest into Shiism and the establishment of the Maṣlaḥat Council. The Maṣlaḥat Council was originally to arbitrate between the Council of Guardians and the Majlis, but it has since taken on the task of expanding legislation beyond matters specifically vetoed by the jurists of the Council of Guardians and of setting up the general policies of the state as the advisory arm of the leader (*rahbar*) or supreme jurist. The solution proposed by the former head of the judiciary, Ayatollah Sayyid Muḥammad Yazdī, for the second set of contradictions was to force the recognition of the supreme jurist as the sole *marjaʿ*. It failed, as did the attempt to restrict the number of *marājiʿ* to seven through semiofficial designation by the Association of the Mudarrisīn (Professors) of Qom.[13]

The current head of the judiciary, Ayatollah Sayyid Maḥmūd Hāshimī Shahrūdī, has strengthened the Legal Office (Idārā-yi ḥuqūqī) of the judiciary and instituted a Research Center in Jurisprudence (Markaz-i taḥqīqāt-i fiqhī) to answer inquiries from the courts and provincial branches of the Ministry of Justice. The center draws on the rulings (*fatwās*) of the seven designated *marāji*ʿ, including the leader, Ayatollah Sayyid ʿAlī Khamenei, but does so alongside the rulings of other living *marāji*ʿ, as well as those of the late Ayatollahs Khomeini and Abū l-Qāsim Khū'ī (Kho'i, 1899–1992) and the classics in Shiite jurisprudence. This Research Center, like the Legal Office of the Ministry of Justice, follows Article 167 of the constitution, consistently upholding the priority of ordinary laws over Shiite jurisprudence. The resort to the latter is thus residual. Furthermore, it is usually inconclusive because the *fatwās* presented to supplement ordinary laws are often contradictory, and categorical instructions seem to be provided only when a pertinent positive law is found additionally.[14] Indeed, the latter seems to make the *fatwās* redundant. For example, four out of five *fatwās* produced in response to the question whether women can be judges according to Shari'a give a negative answer but are overruled by the Legal Office of the Judiciary, which cites an ordinary law of 1374 (1995–96) on the appointment of women as judges.[15]

As for the areas of law where Shari'a is relevant, problems do arise residually in procedural and civil law,[16] but are much more intractable in penal law because of the laws of retribution (*qiṣāṣ*) and blood money and compensation for injuries (*diyāt*) passed in 1981[17] and the law of discretionary punishments (*taʿzīrāt*) passed in 1996, which are now referred to as the Islamic Penal Code (Qānūn-i mujāzāt-i Islāmī). The Penal Code provides inadequate guidelines for the determination of compensation for many parts of the body in cases of injury and malpractice, and it is not self-sufficient and refers the judges to Shiite jurisprudence for procedural rules for the *ḥadd* punishments (including the so-called rights of God, *ḥuqūq Allāh*, and rights of men, *ḥuqūq al-nās*).[18] The inadequacy of the law of discretionary punishments is even more problematic for the courts because sometimes only the upper limits of punishment are specified, and the judge can even pardon the culprit.[19] The *taʿzīrāt* law of 1996 itself was a response to the chaos created by the exercise of the discretionary authority by the Islamicized courts, but it did not eliminate the indeterminacies and ambiguities or the consequent pressure on the branch of the Supreme Court that issues opinions on "procedural unity" (*waḥdat-i rawiyya*) or the Legal Office of the Ministry of Justice.[20] An interesting question here is the extent to which Shiite jurisprudence can in fact fill the gap in the rational-legal framework of the constitutional state. Only a minority of the jurists cited in the recent publications of the Center for Research in Jurisprudence—Khamenei is, predictably, one of them—consciously try to do this by taking a statist position. By contrast, it is striking how rigidly bound are all the jurists, including this minority and Ayatollah ʿAbd al-Karīm Musāwī Ardabīlī, for long a leading member of Iran's ruling elite who is known as a leading advocate of "innovative jurisprudence" (*fiqh-i puyā*), by the *ḥadīth* and the traditional rules of jurisprudence. To give one important example, both Musāwī Ardabīlī and Ayatollah Rūḥallāh Ṣāfī Gulpāyagānī, a longtime member of the Council of Guardians who could also be assumed sympathetic in adapting jurisprudence to its new function within the Islamic state, ignore the requirements of rational judicial administration through the state by confirming that a judge who is a *mujtahid* can pardon a *ḥadd* punishment, but one who is not cannot.[21]

The same inflexibility is apparent in the *fatwā*s concerning the "knowledge (*ʿilm*) of the Judge" as a supplement to the prosecutional evidence (*bayyināt*) used in the Shari'a courts and the possibility of appeal—issues of great importance in view of the enormous discretionary power of the judge, who also acts as the prosecutor and whose verdict is final. The resort to Shiite jurisprudence appears to boost the knowledge of the judge, though the *fatwā*s produced are far from unanimous. In astonishing disregard of procedural rationality, some jurists affirm the well-known personalism of Islamic law by considering the knowledge of the judge before his appointment legitimate grounds for a decision.[22] Others, ignoring the haphazard appeal system the judiciary had been forced to introduce for verdicts considered patently wrong by the judiciary itself, affirm the traditional Islamic position that there is no appeal against the *qāḍī*'s verdict. Last but not least, except for one statist jurist, they do not require the judge to give (written) reasons for his decision.[23] The last point is important in a system where judges have such broad discretionary power. It precludes the development of a jurisprudence based on court opinions as a force for rationalization and increasing the predictability of law.

The effectiveness of the current measures to reconcile ordinary laws and Shari'a is hard to determine at this stage. At any rate, residual resort to Shiite jurisprudence through the supervision and advisory services of the judiciary is a secondary mechanism for ensuring consistency between Shari'a and the constitutional state. The primary institution for performing this function is the Council of Guardians, which has a much longer record that we must now examine. It can be stated categorically that the Council of Guardians has made no contribution to institution building in the Islamic Republic of Iran. I would argue that the main reasons for this failure are the absence of a written jurisprudence remotely comparable with the jurisprudence of other constitutional courts (or the Supreme Court in the United States) and the increasing politicization of judicial review, which preceded the politicization of the judiciary and the use of courts as an instrument of political repression. An incidental feature of its French model, supervision of elections, suggested the Council of Guardians as an instrument of political control to Iran's ruling elite after the death of Khomeini and the end of his charismatic leadership. It interpreted its function of supervising elections as the power to reject the qualification of candidates for all elected offices, including the presidency, without giving its reasons, as is also the case when it vetoes legislation. This resulted in a serious overload of the functions of the Council of Guardians and overwhelmed its functions of judicial review and determination of conformity of legislation with Islamic standards. In fact, it is quite clear that since 2000 the effect of the Council of Guardians on institution building has been negative, consisting in the paralysis of legislation and the near destruction of the Majlis as an institution. This has been done by its blanket extension of inconsistency with Shari'a to such items of legislation as the annual government budget.[24]

The Council of Guardians has not shown any concern with removing abundant internal contradictions of the Constitution of the Islamic Republic of Iran. One obvious contradiction is between Shari'a and the principle of equality of all citizens before ordinary state laws. This contradiction is the basis for the vast majority of complaints by members of religious minorities to the presidential Commission for the Implementation of the Constitution.[25] Nor is this contradiction resolved through the secondary mechanism of Shiite jurisprudence. In a question concerning inheritance the jurists who were consulted advised that the Bahā'ī heirs of a deceased Bahā'ī could inherit from him as infidels only if no Muslim could be found in any category of presumptive heirs.[26] It goes without saying that resolving contradictions between Iranian law and international law is even further removed from the increasingly politicized concerns of the Council of Guardians. What I have in mind here is the fact that the gruesome Shari'a punishments obviously contradict the international human rights instruments that outlaw cruel and inhumane punishments. In January 2002 the Council of Guardians vetoed as contrary to Shari'a bills that were found at variance with the governmental orders of the leader (*rahbar*), the orders of the late imam, and even the regulations of the Supreme Council for Cultural Revolution;[27] and in January 2003 it rejected a Majlis bill against torture on the grounds that it contravened the internal regulations (*ā'in-nāmah*) of state prisons. In August 2003 the Council of Guardians then vetoed the ratification of the UN Convention Against Torture and Other Cruel, Inhuman, or Degrading Treatment or Punishment by the Majlis.

I think I have said enough for the reader to anticipate my negative answer to my last question about resolving the contradictions between legislation and Islamic jurisprudence. The quarter-century experience of the Islamic Republic of Iran does not suggest the possibility of removing these contradictions. A Shari'a-derived Islamic state cannot be a modern constitutional state without serious contradictions. There is no way to modernize the traditional system of the two powers by exempting one of them as sacrosanct. Let me conclude by suggesting that this realization is behind the reformist attack under President Muḥammad Khātamī (1997–2005) on clerical authority as the heir to both kings and prophets.

10 THE NORMATIVITY OF THE FACTUAL: ON THE EVERYDAY CONSTRUCTION OF SHARI'A IN A YEMENI FAMILY COURT

Anna Würth

BECAUSE OF THE SCANT AVAILABILITY OF SOURCES, court practice has not been a prevalent field of inquiry in respect to the normativity of Shari'a. Although analyses of the workings of past and contemporary judicial systems have increased, theory has lagged behind. It was previously assumed that court practice would directly reflect highly unegalitarian Islamic legal provisions, but some scholars now point to the highly flexible and often-accommodating nature of premodern family law rulings, particularly in respect to women. It is often inferred that modern codifications of Islamic law have negatively affected this trait of premodern jurisprudence.[1] Although this thesis is attractive, its validity has not been demonstrated empirically; rather, its appeal flows from the imagined consequences of the codification of law. Other attempts to theorize on the relationship between court practice and Islamic legal traditions have likewise encountered significant difficulties with empirical realities. Observing a Moroccan court during the 1960s, Lawrence Rosen stressed the continuity of contemporary judicial practice with "the" Islamic tradition and mores of litigants and argued that the court's main mode of adjudication was to put persons back on track to negotiating their relationships.[2] This is so broad a description that most civil judicial proceedings worldwide might fall under this rubric. Very much despite himself, Rosen nevertheless established that judicial institutions in the Middle East and North Africa should be treated as what they are: they interpret and thus make law, legitimize state order by offering or imposing services, and serve as one of the forums for dispute settlement and adjudication.

In this sense Shari'a can also be considered to be what judges at the different levels of a judicial system say it is. This will not be an appealing point of view to anyone with a political, legal, or religious stake in how Islamic law is defined. In fact, Ziba Mir-Hosseini relates how Iranian judges discouraged her from looking into court rulings—that would not be the place to find the "real" Shari'a.[3] Whether they are real Shari'a or not, analyses of court proceedings and representative samples of rulings demonstrate how Islamic law works in contemporary courts and what its results are for those subject to it.[4] A user- and result-oriented approach can thus add a less ideological dimension to the highly politicized debates about the normativity of Shari'a.

For several reasons, material from Yemen is particularly interesting for this kind of approach. Although legislation in Yemen is as eclectic as elsewhere, (North) Yemen was never successfully colonized, and republican legislation from the 1970s onward has incorporated Islamic substantive and procedural norms to a much larger extent than, for example, Egyptian legislation. Islamic law is thus not marginalized to personal status; for example, penal law retained the *ḥadd* punishments,[5] and criminal procedure contained many of the protections mitigating against their imposition.[6] Legitimacy of state legislation is explicitly couched in terms of Shari'a[7]—as is opposition to the government, which has grown in numbers and violence during the past ten years. Shari'a is thus very much in evidence in Yemen at different levels of society and politics, in contradictory discourses, and last, in the courts and litigants' perceptions of the courts.

In this chapter I focus on the empirical analysis of who does what at an urban primary family court in Yemen's capital, what actions are brought, and how litigants fare.[8] I argue that court routines and procedures greatly affect Shari'a (whether ideologues like this or not), and litigants are confronted with these routines much more immediately than with the substantive norms that guide the adjudication process. Furthermore, I demonstrate that Yemeni court proceedings are particularly relevant for the urban poor, and although most plaintiffs win their actions somewhat speedily, the overall results of Shari'a jurisprudence are modest in the face of current social and economic problems urban poor women face.

THE SOUTH SANAA COURT AND ITS CLIENTELE

Since the early 1980s the South Sanaa (Ṣanʿāʾ) primary court has been located in the Ṣāfiya neighborhood in the southern part of the Yemeni capital.[9] The court has general jurisdiction and is divided into civil, criminal, and family court chambers, each presided over by a single male judge.[10] Appeals go to the Sanaa

Court of Appeals, and the Yemeni Supreme Court can review rulings for legal accuracy. The South Sanaa court district is much larger than the neighborhood itself, and the court's jurisdiction is exceptionally large in terms of territory and population.[11] The district includes two clearly distinct areas of settlement. The majority of the population lives to the southeast of the district, toward Bāb al-Yaman; this area is older as a site of urban development and is of mixed social structure, but relatively poor.[12] The southwestern part of the district, in contrast, was urbanized only in the late 1970s and 1980s and is on the whole more prosperous than the southeast, representing one of the city's preferred residential neighborhoods.[13]

Most litigants and witnesses who appear at the family court are relatively poor wage earners, and the primary employer is the state.[14] Some are self-employed, including entrepreneurs (shop owners, small-business owners in construction) and very few professionals (attorneys and doctors). Formally self-employed as well are petty contractors (small traders, drivers, and day laborers in construction), but the independence implicit in the term is usually a euphemism for an unstable livelihood. A third of the men appearing before the court are employed by various military units and the security forces. This percentage seems relatively high: according to the available data, the corresponding number nationwide was 5 to 10 percent of working males.[15] This relatively high proportion may be due to the location of the presidential palace and a number of military barracks in the court district.

The employment structure among women appears less heterogeneous than among men, but data on women are much more limited. Only a fifth of all women who appear before the court are recorded as employed. Although it is true that the majority of female litigants may actually not be wage earners, women's professional activities are as a rule irrelevant to the court, so the proportion of employed women might be higher than the data suggest. Women appearing at the court work mainly in the informal sector as domestics and petty merchants, as well as in small and intermediate-sized state-run industries. Even though many of these women have families in the city with whom they can live, some live alone, abandoned by their migrant husbands, and rent a room from their sparse earnings or reside with their employer. In this urban social setting, not every woman has a family to which she can turn in case of marital conflict or economic need.[16]

The occupational structure of the men and women who appear before the court shows that they constitute a typical urban population, no matter how they represent their relationships with their place of origin (*al-balad*).[17] The high proportion of wage-dependent men in the civil service points to this urbanity, just as does the high proportion of those in the automotive and transport sectors, as well as in construction and petty trade. The high percentage of women in the informal sector reinforces this impression. Members of the middle and upper strata appear very rarely before this court, and actions brought by them are in every respect exceptions. The majority of the parties thus belong to the poor and poorest strata in the court district, and many of the conflicts in which they are involved revolve around the shortage of material resources.[18] It thus seems fair to conclude that in a setting such as Yemen where all family-related disputes can theoretically be solved out of court, the family court is an institution particularly relevant to the poor who have—mostly because of their poverty—failed to reach settlements out of court.

ROUTINES AT COURT

The court is located in a decrepit rental apartment building; very few Yemeni primary courts were built as such. A large downstairs reception hall has been chosen as the main courtroom to hear criminal trials. Parties and their lawyers sit on squeaky benches and chairs, the judges on an elevated podium; behind them is a bookcase, devoid of content. The upstairs holds a multitude of small offices where civil and personal-status hearings take place. The attempt to project order and dignity onto the space is clearly visible in the downstairs courtroom, but the upstairs appears pathetic; no office bears a sign, most doors are unhinged, files are in abject disarray, and the few available metal desks and chairs tend to break down. Scribes regularly collected signatures for petitions to the Ministry of Justice, which allocated the courts' budget during the mid-1990s, requesting new chairs, desks, writing paper, and ink. Since the ministry never replied, paper and ink continued to be provided by litigants. Judges are likewise deeply troubled by their pathetic work space; when I started fieldwork, the presiding judge had ordered all hearings to take place in the downstairs room, "not to give the researcher a wrong impression about the Shari'a," as he later acknowledged with a chuckle. When that system soon broke down because of staff and space shortages, judges shrugged in frustration and some embarrassment.

The court and its surroundings are busy and noisy, with men milling about, often shouting and occasionally violently clashing with their opponents. Although most clients in this court are women, they do not hang out there as the men do, and they never come in groups. Almost all women between fifteen and forty-five years of age wear a black *sharshaf* and also veil their faces, even if they wear a different style elsewhere.[19] Whether modesty is a strategy to win over judges or to deflect the attention of the crowds of men hanging out at court is hard to determine. But women's attire at court attempts to convey respectability in a not-so-respectable place and social situation. Upon entering the courthouse, men grudgingly deposit their arms with the soldiers who guard the courthouse and the little bug-infested jail attached to it.[20] As in other governmental buildings, men are to encounter the government as less of a man. In court judges are the only men who carry the ubiquitous dagger (*janbiyya*), in a distinct style connoting their noble descent. They may also carry a gun in the back of the belt that holds the *janbiyya* or in their briefcase. In addition, and quite unlike other government representatives, for example, officials in a ministry, judges in this court (and other primary courts and courts of appeal) do not wear Western-style pants, but neither do at least half the male clients coming to court. Apart from the very distinct and dignified physical appearance of the judges, there is thus little in this courthouse that is not shabby.

All litigants must have their complaints recorded at the registrar's office, where they also pay the necessary court fees. In civil matters the fees are proportional to the amount being contested, while for cases in family court the amount is set at the quite modest sum of 50 Yemeni riyal (YR) or $ 0.70.[21] The party being sued is subsequently notified of the suit in writing and required to respond to the complaint by a specified date. This notice and all subsequent subpoenas are supposed to be served by the court, that is, by soldiers (*muḥḍirūn*) employed by the court for that purpose, and only in exceptional cases is this task to be performed by the plaintiff.[22] In reality, the reverse is the case. The plaintiffs themselves serve the subpoenas, which includes the responsibility of making sure that the papers are served in the presence of the neighborhood chairman (*amīn*) or other witnesses, and that receipt of the papers is confirmed in writing. Plaintiffs sometimes pay the soldiers or the police to do this for them, but that requires a separate payment for which no specific amount has been established. In suits involving small amounts, especially cases requesting support payments, the costs of having the papers served on the defendant can quickly exceed the amount being sought. As for wife-initiated divorce suits, in most cases heard at this court the opposing party cannot be located or is known to be abroad. To serve notice that an action for divorce has been brought, women need to publish a notice three times in the semiofficial daily newspaper *al-Thawra*.[23] In 1995 the cost of each of these notices was YR300, a not-inconsiderable sum for many parties.

These bureaucratic prerequisites of judicial proceedings—the drawing up of complaints and having them recorded, issuing subpoenas to opposing parties and witnesses, responding to complaints, and setting court dates—hardly seem reasonable to most litigants, whether men or women, and not only because they can be expensive. Men in particular understand that they must get the opposing party to court, which sometimes involves paying a fee to the soldiers. It is far less obvious why they must hold to agreed-upon dates and follow procedures. Behind every requirement of this sort litigants suspect chicanery, which they are quick to trace to judicial corruption.

However, a look at all decisions taken by the family court over a period of twelve years reveals that most cases in the family court are dealt with relatively quickly. About 50 percent of the suits result in verdicts within three months—reflecting that most suits are brought by young and recently married couples with no or few children and certainly no property.[24] The majority of suits are won by the parties who bring them; 69 percent of plaintiffs who see their cases through to a conclusion emerge victorious. This high rate of success and the speed with which the decisions are rendered tend not to impress plaintiffs because their court action represents neither the first nor the final stage in the conflict. For those who win the suits, the majority believe that they did so because they were "right" (*ʿalā l-ḥaqq*). If they win quickly, they believe first and foremost that this is merely how things should be, and second that they owe the favorable outcome to their own persistence (*mutābaʿa*). As to the latter, they are not altogether mistaken: the efficiency with which the family court operates derives not from the effort invested in pending trials by the court itself, which is minimal, but from what the involved parties must do to speed the procedures along. Many litigants reflect on these features of court proceedings with some exasperation. "The Shari'a is arduous" (*al-sharīʿa ʿarīḍa wa-ṭawīla*) is an often-heard statement with the connotations of complicated, long-winded, and prone to cause frustration.[25]

In comparison with equivalent courts in Morocco or Egypt at roughly the same time, lower-court procedures in Sanaa appear to be structured relatively simply. The most important type of evidence is testimony from witnesses; the proceedings are oral and do not require extensive documentation or formalized written communications.[26] Thus only 36 percent of parties to lawsuits hired attorneys to represent them, and those with attorneys were not more successful in their suits than those who appeared without legal representation.[27] However, professional legal advice is also expensive, costing between $25 and $100 in 1995.

In complicated cases costs might rise incalculably. Moreover, established lawyers are reluctant to take on family law. It promises comparatively little in the way of earnings, requires a great deal of work, and involves bitter, frequently very personal conflicts between the parties. The legal representation available to the majority of litigants is thus of widely differing and often-questionable quality. On the whole, the legal knowledge of the attorneys and "Shari'a experts" (*wukalā' al-sharīʿa*) tends to be limited.[28] Their real abilities consist in a kind of legal semi-education and knowledge of the people in charge and their routines. Their services are thus less those of legal counsel than of an intermediary who facilitates access to the secretaries and judges. Only in this sense are they actually Shari'a experts, which once again confirms for most litigants that what matters is not only the arguments made in court, or who is right and wrong, but knowing the right people. And in fact it is not the parties to a suit but most attorneys and *wukalā' al-sharīʿa* who are known to the court. Individual judges may be critical of the dishonesty involved in how this or that attorney does business, as attorneys are critical of the judges, and especially of the secretaries, for being susceptible to bribes. But because the costs of corruption and dishonesty are passed on to the parties of the suit, as a rule the interplay between the various members of the legal profession functions fairly smoothly.

CASELOAD

Yemeni primary courts handle criminal, civil, and personal-status cases. In the four primary urban courts criminal cases are the most frequent (five hundred to nine hundred cases per year), while family law cases constitute about one-quarter of the overall annual caseload in Sanaa's primary courts.[29] During the early 1990s the family court in South Sanaa handled an average of two hundred cases per year, but the caseload had more than doubled by 1995/96.[30] Although this increase can be traced directly to the worsening of the economic crisis brought on by the 1994 war, and although the general rise in the number of suits filed correlates with population growth in Sanaa, this increase also points to a growing tendency of the population to submit problems involving marital and social relations to judicial determination.

Not all cases pending in any given judicial year are brought to a conclusion, and by no means all court proceedings, once initiated, end in a formal decision. Thus in the course of a judicial year only 20 to 25 percent of pending suits end either in a verdict or a ruling on nonjurisdiction by the court.[31] The others come to a conclusion, at least temporarily, partly in the form of out-of-court settlements (about 10 percent) and partly as a result of the failure of the plaintiff to appear (32–40 percent). The remainder of pending cases are folded into the following year's business. In an average of 10 percent of all suits annually, the court persuades the parties to settle in court or is informed that the case has been settled out of court (*ṣulḥ*, *taṣāluḥ*). It is sometimes specified in the court register whether such a *ṣulḥ* has resulted from the complaint being withdrawn (*tanāzul*) because of the termination of marriage by repudiation, for instance, or because of other types of settlement. For the court, *ṣulḥ* is thus merely the opposite of a verdict, *ḥukm*, which it would have had to reach itself.[32] As a juridical category, *ṣulḥ* designates neither the actual matter at issue nor the outcome of a conflict. Even if the actual number of settlements may be higher than suggested by the mentioned average of 10 percent, the proportion of cases that end in this way seems relatively small. This is in part because the precondition of an amicable settlement being reached—the physical presence of both parties or their representatives—is frequently not met. Many of the men being sued for divorce have been abroad for years and have broken off all family ties, having emigrated for reasons of employment. Moreover, dissolution of marriage requested by women (*faskh*) cannot be effected by arbitration.[33] An added difficulty, however, is that reaching arbitrated solutions can be a very time-consuming, as well as expensive, process, and most parties who appear in court have already been through it without success; their failure to settle out of court is precisely the reason for their appearance in court. As a result, many parties insist on a court verdict, which does not rule out the possibility that parties may resume attempts to reach a settlement in parallel to the court procedure.

On the other hand, at an annual average of between 32 and 40 percent, the number of cases that have been "suspended" appears relatively high. A case is suspended when the plaintiff fails to appear, whereupon the records are supposed to be marked with the appropriate notation. If the plaintiff then reappears, all it takes for the case to be reopened is for the fee of YR50 to be paid once again. A variety of reasons may explain why a case is dropped. Sometimes filing a suit is enough to motivate a settlement, and the court is simply not informed of the outcome. Other factors may also play a role, such as a lack of the necessary financial resources, of time to devote to the matter, or simply that the plaintiff has too little energy for it. As a whole, however, this high percentage of suspended cases also points to the fact that despite the good chances of prevailing in court and the relative speed with which cases are tried, court procedures always appear quite complicated to those who contemplate them.

FAMILY COURT SUITS

Few litigants formulate their claims on their own or with the help of literate relatives or friends. Most have it done for them in exchange for a small fee by one of the four or five scribes located at the gates to the court building or by the attorneys and Shari'a experts to be found there.[34] How and whether a complaint will result in a claim (*daʿwa*) suited for action by the court and whether this action will correspond to the plaintiff's actual claim thus depend on the quality of services offered by these persons. Neither the efforts of the scribes and attorneys outside the court nor those of the secretaries in the department that registers the complaints are always successful. Thus the family court receives written communications asking the judge "to solve my problem" or to "punish my opponent." When concrete demands are expressed, it is only rarely that the corresponding legal basis will be indicated. Even in the official registry a claim is often not categorized in proper terms. Mistaken or incomplete claims do not lead to the suits being dismissed.[35] Secretaries lend assistance in formulating the claim more precisely or send the plaintiff back to the scribe for corrections.

Suits filed by women for divorce and for support either inside the marriage or after it make up well over half the annual number of all registered cases. Although the number of these cases rose in absolute terms in the mid-1990s, their large share in the overall number of cases filed remained relatively constant over the years, with a yearly average of 28 percent of divorce suits and 25.7 percent of claims for support. Complaints regarding custody constitute not more than 6 percent of cases brought on average annually and are filed exclusively after divorce by both men and women. Inheritance cases likewise are brought by both men and women, but their number is very small; therefore they will not be considered further in the following.[36] Suits on marital obedience (exclusively filed by men) make up an average of almost 18 percent of all suits filed.

Not only do women file a majority of the suits, but three-fourths of the cases in which a judge hands down a verdict stem from suits filed by women. Of the 415 suits that ended in a verdict between 1983 and 1995, 74.2 percent were filed by women, and only 25.8 percent by men. The proportion of verdicts in divorce suits, averaging 60 percent yearly, is markedly higher than the proportion of verdicts regarding claims for support, which averages only 33 percent. Women are thus granted divorces more easily and more quickly before this court than they are awarded support. This stems, first, from the circumstance that nearly two-thirds of divorce cases are uncontested because the husband is "absent," that is, has migrated abroad. Second, however, the low number of decisions in support cases stems from the fact that some husbands react to claims for support by repudiating the marriage and ending it; thus the wife would abandon her action for support. Women and men in nearly equal numbers secure custody judgments after divorce. But most of the verdicts secured by men, half on average, come from complaints filed over marital obedience.[37] Excluding the large number of divorce suits brought by women, women comprise only 54 percent of all plaintiffs. This suggests that both women and men, if to different degrees, make use of the court to enforce their rights during the marriage—64 percent of the plaintiffs who attempt to regulate an existing marriage are men. After a marriage has ended, however, the majority of plaintiffs are again women; they constitute more than 70 percent of the plaintiffs requesting a ruling in postmarital issues.

This usage of the court obviously reflects the legal situation: only women need judicial intervention for divorce, while men may terminate marriage without any judicial or administrative supervision;[38] it is therefore women who need to turn to the court to settle the effects that arise from male divorce. Men, on the other hand, need court intervention solely to bring back a runaway wife[39] and to request the transfer of custody after a divorce.

As mentioned earlier, in most cases at the family court the plaintiff is successful. Women win a total of 79.5 percent of the suits they bring, men about 40 percent.[40] In divorce cases women are successful nearly 90 percent of the time, and decisions are also made in their favor in the majority of cases dealing with postdivorce issues. Only about 50 percent are successful, however—the same percentage as for men—in suits over support payments and marital obedience. In nearly half these verdicts both parties are granted their demands in part.

Overall, the high percentage of successful claimants reflects Yemeni procedural norms, which privilege a plaintiff able to bring credible witnesses. But more generally the South Sanaa family court and probably most other family courts in Yemen function fundamentally as institutions run entirely by upper-class men for poor women wronged by other (poor) men, mostly by their spouses and sometimes their male relatives. Older-generation judges aim to set right what other men have set wrong, and they see Shari'a as administered by them as the main avenue for women to claim and obtain their rights. "Alleviating injustice" (*rafʿ al-ẓulm*) is the trope these judges use to describe this understanding; many, however, are aware that judicial intervention is inept to solve problems raised by poverty. Like all paternalism, judicial paternalism also has a flip side; it turns into disciplining when women appear to overstep what are considered legitimate demands. As I have shown elsewhere, this disciplining side of paternalism comes out most forcefully in custody disputes between middle-class couples,[41] which, to date, are rare in this court but are bound to increase with overall changes in the Yemeni social fabric.

Although it has been detailed that a majority of plaintiffs win their cases, and that women win almost 90 percent of the divorce actions they bring, the question remains what "winning" a divorce suit actually means, particularly in a poor urban jurisdiction. Quite in contrast to all other Arab and North African republics, Yemeni legislation recognizes wife-initiated divorce as a judicially supervised dissolution of marriage (*faskh*).[42] Reasons for judicial dissolution, however, are similar to reasons recognized for judicial divorce (*taṭlīq/tafrīq*) in other Arab states: namely, nonsupport and prolonged absence. In addition, alcohol addiction, an executable verdict for jail time of more than three years, impotence, mental feebleness, and hatred (*karāhiyya*) toward the husband are valid reasons for wife-initiated divorce in Yemen. Assault is not spelled out as a ground for divorce, but husbands are "not to harm their wives, physically and psychologically," according to law.[43] Between 1983 and 1995, 88 percent of all rulings in divorce petitions were based on nonpayment of support, and in more than half the cases, on the absence of the husband. Rarely, then, was a ruling on wife-initiated divorce about other issues. This looks quite different from the perspective of women plaintiffs: for them, financial deprivation and the husband's prolonged absence constituted the reasons for more than two-thirds of their divorce petitions. In addition, however, wives mentioned assault as one main reason for their divorce request in about a quarter of all petitions, but judges acknowledged assault in only 4.4 percent of all rulings.

This reflects a number of related issues; indeed, most marriages that come before this court display several indicators of breakdown. Furthermore, the most straightforward divorce proceedings in terms of evidentiary requirements are those on grounds of nonsupport and/or prolonged absence, while proving assault is far more complicated because it usually occurs behind closed doors with no witnesses. Accordingly, the likelihood that a ruling based on nonpayment of support or absence will be quashed on procedural or material grounds is much lower than if it was based on different, more contentious grounds of divorce.[44] But even with these caveats in mind, it is still safe to assume that jurisprudence stresses men's financial shortcomings more than their other shortcomings, such as violence, alcohol addiction, and general depravity, that are brought forward by women in their claims. Given this emphasis on the material responsibility of men in marriage and child support, it is interesting to note that judges never validated a wife-initiated divorce and ordered the husband to pay the marital support owed. Judges were unanimous that the support is owed even if the wife requests a divorce,[45] but they argued that a ruling on divorce plus payment of owed support is not enforceable and thus does not make sense. The overall result of this interpretation is that wife-initiated divorce for non-support resembled a judicially supervised *khulʿ*, a divorce at the instance of the wife, who must pay compensation, and is comparable with legislation enacted in Egypt in 2000.[46] It thus reinforces the stereotype that only repudiation (*ṭalāq*) guarantees full financial rights and is therefore the preferred form of divorce, particularly for women.

Support payments assessed by the court for wives and children provide another interesting angle to assess the overall results of jurisprudence and what "winning" means in this social context. Judges state that support payments should be adequate and are supposed to amount to half the income of the husband. The rulings, however, diverge quite dramatically from this supposed norm. On average the share of the man's income designated for monthly support payments comes to less than 20 percent, and neither income nor the man's occupation can be used as a definite indicator of the level of support ordered. From this it can be concluded that most husbands' earning potential is so limited that cutting it in half would push them to the edge of a viable subsistence, and judges take this into account. If husbands who appear before the court are unable to meet their personal needs with half their income, however, then women and children, disposing an average maximum of just 20 percent of the husband's income, will also be unable to cover their living costs with these payments. The analysis of the yearly evolution of support payments allotted by judges to a woman with one child shows a slow but steady increase in allotted payments since the early 1990s. However, any increase in support was eaten up by the devaluation of the riyal, and what women received in 1994/95 was worth only a third of what they had received in the late 1980s. Furthermore, after the initial rise in support payments in the early 1990s, support payments declined once again in 1994, even though devaluation assumed truly dramatic proportions during and after the war in 1994: the riyal fell by a third against the U.S. dollar, and the rate of inflation peaked at 120 percent.[47] Legal change likewise played a role: the law of 1992, introduced after the Arab Republic of Yemen and the People's Republic of Yemen unified in 1990, limits the payment of owed support to one year before the claim was brought, whereas the former law in the Arab Republic of Yemen had not contained any such limit. Contrary to numerous other provisions of the 1992 law that remained dead letters, this one was fairly stringently applied by the judges, in effect limiting the amounts women received for owed support in extant marriages. The overall result of how much money judges allotted to women and children during the 1990s was thus a shift of the burden of the economic crisis onto the economically weakest members of society, women and children dependent on support.

"Winning" a divorce petition or a suit for support thus has its limits: winning an action for divorce entails losing all financial rights from marriage but gaining the freedom to try again;[48] winning an action for child support or support during marriage boils down to an entitlement too low to survive on and hard to enforce.

This, then, is essentially what Yemeni Shari'a jurisprudence in a low-income urban court district boils down to. Ideologues, be they reactionary, conservative, or feminist, requesting or arguing against the "application of Shari'a" would be well advised to empirically examine the overall results of jurisprudence in a given place and to assess what exactly would be gained from more or less Shari'a if they want to address socioeconomic and marital problems of lower-class families. Legal populism that appeals to Shari'a as authenticity and tradition glosses over the history and structural weaknesses of the Middle Eastern / North African legal systems and the class relevance of contemporary court use.

AFTERWORD

Roy P. Mottahedeh

IT IS AN HONOR TO COMMENT on this very fine collection of essays on Islamic law in the contemporary context. There was a long tradition of writing about Shari'a without reference to its historical setting or of using an abstracted Shari'a to explain social history. As these essays testify, the social meaning of Shari'a can only be understood when it is situated within the discussion of the jurists and of the actual experience of law in specific communities. And in situating Shari'a in the actual experience of law, the historian of law should, as the essayists have ably tried to do, keep in mind the many alternate paths available to those who want a legal outcome.

We tend to privilege the founding written tradition that survives in existing schools of law, but the social historian must accept as equally valid for Bedouin society the famous codes of Bedouin law that the Bedouin feel to be in conformity with Islam.[1] Many Muslim jurists would, of course, be quick to correct the Bedouin lawyer. The historian of law, however, must accept both the learned written tradition and the Bedouin systems of law as "Islamic" in the sense that Muslims have regarded them as in conformity with—even expressive of—their belief in Islam. Here the term *Islamicate* as defined by Marshall Hodgson might well be useful. He defines Islamicate as referring "not directly to the religion of Islam itself, but to the social and cultural complex historically associated with Islam and the Muslims, both among Muslims themselves and even when found among non-Muslims."[2]

Anna Würth's important chapter in this collection reminds us that a great divide lies between the "rulings" (*aḥkām*) that were the decisions of premodern jurists and judges and the statute law that characterizes the modern state. Her courts seem to dwell somewhere between. She also brings home to us how many paths there must have been to legal outcomes outside courts. The copious discussion of arbitration (*taḥkīm*) and conciliation (*ṣulḥ*) helps us understand how, in a premodern society in which courts were comparatively few, many alternatives to settlement by Muslim judges must have been pursued and perhaps, for certain kinds of cases, preferred. Even in cases brought to court we see the judge's exercise of *istiḥsān*, the judge's or jurist's right to decide in favor of "preference" on the grounds of the material considerations in the case. Some such device must exist in any long-functioning legal system.

It was the contention of many of the reformers mentioned in these chapters, such as Muḥammad ʿAbduh (1849–1905), that much of the written corpus we call Islamic law was in fact "Islamicate," associated with Islam through historical circumstances and, therefore, while not necessarily antithetical to Islam, not necessarily inherent in Islam. Such a discussion can only be carried forward among Muslim thinkers and is not the subject of historians of law. Nevertheless, these competing claims as to the nature of Islamic law remind us that insofar as we talk about a "central" learned tradition of Islamic written law, we are talking in large part about the work of jurists of the first four centuries of the Muslim era, parts of whose work was posthumously sacralized. A problem posed by many of the thinkers discussed in these chapters is how a Muslim deals with a "law" set out in the Qur'an, since the great majority of Muslims hold the Qur'an to be the speech of God. A similar problem is posed by the sacralized material outside the Qur'an, given that the status of "scripture" (including, most notably, canonized *ḥadīth*) is itself as great a problem or an even greater one for modern interpreters of Shari'a. The size and foundational importance for Islamic law of scriptural materials exterior to the Qur'an might be seen as more determinative of the law than the Qur'an itself.

Most of the chapters discuss strategies for dealing with this supposed "immutable core" of the central tradition of Islamic law. The first strategy is suggested by the legal tradition itself, which, as a kind of memorial to its tradition, preserves minority opinions within each of its schools. These minority opinions can be adopted by the exercise of *ijtihād*, independent application of the sources of Islamic law. Also, opinions of other law schools can be imported in a process called "patching up" (*talfīq*). These strategies have been widely used by modern jurists, administrators, and legislatures.

Another strategy was to claim "necessity" (*ḍarūra*). The great majority of jurists accept that necessity overrules the law temporarily, as in the case of the man starving of thirst who is allowed to drink enough wine to save his life (but no more). Other jurists have been liberal in their interpretations, allowing necessity to sanction ongoing institutions, such as the cash endowment (*waqf*) in the Ottoman Empire, that would seem to contradict the elaborate Shari'a provisions against usury.[3] Khomeini said that the *ḥadd* punishments—the harsh punishments for capital offenses such as murder, theft, and highway robbery, but also apostasy from Islam and adultery—would only be appropriate in a perfect society, which could not exist before the return of the Twelfth Imam, the messianic end of history. He meant that "necessity" drove people to crime, and these "necessities" would continue to exist.

The suspension of the law for "necessity" was sometimes explained in terms of *maṣlaḥa*. *Maṣlaḥa* has several legal meanings, which are excellently treated in the chapter by Felicitas Opwis. In its more general meaning, as used by the jurists al-Ṭūfī (d. 1316) and, even more boldly, al-Shāṭibī (d. 1388), *maṣlaḥa* is equivalent to the "good ends" (or "beneficial goals") that Shari'a seeks. These good ends become part of the formal procedure in ruling what Shari'a says in any specific circumstance. This consideration could easily overrule even the specific commands and prohibitions in the Qur'an.

Modernists, such as ʿAllāl al-Fāsī, ably discussed in David L. Johnston's chapter, saw in these jurists an opening to discuss the spirit of the law and to use this spirit in the formation of statute law (a possibility that premodern jurists probably did not contemplate). But the compromises in ʿAllāl al-Fāsī's own position and those of other jurists show how far the modern jurist had to travel to feel comfortable with this position. And, as Gudrun Krämer's learned chapter testifies, many Muslim thinkers are indeed moving toward an establishment of the spirit of the law, although when and where there will be major consensus on these questions remains to be seen.

Gudrun Krämer emphasizes justice as one extremely prominent element in the spirit of the law. The classic question of Islamic theology was how one identifies or acquires the spirit of justice. The same direction of thought is discussed in Frank Griffel's excellent chapter. It analyzes the reintroduction of theological assumptions that human nature, and more particularly human reason, is in accord with and a guide to what we would call "natural law." For this law to have divine promulgation would be theologically consonant with a divinely ordained human nature. Not surprisingly, the hints in the Qur'an and elsewhere about *fiṭra*, approximately translated as "innate human nature," were a natural locus of interest. Curiously, the tradition of legal discussion of "the conduct of reasonable people" (*sīrat al-ʿuqalā'*) exists in the Islamic legal tradition and has echoes in many areas, such as the literature about "human actions" (*ʿamal*) of the Mālikī school of law of Spain and North Africa. One might think of the way that *jus gentium*, "the law of the nations," while remaining separate from natural law, influenced Roman concepts of natural law. But the conduct of reasonable people as derived from earlier discussions of Shari'a does not seem to have many modern echoes.

Because we have three fine chapters on Iranian tradition by Abbas Amanat, Shahrough Akhavi, and Saïd Amir Arjomand, we face the important question as to why the Twelver Shiite tradition, which has remained theologically Muʿtazilite, has failed to produce a full-blown "natural law" tradition. With few exceptions the Twelver Shiite tradition stopped its scholastic theology at the point of proving the necessity of accepting the Islamic revelation. Scholasticism was also used to extend the law, once the basics of it had been discovered through the study of scripture. But to attempt to prove the law fully by *ʿaql* (reason or intellect) was a theoretical challenge that was never met.[4]

I came away from these chapters, even Noah Feldman's careful and encouraging analysis of the political philosophy of the somewhat more conservative Yūsuf al-Qaraḍāwī, with a longing for a deeper discussion of "citizenship" as it might be defined in the modern context. Public participation is everywhere in these chapters, and it, of course, implies citizenship. Shari'a's understanding of what it remains to be "a legal agent" (*mukallaf*) is another source from which this discussion might spring. However, the individual does not emerge as strongly as he or she might in a full discussion of liberal Islamic thinkers. Is this absence the accident of the sources chosen, or is the liberalism of the community constructed more from rights of the individual within the community than from the individual, as a nexus of rights, choosing to join the community? Is there an aspiration that the citizen, regardless of her or his system of values, will be public minded?

These questions are clearly associated with the civic tradition of a community and its expression through civic memory as expressed in such media as history, literature, and ceremonials. It is for the possession of this communal space that nationalism has sometimes battled with and sometimes co-opted Shari'a. Will Shari'a find a strong positive expression of citizenship that defines itself in relation to—and redefines the nature of—modern nation-states?

NOTES

Chapter 1

1. For a discussion of Muslim views on subjects of contemporary moral debates, see *Islamic Ethics of Life: Abortion, War, and Euthanasia*, ed. Jonathan E. Brockopp with a foreword by Gene Outka (Columbia: University of South Carolina Press, 2003).

2. See Majid Khadduri, *The Islamic Law of Nations: Shaybānī's Siyar* (Baltimore: Johns Hopkins University Press, 1966).

3. Al-Ghazālī's writings on this subject have been analyzed by Michael Cook, *Commanding Right and Forbidding Wrong in Islamic Thought* (Cambridge: Cambridge University Press, 2000), 427–59.

4. Hence in this book *Shari'a* (for Arabic *sharīʿa*) is treated as an English word similar to other important Muslim terms, such as *Qur'an*, *Shiite*, or *Ayatollah*, that have become part of the English language. Likewise, in the spelling of some familiar names, such as the Safavids (for Ṣafawids), of Khomeini (for Khumaynī), Khamenei (for Khāmina'ī), and Muhammad (for Muḥammad), we follow common usage rather than correct transcription.

5. In addition, the Arabic verb *sharaʿa*, which seems to be derived from *sharīʿa*, appears twice in the Qur'an. Once God is called "the one who has laid down [*sharaʿa*] for you as religion what He had also appointed to Noah" (Q 42.13). In another verse a group of deviators are polemically asked whether they have companions "who have laid down [*sharaʿa*] for them as religion that which God did not permit" (Q 7.163).

6. See Norman Calder and M. B. Hooker, art. "S͟harīʿa," in *The Encyclopaedia of Islam*, new ed., 11 vols. (London: Luzac & Co.; Leiden: Brill, 1954–2002), 9:321a–328a, esp. 326a; Edward William Lane, *Arabic-English Lexicon*, 8 parts (London and Edinburgh: Williams and Norgate, 1863–85), 4:1535.

7. For a report on the different views of the origins of Islamic jurisprudence, see

Harald Motzki, *The Origins of Islamic Jurisprudence: Meccan Fiqh Before the Classical Schools*; translated from the German by Marion H. Katz (Leiden: Brill, 2002), 1–49. A quite different view is offered by Wael B. Hallaq, *The Origins and Evolution of Islamic Law* (Cambridge: Cambridge University Press, 2005).

8. The highest legal authority apart from the Prophet is often held by an eponymous founding figure of the school. Abū Ḥanīfa (d. 767), for instance, is regarded as the founder of the legal tradition of the Hanafite school, Mālik ibn Anas (d. 796) as the founder of the Malikite school, al-Shāfiʿī (d. 820) as the founder of the Shafi'ite school of law, and Aḥmad ibn Ḥanbal (d. 855) as that of the Hanbalite school. On the development of legal methodology in Sunni Islam, see Wael B. Hallaq, *A History of Islamic Legal Theories: An Introduction to Sunnī Uṣūl al-Fiqh* (Cambridge: Cambridge University Press, 1997).

9. On these collections and their content, see Arent Jan Wensinck, *A Handbook of Early Muhammadan Tradition, Alphabetically Arranged* (Leiden: Brill, 1927; 2nd ed., 1960; 3rd ed., 1971).

10. In the case of Sunni theological literature—which follows rules of discourse similar to those of legal literature—this case has been made by Norman Calder, "The Limits of Islamic Orthodoxy," in *Intellectual Traditions in Islam*, ed. Farhad Daftary (London: I. B. Tauris, 2000), 66–86.

11. Timothy Mitchell, *Colonising Egypt* (Cambridge: Cambridge University Press, 1988), 101.

12. The central verb in Arabic is *sharaʿa*, which may be translated as "ordaining law through revelation." The Arabic *sharʿ* is the verbal noun of the process of revelation, i.e., God's ordaining that man shall act such and such. *Sharīʿa* is the systematic formulation of the ordinances; it is that by which man knows that he is obligated (Wilfred C. Smith, *On Understanding Islam: Selected Studies* [The Hague: Mouton, 1981], 96–99, 105). When the Jewish theologian Saʿadya Gaon (d. 933) translates the Hebrew Bible into Arabic, he often uses *sharīʿa* as a translation of the Hebrew word *torah* in the meaning of the law that has been revealed to Moses. Note that according to this understanding, Shari'a is created through revelation. It does not exist in an ideal divine form regardless of whether it has been revealed or not, as some modern understandings of Shari'a propose.

13. Plato, *Laws*, X, 884d–912a, esp. 907b–e.

14. Joseph Vining, *The Authoritative and the Authoritarian* (Chicago: University of Chicago Press, 1986), 187–201.

15. Ibid., 190.

16. Harry A. Wolfson, *The Philosophy of the Kalam* (Cambridge, MA: Harvard University Press, 1976), 244–48.

17. These are the words of one of the earliest researchers of Islamic law in the West, Gotthelf Bergsträsser, *Grundzüge des islamischen Rechts*, ed. Joseph Schacht (Berlin and Leipzig: de Gruyter, 1935), 1. In English literature they have been introduced by H. A. R.

Gibb, *Mohammedanism: An Historical Survey* (London and New York: Oxford University Press, 1949), 106.

18. See Muḥammad ʿAbduh in the first edition of his *Risālat al-Tawḥīd*, in *al-Aʿmāl al-kāmila li-l-imām Muḥammad ʿAbduh*, ed. Muḥammad ʿAmāra, 6 vols. (Beirut: al-Mu'assasa al-ʿArabiyya li-l-Dirāsāt wa-l-Nashr, 1972–74), 3:353–476, 378. The book was published in 1897 and is based on twelve lectures given in Beirut in 1886. On the objections to ʿAbduh's teachings, see Muḥammad Rashīd Riḍā, *Ta'rīkh al-ustādh al-imām Muḥammad ʿAbduh*, 2nd ed., 3 vols. (Cairo: Dār al-Manār, 1350/1931), 1:966.

19. Muḥammad ʿAbduh, *Risālat al-Tawḥīd*, 2nd ed., ed. M. Rashīd Riḍā (Cairo: Dār al-Manār, 1326 [1908–9]), 36–37. Cf. the English translation, *The Theology of Unity*, trans. I. Musaʿad and K. Cragg (London: Allen & Unwin, 1966), 53, which has the text of the second edition without Rashīd Riḍā's footnote.

20. Felicitas Opwis, "Changes in Modern Islamic Legal Theory: Reform or Reformation?" in *An Islamic Reformation?* ed. Michaelle Browers and Charles Kurzman (Lanham, MD: Lexington Books, 2004), 28–53, 30. For an overview of differences among the reform programs in the Muslim countries, see Ira M. Lapidus, *A History of Islamic Societies*, 2nd ed. (Cambridge: Cambridge University Press, 2002), 457–68.

21. Opwis, "Changes in Modern Islamic Legal Theory," 31–32. The Mejelle was based on rulings within the Hanafite school of law.

22. Nathan Brown, "Shariʿa and State in the Modern Muslim Middle East," *International Journal of Middle East Studies* 29 (1997): 359–76, esp. 360–63, 369.

23. Ibid., 366.

24. Joseph Schacht, *An Introduction to Islamic Law* (Oxford: Clarendon Press, 1964), 100–111, esp. 101.

25. Daniel Crecelius, "Nonideological Responses of the Egyptian Ulama to Modernization," in *Scholars, Saints, and Sufis: Muslim Religious Institutions in the Middle East Since 1500*, ed. Nikki R. Keddie (Berkeley: University of California Press, 1972), 167–209, 189.

26. Nathan J. Brown, *The Rule of Law in the Arab World: Courts in Egypt and the Gulf* (Cambridge: Cambridge University Press, 1997), 61–69; Schacht, *Introduction to Islamic Law*, 107.

27. On the impact of the introduction of the printing press during the nineteenth century on the understanding of Shari'a, see Opwis, "Changes in Modern Islamic Legal Theory," 33–36.

28. Muḥammad Rashīd Riḍā, *al-Khilāfa aw l-imāma al-uẓmā* (Cairo: Dār al-Manār, 1341 [1923]), 90–91; French translation by Henri Laoust, *Le califat dans la doctrine de Rašīd Riḍā* (Beirut: Memoires de l'Institut français de Damas, 1938), 151–54; ʿAbd al-Razzāq al-Sanhūrī, *Le califat: Son évolution vers une société des nations orientales* (Paris: P. Geuthner, 1926); Hamid Enayat, *Modern Islamic Political Thought* (Austin: University of Texas Press, 1982), 77–79, 81; Brown, "Shariʿa and State in the Modern Muslim Middle East," 370.

29. ʿAbd al-Qādir ʿAwda, *al-Islām wa-awḍāʿunā al-qānūniyya* (Cairo: Dār al-Kitāb al-ʿArabī, 1951); English translation by S. M. Hasnain, *The Islamic System of Justice* (Karachi: International Islamic Publications, 1982); Richard P. Mitchell, *The Society of the Muslim Brothers*, 2nd ed. (New York and Oxford: Oxford University Press, 1993), 235–50. At the same time, ʿAwda and many of the Brotherhood's leaders admitted that the laws imported into Egypt were, with the exception of some provisions in penal law, in agreement with Shari'a and did not violate its general principles (Mitchell, 241).

30. Sayyid Quṭb, *Maʿālim fī l-ṭarīq* (Cairo: n.p., 1383/1964); English translation, *Milestones* (Indianapolis: American Trust Publications, 1990).

31. The texts were also published as a book: Ibn Taymiyya, *Majmūʿat al-rasā'il wa-l-masā'il*, ed. M. Rashīd Riḍā (Cairo: Manshī Majallat al-Manār, 1341–49 [1922–30]).

32. Sayyid Quṭb, *Fī ẓilāl al-Qur'ān*, 6 vols. (Beirut and Cairo: Dār al-Shurūq, 1493–94/1973–74). The commentary was first published in installments during the years after 1960. Parts of it have been translated into English by M. Adil Salahi and Ashur A. Shamis, *In the Shade of the Qur'an* (London: MWH, 1979–).

33. Mitchell, *Society of the Muslim Brothers*, 237.

34. Monique C. Cardinal surveys the courses of study on *uṣūl al-fiqh* at al-Azhar, al-Qarawiyyīn, Zaytūna (Tunis), Damascus University, and Jordan University in "Islamic Legal Theory Curriculum: Are the Classics Taught Today?" *Islamic Law and Society* 12 (2005): 224–72.

35. Ibid., 246–53.

36. ʿAbd al-Qādir ʿAwda's *al-Tashrīʿ al-jināʾī al-Islāmī muqāranan bi-l-qānūn al-waḍʿī* first appeared in 1949. Its second expanded edition came out in two volumes (Cairo: Dār al-Urūba, 1959) and has often been reprinted. The book has been translated into other Muslim languages, including English: *Criminal Law of Islam* (Karachi: International Islamic Publishers, 1987).

37. See, for instance, al-Bukhārī, *al-Ṣaḥīh, kitāb al-jihād, bāb* no. 149, or *kitāb al istitāba, bāb* no. 2; Ibn Māja, *al-Sunan, kitāb al-ḥudūd, bāb* no. 2; Mālik ibn Anas, *al-Muwaṭṭā', kitāb al-aqḍiya, bāb* no. 18; and Aḥmad ibn Ḥanbal, *al-Musnad*, 6 vols. (Cairo: al-Maṭbaʿa al-Maymaniyya, 1311–13 [1893–95]), 1:2, 7, 217, 282, 323.

38. On the law of apostasy and the institution of *istiṭāba*, see my "Toleration and Exclusion: al-Shāfiʿī and al-Ghazālī on the Treatment of Apostates," *Bulletin of the School of Oriental and African Studies* (London) 64 (2001): 339–54; and my article on "Apostasy" in the forthcoming *Encyclopaedia of Islam*, 3rd ed., executive editors Marc Gaborieau, Gudrun Krämer, John Nawas, and Everett Rawson, vol. 1 (Leiden: Brill).

39. Another example is the age of consent, which is practically unknown in Shari'a. Marrying a child, particularly a girl, is still practiced in some rural parts of the Muslim world. But this part of Shari'a is generally not what proponents want to revive.

40. See, for instance, Arzina R. Lalani, "Judgement," in *Encyclopaedia of the Qur'ān*, ed. Jane Dammen McAuliffe, 5 vols. (Leiden: Brill, 2001–7), 3:64–68.

41. For a Muslim theological critique of the idea of *ḥākimiyya* in the writings of Abū l-Aʿlā Mawdūdī, see Fazlur Rahman, "Implementation of the Islamic Concept of State in the Pakistani Milieu," *Islamic Studies* 6 (1967): 205–24.

42. Smith, *On Understanding Islam*, 88–95, observes that a proper treatment of the term *sharīʿa* is conspicuously absent from Muslim theological literature of the early classical period (750–1400). His result must be read with caution, however, since he did not survey legal literature on any works after 1500. In addition, the concept of Shari'a as divine law is clearly present in influential methodological works of Muslim jurisprudence, such as al-Ghazālī's *al-Mustaṣfā min ʿilm al-uṣūl*, 2 vols. (Būlāq: al-Maṭbaʿa al-Amīriyya, 1322–24 [1904–6]).

Chapter 2

In preparing my chapter, I have benefited from discussions with participants in the Yale Symposium and with the fellows of Max-Weber-Kolleg, Erfurt, Germany, during my stay there in 2004–5.

1. Ze'ev Maghen, "Much Ado About Wuḍū'," *Der Islam* 76 (1999): 205–52 (the quotes are from 224, 216, and 221, respectively). The italics are mine.

2. In this context "Muslim scholars" refers exclusively to the *ʿulamāʾ*, not just any scholar who happens to be a Muslim.

3. The element of competition that marked relations between Islam and other religious communities from the very beginning has been highlighted by Jonathan P. Berkey, *The Formation of Islam: Religion and Society in the Near East, 600–1800* (Cambridge: Cambridge University Press, 2003).

4. For a spirited critique of these assumptions, see Muhammad Khalid Masud, *Muslim Jurists' Quest for the Normative Basis of Sharīʿa* (Leiden: ISIM Lectures, 2001).

5. Many Muslims reject any attempt to divide Islam into conservative and progressive, rightist and leftist, Middle Eastern or European. Still, for analytical purposes it makes perfect sense to classify Muslim authors and activists who offer readings of Islam, not Islam "as such," according to their philosophical and political preferences and practices; see Leonard Binder, *Islamic Liberalism: A Critique of Development Ideologies* (Chicago: University of Chicago Press, 1988); Charles Kurzman, *Liberal Islam: A Sourcebook* (New York: Oxford University Press, 1998); and Abdou Filali-Ansary, "What Is Liberal Islam? The Sources of Enlightened Muslim Thought," *Journal of Democracy* 14 (2003): 19–33.

6. For different perspectives, see notably Mohammad Hashim Kamali, *Principles of Islamic Jurisprudence*, rev. ed. (Cambridge: Islamic Texts Society, 1991); Wael B. Hallaq, *A History of Islamic Legal Theories: An Introduction to Sunnī Uṣūl al-Fiqh* (Cambridge: Cambridge University Press, 1997); Bernard G. Weiss, *The Spirit of Islamic Law* (Athens: University of Georgia Press, 1998); Devin J. Stewart, *Islamic Legal Orthodoxy: Twelver*

Shiite Responses to the Sunni Legal System (Salt Lake City: University of Utah Press, 1998); and Baber Johansen, *Contingency in a Sacred Law* (Leiden: Brill, 1999). On the *qawāʿid*, see also Muḥammad al-Rūkī, *Naẓariyyat al-taqʿīd al-fiqhī wa-atharuhā fī ikhtilāf al-fuqahāʾ* (Rabat: Kulliyyat al-Adab wa-l-ʿUlūm al-Insāniyya bi-l-Ribāṭ, 1994). See further Khaled El-Rouayheb, "Sunni Muslim Scholars on the Status of Logic, 1500–1800," *Islamic Law and Society* 11 (2004): 213–32.

7. David L. Johnston approaches this phenomenon from a different angle: "A Turn in the Epistemology and Hermeneutics of Twentieth Century *Uṣūl al-Fiqh*," *Islamic Law and Society* 11 (2004): 233–82.

8. See notably Weiss, *Spirit of Islamic Law*, chaps. 4 and 7; Hallaq, *History*, 112–13, 132, 162–206, 214–31; Kamali, *Principles of Islamic Jurisprudence*, 267–82; Kemal A. Faruki, *Islamic Jurisprudence* (New Delhi: Deep & Deep Publications, 1988), 22–33, 75–165; also Muhammad Khalid Masud, *Shatibi's Philosophy of Islamic Law*, rev. and enlarged ed. (Islamabad: Islamic Research Institute, 1995), esp. 127–68; Sherman A. Jackson, *Islamic Law and the State: The Constitutional Jurisprudence of Shihāb al-Dīn al-Qarāfī* (Leiden: Brill, 1996), esp. 57–64; Muṣṭafā Zayd, *al-Maṣlaḥa fī l-tashrīʿ al-Islāmī wa-Najm al-Dīn al-Ṭūfī* (Cairo: Dār al-Fikr al-ʿArabī, 1954). The concept of necessity (*ḍarūra*) as it was expressed, among others, in the legal principle of *lā ḍarar wa-lā ḍirār* (no injury or counterinjury) has to be seen in the same context of jurists attempting to rationally assess and balance the weight of explicit scriptural injunctions against countervailing considerations (*muʿāriḍāt*), opportunity, and utility. On *maṣlaḥa* in classical and modern legal thinking, see also Jamāl al-Dīn ʿAṭiya Muḥammad, *Naḥwa tafʿīl maqāṣid al-sharīʿa* (Damascus and Beirut: Dār al-Fikr, 2001); and Felicitas Opwis, "*Maṣlaḥa* in Contemporary Islamic Legal Theory," *Islamic Law and Society* 12 (2005): 182–223, as well as her contribution to this volume.

9. See, e.g., ʿAbd al-Wahhāb Khallāf, *ʿIlm uṣūl al-fiqh* (Cairo: n.p, n.d. [1940]); ʿAllāl al-Fāsī, *Maqāṣid al-sharīʿa al-Islāmiyya wa-makārimuhā*, 5th rev. ed. (Beirut: Dār al-Gharb al-Islāmī, 1993).

10. This kind of reasoning is characteristic of contemporary discourse dealing with the ideal Islamic state or order (*niẓām Islāmī*); for more detail, see my *Gottes Staat als Republik: Reflexionen zeitgenössischer Muslime zu Islam, Menschenrechten und Demokratie* (Baden-Baden: Nomos, 1999), 73–95, or, with less reserve concerning Islamist credentials, Ahmad S. Moussalli, "Modern Islamic Fundamentalist Discourses on Civil Society, Pluralism and Democracy," in *Civil Society in the Middle East*, ed. A. R. Norton, 2 vols. (Leiden: Brill, 1995), 1:79–119. Islamist writers such as Muḥammad ʿAmāra, *al-Dawla al-Islāmiyya bayna al-ʿalmāniyya wa-l-sulṭa al-dīniyya* (Cairo and Beirut: Dār al-Shurūq, 1988); or Fahmī Huwaydī, *al-Qurʾān wa-l-sulṭān: humūm Islāmiyya muʿāṣira* (Cairo and Beirut: Dār al-Shurūq, 1982), as well as Muslim jurists such as Muḥammad Salīm al-ʿAwwā, *Fī l-niẓām al-siyāsī lil-dawla al-Islāmiyya*, 2nd rev. ed. (Cairo and Beirut: Dār al-Shurūq, 1989), chap. 4; Abdur Rahman I.

Doi, *Sharī'ah: The Islamic Law* (London: Ta Ha Publishers, 1984); or Mohammad Kamali, *Principles of Islamic Jurisprudence*, provide good examples of the value-oriented approach that does not underrate the importance of proper conduct. For a more general discussion of Islamic ethics, see notably Toshihiko Izutsu, *Ethico-religious Concepts in the Qur'ān* (Montreal: McGill University Press, 1966); *Ethics in Islam: Ninth Giorgio Levi della Vida Biennial Conference*, ed. R. G. Hovannisian (Malibu, CA: Undena Publications, 1985); Majid Fakhry, *Ethical Theories in Islam*, 2nd enlarged ed. (Leiden: Brill, 1994); Daniel Brown, "Islamic Ethics in Comparative Perspective," *Muslim World* 89 (1999): 181–92.

11. Weiss, *Spirit of Islamic Law*, esp. chaps. 4 and 7, helps grasp the epistemological differences between mainstream Sunni *fiqh* and modern conceptions of the vital interests or basic values of Islam. See also Syed Nawab Haider Naqvi, *Perspectives on Morality and Human Well-Being: A Contribution to Islamic Economics* (Leicester: Islamic Foundation, 2003), esp. 129, where he argues, "True, these *maqāṣid*, i.e., (a) faith; (b) life; (c) progeny; (d) intellect; and (e) wealth, must have made an interesting list of objectives, in the time these were formulated, to address legal and metaphysical issues; yet they need to be refocused, expanded and amended to become useful guides for public policy in modern times. Leaping between totally different eras and time zones to cull nuggets of tradition wisdom is, at best, an exercise in futility."

12. Lawrence Rosen, art. "Justice," in *The Oxford Encyclopedia of the Modern Islamic World*, ed. J. L. Esposito (New York: Oxford University Press, 1995), 2:388–91, 391. See also Rosen, *The Anthropology of Justice: Law as Culture in Islamic Society* (Cambridge: Cambridge University Press, 1989); Rosen, "Justice in Islamic Culture and Law," in *Perspectives on Islamic Law, Justice, and Society*, ed. Ravindra S. Khare (Lanham, MD: Rowman & Littlefield, 1999), 33–52; and Rosen, *The Justice of Islam* (New York: Oxford University Press, 2000). Rosen's tendency to generalize on the basis of his Moroccan case studies and to make sweeping statements concerning Arabs and Muslims or Islam, respectively, need not concern us here.

13. For general surveys, see notably Franz Rosenthal, "Political Justice and the Just Ruler," *Israel Oriental Studies* 10 (1982): 92–101; Majid Khadduri, *The Islamic Conception of Justice* (Baltimore: Johns Hopkins University Press, 1984); Fakhry, *Ethical Theories*. There seems to be slightly more on the concept of freedom despite the fact that when trying to translate Western political terms into Arabic, Shaykh Ṭahṭāwī argued that what the French called freedom was known to Muslims as justice or equity (quoted from Bernard Lewis, *The Political Language of Islam* [Chicago: University of Chicago Press, 1988], 143n60). Mohammad Hashim Kamali's approach is particularly relevant here; see his *Freedom of Expression in Islam*, rev. ed. (Cambridge: Islamic Texts Society, 1997); and *The Dignity of Man: An Islamic Perspective* (Cambridge: Islamic Texts Society, 2002).

14. Rosen, art. "Justice," 390; see also Otfried Höffe, *Gerechtigkeit: Eine philosophische Einführung* (Munich: Beck, 2001), 112–13.

15. Rosenthal, "Political Justice," 100, suggests that Muslims were too much aware of "human frailty" and political realities to spend much time and effort on systematic thought, research, and redefinition of justice, which they thought to be attainable only in the age of the *mahdī* and the hereafter. On Miskawayh, see Mohammed Arkoun, *Contribution à l'étude de l'humanisme arabe au IVe/Xe siècle: Miskawayh (320/325–421) = (932/936–1030), philosophe et historien* (Paris: J. Vrin, 1970), esp. 113–14, 292–307; Khadduri, *Islamic Conception of Justice*, chap. 5, esp. 110–13; Fakhry, *Ethical Theories*, chap. 6, esp. 113–15.

16. For studies dealing with different areas and historical periods, see Ann K. S. Lambton, "Justice in the Medieval Persian Theory of Kingship," *Studia Islamica* 17 (1962): 91–119; Lambton, "Changing Concepts of Justice and Injustice from the 5th/11th Century to the 8th/14th Century in Persia: The Saljuq Empire and the Ilkhanate," *Studia Islamica* 68 (1988): 27–60; Azim Nanji, "Between Metaphor and Context: The Nature of the Fāṭimid Ismāʿīlī Discourse on Justice and Injustice," *Arabica* 37 (1990): 234–39; Riḍwān al-Sayyid, "Mas'alat al-ʿadl fī l-fikr al-Islāmī al-ḥadīth wa-l-muʿāṣir," in al-Sayyid, *Siyāsiyyāt al-Islām al-muʿāṣir: murājaʿāt wa-mutābaʿāt* (Beirut: Dār al-Kitāb al-ʿArabī, 1997), 279–97. Boğaç A. Ergene, "On Ottoman Justice: Interpretations in Conflict (1600–1800)," *Islamic Law and Society* 8 (2001): 52–87, is of particular interest here.

17. For case studies analyzing legal practice, ranging from Ottoman Anatolia, Syria, and Palestine to modern Egypt, Yemen, and Malaysia, see Ron Shaham, *Family and the Courts in Modern Egypt: A Study Based on Decisions by the Shari'a Courts, 1900–1955* (Leiden: Brill, 1997); Judith E. Tucker, *In the House of the Law: Gender and Islamic Law in Ottoman Syria and Palestine* (Berkeley: University of California Press, 1998); Anna Würth, *Aš-Šarīʿa fī Bāb al-Yaman: Recht, Richter und Rechtspraxis an der familienrechtlichen Kammer des Gerichts Süd-Sanaa, (Republik Jemen), 1983–1995* (Berlin: Duncker & Humblot, 2000); Michael G. Peletz, *Islamic Modern: Religious Courts and Cultural Politics in Malaysia* (Princeton: Princeton University Press, 2002); Leslie Peirce, *Morality Tales: Law and Gender in the Ottoman Court of Aintab* (Berkeley: University of California Press, 2003). In his study of two courts in seventeenth- and eighteenth-century Ottoman Anatolia, Boğaç A. Ergene focused on social rank and status rather than gender as a major factor in negotiating justice: *Local Court, Provincial Society, and Justice in the Ottoman Empire: Legal Practice and Dispute Resolution in Çankırı and Kastamonu (1652–1744)* (Leiden: Brill, 2003). Uriel Heyd in his classic *Studies in Old Ottoman Criminal Law* (Oxford: Clarendon Press, 1973) already highlighted the relevance of wealth and social status to legal sanctions.

18. For a transcultural comparison that, however, does not include Islam, see Höffe, *Gerechtigkeit*. For Islam, Rosenthal, "Political Justice," and Khadduri, *Islamic Conception of Justice*, provide the broadest overviews.

19. This is obviously not the place to go into Muslim theology and, more specifically, speculations regarding divine justice that excluded the possibility of God acting

unjustly; for first introductions, see Khadduri, *Islamic Conception of Justice*, chap. 3; and Fakhry, *Ethical Theories*, 14–17, 55–58; for greater depth, see A. Kevin Reinhart, *Before Revelation: The Boundaries of Muslim Moral Thought* (Albany: State University of New York Press, 1995).

20. See also Khadduri, *Islamic Conception of Justice*, 7–11. Rosenthal, "Political Justice," 95–96, draws attention to the fact that the Sunna has very little to say on the subject.

21. For a learned exposition of the theory, see Ibrāhīm Āl Sulaymān al-ʿĀmilī, *al-ʿAdāla wa-mawāriduhā: risāla fiqhiyya istidlāliyya* (Beirut: author, 1993).

22. On justice and equity in Islamic legal reasoning, see Hervé Bleuchot, "Les voies de l'équité et le droit musulman," *Droit et Cultures* 38 (1999): 111–35; John Makdisi, "Legal Logic and Equity in Islamic Law," *American Journal of Comparative Law* 33 (1985): 63–92; Kamali, *Principles of Islamic Jurisprudence*, 245–66. Chafik Chehata, "L'équité' en tant que source du droit hanafite," *Studia Islamica* 25 (1966): 123–38, deals with *istiḥsān*, which he defines not as equity, entailing certain knowledge of what is just and good, *ḥasan*, a certainty unobtainable according to most premodern *ʿulamāʾ*, but rather as judicial clemency, *benignitas* or *bonté bienveillante* (137–38). On the question of certainty, see with different evaluations Weiss, *Spirit of Islamic Law*; and Reinhart, *Before Revelation*.

23. Charity and poverty relief are receiving growing attention among Middle Eastern historians; see notably *Pauvreté et richesse dans le monde musulman et méditerranéen / Poverty and Wealth in the Muslim Mediterranean World*, ed. Jean-Paul Pascual (Paris: Maisonneuve & Larose, 2003); *Poverty and Charity in Middle Eastern Contexts*, ed. Michael Bonner, Mine Ener, and Amy Singer (Albany: State University of New York Press, 2003). For almsgiving and the religious endowments, see arts. "zakāt" and "waḳf" in *The Encyclopaedia of Islam*, new ed., 11 vols. (London: Luzac & Co.; Leiden: Brill, 1956–2002). For comparison, see also Mark R. Cohen, *Poverty and Charity in the Jewish Community of Medieval Egypt* (Princeton: Princeton University Press, 2005).

24. For very different perspectives, see Aziz Al-Azmeh, *Muslim Kingship: Power and the Sacred in Muslim, Christian and Pagan Polities* (London: I. B. Tauris, 1997), esp. 87, 128–29; and the Egyptian Muslim Brother ʿAlī Jarīsha, *al-Mashrūʿiyya al-Islāmiyya al-ʿulyā*, 2nd ed. (Cairo: Dār al-Wafāʾ, 1406/1986), esp. 169ff., 177–79.

25. See esp. Izutsu, *Ethico-religious Concepts*; Lewis, *Political Language*; Bleuchot, "Voies," 119; also Khaled Abou El Fadl, *Rebellion and Violence in Islamic Law* (Cambridge: Cambridge University Press, 2001).

26. For a brief introduction, see Azim N. Nanji, "Ethics and Taxation: The Perspective of the Islamic Tradition," *Journal of Religious Ethics* 13 (1985): 161–78. Empirical studies of the scholarly critique of and popular resistance to "unjust" taxation would be required to substantiate the general assumptions concerning notions of justice and oppression in Muslim societies.

27. See, e.g., Mahmoud Ayoub, "The Islamic Concept of Justice," in *Islamic Identity and the Struggle for Justice*, ed. Nimat Hafez Barazangi, M. Raquibuz Zaman, and Omar

Afzal (Gainesville: University Press of Florida, 1996), 19–26, 25; also Lambton, "Changing Concepts"; and Lewis, *Political Language.*

28. See Louis Gardet, art. "fitna," in *The Encyclopaedia of Islam,* new ed. Ahmed as-Sirri, *Religiös-politische Argumentation im frühen Islam (610–685): Der Begriff Fitna; Bedeutung und Funktion* (Frankfurt: Peter Lang, 1990), highlights the many uses and abuses of the concept within the early community.

29. The possibilities of exploiting this approach in order to justify authoritarian rule have been explored by, among others, Lewis, *Political Language.* For a modern Islamist critique, see Jarīsha, *al-Mashrūʿiyya al-Islāmiyya al-ʿulyā,* 170–71.

30. Out of the rich literature on royal justice, see notably Jocelyne Dakhlia, *Le divan des rois: Le politique et le religieux dans l'Islam* (Paris: Aubier, 1998); and Al-Azmeh, *Muslim Kingship*; also Patricia Crone and Martin Hinds, *God's Caliph: Religious Authority in the First Centuries of Islam* (Cambridge: Cambridge University Press, 1986); Lambton, "Changing Concepts"; Roy P. Mottahedeh, *Loyalty and Leadership in an Early Islamic Society* (Princeton: Princeton University Press, 1980), chap. 4; or Khaliq Ahmad Nizami, *Royalty in Medieval India* (New Delhi: Munshiram Manoharlal Publishers, 1997). It should be noted that contrary to what is often said, these were not just pre-Islamic notions, but notions held by contemporaries of the Muslim scholars and bureaucrats who were defining their version of the "circle of justice."

31. On (in)equality, see Louise Marlow, *Hierarchy and Egalitarianism in Islamic Thought* (Cambridge: Cambridge University Press, 1997).

32. Quoted from Rosenthal, "Political Justice," n12; see esp. Mottahedeh, *Loyalty and Leadership,* 178: "An important part of the king's role, therefore, was to keep people in their place." The formula is repeated by the sixteenth-century Ottoman scholar and bureaucrat Muṣṭafā ʿAlī in his *Counsel for Sultans,* quoted from Ergene, "On Ottoman Justice," 75 ("putting things in the places where they belong").

33. Commonly attributed to the Roman jurist Domitius Ulpianus (ca. 170–228), it was included in Justinian's Corpus Iuris Civilis: "Iuris praecepta sunt haec: honeste vivere, alterum non laedere, suum cuique tribuere" (The prescriptions of justice / the law are the following: to live honorably, not to harm others, and to give everyone his or her due). See Höffe, *Gerechtigkeit,* 49–53.

34. This point is emphasized in most studies of conflict resolution in Muslim societies, both within and outside formal courts; see esp. the works of Rosen, Würth, and Peirce; also Heyd, *Studies in Old Ottoman Criminal Law,* esp. 95–103, 179–80, 286–89; Ergene, *Local Court,* esp. 189–211.

35. Ergene ("On Ottoman Justice," 86–87) stresses the fact that the preservation of justice was not necessarily premised on the intervention of the ruler, but that reference to justice as established by Shari'a could equally be used to contest government policies. In neither case did this involve the notion of equality: "For these people [the participants in the 1703 rebellion] justice meant the protection of the legitimate order and the proper

stratification of a society in which the mutual rights and obligations of interacting parties were recognized. Accordingly, political justice had nothing to do with the benevolence of the ruler or the state, but depended upon the acknowledgment of the authority of the holy law and the eminence of the hierarchical social order. The emphasis on the sharia was instrumental in enabling dissidents . . . to approach the sultan as equals under the laws of God, rather than impotent slaves subject to the absolute control of the state."

36. Referring to the (Islamist) jurist Muḥammad Salīm al-ʿAwwā, Farīd ʿAbd al-Khāliq tried to draw a sharp line between *ʿadl* (justice) and *ʿadāla* (moral probity and/or abidance by the law as defined by Islamic *fiqh*) in his *Fī l-fiqh al-siyāsī al-Islāmī: mabādiʾ dustūriyya; al-shūrā, al-ʿadl, al-musāwāt* (Cairo and Beirut: Dār al-Shurūq, 1998), 201; see also al-ʿAwwā, *Fī l-niẓām*, 208n2. For the standard view (Shari'a is justice, *ʿadl*), see Jarīsha, *al-Mashrūʿiyya al-Islāmiyya al-ʿulyā*, 169ff.

37. For a critique of orientalist views that, following Joseph Schacht (see notably his "Zur soziologischen Betrachtung des islamischen Rechts," *Der Islam* 22 [1935]: 207–38), portray Islamic law as being undifferentiated from Islamic ethics, see Baber Johansen, "Die sündige, gesunde Amme: Moral und gesetzliche Bestimmung (*ḥukm*) im islamischen Recht," *Die Welt des Islams* 28 (1988): 264–82; but see also Weiss, *Spirit of Islamic Law*, chap. 7 ("The Moralistic Bent"), esp. 167–71 with n17. Höffe, *Gerechtigkeit*, sees the lack of differentiation as characteristic of all premodern concepts of justice.

38. ʿAbd al-Khāliq, *Fī l-fiqh al-siyāsī*, 195–205, esp. 195, 202. Al-ʿAwwā, whom ʿAbd al-Khāliq repeatedly quotes, offers similar views in much briefer form: *Fī l-niẓām*, 205–10. Like many other Muslim authors, al-ʿAwwā insists on the superior status and quality of justice in Islam compared with any other sociopolitical theory or legacy, Western democracy included.

39. The subject has been exhaustively treated by Michael Cook, *Commanding Right and Forbidding Wrong in Islamic Thought* (Cambridge: Cambridge University Press, 2000); for contemporary Islamist conceptions of its status and meaning, see also Krämer, *Gottes Staat als Republik*.

40. For more detail, see Krämer, *Gottes Staat als Republik*, esp. 54–58.

41. ʿAbd al-Khāliq, *Fī l-fiqh*, 199; al-ʿAwwā, *Fī l-niẓām*, 139–43.

42. Doi, *Sharī'ah*, 2–11; the quotes are from 3 and 5, respectively. The italics are mine.

43. For a strong argument in favor of equality (not just of Muslims, but of all human beings) as a general principle of Islam, see al-ʿAwwā, *Fī l-niẓām*, 226–31. He does not go into the legal status of women, whereas the status of non-Muslims is discussed (in a rather interesting and innovative way) later in the study (246–64); see also the interview with al-ʿAwwā in *al-Munṭalaq*, 1996, 95–102.

44. Doi, *Sharī'ah*, 3. The italics are mine.

45. For non-Muslims, see my *Gottes Staat als Republik*, 162–79; and Gudrun Krämer, "Dhimmi or Citizen? Muslim-Christian Relations in Egypt," in *The Christian-Muslim Frontier: Chaos, Clash or Dialogue?* ed. Jørgen S. Nielsen (London: I. B. Tauris, 1998), 33–49.

46. This is not the place to offer a full discussion of Q 4.3. It is worth quoting, though, for not only does it deal with polygyny within the context of providing for (female) orphans, allowing for the possibility to restrict its normativity by placing it in this specific context only (Asma Barlas, *"Believing Women" in Islam: Unreading Patriarchal Interpretations of the Qur'ān* [Austin: University of Texas Press, 2002], 190–92, presents a perfect example of this kind of reasoning); but it also includes both *ʿadl* and *qisṭ*: "wa-in khiftum allā tuqsiṭū fī l-yatāmā fa-nkiḥū mā ṭāba lakum mina l-nisā'i mathnā wa-thulātha wa-rubāʿa fa-in khiftum allā taʿdilū fa-wāḥidatan." In this context, al-ʿAwwā (*Fī l-niẓām*, 209) refers to the principle of necessity/utility (*lā ḍarar wa-lā ḍirār*, no injury or counterinjury).

47. For a very useful overview of the relevant debates, see Barbara F. Stowasser, *Women in the Qur'ān, Traditions, and Interpretation* (New York: Oxford University Press, 1994); with a different focus, see also *Windows of Faith: Muslim Women Scholar-Activists in North America*, ed. Gisela Webb (Syracuse, NY: Syracuse University Press, 2000); and the critical review by the Egyptian scholar-activist Umayma Abū Bakr, *al-Mar'a wa-l-gender: ilghā' al-tamyīz al-thaqāfī wa-l-ijtimāʿī bayna l-jinsayn*, ed. U. Abū Bakr and S. Shukrī (Damascus and Beirut: Dār al-Fikr, 1423/2002), 11–77; also Nasaruddin Umar, "Gender Biases in Qur'ānic Exegesis: A Study of Scriptural Interpretation from a Gender Perspective," *Hawwa* 2 (2004): 338–62. Amina Wadud, one of the most prominent Muslim American scholars, appears to accept a certain degree of inequality as consistent with justice; see her *Qur'ān and Woman: Rereading the Sacred Text from a Woman's Perspective* (New York: Oxford University Press, 1999), esp. 82–85. Basing herself on Wadud, Asma Barlas, *"Believing Women,"* 190–91, argues in a similar way. For a rather simplistic identification of divine justice with gender equality, see Riffat Hassan, "Challenging the Stereotypes of Fundamentalism: An Islamic Feminist Perspective," *Muslim World* 91 (2001): 55–69; for a scathing attack on (patriarchal) Muslim practices as against Qur'anic teachings, see her "Rights of Women Within Islamic Communities," in *Religious Human Rights in Global Perspective*, ed. Johan D. van der Vyver and John Witte Jr. (The Hague: Martinus Nijhoff Publishers, 1996), 361–86.

48. See Wadud, *Qur'ān and Woman*, 66–74. Barlas, *"Believing Women,"* 184–87, opts for a reading in which men in their capacity as breadwinners are enjoined to protect and maintain women, or at any rate those women who are not economically independent. See also Azizah Yahia Al-Hibri, "Muslim Women's Rights in the Global Village: Challenges and Opportunities," *Journal of Law and Religion* 15 (2000–2001): 37–66, esp. 50–51; or, for an interesting statement by a (male) German Muslim arguing in favor of male protection rather than female subjection, Murad Hofmann, *Der Islam als Alternative* (Munich: Eugen Diederichs, 1993), 36, 163–83.

49. See Wadud, *Qur'ān and Woman*, 74–78; Barlas, *"Believing Women,"* 187–202; also Muḥammad Ṭālibī, *Ummat al-wasaṭ: al-Islām wa-taḥaddiyyāt al-mu'āṣara* (Tunis: Sirās li-l-Nashr, 1996), esp. 115–41.

50. Quote from Barlas, "*Believing Women,*" 188. In this context Abū Bakr's reference to Q 9.71 to emphasize mutual responsibility of men and women for the preservation of Islamic precepts (*wa-l-mu'minūna wa-l-mu'minātu baʿḍuhum awliyā'u baʿḍin*), presupposing female agency, is of particular interest (Abū Bakr, *al-Mar'a wa-l-gender*, 72).

51. See, e.g., Barlas, "*Believing Women,*" 197–200.

52. The *daraja* (step, degree) mentioned in the Qur'anic verse cited.

53. Saʿīd Ramaḍān, *Maʿālim al-ṭarīq* (Cairo: Dār al-Nashr wa-l-Tawzīʿ al-Islāmiyya, 1987), 44.

54. Wadud's translation (*Qur'ān and Woman*, 68) makes the meaning quite clear: "And [(the rights) due to the women are similar to (the rights) against them, (or responsibilities they owe) with regard to] the *maʿrūf*, and men have a degree [*darajah*] above them (feminine plural)." Basing herself on English translations, Barlas, "*Believing Women,*" 195–96, supports Ramaḍān's reading.

55. On this point, see also Tucker, *In the House of the Law*, 37–46; and Bettina Dennerlein, *Islamisches Recht und sozialer Wandel in Algerien: Zur Entwicklung des Personalstatuts seit 1962* (Berlin: Klaus Schwarz, 1998), esp. 202–18, where she elaborates on the specifically modern concept of family on which Algerian legislators based their revised family code. The contributions to *Family History in the Middle East: Household, Property, and Gender*, ed. Beshara Doumani (Albany: State University of New York Press, 2003), illustrate the great variety and variability of family and household patterns in eighteenth- to twentieth-century Middle Eastern societies that the legal and moral discourses I have focused on tend to ignore.

56. Krämer, "Dhimmi or Citizen?" and *Gottes Staat als Republik*, 162–79. For religious discrimination, see the concise statement by Muhammad Asad, *The Principles of State and Government in Islam* (Berkeley: University of California Press, 1961), 40–41.

57. Farhad J. Ziadeh, "Equality (Kafā'ah) in the Muslim Law of Marriage," *American Journal of Comparative Law* 6 (1957): 503–17; for two case studies covering Muslim societies often neglected in theorizing about Islamic law, morals, and social structures, the Western Sahara and Southeast Asia, respectively, see Rainer Oßwald, *Schichtengesellschaft und islamisches Recht: Die Zawāyā und Krieger der Westsahara im Spiegel von Rechtsgutachten des 16–19. Jahrhunderts* (Wiesbaden: Harrassowitz, 1993); and Engseng Ho, "Le don précieux de la généalogie," in *Emirs et présidents: Figures de la parenté et du politique dans le monde arabe*, ed. Pierre Bonte, Édouard Conte, and Paul Dresch (Paris: CNRS, 2001), 79–110; for modern legislation, see *Islamic Family Law in a Changing World: A Global Resource Book*, ed. Abdullahi A. An-Na'im (London: Zed Books, 2002); for legal practice, see the studies by Tucker, Würth, and Peirce. Regulations regarding blood money, *diya*, could provide an equally rewarding field of investigation.

58. As far as I am aware, the best introduction, covering classical definitions, as well as modern controversies and practical experiments in "applying" *zakāt* in contemporary Egypt and Pakistan, is Olaf Farschid, "Islamische Ökonomik und Zakāt" (Ph.D. diss.,

Free University of Berlin, 1999), which also provides useful information on the discursive community of "Islamic economists," who, incidentally, seem to be all male; I have not been able to identify a single female participant. See also art. "*zakāt*" in *The Encyclopaedia of Islam*, new ed.

59. For a highly critical assessment, see Timur Kuran, "On the Notion of Economic Justice in Contemporary Islamic Thought," *International Journal of Middle East Studies* 21 (1989): 171–91; on Quṭb, see William E. Shepard, *Sayyid Qutb and Islamic Activism: A Translation and Critical Analysis of Social Justice in Islam* (Leiden: Brill, 1996); on Bāqir al-Ṣadr, see Chibli Mallat, *The Renewal of Islamic Law* (Cambridge: Cambridge University Press, 1993); for private enterprises, see, e.g., Steffen Wippel, *Islamische Wirtschafts- und Wohlfahrtseinrichtungen in Ägypten zwischen Markt und Moral* (Münster: Lit, 1996).

60. See notably Asghar Schirazi, *The Problem of the Land Reform in the Islamic Republic of Iran: Complications and Consequences of an Islamic Reform Policy* (Berlin: Der Arabische Buch, 1987).

61. *Studies in Islamic Economics*, ed. Khurshid Ahmad (Leicester: Islamic Foundation, 1400/1980), is, I think, representative of this search for an Islamic moral economy or Islamic moral economics; see also Farschid, "Islamische Ökonomik," 135–75.

62. See the discussion in Farschid, "Islamische Ökonomik," 147–53 and 177–85.

63. See notably Naqvi, *Perspectives on Morality and Human Well-Being*; for an evaluation of his earlier work, see Farschid, "Islamische Ökonomik," 137–40.

64. Khurshid Ahmad, introduction to Naqvi, *Perspectives on Morality and Human Well-Being*, xiii. Ahmad's critique of what he believes are Muʿtazilite influences on Naqvi (xii) merits special attention: it is not based on any intrinsic weakness of Muʿtazilite thinking, but on its extrinsic source of inspiration: Greek philosophy. For him, that is enough to disqualify Muʿtazilite ideas as a basis for reconstructing Islamic thought that is fully authentic and for that very reason acceptable to the Muslim masses.

65. The influential scholar Fazlur Rahman provides a prime example of this approach; see notably his "Islamic Modernism: Its Scope, Method and Alternatives," *International Journal of Middle East Studies* 1 (1970): 317–33. The debate on polygyny is a case in point.

66. In modern times *ijtihād* has almost universally come to be seen in such a positive light that it may be necessary to point to the "social logic" of *taqlīd*, which, at least in the legal sphere, served the important function of securing predictability of procedure and outcome; see Mohammad Fadel, "The Social Logic of *Taqlīd* and the Rise of the *Mukhataṣar* [*sic*]," *Islamic Law and Society* 3 (1996): 193–233.

Chapter 3

1. Emilio Platti, "La théologie de Abū l-Aʿlā Mawdūdī," in *Philosophy and Arts in the Islamic World: Proceedings of the Eighteenth Congress of the Union Européenne des Arabisants et Islamisants*, ed. U. Vermeulen and D. De Smet (Leuven: Peeters, 1998), 242–51.

2. Abū l-Aʿlā Mawdūdī, *The Islamic Way of Life* (Islām ka-niẓām-i ḥayāt), trans. and ed. K. Ahmad and K. Murad (Leicester: Islamic Foundation, 1986). The book consists of a series of radio talks Mawdūdī gave in 1948.

3. Abū l-Aʿlā Mawdūdī, *The Islamic Law and Constitution*, 2nd ed. (Lahore: Islamic Publications, 1960). The book is a collection from Mawdūdī's papers and speeches during the 1950s, gathered, edited, and translated into English by Khurshīd Aḥmad in collaboration with Mawdūdī. Platti refers to the paper "The Role of Ijtihad and Scope of Legislation in Islam" given at a conference in Lahore in 1958.

4. Mawdūdī, *Islamic Law and Constitution*, 75. On Mawdūdī's holistic understanding of Islam as absolute obedience to God, see Seyyid V. Reza Nasr, *Mawdudi and the Making of Islamic Revivalism* (New York: Oxford University Press, 1996), 57–63.

5. "Ce fut l'obstacle majeur à ce qu'il devienne réellement un théologien innovateur efficace et non pas la source d'un fondamentalisme aberrant." Platti, "Théologie de Abū l-Aʿlā Mawdūdī," 249.

6. William E. Shepard, "Islam as a 'System' in the Later Writings of Sayyid Qutb," *Middle Eastern Studies* 25 (1989): 31–50.

7. On Mawdūdī's influence on Sayyid Quṭb, see William E. Shepard, *Sayyid Qutb and Islamic Activism* (Leiden: Brill, 1996), xxv–xxvi; Emmanuel Sivan, *Radical Islam*, 2nd ed. (New Haven: Yale University Press, 1990), 22–23; Gudrun Krämer, *Gottes Staat als Republik: Reflexionen zeitgenössischer Muslime zu Islam, Menschenrechten und Demokratie* (Baden-Baden: Nomos, 1999), 218–19; Olivier Carré, *Mystique et politique: Lecture révolutionnaire du Coran par Sayyid Quṭb, frère musulman radical* (Paris: Les editions du Cerf, 1984), 35–36; expanded English translation by C. Artigues, *Mysticism and Politics: A Critical Reading of Fī Ẓilāl al-Qur'ān* (Leiden: Brill, 2003), 25.

8. "We hold these truths to be self-evident, that all men are created equal, that they are endowed by their Creator with certain unalienable Rights, that among these are Life, Liberty and the Pursuit of Happiness."

9. E. Wolf, R. Specht, A. Hügli, R. Ruzicka, and K. Kühl, "Naturrecht," in *Historisches Wörterbuch der Philosophie*, ed. J. Ritter and K. Gründer, 12 vols. (Basel: Schwabe & Co., 1971–), 6:559–623.

10. Aristotle, *Nicomachean Ethics*, V.7, 1134b 18.

11. *Thesaurus linguae Latinae* (Leipzig: B. G. Teubner, 1900–), 10.2:90–91 sub "positivum."

12. Helmut Koester, "NOMOS PHYSEOS: The Concept of Natural Law in Greek Thought," in *Religions in Antiquity: Essays in Memory of Erwin Ramsdell Goodenough*, ed. J. Neusner (Leiden: Brill, 1968), 521–41, 526. See also Plato, *Laws*, X, 890d, where laws are derived "from nature, or from something which is no less than nature, in as such as they are products of rightful thinking (*gennemata kata logon orthon*)."

13. Aristotle, *Politics*, I.4, 1253b 14–15; I.5, 1254b 18–20.

14. Ibid., I.3, 1253b 20.

15. Philo of Alexandria, *De opificio mundi*, 3; *Questiones et solutiones in Exodum* II, 42; *De specialibus legibus* II, 129. See Markus Bockmuehl, "Natural Law in Second Temple Judaism," *Vetus Testamentum* 45 (1995): 17–44, 39ff.; Klaus M. Girardet, "Naturrecht und Naturgesetz: Eine grade Linie von Cicero zu Augustinus?" *Rheinisches Museum für Philologie* 138 (1995): 266–98, 293–98; Harry A. Wolfson, *Philo: Foundations of Religious Philosophy in Judaism, Christianity, and Islam*, 5th ed., 2 vols. (Cambridge, MA: Harvard University Press, 1982), 2:189–94, 304–24, 447–55.

16. On the dispute whether Philo regarded the Torah as a copy of the law of nature or rather as something derived from it, see Valentin Nikiprowetzky, *Le commentaire de l'écriture chez Philon d'Alexandre* (Leiden: Brill, 1977), 117–20. More traditional Jewish theologians held that the ethical rules that existed before God revealed the Torah to Moses went back to seven maxims that Noah received after the Flood and that thus constituted ethical rules for all humankind. See Aaron Lichtenstein, *The Seven Laws of Noah* (New York: Rabbi Jacob Joseph School Press, 1981).

17. Romans 2.14–15.

18. Girardet, "Naturrecht und Naturgesetz," 288ff.

19. Gratian, *Decree* (*Concordia discordantium canonum*), Decretum 1, distinctio 1; English translation by A. Thompson, *The Treatise on Laws (Decretum DD. 1–20)* (Washington, DC: Catholic University of America Press, 1993), 3. The passage in Matthew 7.12 appears within Jesus' Sermon on the Mount and identifies the Golden Rule as the gist of the Torah and the books of the Prophets: "Therefore all things whatsoever ye would that men should do to you, do ye even so to them, for this is the Law and the Prophets." (See also Matthew 22.36–40 and Romans 13.8–10, which identify the imperative to love God and one's neighbor as the gist of the Torah and the Prophets.)

20. Gratian, *Decree*, Decretum 1, distinctio 1.1; English translation, 3–4.

21. Ibid., Decretum 1, distinctio 5; Decretum 1, distinctio 1.7 § 2; English translation, 15–16, 6.

22. *Nomos physeôs* equals *lex naturae/lex naturalis; ius naturale; ius positivum; ius divinum*. The notions of natural law and positive law and their relationship to one another are most prominently introduced in the *Digesta* (50.17.1; I.1.1), a collection of texts on jurisprudence collected from earlier writings under the Roman emperor Justinian (527–565 C.E.). The *Digesta* became part of the Corpus Iuris Civilis or Codex Iustinianus. The authors of the *Digesta* drew on Stoic notions of natural law, particularly those found in the writings of Cicero (106–43 BCE).

23. The word *fiṭra* does not appear in any known testimony of Arabic before the Qur'an. Theodor Nöldeke, *Neue Beiträge zur semitischen Sprachwissenschaft* (Strassburg: Trübner, 1910), 49; and Friedrich Schwally, "Lexikalische Studien," *Zeitschrift der Deutschen Morgenländischen Gesellschaft* 53 (1899): 197–201, 199–201, considered it a loanword from Ethopian meaning "the way and manner of being created." On *fiṭra*, cf. Geneviève Gobillot, *La fiṭra: La conception originelle, ses interpretations et functions chez*

les penseurs musulmans (Damascus: Institut français d'archéologie orientale, 2000); William M. Watt's article, "*Fiṭra*," in *The Encyclopaedia of Islam*, new ed., 11 vols. (London: Luzac & Co.; Leiden: Brill, 1954–2003), 3:165a–166b; and Duncan Black MacDonald's earlier article in *The Encyclopaedia of Islam*, 4 vols. (London: Luzac & Co.; Leiden: Brill, 1913–34), 2:115–116. Abu al-Fazl Ezzati, *Islam and Natural Law* (London: ICAS Press, 2002), 93–109, presents the notion of *fiṭra* from an Islamist perspective.

24. Uri Rubin, art. "Ḥanīf," in *Encyclopaedia of the Qur'ān*, ed. Jane Dammen McAuliffe, 6 vols. (Leiden: Brill, 2001–6), 2:402–4.

25. Arent J. Wensinck, *The Muslim Creed* (Cambridge: Cambridge University Press, 1932), 42–46; Josef van Ess, *Zwischen Ḥadīṯ und Theologie: Studien zum Entstehen prädestinatianischer Überlieferung* (Berlin: Walter de Gruyter, 1975), 101–14.

26. Arent J. Wensinck et al., *Concordance et indices de la tradition musulmane*, 8 vols. (Leiden: Brill, 1936–88), 5:180a.

27. Arabic *wulida ʿalā l-fiṭra.*

28. Gobillot, *La fiṭra*, 14ff.

29. Wensinck, *Muslim Creed*, 214–15; Josef van Ess, *Theologie und Gesellschaft im 2. und 3. Jahrhundert Hidschra: Eine Geschichte des religiösen Denkens im frühen Islam*, 6 vols. (Berlin and New York: de Gruyter, 1991–97), 4:361; A. Kevin Reinhart, *Before Revelation: The Boundaries of Muslim Moral Thought* (Albany: State University of New York Press, 1995), 153–56; Harry A. Wolfson, *The Philosophy of the Kalam* (Cambridge, MA: Harvard University Press, 1976), 616ff.

30. Ess, *Theologie und Gesellschaft*, 2:172, 376–77, 4:361, 566.

31. al-Ashʿarī, *Kitāb al-Lumaʿ*, ed. R. McCarthy (Beirut: Imprimerie Catholique, 1953), § 170; Ibn Fūrāq, *Mujarrad maqālāt al-Ashʿarī*, ed. D. Gimaret (Beirut: Librairie Orientale, 1987), 15.5–7; Reinhart, *Before Revelation*, 63.

32. Richard M. Frank, "Moral Obligations in Classical Muslim Theology," *Journal of Religious Ethics* 11 (1983): 205–23, 207–10.

33. The Ashʿarite theologian al-Juwaynī (d. 1085) was very explicit about this in his *al-Irshād ilā qawāṭiʿ al-adilla fī uṣūl al-iʿtiqād*, ed. M. Y. Mūsā and ʿA. ʿA. ʿAbd al-Ḥamīd (Cairo: Maktabat al-Khānjī, 1369/1950), 258; English translation by P. E. Walker, *A Guide to Conclusive Proofs for the Principles of Belief* (Reading: Garnet Publishing, 2000), 140.

34. George F. Hourani, "Juwaynī's Criticism of Muʿtazilite Ethics," *Muslim World* 65 (1975): 161–73, reprinted in Hourani, *Reason and Tradition in Islamic Ethics* (Cambridge: Cambridge University Press, 1985), 124–34; Reinhart, *Before Revelation*, 68.

35. al-Juwaynī, *al-Irshād*, 304; English translation, 165–66.

36. On the philosophical understanding of *fiṭra*, see Gobillot, *Fiṭra*, 118–25; on Ibn Sīnā's understanding, see his *Livre de definitions*, ed. and trans. A. M. Goichon (Cairo: Publications de l'IFAOC, 1963), 11/13. (This passage is copied by al-Ghazālī, *Miʿyār al-ʿilm fī fann al-manṭiq*, ed. M. Ṣabrī al-Kurdī, 2nd ed. [Cairo: al-Maṭbaʿa al-ʿArabiyya, 1346/1927], 183.) On Ibn Sīnā, see also Amélie Marie Goichon, *Lexique de la langue*

philosophique d'Ibn Sīnā (Avicenne) (Paris: Desclée de Brouwer, 1938), 274–76. On Ibn Sīnā's identification of *fiṭra* and *ḥads* ("intuition"), see Dimitri Gutas, *Avicenna and the Aristotelian Tradition* (Leiden: Brill, 1988), 170.

37. "Every human is originally created with (*fuṭira ʿalā*) the belief in the one God." al-Ghazālī, *Iḥyā ʿulūm al-din,* 4 vols. (Cairo: M. al-Bābī al-Ḥalabī wa-Awlādihi, 1346 [1927–28]), 1:77 (I.6.2).

38. Ibid.; see also al-Ghazālī, *Al-Munqidh min al-ḍalāl / Erreur et délivrance*, ed. and trans. F. Jabre, 3rd ed. (Beirut: Commission libanaise pour la traduction des chefs-d'oeuvre, 1969), 10–11; English translation by R. J. McCarthy, *Deliverance from Error* (Louisville: Fons Vitae, 2000), 55.

39. al-Ghazālī, *al-Iqtiṣād fī l-iʿtiqād*, ed. H. Atay and I. A. Çubukçu (Ankara: Nur Matbaasi, 1962), 24–35.

40. al-Ghazālī, *al-Mustaṣfā min ʿilm al-uṣūl*, 2 vols. (Būlāq: al-Maṭbaʿa al-Amīriyya, 1322–24 [1904–6]), 1:5–7.

41. George F. Hourani, "Ghazālī on the Ethics of Action," *Journal of the American Oriental Society* 96 (1976): 69–88 (reprinted in Hourani, *Reason and Tradition in Islamic Ethics*, 135–66); Reinhart, *Before Revelation*, 70–75.

42. Malcolm Kerr, *Islamic Reform: The Political and Legal Theories of Muḥammad ʿAbduh and Rashīd Riḍā* (Berkeley: University of California Press, 1966), 58–60, points to another reason why Ashʿarites have not developed the notion of natural law, namely, their occasionalism. This, however, is not convincing. The distinction of whether the laws of nature are "God's customs" or necessary by themselves need not play a role in the acknowledgment of their existence (see the section "Natural Law and the Law of Nature," earlier in this chapter). This point is implicitly accepted by Kerr in his analysis of Muḥammad ʿAbduh's position (*Islamic Reform*, 119–21).

43. Ibn Taymiyya, *Dar' taʿāruḍ al-ʿaql wa-l-naql,* ed. M. Rashād Sālim, 11 vols. (Beirut: Dār al-Kunūz al-Adabiyya, n.d.), 8:382–90, 444–48, 463–64. See Yasien Mohamed, *Fitrah: The Islamic Concept of Human Nature* (London: Ta Ha Publishers, 1416/1996), 41–44.

44. Ibn Taymiyya, *Dar' taʿāruḍ al-ʿaql wa-l-naql*, 8:383–84.

45. Ibid., 385.

46. Ibid., 445–46; see also 463.

47. al-Bājūrī (also known as al-Bayjūrī), *Sharḥ Jawharat al-tawḥīd al-musammā Tuhfat al-murīd* (Beirut: Dār al-Kutub al-ʿIlmiyya, 1416/1995), 30–31. The book is a commentary on the popular didactic poem *Jawharat al-tawḥīd* (The Essence of the Tawḥīd) by one of al-Bājūrī's predecessors at al-Azhar, Ibrāhīm al-Lāqānī (d. 1631).

48. See Sayyid Quṭb's own account in his autobiography *Ṭifl min al-qarya* (Child from a Village) (Cologne: Al-Kamel, 1999), 18–19. The book was first published in 1946.

49. The articles appeared in the weekly journal *al-Risāla* between November 1951 and November 1952 and are reprinted in Ṣalāḥ ʿAbd al-Fatāḥ al-Khālidī, *Amrīkā min al-dākhil bi-manẓūr Sayyid Quṭb*, 2nd ed. (Jeddah: Dār al-Manār, 1406/1986), 93–147; English trans-

lation *America in an Arab Mirror: Images of America in Arabic Travel Literature; An Anthology, 1895–1995*, ed. K. Abdel-Malek (New York: St. Martin's Press, 2000), 9–27.

50. On Sayyid Quṭb's life, see Shahrough Akhavi's article in *The Oxford Encyclopedia of the Modern Islamic World*, ed. J. L. Esposito (New York: Oxford University Press, 1995), 3:400–404; and Shepard, *Sayyid Qutb and Islamic Activism*, xi–xxiii. For a bibliography of Sayyid Quṭb's works, see Shepard, 357–58.

51. Muḥammad ʿAbduh, *Risālat al-Tawḥīd*, in *al-Aʿmāl al-kāmila li-l-imam Muḥammad ʿAbduh*, ed. M. ʿAmāra, 6 vols. (Beirut: al-Mu'assasa al-ʿArabiyya li-l-Dirāsat wa-l-Nashr, 1972–74), 3:353–483, 390–99; English translation *The Theology of Unity*, trans. I. Musaʿad and K. Cragg (London: Allen & Unwin, 1966), 66–76; Kerr, *Islamic Reform*, 108, 121, 123–25.

52. See the review of the contributions in this direction in Thomas Hildebrandt, "Waren Ğamāl ad-Dīn al-Afġānī und Muḥammad ʿAbduh Neo-Muʿtaziliten?" *Welt des Islams* 42 (2002): 207–62.

53. ʿAbduh, *Risālat al-Tawḥīd*, 403–10; English translation, 80–88.

54. Ibid., 410–14; English translation, 88–93. This analysis runs counter to Malcolm Kerr's analysis of ʿAbduh's teaching (*Islamic Reform*, 126–27). Kerr understood ʿAbduh to express the Māturīdī position that the moral values of human actions are known to humans, but that the obligatory character of the laws is not known without revelation. A close reading of ʿAbduh's *Risāla al-Tawḥīd*, however, reveals that this is not what he teaches.

55. See Ibn Sīnā, *Avicenna's De Anima: Being the Psychological Part of Kitāb al-Shifā'*, ed. F. Rahman (London: Oxford University Press, 1959), 171–78, 248–50. See also Fazlur Rahman, *Prophecy in Islam: Philosophy and Orthodoxy* (London: Allen & Unwin, 1958), 30ff.

56. Sayyid Quṭb, *Fī ẓilāl al-Qur'ān*, 6 vols. (Beirut and Cairo: Dār al-Shurūq, 1493–94/1973–74), 5:2767.

57. The term *nāmūs* is a transliteration of the Greek *nomos*. It entered Arabic with the translation of Greek philosophical literature in the eighth and ninth centuries. In modern Arabic it is used to refer to a secular law that is not based on revelation, while Shari'a refers to divinely revealed law.

58. See also Q 38.71–72: "I am about to create men from clay and when I have formed him and breathed into him of my spirit." Sayyid Quṭb, *Fī ẓilāl al-Qur'ān*, 6:3917.

59. Sayyid Quṭb, *Fī ẓilāl al-Qur'ān*, 6:3917.

60. Ibid.

61. Mohamed, *Fitrah*, 57.

62. Sayyid Quṭb, *Fī ẓilāl al-Qur'ān*, 6:3918.

63. Ibid.

64. Ibid.

65. For Sayyid Quṭb's views on human *fiṭra* and its disposition to let humans be God's viceregents (*khilāfa*) on earth, see William Shepard's translations from *Fī ẓilāl al-Qurʿān*, 4:2296, in Carré, *Mysticism and Politics*, 321–22.

66. This motive in Sayyid Quṭb's anthropology is further developed by his brother Muḥammad in his book *al-Insān bayna l-māddiyya wa-l-Islām*, 4th ed. (Cairo: Dār Iḥyā' al-Kutub al-ʿArabiyya, 1965), esp. 80ff. The book was first published in 1962. English translation by S. A. Kandhlawi, *Islam and the Modern Materialistic Thought* (Delhi: Hindustan Publications, 1985), 94ff. After the second crackdown on the Muslim Brotherhood in 1965, Muḥammad Quṭb left Egypt and eventually became a professor at King ʿAbd al-Azīz University in Jedda, Saudi Arabia. His works are an important supplement to his brother Sayyid's. Muḥammad Quṭb made himself significantly familiar with Western schools of thought such as Marxism and psychoanalytic theory to compare their anthropology with that developed by his brother; see Muḥammad Quṭb, *Dirāsāt fī l-nafs al-insāniyya* (Studies on the Human Soul) (Beirut and Cairo: Dār al-Shurūq, 1394/1974), esp. 211–44 ("al-Dīn wa-l-fiṭra.") See also Muḥammad Quṭb, *Fī l-nafs wa-l-mujtamaʿ* (On the Soul and Society) (Beirut and Cairo: Dār al-Shurūq, 1393/1973).

67. Sayyid Quṭb, *Hādhā l-dīn* (Beirut: Dār al-Shurūq, 1403/1983), 58–78.

68. On Sayyid Quṭb's view about a "Qur'anic emancipation" of women, cf. Carré, *Mystique et politique*, 75–92; expanded English translation, 125–51.

69. Sayyid Qutb, *Fī ẓilāl al-Qur'ān*, 1:576.

70. Ibid., 1:579.

71. Ibid., 1:579–80.

72. Ibid., 1:581.

73. Muḥammad Quṭb, *Shubuhāt ḥawla l-Islām*, 6th ed. (Beirut and Cairo: Dār al-Shurūq, 1393/1973), 110–58. English translation *Islam, the Misunderstood Religion*, 14th ed. (Lahore: Islamic Publications, 1998), 90–132. The English translation first appeared in 1967 in Kuwait, published by the Ministry of Awqaf and Islamic Affairs. All English translations in this chapter are by the author.

74. Ibid., 128; English translation, 107.

75. Sayyid Quṭb, *Maʿālim fī l-ṭarīq* (Cairo: n.p., 1386/1967), 97–104; English translation *Milestones* (Indianapolis: American Trust Publications, 1990), 73–78. The English translations in this chapter are by the author.

76. Ibid., 102; English translation, 76.

77. Ibid.

78. Ibid., 98–99; English translation, 74.

79. Ibid., 99; English translation, 74.

80. Ibid., 100; English translation, 75.

81. Ibid., 101–2; English translation, 75–76.

82. The higher goal (*al-ghāya al-ʿulyā*) of Islam is, in Muḥammad Quṭb's words, the establishment of equilibrium (*tawāzun*) in the soul of the individual, in his society, and in humanity as a whole (*al-Insān bayna l-māddiyya wa-l-Islām*, 81; English translation, 95). On this equilibrium between the known and the unknown and the inner balance of Islam, see Sayyid Quṭb, *Khaṣā'iṣ al-taṣawwur al-Islāmī wa-muqawwimatuhu* (Cairo: ʿĪsā

al-Bābī al-Ḥalabī, 1962), 134–69; English translation by M. M. Siddiqui, *The Islamic Concept and Its Characteristics* (Indianapolis: American Trust Publications, 1991), 109–43.

83. Sayyid Quṭb, *Maʿālim fī l-ṭarīq*, 97; English translation, 73.

84. For a programmatic treatment of the notion of natural law from an Islamist perspective, including a history of natural law in the Western tradition, see Ezzati, *Islam and Natural Law*, esp. 60–92.

85. Mawdūdī, *Islamic Way of Life*, 17.

86. Ibid.

87. For Mawdūdī, see *Islamic Way of Life*, 21: "A moral sense is inborn in man and, through the ages, it has served as the common man's standard of moral behavior." For Ibn Taymiyya, see *Darʾ taʿāruḍ al-ʿaql wa-l-naql*, 8: 445–46, where human *fiṭra* includes four elements: the faculty to lean toward knowledge and belief, the capacity to receive the judgments of what are good actions, the "state of readiness" (*istiʿdād*) to do good, and the capacity (*ṣalāḥiyya*) to do so.

88. Sayyid Quṭb, *Maʿālim fī l-ṭarīq*, 102; English translation, 77.

89. Mawdūdī, *Islamic Law and Constitution*, 75.

90. Abū l-Aʿlā Mawdūdī, *Fī maḥkamat al-ʿaql* (Cairo: Dār al-Sharq al-Awsaṭ, 1980), 57. This short pamphlet contains Arabic translations of speeches and radio addresses by Mawdūdī on the subject of human rationalism and its relationship to Shari'a. The notions expressed in these texts show an influence from Ashʿarite theology that is not present in Sayyid Quṭb. This particular passage is from a radio address in Lahore in November 1943.

91. Sayyid Quṭb, *Maʿālim fī l-ṭarīq*, 102; English translation, 77.

92. Sayyid Quṭb, *Fī ẓilāl al-Qur'ān*, 2:806. On this relationship between reason and revelation in Sayyid Quṭb, see Ibrahim M. Abu-Rabiʿ, *Intellectual Origins of Islamic Resurgence in the Modern Arab World* (Albany: State University of New York Press, 1996), 191–92.

93. See, for instance, Muḥammad Quṭb's attempt to legitimize Shari'a's prescription of capital punishment for apostasy from Islam as a ruling necessary for the benefit of all societies, not only those with a majority of Muslims, in *al-Insān bayna l-māddiyya wa-l-Islām*, 194–96; English translation, 223–25.

94. Sivan, *Radical Islam*, 67.

Chapter 4

I want to thank Frank Griffel and Ahmad Dallal for their careful reading of earlier drafts of this chapter. Their valuable comments and my husband Joseph's gentle rephrasing of German-style sentences into readable English contributed in no small manner to this chapter.

1. See Daniel Brown, *Rethinking Tradition in Modern Islamic Thought* (Cambridge: Cambridge University Press, 1996), 122.

2. See John L. Esposito and John O. Voll, *Makers of Contemporary Islam* (New York: Oxford University Press, 2001), 192.

3. *Maṣlaḥa*, in my view, should be translated as "public interest" only when it refers to the permissibility of the political authorities to issue rulings that concur with the public good within the sphere of governance (*siyāsa*). When, however, a *muftī* gives a legal opinion on the grounds of *maṣlaḥa*, this has little to do with "public" well-being and is primarily based on considerations of a single, private case.

4. I address the historical and personal circumstances influencing the interpretation of *maṣlaḥa* only for jurists of the modern period. The interpretation of *maṣlaḥa* by jurists from the eleventh to the fourteenth century depended additionally on intellectual developments in legal logic and epistemology. Taking these developments into account warrants more space than is available in this chapter.

5. The potential for legislative revision does not necessarily mean that the law itself undergoes much change. For example, despite more than ten thousand proposals for amending the U.S. Constitution, only twenty-seven amendments have been ratified in its two-hundred-year history.

6. Because in this chapter I am not concerned with the development of Sunna and the *ḥadīth*, I treat Sunna as a body of textual material and consider it, together with the Qur'an, as scripture.

7. I follow Hourani, who called the approach of these two groups toward ethical knowledge rationalistic objectivism and theistic subjectivism; George F. Hourani, *Islamic Rationalism: The Ethics of ʿAbd al-Jabbār* (Oxford: Clarendon Press, 1971), 3, 8–13.

8. Ibid., 69–75, 104–15, 121–25; A. Kevin Reinhart, *Before Revelation: The Boundaries of Muslim Moral Thought* (Albany: State University of New York Press, 1995), 38–61. The terms scholars used to describe benefit and similar meanings are *nafʿ*, *manfaʿa*, *ṣalāḥ*, and *maṣlaḥa*, and for harm *ḍarra*, *maḍarra*, and *mafsada*.

9. It needs to be noted that the Ashʿarite position of theistic subjectivism had developed before al-Ashʿarī (d. 935) and in its essence was held by such jurists as al-Shāfiʿī (d. 820) and Ahmad ibn Ḥanbal (d. 855) (cf. Hourani, *Islamic Rationalism*, 3, 9–12). Likewise, rationalistic objectivism was not advocated only by people who would be counted among Muʿtazilite theologians. Ibn al-Muqaffaʿ (d. 756), the advisor to the caliph al-Manṣūr, espoused similar ideas (cf. ʿAbd Allāh Ibn al-Muqaffaʿ, "Risāla fī l-ṣaḥāba," in *Āthār Ibn al-Muqaffaʿ*, ed. ʿUmar Abū l-Naṣr [Beirut: Dār Maktabat al-Ḥayāt, 1966], 348–49, 354–55, 360). And some Muʿtazilite theologians, such as Abū l-Qāsim al-Balkhī al-Kaʿbī (d. 931), held views on moral knowledge that were close to al-Ashʿarī's (cf. Reinhart, *Before Revelation*, 14–27, 31–32).

10. Reinhart, *Before Revelation*, 62–76.

11. See Hourani, *Islamic Rationalism*, 132–37.

12. The Ẓāhirī school of law is an example of an extreme theistic subjectivism. The Ẓāhirīs accepted as valid only rulings directly derived from the manifest meaning of the

Qur'an and Sunna, rejecting legal analogy, as well as other methods of law-finding. The inability to deliver solutions to unprecedented situations resulted ultimately in their disappearance.

13. Reinhart attributes the triumph of Ashʿarism also to demographic changes; Muslims were no longer the minority in the lands under Islamic rule but had become the majority. The success of the Islamic civilization resulted in emphasizing its historical uniqueness and stressing revelation as the only standard of authority (Reinhart, *Before Revelation*, 177–82).

14. Although claims that rulings are only valid when they are derived from scripture had been voiced by jurists since at least the early ninth century (e.g., al-Shāfiʿī and Ibn Ḥanbal), it was not until the tenth and especially the eleventh century that these demands were conceptualized into a coherent legal theory; see Wael B. Hallaq, *A History of Islamic Legal Theories* (Cambridge: Cambridge University Press, 1997), 29–37; Reinhart, *Before Revelation*, 14–30.

15. For a detailed analysis of the development of *maṣlaḥa* in Islamic legal theory from the tenth to the late fourteenth century, see Felicitas Opwis, "Maṣlaḥa: An Intellectual History of a Core Concept in Islamic Legal Theory" (Ph.D. diss., Yale University, 2001).

16. The technical term used in these legal writings was usually *istiḥsān*, not *maṣlaḥa*. See, e.g., Sahnūn ibn Saʿīd, *al-Mudawwana al-kubrā*, 16 pts. in 8 vols. (Cairo: Maṭbaʿat al-Saʿāda, 1323/1904–5), pts. 14:134, 16:217. Ibn al-Muqaffaʿ, in his advice to the caliph al-Manṣūr, used the verb *istaṣlaḥa* to describe how jurists should decide people's affairs when no textual ruling existed (Ibn al-Muqaffaʿ, "Risāla fī l-ṣaḥāba," 360).

17. See Aḥmad ibn ʿAlī al-Jaṣṣāṣ, *al-Fuṣūl fī l-uṣūl* (Lahore: al-Maktaba al-ʿIlmiyya, 1981), 133–35.

18. al-Ghazālī, *al-Mustaṣfā min ʿilm al-uṣūl*, 4 vols. (Jedda: Sharikat al-Madīna al-Munawwara, n.d. [1993]), 2:481–82. Al-Ghazālī's concept and definition of *maṣlaḥa* may have been influenced by Muʿtazilite theories that established beneficence as a criterion for recognizing good and for imposing obligation; see Hourani, *Islamic Rationalism*, 121–26; Robert Brunschvig, "Muʿtazilisme et Optimum (al-aṣlaḥ)," *Studia Islamica* 39 (1974): 5–23, 15. Whether there was such a connection needs further investigation.

19. al-Ghazālī, *al-Mustaṣfā*, 2:488.

20. al-Ghazālī, *Shifāʾ al-ghalīl* (Baghdad: Maṭbaʿat al-Irshād, 1390/1971), 146; Fakhr al-Dīn al-Rāzī, *al-Maḥṣūl fī ʿilm uṣūl al-fiqh*, 2 vols. (Beirut: Dār al-Kutub al-ʿIlmiyya, 1408/1988), 2:139–40.

21. See al-Rāzī, *al-Maḥṣūl*, 2:324–25.

22. al-Ghazālī, *al-Mustaṣfā*, 2:502–3.

23. Ibid., 3:620–33; al-Ghazālī, *Shifāʾ al-ghalīl*, 146–94.

24. al-Ghazālī, *al-Mustaṣfā*, 2:487, 489.

25. See al-Rāzī, *al-Maḥṣūl*, 2:327–32.

26. See ibid., 2:319–27; 2:385–92; 2:480–82; 2:578–81.

27. al-Ghazālī, *al-Mustaṣfā* 2:488. Al-Ghazālī's restrictions on using *maṣlaḥa* to derive laws were not always consistent. Although he clearly stated that a legally valid *maṣlaḥa* had to be certain and universal and refer to one of the five essential elements of human existence, his examples for such cases in *al-Mustaṣfā* and *Shifā' al-ghalīl* do not always fulfill these stipulations. The inconsistency may be resolved by looking at whether *maṣlaḥa* is used to extend or adapt the law. In the example of the Muslim prisoners, in which the ruling based on an unattested *maṣlaḥa* contradicts a clear Qur'anic injunction, al-Ghazālī's conditions were met, and the existing law was adapted. In contrast, al-Ghazālī's rationalization for the *ḥadd* punishment of eighty lashes for drinking wine on account of *maṣlaḥa* is a case of finding a ruling about which the scripture is silent. In this example of extending the law, al-Ghazālī considered the ruling valid despite the fact that the conditions of universality and certainty were not fulfilled (cf. ibid., 2:488; al-Ghazālī, *Shifā' al-ghalīl*, 212–18).

28. See al-Qarāfī, *al-Dhakhīra* (Cairo: Maṭbaʿat Kulliyyāt al-Sharīfa, 1381/1961), 1:119–30; al-Qarāfī, *Sharḥ Tanqīḥ al-fuṣūl fī khtiṣār al-Maḥṣūl fī l-uṣūl* (Cairo: Dār al-Fikr, 1393/1973), 383–94.

29. See al-Qarāfī, *al-Dhakhīra*, 1:127, 144–46; al-Qarāfī, *al-Furūq wa-bi-hāmish al-Kitābayn Tahdhīb al-furūq wa-l-Qawāʿid al-saniyya fī l-asrār al-fiqhiyya*, 4 pts. in 2 vols. (Beirut: ʿĀlam al-Kutub, n.d.), 2:32–34; idem, *Sharḥ Tanqīḥ*, 85–87, 415–16, 448–50. It should be noted that al-Rāzī, whose model of *maṣlaḥa* al-Qarāfī otherwise adopted, did not explain legal licenses in terms of *maṣlaḥa*.

30. See Muṣṭafā Zayd, *al-Maṣlaḥa fī l-tashrīʿ al-Islāmī wa-Najm al-Dīn al-Ṭūfī*, 2nd ed. (Cairo: Dār al-Fikr al-ʿArabī, 1384/1964), 206–17. Zayd critically edited al-Ṭūfī's commentary on the *ḥadīth* "lā ḍarar wa-lā ḍirār," which contains his theory of *maṣlaḥa* (ibid., 206–40).

31. Ibid., 231.

32. Ibid., 210, 232–38.

33. Ibrāhīm ibn Mūsā al-Shāṭibī, *al-Muwāfaqāt fī uṣūl al-sharīʿa*, 4 vols. (Cairo: Dār al-Fikr al-ʿArabī, n.d.), 3:366–68, 3:406, 4:20–22.

34. Ibid., 1:34–41.

35. Ibid., 1:29–31, 3:15–17.

36. Ibid., 1:39–40, 2:283–86, 2:297–98, 3:77.

37. Ibid., 4:194–95.

38. Ibid., 3:9–13, 3:17–18, 3:261–62, 4:299–302.

39. Al-Shāṭibī argued that acts for which no textual ruling existed but that were likely to have occurred during the lifetime of the Prophet Muhammad were legally treated as acts for which no ruling was intended. For example, to abstain from talking during the fast constituted, in al-Shāṭibī's eyes, a prohibited innovation since the Prophet himself had made no indication about that practice whatsoever, nor did the early community agree upon it (ibid., 2:410–13).

40. Ibid., 2:396, 2:409–12, 3:56, 3:64–70, 3:74.

41. Ibid., 2:284–85, 297–98.

42. It should be mentioned that al-Shāṭibī's understanding of the relationship between the early and later revelations, in association with his postulate that a universal or general law prevailed over a particular or specific law, differed from the traditional concept of the revelation and the strength of legal indicants.

43. See Opwis, "Maṣlaḥa," 158–60, 246–50, 340–52; Wael Hallaq, "On Inductive Corroboration, Probability and Certainty in Sunnī Legal Thought," in *Islamic Law and Jurisprudence*, ed. N. L. Heer (Seattle: University of Washington Press, 1990), 3–31; Bernard Weiss, "Knowledge of the Past: The Theory of Tawātur According to Ghazālī," *Studia Islamica* 61 (1985): 81–105.

44. See Opwis, "Maṣlaḥa," 194–95; Muhammad Khalid Masud, *Islamic Legal Philosophy: A Study of Abū Isḥāq al-Shāṭibī's Life and Thought* (Delhi: International Islamic Publishers, 1989), 103–5, 322–26.

45. For an analysis of al-Qāsimī's life and thought, see David Dean Commins, *Islamic Reform: Politics and Social Change in Late Ottoman Syria* (New York: Oxford University Press, 1990).

46. On Muḥammad Rashīd Riḍā's political and legal thought, as well as his life, see Malcolm H. Kerr, *Islamic Reform: The Political and Legal Theories of Muḥammad ʿAbduh and Rashīd Riḍā* (Berkeley: University of California Press, 1966), esp. 153–223.

47. See Commins, *Islamic Reform*, 112–13; Malcolm Kerr, "Rashīd Riḍā and Islamic Legal Reform: An Ideological Analysis," *Muslim World* 50 (1960): 99–108, 170–81, 108, 171, 179; Kerr, *Islamic Reform*, 55, 198–99; Muḥammad Rashīd Riḍā, "al-Muḥāwarāt bayna l-muṣliḥ wa-l-muqallid," *al-Manār* 4 (1318–19/1901–2): 859; "Bāb Uṣūl al-fiqh," *al-Manār* 9 (1324/1906): 745–46, 753n1, 768n1; Muḥammad Rashīd Riḍā, *Yusr al-Islām wa-uṣūl al-tashrīʿ al-ʿāmm* (Cairo: Maktabat al-Salām al-ʿĀlamiyya, 1984), 145–46, 151–52, 159. Both al-Qāsimī and Rashīd Riḍā were familiar with the other models of *maṣlaḥa* (see Commins, *Islamic Reform*, 171n33; al-Qāsimī's notes in his edition of al-Ṭūfī's treatise on *maṣlaḥa* in *al-Manār*, 9 [1324/1906], 746–70; Rashīd Riḍā, *Yusr al-Islām*, 141–52). Al-Shāṭibī's influence on Rashīd Riḍā's conception of *maṣlaḥa* is evident in his work *Yusr al-Islām* (145–46, 157).

48. Commins, *Islamic Reform*, 12–20; Kerr, "Rashīd Riḍā," 170.

49. Commins, *Islamic Reform*, 29, 32, 48, 66–68; Kerr, "Rashīd Riḍā," 104, 170, 180; Kerr, *Islamic Reform*, 55.

50. See Commins, *Islamic Reform*, 32–33, 48, 65–67; Kerr, *Islamic Reform*, 107, 157; Rashīd Riḍā, "al-Muḥāwarāt," 216; Rashīd Riḍā, *Yusr al-Islām*, 147.

51. See Commins, *Islamic Reform*, 71; Kerr, *Islamic Reform*, 17; Rashīd Riḍā, "al-Muḥāwarāt," 861; Rashīd Riḍā, *Yusr al-Islām*, 16–19, 50, 153.

52. Mazheruddin Siddiqi, *Modern Reformist Thought in the Muslim World* (Islamabad, Pakistan: Islamic Research Institute, 1982), 74–75.

53. Rashīd Riḍā, "al-Muḥāwarāt," 866.

54. Commins, *Islamic Reform*, 65, 69, 71–73; Kerr, "Rashīd Riḍā," 107–8; Rudolph Peters, "Idjtihād and Taqlīd in 18th and 19th Century Islam," *Die Welt des Islams* 20 (1980): 131–44, 141; Siddiqi, *Modern Reformist Thought*, 75.

55. Commins, *Islamic Reform*, 44–45; Kerr, *Islamic Reform*, 207.

56. See Kerr, "Rashīd Riḍā," 108, 173–74; Kerr, *Islamic Reform*, 155, 165, 183, 187, 189–90, 197–99, 202–3; Rashīd Riḍā, "al-Muḥāwarāt," 859, 866; Rashīd Riḍā, *Yusr al-Islām*, 46, 48, 83, 91, 153, 159–60.

57. See Commins, *Islamic Reform*, 48, 66, 69, 78, 142.

58. See Wolfhart Heinrichs, " Ǧadal bei aṭ-Ṭūfī: Eine Interpretation seiner Beispielsammlung," in *ZDMG Supplement III/19: Deutscher Orientalistentag 1975*, ed. Wolfgang Voigt, 2 vols. (Wiesbaden: Steiner, 1977), 1:463–73, 468–69; Zayd, *al-Maṣlaḥa*, 215, 226–32.

59. See Commins, *Islamic Reform*, 65–73, 141; Rashīd Riḍā, *Yusr al-Islām*, 159.

60. Rashīd Riḍā, "al-Muḥāwarāt," 205.

61. Commins, *Islamic Reform*, 69.

62. See ibid., 65–66, 69, 141–42; Ahmad Dallal, "Appropriating the Past: Twentieth-Century Reconstruction of Pre-modern Islamic Thought," *Islamic Law and Society* 7 (2000): 333–42, 335–36, 357; Rashīd Riḍā, *Yusr al-Islām*, 159.

63. See Badrān Abū l-ʿAynayn Badrān, *Uṣūl al-fiqh al-Islāmī* (Alexandria: Mu'assasat Shabāb al-Jāmiʿa, 1984), 213; Jallāl al-Dīn ʿAbd al-Raḥmān Jallāl, *al-Maṣāliḥ al-mursala wa-makānatuhā fi-l-tashrīʿ* (Cairo: Maṭbaʿat al-Saʿāda, 1403/1983), 57, 64, 67, 95–96; Kerr, "Rashīd Riḍā," 176, 179; ʿAbd al-Wahhāb Khallāf, *Maṣādir al-tashrīʿ al-Islāmī fīmā lā naṣṣa fīhi*, 6th ed. (Kuwait: Dār al-Qalam, 1414/1993), 101; Gudrun Krämer, "Kritik und Selbstkritik: Reformistisches Denken im Islam," in *Der Islam im Aufbruch? Perspektiven der arabischen Welt*, ed. Michael Lüders (Munich: Piper, 1992), 209–24, 224.

64. See Joseph Schacht, *An Introduction to Islamic Law* (Oxford: Clarendon Press, 1964), 100–111.

65. For a biographical sketch of Maḥmaṣānī's life, see Nabil Saleh, "Biographical Notes on the Late Dr. Sobhi Mahmassani (1909–86)," *Middle East Commercial Law Review* 2, no. 6 (1996): 183; Muḥammad Khayr Ramaḍān Yūsuf, *Tatimmat al-Aʿlām li-l-Ziriklī*, 2 vols. (Beirut: Dār Ibn Ḥazm, 1418/1998), 1:242–43. Yūsuf and Saleh give different birthdates for Maḥmaṣānī, 1906 and 1909, respectively. Since Saleh provided a specific day, January 29, I followed his dates.

66. Saleh, "Biographical Notes," 183; Yūsuf, *Tatimmat al-Aʿlām*, 1:242–43.

67. Interestingly, Maḥmaṣānī differentiated between *maṣlaḥa* and the purposes of the law, mentioning both side by side. However, nowhere in his book on the philosophy of Islamic legislation did he elaborate on the difference between these or define the purposes of the law.

68. Ṣubḥī Rajab Maḥmaṣānī, *Falsafat al-tashrīʿ fī-l-Islām*, 3rd ed. (Beirut: Dār al-ʿIlm li-l-Malāyīn, 1380/1961), 163, 176, 199, 204, 219, 262.

69. Ibid., 176–77.

70. Ibid., 217, 262.

71. Ibid., 200–202, 204–5, 212, 214, 217–19.

72. At the beginning of his book on Islamic legislation Maḥmaṣānī argued that a Shari'a ruling (*ḥukm*), like a state law (*qānūn*), refers to the genus and not to a specific individual or specified situation (ibid., 19, also 269).

73. Ibid., 262–63. Examples of universal rulings are the principle of the prohibition to kill wrongfully, to misappropriate another person's property, and to engage in fornication (ibid., 262).

74. Maḥmaṣānī served on Lebanon's Court of Appeals (Saleh, "Biographical Notes," 183).

75. In the secondary literature one finds different dates for al-Fāsī's life, varying from 1906, 1907, 1908, and 1910 for the year of his birth to 1973 or 1974 for his death; see Amnon Cohen, "ʿAllāl al-Fāsī: His Ideas and His Contribution Towards Morocco's Independence," *Asian and African Studies*, 3 (1967): 121–64, 121; Ali Merad, art. "Iṣlāḥ," in *The Encyclopaedia of Islam*, new ed., vol. 4 (Leiden: Brill, 1973), 141–63; Laurence O. Michalek, art. "Fāsī, Muḥammad ʿAllāl al-," in *The Oxford Encyclopedia of the Modern Islamic World*, ed. J. Esposito, 4 vols. (Oxford: Oxford University Press, 1995), 2:4–5; Khayr al-Dīn Ziriklī, *al-Aʿlām*, 11 vols. (Beirut: Dār al-ʿIlm li'l-Malāyīn, 1992), 4:246.

76. For his role in the Moroccan independence movement before 1956, see Cohen, "ʿAllāl al-Fāsī," 121–64.

77. See ʿAllāl al-Fāsī, *Maqāṣid al-sharīʿa al-Islāmiyya wa-makārimuhā* (Casablanca: Maktabat al-Waḥda al-ʿArabiyya, n.d. [1963]), 209–17.

78. Ibid., 43, 159.

79. Ibid., 138–44.

80. For similar criticism of al-Fāsī's thought, see Hallaq, *History of Islamic Legal Theories*, 224–26; and Cohen, "ʿAllāl al-Fāsī," 163.

81. ʿAbd al-Wahhāb Khallāf, *ʿIlm uṣūl al-fiqh* (Alexandria: Mu'assasat Shabāb al-Jāmiʿa, 1984), 4.

82. Muḥammad ʿIzzat al-Ṭahṭāwī, *Min ʿulamā' al-ruwwād fī riḥāb al-Azhar* (Cairo: Maktabat Wahba, 1990), 141–52.

83. Khallāf, like Rashīd Riḍā before him, saw in Shari'a a means to unify the Arab nations (Khallāf, *Maṣādir al-tashrīʿ*, 6).

84. Khallāf (ibid., 101) attacked al-Ṭūfī's theory of *maṣlaḥa*, arguing that it constituted abrogation of the sacred texts by arbitrary opinion.

85. Ibid., 156–57.

86. See the section "The Concept of *Maṣlaḥa* in Classical Islamic Legal Theory" in this chapter. Khallāf, *Maṣādir al-tashrīʿ*, 18–28, 51, 56–58. Khallāf was not categorical about the order or even the elements falling under the category of necessities; sometimes he listed five (religion, life, intellect, property, and honor), sometimes fewer, and he

alternated between mentioning progeny together with life and substituting honor (*ʿirḍ*) for it.

87. Khallāf, *Maṣādir al-tashrīʿ*, 85.

88. Ibid., 59–61.

89. See also Hallaq, *History of Islamic Legal Theories*, 220–24.

90. Khallāf, *Maṣādir al-tashrīʿ*, 102–3.

91. Ibid., 89.

92. Andreas Christmann, "Islamic Scholar and Religious Leader: Shaikh Muhammad Saʿid Ramadan al-Buti," in *Islam and Modernity: Muslim Intellectuals Respond*, ed. J. Cooper, R. L. Nettler, and M. Mahmoud (London and New York: I. B. Tauris, 2000), 57–81, esp. 58–60.

93. Christmann, "Islamic Scholar," 58.

94. Muḥammad Saʿīd Ramaḍān al-Būṭī, *Ḍawābiṭ al-maṣlaḥa fī l-sharīʿa al-Islāmiyya*, 4th ed. (Beirut: Mu'assasat al-Risāla, 1402/1982), 11–15. Interestingly, al-Būṭī in this instance does not count consensus (*ijmāʿ*) among the sources of Islamic law.

95. Ibid., 48, 50, 58–61, 65–66.

96. Ibid., 15, 25–28, 60.

97. Al-Būṭī criticized al-Ṭūfī repeatedly and at length (see ibid., 129, 140, 202–15).

98. Ibid., 12; Khallāf, *Maṣādir al-tashrīʿ*, 90, 101, 160.

99. al-Būṭī, *Ḍawābiṭ al-maṣlaḥa*, 119.

100. Ibid., 216–32.

101. For a detailed exposition of these determinants, see ibid., 129–247.

102. Ibid., 139–40, 173, 197, 276–79. Al-Būṭī's use of legal precepts resembled that of al-Qarāfī, with the difference that he did not tie them to *maṣlaḥa* but to statements in the Qur'an or Sunna.

103. See ibid., 139–40, 173, 197, 276–79.

104. In case an attested *maṣlaḥa* was in opposition to an unattested *maṣlaḥa*, al-Būtī always gave priority to the former. He considered the unattested *maṣlaḥa* then to be illusory because he held that God did not neglect a *maṣlaḥa* in His law (ibid., 67).

105. See ibid., 248–61.

106. See Zayd, *al-Maṣlaḥa*, 235–40; Opwis, "Maṣlaḥa," 216–35. Although al-Rāzī also had a similar scale of preponderance, al-Būṭī's language resembles more that of al-Ṭūfī (see al-Rāzī, *al-Maḥṣūl*, 2:480–82; Opwis, "Maṣlaḥa," 91–94).

107. al-Būṭī, *Ḍawābiṭ al-maṣlaḥa*, 266, 270.

108. See ibid., 330–31.

109. Ibid., 166–67.

110. There are, of course, exceptions to this rule. For example, Ibn Taymiyya understood *maṣlaḥa* almost exclusively from the standpoint of substantive rationality, but he rejected the use of human reasoning unaided by revelation (cf. Opwis, "Maṣlaḥa," 161–79).

111. The concept of *maṣlaḥa* frequently became a vehicle to justify novel institutions, such as the Ottoman constitution, or secular laws that were contrary to rulings derived from the Islamic scripture, such as Tunisia's abolition of polygamy. See Commins, *Islamic Reform*, 126–27; J. N. D. Anderson, "The Tunisian Law of Personal Status," *International and Comparative Law Quarterly* 7 (1958): 262–79, 267; Fazlur Rahman, "A Survey of Modernization of Muslim Family Law," *International Journal of Middle East Studies* 11 (1980): 451–65, 457.

Chapter 5

1. Abderrahim Lamchichi, *Islam et contestation au Maghreb* (Paris: Editions l'Harmattan, 1989), 169; and Emad Eldin Shahin, *Political Ascent: Contemporary Islamic Movements in North Africa* (Boulder, CO: Westview Press, 1997), 48–56.

2. Because of the strong influence of French culture in North Africa, names in the literature are usually written in their French form—thus Abdelkrim (or Abdel-Krim) al-Khattabi, instead of ʿAbd al-Karīm al-Khaṭṭābī.

3. The Berber Rif area in northern Morocco became a Spanish protectorate in 1912. France, which held the larger part of Morocco as a protectorate, helped the Spanish defeat al-Khattabi in 1926, three years after his initial victory over the Spanish troops.

4. Lamchichi, *Islam et contestation au Maghreb;* Mohamed El Alami, *Allal El Fassi: Patriarche du nationalisme morocain* (Casablanca: Dar El Kitab, 1975), 48–49; Attilio Gaudio, *Allal El Fassi ou l'histoire de l'Istiqlal* (Paris: Editions Alain Moreau, 1972), 34; Shahin, *Political Ascent*, 33–39.

5. El Alami notes that of the three at this point the undeniable leader was Mohamed Hassan El Ouezzani, who had just graduated that year from a French university with a degree in political science and who had been for a while secretary to the famous pan-Arabist writer and activist Chakib Arsalane in Geneva (El Alami, *Allal El Fassi,* 49). He continued to play a major political role, mostly in competition with al-Fāsī, as representing the more bicultural nationalist tendency.

6. The importance of the bloodline is evidenced in the El Alami's biography by a whole chapter devoted to his genealogy (ibid., 13–37).

7. There is no book devoted to him in English or German, and only one article I have found so far in English: Amnon Cohen, "ʿAllal al-Fasi: His Ideas and His Contribution Towards Morocco's Independence," *Asian and African Studies* 3 (1967): 121–64. Surprisingly, this lack is also glaring in a recent French research publication, *Parcours d'intellectuels maghrébins: Scolarité, formation, socialisation et positionnements*, ed. Aïssa Kadri (Paris: Kartala and Institut Maghreb-Europe, 1999), where he is only mentioned in passing in the first essay on higher education during the Protectorate.

8. Cohen, "ʿAllal al-Fasi," 30.

9. Shahin notes that, unlike Algeria and Tunisia, the three traditional centers of power in Morocco are the monarchy, the *ʿulamāʾ*, and the Sufi orders. It was the Salafiyya

reform movement, originated in the east by Jamāl al-Dīn al-Afghānī and Muḥammad ʿAbduh and strongly represented by al-Fāsī's teachers ʿAbdallāh Idrīs al-Sanūsī, Abū Shuʿayb al-Dukkālī, and al-ʿArabī al-ʿAlāwī at al-Qarawiyyīn, that largely sapped the authority and influence of the Sufi brotherhoods for the younger generation (Shahin, *Political Ascent*, 31–35).

10. El Alami, *Allal El Fassi*, 35.

11. In 1929 Mohamed Ben Abbès El Kabbaj included many of al-Fāsī's poems in his book *La litérature arabe au Maroc* and introduced him as one who, by his will, sincerity, and competence, had been recognized as "poet of the young generation" (El Alami, *Allal El Fassi*, 39–40).

12. El Alami, *Allal El Fassi*, 50–53. His official title *ʿalīm* (singular of *ʿulamāʾ*) was actually not given to him upon his graduation because he and two colleagues refused to sign a statement apologizing for their part in the 1930 protest of the Berber *ẓahīr*.

13. El Alami, *Allal El Fassi*, 61, attributes the greater boldness of Sultan Muhammad V to the letter the CAM youth sent to him the year before, congratulating him on the occasion of the first Feast of the Throne in 1933, and to the protests the CAM helped organize against the Daladier government in France, which had just subsumed the administration of Morocco under the Ministry of France Overseas (ibid., 60–61). Shahin confirms that the king expressed gratitude to the nationalist movement by quietly supporting it, "finding in it a means to protect the integrity of the throne." After World War II the sultan became closely associated with the cause of the Istiqlāl Party (Shahin, *Political Ascent*, 34).

14. Gaudio, *Allal El Fassi*, 37–39; El Alami, *Allal El Fassi*, 65–73.

15. On the Islamic concept of *fiṭra* and its understanding as the way God created humans, see Chapter 3 in this book by Frank Griffel.

16. ʿAllāl al-Fāsī, *Nidāʾ al-Qāhira* (Rabat: Maṭbaʿat al-Risāla, 1981), 159.

17. For the lexicographic background on *nāmūs*, see note 57 in Chapter 3 of this book.

18. al-Fāsī, *Nidāʾ al-Qāhira*, 170–71. For parallels with Sayyid Quṭb's thought, see note 82 in Chapter 3.

19. Some scholars, such as Cohen, "ʿAllal al-Fasi," 143, 147, and Reinhard Schulze, *A Modern History of the Islamic World* (New York: New York University Press, 2000), 95, 121, characterize al-Fāsī's movement as "neo-Salafiyya" because it has added the nationalist element to the religious foundation. Although this is true, Cohen's study does not look at al-Fāsī's books on Islamic legal matters and therefore misses much of what is truly distinctive in his vision of Islam.

20. ʿAllāl al-Fāsī, *al-Naqd al-dhātī* (Rabat: Maṭbaʿat al-Risāla, 1979). The book was first published in 1952.

21. Significantly, the most common Arabic term used for "nation" in his book is *umma*, which usually refers to the worldwide Islamic community. This may be at once

a "reformist" code word meant as a deliberate reinterpretation of traditional Islamic discourse and a reaffirmation of the Islamic character of the Moroccan collective psyche, a point he drives home throughout.

22. al-Fāsī, *al-Naqd al-dhātī*, 22 (chap. 3, "Thinking in a Social Way").

23. Ibid., 28. Al-Fāsī expresses a bold critique of his host country Egypt as well. Even "in the country of Muḥammad ʿAbduh and Jamāl al-Dīn al-Afghānī there are still spiritual shortcomings, and in spite of the beneficial influence of al-Azhar, there is still much traditionalism. But worse yet, the religious schools are full of peasants with little ability to exercise critical thinking, unlike the more educated, open-minded urbanites" (ibid., 27).

24. Ibid., 45.

25. Ibid., 49.

26. Ibid., 62.

27. Ibid., 67.

28. Ibid., 103.

29. The third part is called "Economic Thinking," and the fourth, "Social Thinking," with eight and thirty-two chapters, respectively. Though both parts have one or two chapters on specifically Islamic subjects, references to Islam are peppered throughout, but not anywhere in the quantity found among contemporary Islamist writers. What is striking, as said earlier, is how rarely al-Fāsī refers to specific Islamic sources.

30. Al-Fāsī is not thereby denying the early conquests but probably is pointing to the spirit of the Meccan period of the Qur'an, yet without dealing directly with the issue he raises. Were the conquests a mistake, as he seems to be implying? He never answers directly. In one of the last chapters ("The Islamic Party"—*ṭā'ifa*) he claims that the Umayyads departed from Islamic principles. In a similar way al-Fāsī revisits the Islamic roots of Moroccan history. He sees Ibn Khaldūn (d. 1406) as having a personal interest in the instability of regimes and in their autocratic nature, while for him the founder of Muslim Morocco, Idrīs I (d. 791) was very sincere in his faith. Sadly, the masses in this period knew little or nothing of Islam and, in their natural Berber mentality, easily fell into the kind of personality cult that affects Islam in Morocco. However, only a single fact is constant throughout history: the Moroccan psyche was characterized by an inalterable thirst for independence and a distinctive nationalist stance.

31. al-Fāsī, *al-Naqd al-dhātī*, 124.

32. Literally "reversals into being and nonbeing, as they say" (ibid., 125).

33. Ibid.

34. Muslim nations, observes al-Fāsī, are on a par with other nations when it comes to bowing to progress—do Muslims not say that a renewer must come every hundred years? They are in constant need of renewal. But more than just repair and reformation, what is genuinely needed today is a radical change. It is the kind of spirit that animated ʿAlī ibn Abī Ṭālib (d. 661) when he said, "Teach your children, for they were created for

another generation (not yours)" (al-Fāsī, *al-Naqd al-dhātī,* 127), thus indicating that changes must take place in each generation. Each new generation must rethink how it will apply the foundation it has inherited. This progressive spirit, he argues, enabled the *salaf* to build an impressive civilization that was mostly characterized by its humanism and its open spirit to other civilizations, showing full respect for human values found elsewhere.

35. Ibid., 128.

36. Al-Fāsī had started on this project earlier with two works on Islamic law that are mentioned by the Istiqlāl publishing house in an advertisement at the end of his *Maqāṣid al-sharīʿa.* These two works, however, were published years after his death: *Al-Madkhal li-dirāsa al-naẓariyya al-ʿāmma li-l-fiqh al-Islāmī wa-muqāranatuhu bi-l-fiqh al-ajnabī* (Introduction to a Theoretical and General Study of Islamic Law and Its Comparison with Foreign Jurisprudence) (Rabat: Mu'assasat ʿAllāl al-Fāsī, 1985); and *Tārīkh al-tashrīʿ al-Islāmī* (History of Islamic Legislation) (Rabat: Kitāb al-ʿIlm, 1990). Of over twenty books he wrote, the fact that four bore directly on Shari'a shows his great concern as an *ʿalīm* to see Islamic law adapted and applied in his newly independent country. The next greatest interest that is reflected in his publications is the recent history of North African independence movements.

37. ʿAllāl al-Fāsī, *Maqāṣid al-sharīʿa al-Islāmiyya wa-makārimuhā,* 2nd ed. (Rabat: Maṭbaʿat al-Risāla, 1979). The book took him four years to write, while working on other projects simultaneously, as he mentions in his preface. He very likely put the finishing touches on it during his tenure as minister of Islamic affairs (June 1961–January 1963). It was first published in 1963.

38. Very probably the same publisher as his other titles at the time (Rabat: Maṭbaʿat al-Risāla). I have not yet been able to obtain a copy of the Arabic original, and it is mentioned neither in Gaudio's biography nor in El Alami's. I am using the French translation, *Défense de la loi islamique,* trans. Charles Samara (Rabat: Commission du Patrimoine de Feu Allal El Fassi, 1977).

39. See his discussion of the feasibility of reapplying Shari'a law in Morocco (al-Fāsī, *Défense de la loi islamique,* 270–74). He is for a progressive return, even if the application of some of the *ḥudūd* (penal law) has to wait.

40. He states this in many places. In *Maqāṣid al-sharīʿa al-Islāmiyya,* for instance, al-Fāsī traces the history of human legal codes from prehistory to the Greek and Roman periods and from Christian medieval canon law to British law, showing that in all of them justice is at the heart of the jurists' concerns. But whereas justice is an external factor for all these "human" systems, it is at the heart of Shari'a because it is revealed by God as the main purpose of his commands (al-Fāsī, *Maqāṣid al-sharīʿa al-Islāmiyya,* 41). Further, he states, "Thus Islamic legislation in the stages of its development parallels the developments of Western positive law, that is, insofar as both hold firmly to their specific ethos and direct sources (*maṣādiruhu al-mubāshira*) for the sake of justice and the

spread of fairness (*inṣāf*) among people" (ibid., 58). See also al-Fāsī, *Défense de la loi islamique*, 93–95, 153, 158, 166.

41. Al-Fāsī opposes the view of some contemporary Muslim rationalists who say that the Muʿtazilites were pointing to a kind of natural law, thus anticipating modern Western thought. Not at all, he counters, for Christian thought teaches that the human mind was debilitated by the fall, whereas Muslims believe that it is intact. The Muʿtazilites go too far, however, in positing reason above revelation (al-Fāsī, *Maqāṣid al-sharīʿa al-Islāmiyya*, 49).

42. One of al-Fāsī's own definitions of *ijtihād* is worth quoting. *Ijtihād* is "the particular effort a competent person expends in order to understand Shari'a's injunctions (*aḥkām*) and to infer its detailed laws [literally "evidences," *adilla*]" (ibid., 159).

43. Ibid., 58.

44. Al-Fāsī quotes from Ibn Rushd's *al-Kashf ʿan manāhij al-adilla fī ʿaqā'id al-milla* (The Exposition of the Methods of Proof in the Doctrines of Religion). This discussion spans two sections ("The Third Question: On Divine Decree and Predestination" and "The Fourth Question: On Divine Justice and Injustice"); see Averroes, *Faith and Reason in Islam: Averroes' Exposition of Religious Arguments*, trans. I. Najjar (Oxford: Oneworld, 2001), 105–21.

45. Al-Fāsī chooses to ignore the scholastic arguments put forth by Ibn Rushd, namely, that our actions can be imputed both to our will and to God's will through the faculties with which He endowed humans and through the order that He created in the universe. Thus our choosing between opposite courses of action "cannot be accomplished except through the propitiousness of the causes that God made subservient to us from outside, and after the removal of their impediments. . . . If this is the case, then the actions imputed to us are performed through our will, together with the propitiousness of external forces, and that is what is referred to as God's decree. These external causes that God has made subservient to us do not only complement or impede the actions we want to do, they are also the causes of our choice of one of the two opposites" (Averroes, *Faith and Reason*, 108–9).

46. Ibid., 118.

47. al-Fāsī, *Défense de la loi islamique,* 61.

48. Ibn Ḥazm was the best-known proponent of the relatively short-lived Ẓāhirī school of Islamic jurisprudence.

49. al-Fāsī, *Défense de la loi islamique*, 63, referring to Ibn Ḥazm's *al-Iḥkām fi uṣūl al-aḥkām* (Method of Ruling Regarding the Root of the Laws). It seems that al-Fāsī consciously privileges Andalusian and Maghrebian (North African) scholars in his writings. This is likely tied to his lifelong efforts to promote the unity and revival of the "Great Maghreb" and to bolster the self-image of his Moroccan readers.

50. Two pages earlier al-Fāsi had marshaled the thought of the Danish physicist Niels Bohr (1885–1962) to show that twentieth-century quantum physics and relativity theory disprove any notion of strict determinism.

51. al-Fāsī, *Défense de la loi islamique*, 64.

52. Literally, "custom," or "habit," but here referring to al-Shāṭibī's distinction between *al-ʿawā'id* (plural of *ʿāda*, meaning roughly human civilization and culture) and *al-taʿabbudāt* (synonymous with *al-ʿibādāt* and referring to the ritual duties of Islam). For a detailed exposition of this concept, see Muhammad Khalid Masud, *Islamic Legal Philosophy: A Study of Abū Isḥāq al-Shāṭibī's Life and Thought* (Delhi: International Islamic Publishers, 1989), 293–99.

53. al-Fāsī, *Maqāṣid al-sharīʿa al-Islāmiyya,* 67.

54. Quoting from Ibn Sīnā's *al-Najāt* (Book of Salvation) and *al-Shifā'* (Book of Healing).

55. al-Fāsī, *Maqāṣid al-sharīʿa al-Islāmiyya,* 68.

56. Al-Fāsī quotes from al-Fārābī's *Mabādi' ārā' ahl al-madīna al-fāḍila* (Principles of the Opinions of the People of the Virtuous City).

57. al-Fāsī, *Maqāṣid al-sharīʿa al-Islāmiyya,* 69.

58. Ibid., 70. Cf. also al-Fāsī, *Défense de la loi islamique*, 175.

59. Malcolm Kerr, *Islamic Reform: The Political and Legal Theories of Muḥammad ʿAbduh and Rashīd Riḍā* (Berkeley: University of California Press, 1966), 109.

60. al-Shāṭibī, *al-Muwāfaqāt fi uṣūl al-sharīʿa,* ed. ʿAbdallāh Dirāz, 2nd ed., 4 vols. (Cairo: al-Maktaba al-Tijāriyya al-Kubrā, 1975), 2:25. One has to bear in mind that both al-Shāṭibī and al-Fāsī are from the Mālikī school of Islamic jurisprudence, founded by Mālik ibn Anas (d. 795). In its early days the Mālikī school favored the use of *istiṣlāḥ*, or *maṣlaḥa mursala* (unattested *maṣlaḥa*, not suggested by the legislative text). This particular edition of al-Shāṭibī's *al-Muwāfaqāt* had a great influence, mainly because of Dirāz's introduction and notes. Dirāz was a respected teacher at al-Azhar seminary in Cairo. Al-Fāsī quotes approvingly from Dirāz's introduction (*Maqāṣid al-sharīʿa al-Islāmiyya*, 9), saying that relying on the Shari'a's purposes was considered by many *uṣūlīs* a valid juristic technique. But the *maqāṣid* were reduced to a "means" (*waṣīla*) for a *mujtahid* to infer certain laws in situations where there were no Qur'anic injunctions (*maṣlaḥa mursala*). In his introduction to al-Shāṭibī's *al-Muwāfaqāt*, Dirāz writes that this approach is like a person teaching another person to weave by only showing some parts of the loom—nobody will learn to weave a cloth that way! But for al-Shāṭibī, as Dirāz understood him to mean, *fiqh* has two pillars: the first is the right use of the Arabic language and the second a discernment of the *maqāṣid*. Dirāz has strong words for those stuck in their traditional ways: [*al-Muwāfaqāt*] is like "a fly swatter chasing away those boastful swindlers who live like parasites off the various disciplines of the holy Shari'a, who claim to be masters of *ijtihād*, though without any of the means to reach it" (in al-Shāṭibī, *al-Muwāfaqāt*, 1:10).

61. See also al-Fāsī, *Maqāṣid al-sharīʿa al-Islāmiyya*, 43, where he quotes Ibn Qayyim al-Jawziyya (d. 1350), a younger contemporary of al-Shāṭibī: "Shari'a is built and founded upon judgment (*ḥukm*) and the benefits (*maṣāliḥ*) of people in this and the next life. It is all justice, all mercy, and all wisdom."

62. al-Fāsī, *Maqāṣid al-sharīʿa al-Islāmiyya*, 41.

63. Ibid.

64. Ibid., 43. See also al-Fāsī, *Défense de la loi islamique*, 159, 172.

65. al-Fāsī, *Maqāṣid al-sharīʿa al-Islāmiyya*, 52 and 54. Lack of space forbids me to discuss his Mālikī emphasis on the *ʿamal* ("legal practice") of Medina and its assimilation to what he considers virtually two synonyms, *ʿāda* and *ʿurf*, that is, the freedom of *ijtihād* in the sociopolitical and economic spheres. Here al-Fāsī anticipates the conservative thesis of a recent book that examines Mālik's *Muwaṭṭa'* and the concept of Medinan jurisprudence: Yasin Dutton, *The Origins of Islamic Law: The Qur'an, the Muwatta' and Madinan ʿAmal* (Richmond: Curzon, 1999).

66. See also al-Fāsī, *Défense de la loi islamique*, 107, and especially 130 and 175 for succinct statements on how Shari'a is perfect, but through the necessary effort of *ijtihād*, *fiqh* is a form that evolves over time.

67. Al-Fāsī's *Maqāṣid al-sharīʿa al-Islāmiyya* is really a modified *uṣūl al-fiqh* manual. The main differences are that (1) al-Fāsī has a long comparative history of law, (2) he avoids most of the semantic and hermeneutic rules for the interpretation of the texts, and (3) the last fourth of the book is devoted to the political dimension, i.e., the relationship between Islam and human rights.

68. In addition to these two exceptions, one could mention the stunning absence of what now is considered a standard *maqāṣid al-sharīʿa* presentation of the three levels of *maṣlaḥa*: the *ḍarūriyyāt*, which are the guarantee of preservation of the five categories of human existence; the *ḥājiyyāt*, or the *maṣāliḥ* that, without being essential, are nevertheless necessary in order to achieve overall *maṣlaḥa*; and the *taḥsīnāt* or *tazyīnāt*, which contribute to the improvement of human life. Al-Fāsī does mention the five "necessary" objectives in passing in *Défense de la loi islamique*, 238.

69. Ibid., 143–47.

70. Al-Fāsī traces al-Ṭūfī's rise to prominence in the modern period to the writings of the Syrian Salafī writer Jamāl al-Dīn al-Qāsimī (1866–1914) and to Muḥammad Rashīd Riḍā. The latter quotes from al-Ṭūfī repeatedly in his articles in the journal *al-Manār*. From here, al-Ṭūfī's influence spread further through a dissertation by Muṣṭafā Zayd and finally by the activity of the influential *uṣūlī* Muḥammad ʿAbd al-Wahhāb Khallāf (1888–1956). Al-Shāṭibī is more influential in Khallāf's thought. Al-Fāsī also quotes from him, but from an earlier work than al-Khallāf's two most famous books, *ʿIlm uṣūl al-fiqh* (published in 1942) and *Maṣādir al-tashrīʿ al-Islāmī fīmā lā naṣṣa fīhi* (published in 1955).

71. al-Fāsī, *Maqāṣid al-sharīʿa al-Islāmiyya*, 147.

72. Ibid., 240.

73. Ibid., 241.

74. Hans Wehr, *A Dictionary of Modern Written Arabic*, ed. J. Milton Cowan (Wiesbaden: Harrassowitz, 1974), 259, translates the expression *makārim al-akhlāq* as "noble manners, high moral standard."

75. The section bears this long title: "Noble Ethical Standards as the Criterion for Every General Benefit [*maṣlaḥa*] and Foundation of Every Purpose of Islam."

76. al-Fāsī, *Maqāṣid al-sharīʿa al-Islāmiyya*, 190.

77. The use of *al-maʿrūf* here represents a widening of its traditional meaning. In the Qur'an it refers to honorable conduct and typifies the ethical wisdom of God's commands in the expression *al-amr bi-l maʿrūf wa'l nahy ʿan al-munkar*. In essence, by redefining this "good" (specific to the Arabian culture of Muhammad's day) as the minimum ethical common ground among humanity today, al-Fāsī is seeking to bolster his apologetic argument that Islam already encompasses the ethical standards recognized by all peoples. There is some Qur'anic precedent for this, however: "Ye are the best of peoples, evolved for mankind, enjoining what is right, forbidding what is wrong, and believing in God" (Q 3.110).

78. al-Fāsī, *Maqāṣid al-sharīʿa al-Islāmiyya*, 192.

79. Ibid., 193.

80. Ibid., 194.

81. Cf., for instance, Muḥammad ʿAbduh's commentary on Q 2.30, the principal verse affirming Adam's *khilāfa*, in Muḥammad Rashīd Riḍā, *Tafsīr al-Qur'ān al-ḥakīm al-shahīr bi-Tafsīr al-Manār*, 12 vols. (Beirut: Dār al-Maʿrifa, 1990), 1:251–369.

82. In his Qur'an commentary, *Fī ẓilāl al-Qur'ān*, Sayyid Quṭb begins with the "primordial covenant" verse (Q 7.172): "And now in this lesson the issue of *tawḥīd* is presented from a different angle, an angle of depth . . . it is presented from the angle of the original human nature (*al-fiṭra*), with which God created (*faṭara*) humanity; and through it He concluded the covenant with them in their very souls, their very essence (*wa-dhāt takwīnihim*), while they were still in the world of particles. Indeed, the confession of God's sole lordship is the *fiṭra* of the human being—a *fiṭra* that the Creator has deposited into this being. . . . Truly, *tawḥīd* is the covenant (*al-mīthāq*) made between the *fiṭra* of humanity and its Creator since their first appearance in the realm of existence" (Sayyid Quṭb, *Fī ẓilāl al-Qur'ān*, 4 vols. [Beirut and Cairo: Dār al-Shurūq, 1493–94/1973–74], 3:1391). This story, he contends, is not to be taken literally (to do so would be on the basis of dubious *Isra'īliyyāt*) but "is the representation of a state that has been repeated in each soul throughout history" (ibid.). Nevertheless, after three more pages of discussion he cautiously concludes that only God knows (the literal reading cannot be ruled out). In his commentary on Q 2.30 (ibid., 1:56) Quṭb links this *mīthāq* to humanity's *khilāfa* (caliphate), but unlike al-Fāsī, Quṭb ties it directly to the solemn oath of the human souls before birth that they accept the one God as their Lord. This means that in his case *khilāfa* is always linked to *tawḥīd*, leaving us with the suspicion that this *khilāfa* is in fact reserved for radical Muslims like himself, as opposed to the rest who are still in a state of *jāhiliyya* (ignorance, like the pre-Islamic Arabians mentioned in the Qur'an). On this subject, see also Chapter 3 in this book by Frank Griffel.

83. *ʿAmārat al-arḍ*, an expression that is often called upon by Muḥammad ʿAbduh and Sayyid Quṭb and even more by al-Fāsī. It is difficult to translate. The three main meanings of the underlying verb *ʿamara* are (1) to build upon, (2) to inhabit, and (3) to cultivate. In the context of these writings they coalesce to express "civilizing," similar to God's command in Genesis 1 and 2 to fill the earth and cultivate or wisely manage its resources. The only Qur'anic attestation of this root used in this sense is the appearance of the tenth form of *ʿamara* in Q. 11.61: "He who produced you from the earth and has given you to live therein (*istaʿmarakum fīhi*)." Al-Fāsī has already quoted this verse earlier (*Maqāṣid al-sharīʿa al-Islāmiyya*, 42). *Istaʿmara* is the Arabic verb used today for colonizing, a good indication that "populate" is not strong enough.

84. al-Fāsī, *Maqāṣid al-sharīʿa al-Islāmiyya*, 192 (cf. *Défense de la loi islamique*, 41–43, 232–33). See his first discussion of this *ḥadīth*, "God created Adam in His image," a direct parallel to Genesis 1.26–27. Interestingly, he is one of the few Muslims in this context (al-Ghazālī was another) who makes use of this tradition. Gudrun Krämer, for instance, claims that it is nowhere to be found among contemporary writers (*Gottes Staat als Republik: Reflexionen zeitgenössischer Muslime zu Islam, Menschenrechten and Demokratie* [Baden-Baden: Nomos, 1999], 74).

85. Particularly in the sections on the necessity of setting up an Islamic state (*al-dawla al-Islāmiyya*) one finds some ambiguity (e.g., al-Fāsī, *Maqāṣid al-sharīʿa al-Islāmiyya*, 205–320; *Défense de la loi islamique*, 121–23). This is mainly the case because in following Rashīd Riḍā he advocates a kind of parliament composed of persons who know both *sharīʿa* and contemporary issues well (*ahl al-ḥall wa-l-ʿaqd*). The ambiguities and tension also stem from his attraction to several Islamist figures. For instance, in his *Défense de la loi islamique* al-Fāsī quotes approvingly from Mawdūdī (161–66) and Muḥammad Quṭb (176–81) on issues of Islam, the state, and human nature.

86. A deliberate choice of word that makes room for all human legal codes with a solid ethic.

87. al-Fāsī, *Maqāṣid al-sharīʿa al-Islāmiyya*, 9.

88. Ibid., 224–27.

89. Ibid., 228.

90. Ibid., 233.

91. Al-Fāsī devotes a brief section to women's rights (*Maqāṣid al-sharīʿa al-Islāmiyya*, 241–44). A large portion of that is used to berate the Christian doctrine of original sin with woman as the one to blame. By his time, al-Fāsī argues, the West has experienced a backlash with an equally unacceptable sexual revolution. The Arabs and oriental people in general suffer from a traditional culture that, under the pretext that women are weak and threaten a family's honor, has kept them subjugated. Islam, declares al-Fāsī, came to liberate women. They have all the privileges and duties of men in every area. They are to be partners with men at home, at work, and in the political arena. Sadly, he adds, most Muslims have not yet caught up with the revolutionary message of Islam in this area.

92. Ibid., 249–351.

93. The Bahā'ī religion was founded in the mid-nineteenth century in Iran by Mīrzā Ḥusayn ʿAlī Nūrī (1817–92), known as Bahā' Allāh (Glory of God). Most early converts to Bahā'ism were Muslims, which meant that from the viewpoint of Muslim jurists they became subject to the law of apostasy from Islam once they joined the Bahā'ī faith. Bahā'ī faith considers all religions, including Islam, as teaching essentially an identical truth.

94. John Waterbury, "Kingdom-Building and the Control of the Opposition in Morocco: The Monarchical Uses of Justice," *Government and Opposition* 5, no. 1 (Winter 1969–70): 54–66, 64.

95. al-Fāsī, *Maqāṣid al-sharīʿa al-Islāmiyya*, 266. Shari'a divides the world into *dār al-islām*, *dār al-ṣulḥ* (or *'ahd*), and *dār al-ḥarb*.

96. See Azzam S. Tamimi, *Rachid Ghannouchi: A Democrat Within Islamism* (New York: Oxford University Press, 2001). al-Ghannūshī, although quoting al-Fāsī's *Maqāṣid al-sharīʿa al-Islāmiyya* and following al-Fāsī's method, argues against the death penalty for apostasy and is much more specific on norms of democracy and pluralism. See David L. Johnston, "Fuzzy Reformist-Islamist Borders: Malek Bennabi and Rachid al-Ghannoushi on Civilization," *Maghreb Review* 29 (2004): 123–52.

97. Cf. Felicitas Opwis's contribution to this volume.

Chapter 6

Thanks to Louise Feld for excellent research assistance.

1. Comparatively little secondary literature exists on al-Qaraḍāwī. There is a discussion in Armando Salvatore, *Islam and the Political Discourse of Modernity* (London: Ithaca Press, 1997), 197–216; see also Reuven Paz, "Shaykh Dr. Yousef al-Qaradawi: Dr. Jekyll and Mr. Hyde," *Policywatch,* no. 576 (Washington, DC: Washington Institute for Near East Policy, October 18, 2001), available at http://www.washingtoninstitute.org/templateC05.php?CID=1454.

2. Noah Feldman, *After Jihad: America and the Struggle for Islamic Democracy* (New York: Farrar, Straus & Giroux, 2003).

3. See Yūsuf al-Qaraḍāwī, *Min fiqh al-dawla fī-l-Islām* (Cairo: Dār al-Shurūq, 1997), 131 (referring to democracy as the thing in which "many of the *Islāmiyyūn* see the desirable means to check the recalcitrance of autocratic government"). Translations in this chapter are my own, and only after finishing this chapter did I discover an English version of *Min fiqh al-dawla*: Dr. Yūsuf al-Qaraḍāwī, *State in Islam*, anonymous translator (Cairo: el-Falah for Translation, Publishing and Distribution, 1998). The translation is spotty and unidiomatic but useful and on the whole faithful.

4. Yūsuf al-Qaraḍāwī, *Priorities of the Islamic Movement*, at 1. The text was available in 2003 at http://www.wponline.org/vil/Books/Q_Priorities/.

5. See interview with Maher Abdullah, *al-Fiqh al-Islāmī fī muwājahat al-taṭawwur*, at http://www.Qaradawi.net/site/topics/article.asp?cu_no=2&item_no=2987&version=1&template_id=105&parent_id=16 (hereafter Maher Abdullah interview).

6. *Liberal Islam: A Sourcebook*, ed. Charles Kurzman (New York: Oxford University Press, 1998).

7. See, e.g., Paz, "Shaykh Dr. Yousef al-Qaradawi."

8. Fouad Ajami, *The Foreigner's Gift: The Americans, the Arabs, and the Iraqis in Iraq* (New York: Free Press, 2006), 74–75.

9. See Maher Abdullah interview.

10. Ibid.

11. Ibid.

12. Abū Isḥāq al-Shāṭibī (d. 1388), an important jurist of the Nāṣrid period in al-Andalus, has become influential because he considered *maṣlaḥa* (common benefits) a legitimate and important motive in *fiqh*. On some of his innovative views regarding *maṣlaḥa*, see Felicitas Opwis's chapter in this book.

13. Maher Abdullah interview.

14. Ibid.

15. Ibid.

16. In a subtly polemical mode al-Qaraḍāwī adds that contrary to widespread belief, the Ḥanbalī legal scholar Ibn Taymiyya (d. 1328) and his student Ibn Qayyim al-Jawziyya (d. 1350) were ends-based jurists. Indeed, al-Qaraḍāwī argues, it is even mistaken to associate the Ḥanbalī legal school with literalism. See Maher Abdullah interview.

17. Yūsuf al-Qaraḍāwī, *The Islamic Movement in the Field of Intellect and Knowledge*, chap. 1. The text was available in 2003 at http://www.wponline.org/vil/Books/Q_Priorities/ch1p1.htm.

18. Ibid.

19. al-Qaraḍāwī, *Min fiqh al-dawla fī-l-Islām*, 130.

20. Ibid., 132.

21. Ibid.

22. Ibid.

23. Most famously expressed by ʿAlī ʿAbd al-Rāziq (1888–1966) in his book *al-Islām wa-uṣūl al-ḥukm* (Cairo: Maṭbaʿat Miṣr, 1343–44/1925).

24. al-Qaraḍāwī, *Min fiqh al-dawla fī l-Islām*, 133–34.

25. Ibid., 134.

26. Ibid., 136.

27. Ibid., 136–37.

28. Ibid., 137.

29. Ibid., 138.

30. Ibid., citing Yūsuf al-Qaraḍāwī, *al-Ḥall al-Islāmī: farīḍa wa-ḍarūra*, 3rd ed. (Cairo: Maktabat Wahba, 1977).

31. al-Qaraḍāwī, *Min fiqh al-dawla fī l-Islām*, 138.

32. It is important that al-Qaraḍāwī does not deny the non-Islamic origins of democracy but rather acknowledges them while rendering the foreign origin irrelevant for purposes of practical *fiqh*. I will return to this point later.

33. al-Qaraḍāwī, *Min fiqh al-dawla fī l-Islām*, 138–39.

34. See, for example, Rajā Bahlūl, *Ḥukm Allāh, ḥukm al-shaʿab: ḥawla al-ʿalāqa bayna l-dīmuqrāṭiyya wa-l-ʿilmaniyya* (Amman: Dār al-Shurūq, 2000). This sophisticated work seeks to disentangle democracy from liberal democracy in the process of its inquiry.

35. al-Qaraḍāwī, *Min fiqh al-dawla fī l-Islām*, 139.

36. The Khārijites were one of the sects of early Islam. Their strong moralistic theology was later regarded as one of main factors that brought disunity into the generation of Muhammad's companions. They are today regarded as radicals and heretics.

37. al-Qaraḍāwī, *Min fiqh al-dawla fī l-Islām*, 140.

38. Ibid., 141.

39. Ibid.

40. Ibid., 142.

41. Notwithstanding its technical, historical meaning, which is explained by Felicitas Opwis in Chapter 4 of this book, *mursala maṣlaḥa* is deployed in the writings of modernist Islamists—following some orientalist writers—to mean something like public interest.

42. al-Qaraḍāwī, *Min fiqh al-dawla fī l-Islām*, 142.

43. Ibid.

44. Ibid., 145.

45. Ibid., 145–46.

46. Ibid., 146.

47. Ibid. Obviously al-Qaraḍāwī does not follow the classic identification of the "people of binding and loosing" with Muslim legal scholars in this context.

48. Ibid.

49. Ibid., 145 and 137–38.

50. Ibid., 145.

51. Ibid., 138.

52. See Feldman, *After Jihad*.

53. al-Qaraḍāwī, *Min fiqh al-dawla fī l-Islām*, 137.

54. Ibid., 132.

Chapter 7

The first version of this chapter was presented to the Yale Law School's Middle East Legal Studies Seminar in January 2003 in Granada, Spain. A shorter version of it appeared in the online journal *Logos* (Summer 2003).

1. Aghājārī's speech was delivered in the Muʿallam Lecture Hall in Hamadan on 29 Khurdād 1381 / June 19, 2002. It was first published in the monthly *Bīnish-i sabz* (Tehran, 9th Amurdād 1381 / July 31, 2002) and in the weekly *Umīd-i jawān*, no. 306 (Tehran, Daymāh 1381 / January 2003) and was widely cited in papers and on the Internet. The full text appears in *Aghājārī: Matn-i kāmil-i sukhanrānī-yi Hamadān*, ed. Pūriyā Hājizādah (Tehran: Intishārāt-i Jāmahdarān, 1382/2003), 36–37. Although refreshing and courageous for the Islamic Republic, Aghājārī's speech draws a rather pedestrian and largely unhistorical comparison between Christianity and Islam. He portrays ʿAlī Sharīʿatī as a prophet of Protestant Islam while seeking in his thoughts and his life story a "humanist" message.

2. For institutional and historical obstacles to development of the *marjaʿiyya* in the nineteenth and twentieth centuries, see Abbas Amanat, "In Between the *Madrasa* and the Marketplace: The Designation of Clerical Leadership in Modern Shi'ism," in *Authority and Political Culture in Shi'ism*, ed. Saïd A. Arjomand (Albany: State University of New York Press, 1988), 98–132. See also *The Most Learned of the Shi'a: The Institution of the Marja' Taqlid*, ed. Linda S. Walbridge (New York: Oxford University Press, 2001); Ann K. S. Lambton, "A Reconsideration of the Position of the *Marja' al-Taqlid* and the Religious Institution," *Studia Islamica* 20 (1964): 115–35.

3. For the doctrine of occultation (*ghayba*) in Shiism, see, for example, Saïd A. Arjomand, "Crisis of the Imamate and the Institution of Occultation in Twelver Shi'ism: A Sociohistorical Perspective," *International Journal of Middle East Studies* 28 (1996): 491–515; Arjomand, "The Consolation of Theology: The Shi'ite Doctrine of Occultation and the Transition from Chiliasm to Law," *Journal of Religion* 76 (1996): 548–71; Etan Kohlberg, "From Imāmiyya to Ithna-ʿashariyya," *Bulletin of the School of Oriental and African Studies* 39 (1976): 521–34. See also Abbas Amanat, *Resurrection and Renewal: The Making of the Babi Movement in Iran, 1844–1850* (Ithaca, NY: Cornell University Press, 1989), 1–29, and the sources cited there.

4. For the historical evidence in the Safavid and Qajar periods, see, for example, Amanat, *Resurrection and Renewal*, 33–69; Saïd A. Arjomand, *The Shadow of God and the Hidden Imam: Religion, Political Order, and Societal Change in Shi'ite Iran from the Beginning to 1890* (Chicago: University of Chicago Press, 1984), 171–201, 238–59.

5. The development of *ijtihād* in Shiism still awaits a full modern treatment. See Mohammed Arkoun, "The Concept of Authority in Islamic Thought: *Lā ḥukūma illā lillāh*," in *Islam: State and Society*, ed. Klaus Ferdinand and Mehdi Mozaffari (London: Curzon Press, 1988), 53–73; Robert Brunschvig, "Les usûl al-fiqh imâmites à leur stade ancien (Xe et XIe siècles)," in *Le Shî'isme imâmite: Colloque de Strasbourg (6–9 mai 1968)* (Paris: Presses universitaires de France, 1970), 201–13; Norman Calder, "Doubt and Prerogative: The Emergence of an Imāmī Shīʿī Theory of *Ijtihād*," *Studia Islamica* 70 (1989): 57–77; Wilferd Madelung, "Authority in Twelver Shiism in the Absence of the Imam," in Madelung, *Religious Schools and Sects in Medieval Islam* (London: Variorum Reprints,

1985), 163–73; and Aron Zysow, art. "Ejtehād," in *Encyclopaedia Iranica*, ed. Ehsan Yarshater (London: Routledge & Kegan Paul., 1982–), 8:281–86. For theological debates in early Shiism, see Hossein Modarressi, *Crisis and Consolidation in the Formative Period of Shiite Islam: Abū Jaʿfar ibn Qiba al-Rāzī and His Contribution to Imāmite Shīʿite Thought* (Princeton: Darwin Press, 1993); and Andrew J. Newman, *The Formative Period of Twelver Shīʿism: Ḥadīth as Discourse Between Qum and Baghdad* (Richmond: Curzon Press, 2000).

6. For Safavid conversion to Twelver Shiism, see Arjomand, *Shadow of God*, 105–214; Rula Jurdi Abisaab, *Converting Persia: Religion and Power in the Safavid Empire* (London: I. B. Tauris, 2004); and Rasūl Jaʿfariyān, *Dīn wa-siyāsat dar dawrah-yi Ṣafawī* (Qom: Anṣāriyān, 1370 [1991]). Abisaab demonstrates the emergence of the *akhbārī* school as the outcome of a complex interplay between the Arabic-speaking *ʿulamā'*, as well as their descendants and the Persian *ʿulamā'* of the Safavid period.

7. For the *akhbārī-uṣūlī* controversy, see Robert Gleave, *Inevitable Doubt: Two Theories of Shi'i Jurisprudence* (Leiden: Brill, 2000); Andrew J. Newman, "The Nature of the Akhbārī/Uṣūlī Dispute in Late Ṣafawid Iran," *Bulletin of the School of Oriental and African Studies* 55 (1992): 22–51, 250–61; Newman, "Anti-Akhbārī Sentiments Among the Qajar ʿUlamā': The Case of Muḥammad Bāqir al-Khwānṣārī, d. 1313/1895," in *Religion and Society in Qajar Iran*, ed. Robert Gleave (London: RoutledgeCurzon, 2005), 155–73.

8. The extensive patronage networks in Shiite Iraq in the nineteenth century are examined in Meir Litvak, *Shi'i Scholars of Nineteenth-Century Iraq: The ʿUlama' of Najaf and Karbala'* (Cambridge: Cambridge University Press, 1998). See also Amanat, "In Between the *Madrasa* and the Marketplace."

9. The conventional treatment of clerical and state relations in the nineteenth century is Hamid Algar, *Religion and State in Iran, 1785–1906: The Role of the Ulama in the Qajar Period* (Berkeley: University of California Press, 1969). Algar, like most scholars in the 1960s, is inclined to portray the *ʿulamā'* as a unanimous voice of opposition to the Qajar state, who questioned its legitimacy and enjoyed the support of their constituency in challenging the state, but even the selective evidence in Algar's study points to a pattern of greater collaboration between the *ʿulamā'*s and the state rather than confrontation. To preserve their vested interests, prevail in intraclerical rivalries, and maintain power and prestige, the *ʿulamā'* frequently sought collaboration with the state. From the theoretical perspective, during the Qajar and most of the Pahlavi periods the *ʿulamā'* did not produce any substantive account of a theory of government—or even any oral pronouncement of any substance—that denies the legitimacy of the Shiite state. For a more nuanced view of the relation, see, for example, Arjomand, *Shadow of God*; and Amanat, *Resurrection and Renewal.*

10. Aspects of clerical transformation under the Pahlavis are studied in Shahrough Akhavi, *Religion and Politics in Contemporary Iran: Clergy-State Relations in the Pahlavi Period* (Albany: State University of New York Press, 1980); and Michael M. J. Fischer,

Iran: From Religious Dispute to Revolution (Cambridge, MA: Harvard University Press, 1980). See also two recent accounts with new details but with proclerical bias: Ḥā mid Baṣīrat-Mansih, *ʿUlamāʾ wa-rizhīm-i Rizā Shāh: Naẓarī bar ʿamalkard-i siyāsī-farhangī-yi rūḥāniyyūn dar sālhā-yi 1305–1320sh.* (Tehran: ʿUrūj, 1376 [1997]); and Rasūl Jaʿfariyān, *Jarayānhā wa-sāzmānhā-yi madhhabī-siyāsī-yi Īrān: Az rūyi kār amadan-i Muḥammad Rizā Shāh tā pīrūzī-yi Inqilāb-i Islāmī: 1320–1357*, 6th ed. (Qom: 1384 [2005]).

11. Among the few exceptions was Muḥammad Bāqir al-Ṣadr's (1935–80) trilogy on politics, society, and economics from the perspective of Shiite jurisprudence, though here too al-Ṣadr's attempt takes more a rhetorical turn toward apologia than a serious reconstruction of the legal theory. See Chibli Mallat, *The Renewal of Islamic Law: Muhammad Baqer es-Sadr, Najaf, and the Shi'i International* (Cambridge: Cambridge University Press, 1993). For an English translation and extensive commentary on al-Ṣadr's work on *uṣūl al-fiqh* (*Durūs fī ʿilm al-uṣūl*), see Muḥammad Bāqir al-Ṣadr, *Lessons in Islamic Jurisprudence*, trans. Roy P. Mottahedeh (Oxford: Oneworld, 2003).

12. A collection of papers of this conference appeared in *Baḥthī dar bārah-yi marjaʿiyyat wa-rūḥāniyyat*, ed. Muḥammad Ḥusayn Ṭabāṭabāʾī et al. (Tehran: Shirkat-i Intishār, 1342 [1963]). Ann K. S. Lambton was among the few from outside Iran to discuss the new debate in her "Reconsideration of the Position of the *Marjaʾ al-taqlīd.*"

13. See, for example, *Matn-i kāmil-i khāṭirāt-i Ayātallāh Ḥusayn ʿAlī Muntaẓirī* (Essen, Germany: Nima, 2001), 42–102.

14. See Jaʿfariyān, *Jarayānhā*, 703–54. Khomeini's *Kashf al-asrār* (first published in Tehran in 1323/1944) was in response to Shiite revisionist trends. It was a refutation of Ḥakamzādah's anticlerical tract *Asrār-i hazār sāliḥ*, which appeared in Tehran in the same year.

15. Most of Murtazā Mutahharī's work in the late 1960s and during the 1970s is devoted to popularizing Islamic (and to a lesser extent Shiite) theology, fundamentals of religion (*uṣūl-i ʿaqāʾid*), Islamic philosophy (*ḥikmat*), and exegesis (*tafsīr*) rather than jurisprudence and *uṣūl al-fiqh*. His lectures at the Ḥusayniyya Irshād in Tehran and at other places, and the bulk of his writings, even when implicitly refuting ʿAlī Sharīʿatī's revolutionary reading of Shiism, are shaped by an Islamic modernist discourse that was safely distant from the traditional teachings of the *ḥawza*. To a lesser extent other radical clerics of Qom and other centers, many of them Khomeini's students, moved away from *fiqh*. Murtazā Mutahharī's collected works, *Majmūʿah-yi athār-i ustad-i shahīd Mutahharī*, 7 vols. (Tehran: Intishārāt-i Ṣadrā, 1369–74/1989–95), clearly reflect this modernist tendency.

16. Khomeini's thirteen lectures in Najaf on the "authority of the jurist" (*wilāyat-i faqīh*) in early 1970 were apparently delivered at the request of Jalāl al-Din Farsī, an Islamic activist and author of a number of works on political Islam. Farsī first published the Persian lectures in Beirut in 1349/1970, and later they were also published in Qom, Najaf, and Tehran. The idea of *wilāyat-i faqīh* was not entirely unknown to the Shiite dissident circles since the early 1950s, though it was Khomeini who first developed it as

a political doctrine. See, for example, Ja'fariyān, *Jarayānhā*, 237–49. For an English translation of Khomeini's lectures, see Hamid Algar, *Islam and Revolution: Writings and Declarations of Imam Khomeini* (Berkeley, CA: Mizan Press, 1981). See also Michael M. J. Fischer's critical review of Algar's book in *Iranian Studies* 14 (1981): 263.

17. Algar, *Islam and Revolution*, 29.

18. This assertion comes despite the fact that Khomeini himself had produced one such "practical treatise of jurisprudence" with all the familiar conventionalities and customary preoccupations with ritual acts, cleanliness (*ṭahārāt*), and similar debates. See Rūḥallāh Khomeini, *Risālah-yi tawḍīḥ al-masā'il* (first published in Qom 1381/1962), which is a commentary on Ayatollah Burūjirdī's voluminous work on the subject. It is translated as *A Clarification of Questions: An Unabridged Translation of Resaleh Towzih al-Masael*, trans. J. Borujerdi (pseudonym) with a foreword by Michael M. J. Fischer and Mehdi Abedi (Boulder, CO: Westview Press, 1984). Moreover. Khomeini produced at least twenty-seven titles on *fiqh* and *uṣūl al-fiqh* in Arabic and Persian on all aspects of *furū'*. For an annotated list, see *Pāygāh-i iṭṭilā'rasānī-yi Imām Khumaynī* (http://www.imam-khomeini.com) under "athār wa-'ashā'ir-i Imām." See also Ḥamīd Rūḥānī (Ziyāratī), *Bar'rasī wa-taḥlīlī az nahzāt-i Imām Khumaynī*, 11th ed., 2 vols. (Tehran: Daftar-i Intishārāt-i Islāmī, 1360 [1981]), 1:55–62. For a discussion of Khomeini's early interests in jurisprudence, see Hamid Algar, "Imam Khomeini: Pre-revolutionary Years, 1902–1962," in *Islam, Politics, and Social Movements*, ed. Edmund Burke III and Ira M. Lapidus (Berkeley: University of California Press, 1989), 263–88.

19. The early references to Khomeini as imam appear in the tracts of the Najaf-based clandestine publisher Intishārāt-i Pānzdahum-i Khurdād (better known as Dawāzdahum-i Muḥarram) operated by Khomeini's students Maḥmūd Dū'ā'ī, 'Alī Akbar Muhtashimipūr, and others. Among its publications were the Arabic *Mawqif al-Imām al-Khumaynī tujāha Isrā'īl* (Najaf, 1971?) and a two-volume Persian propagandistic biography of Khomeini, *Bīyugrāfī-yi pīshwā*, 2 vols. (n.p. [Najaf?]: Intishārāt-i Pānzdahum-i Khurdād, 1394 [1974]), where the aforementioned *qaṣīda* appears at the beginning of the first volume (7–11). The authors in this work repeatedly refer to Khomeini with the title *pīshwā*, a term ominously used in Persian since the 1930s for the German *Führer*. The Persian editions of Khomeini's *Ḥukūmat-i Islāmī* published in the early 1970s appeared under the pseudonym "Imam Kāshif al-Ghiṭā'," a camouflage under the cover of the well-known anti-British Iraqi Shiite leader of the 1920s. One other example in the 1970s of Shiite adoption of the term *imam* is the case of the Iranian-Lebanese Shiite leader Imam Mūsā al-Ṣadr (1928–78?).

20. On the relationship of the *wilāyat-i faqīh* to social contract theories, see Shahrough Akhavi's contribution in Chapter 8 of this volume.

21. Muḥsin Kadīwar, *Ḥukūmat-i wilā'ī* (Tehran: Nashr-i Nay, 1377 [1998]).

22. Muḥsin Kadīwar, *Naẓariyyahā-yi dawlat dar fiqh-i Shī'ah* (Tehran: Nashr-i Nay, 1376 [1997]).

23. Muḥammad Taqī Miṣbāḥ Yazdī, *Nigāhi guzarā bih naẓariyyah-yi wilāyat-i faqīh* (Qom: Mu'assasah-yi Āmūzishī wa-Pizhūhishī-yi Imām Khumaynī, 1378 [1999]).

24. For the indictment against Aghājārī and his defense, see *Aghājārī: Matn-i kāmil-i sukhanrānī-yi Hamadān*, 47–170.

Chapter 8

1. As an imported idea, it would be considered *bidʿa* or *ibtikār* (unwarranted innovation) by Muslim traditionalists. On Rifāʿat al-Ṭahṭāwī's (d. 1873) and Mehmet Namık Kemal's (d. 1888) interest in social contract and natural law, see, respectively, Albert Hourani, *Arabic Thought in the Liberal Age, 1798–1939* (London: Oxford University Press, 1962), 69–70, 75; and Serif Mardin, *The Genesis of Young Ottoman Thought* (Princeton: Princeton University Press, 1962), 289–336.

2. In the introduction to his edition and translation of *Social Contract: Essays by Locke, Hume and Rousseau* (New York: Oxford University Press, 1960), viii, Ernest Barker argues that Aquinas was an important precursor of social contract theory because he reflected liberalism rooted in a blend of the Bible, Roman law, and Aristotelian concepts of politics. Although Aquinas is significant for the later development of the theory of social contract, we are not likely to call him a social contract theorist. Similarly, the writings of an Azharite scholar may lend themselves to certain arguments in social contract theory, but that would not warrant considering that individual a social contractarian.

3. Murray Forsyth, "Hobbes's Contractarianism: A Comparative Analysis," in *The Social Contract from Hobbes to Rawls*, ed. David Boucher and Paul Kelly (New York: Routledge, 1994), 35–50, 38.

4. Majid Khadduri, *War and Peace in the Law of Islam* (Baltimore: Johns Hopkins University Press, 1955), 7–9; Mardin, *Genesis of Young Ottoman Thought*, 82–92.

5. Marcus Tullius Cicero, *On the Commonwealth*, trans. George H. Sabine and Stanley B. Smith (Columbus: Ohio State University Press, 1929), 215.

6. Barker, *Social Contract*, x.

7. Hourani, *Arabic Thought in the Liberal Age*, 136.

8. Malcolm Kerr, *Islamic Reform: The Political and Legal Theories of Muḥammad ʿAbduh and Rashīd Riḍā* (Berkeley: University of California Press, 1966), 104–5.

9. Ibid., 138.

10. Ibid., 161–62.

11. Ibid., 162.

12. Ibid.

13. Muḥammad ʿAmārah, *Maʿrakat al-Islam wa-uṣūl al-ḥukm* (Cairo and Beirut: Dar al-Shurūq, 1989), 152–62.

14. Leonard Binder, *Islamic Liberalism: A Critique of Development Ideologies* (Chicago: University of Chicago Press, 1988), 261.

15. Shahrough Akhavi, "Sunni Modernist Theories of Social Contract in Contemporary Egypt," *International Journal of Middle East Studies* 35 (2003): 23–49.

16. Rūḥallāh Khomeini, *Ḥukūmat-i Islamī*, 3rd ed. (Najaf: n.p., 1971), 121.

17. Ibid., 112.

18. Ibid., 121.

19. Rūḥallāh Khomeini, *Kitāb al-Bayʿ*, 5 vols. (Qom: Maṭbaʿah-yi Ismāʿīliyān, 1409/1988), 2:478–82. The book was orginally published in 1970. Khomeini, *Ḥukūmat*, 121.

20. Saïd Arjomand, *The Turban for the Crown* (New York: Oxford University Press, 1988), 177–78.

21. Niʿmatullāh Ṣāliḥī Najafābādī, *Wilāyat-i faqīh: Ḥukūmat-i ṣāliḥān* (Tehran: Mu'assasah-yi Khadamāt-i Farhang-i Rasā, 1363/1984), 45–46, 22–23.

22. Ibid., 31–32.

23. Ibid., 36.

24. Ibid., 38.

25. Ibid., 36–37.

26. Ibid., 46–47.

27. Ibid., 50.

28. Ibid., 106–7, 123–25.

29. Mahdī Ḥā'irī, *Ḥikmat wa-ḥukūmat* (London: Intishārāt-i Shādī, 1995), 54.

30. On the meaning of the Arabic verb *ḥakama* and its significance for this debate, see the section "Shari'a in the Contemporary Context" in Chapter 1 of this book.

31. Mahdī Ḥā'irī, *Ḥikmat wa-ḥukūmat*, 54–55.

32. Ibid., 55.

33. Ibid., 58.

34. Ibid., 61–62.

35. Ibid., 62.

36. Ibid., 63–64.

37. Ibid., 65.

38. Ibid., 70–82.

39. Ibid., 84–85.

40. Ibid., 89–90.

41. Ibid., 91–92.

42. Ibid., 92–95.

43. Ibid., 97–102.

44. Ibid., 102–5.

45. Ibid., 105–8.

46. Ibid., 108–9.

47. Muʿtazilites argued that one can demonstrate the validity of revelation by reason rather than having simply to accept it as God's entitlement, but this was a marginal development and was suppressed.

Chapter 9

1. Hamilton A. R. Gibb, "The Heritage of Islam in the Modern World (I)," *International Journal of Middle East Studies* 1 (1970): 3–17, 11.

2. Saïd Amir Arjomand, "Medieval Persianate Political Ethic," *Studies on Persianate Societies* 1 (2003): 3–28.

3. Saïd Amir Arjomand, *The Shadow of God and the Hidden Imam: Religion, Political Order, and Societal Change in Shi'ite Iran from the Beginning to 1890* (Chicago: University of Chicago Press, 1984).

4. The royal librarian, Muḥammad Nadīm Bārfurūshī (d. 1825), for example, states, "[God] has chosen two classes among mankind and given them the crown of sovereignty and the ring of superiority. The first are the prophets. . . . the second class consists of the rulers of the earth and the just kings. . . . After the rank of prophecy, there shall be no position higher than kingship." (Cited in ʿAbd al-Hādī Ḥā'irī, *Nukhustīn rūyārū'ihā-yi andīshagarān-i Īrān bā-daw raviyah-i tamaddun-i bourgeoisie-yi gharb* [Tehran: Amīr Kabīr, 1988], 355.)

5. Nader Shohrabi, "Revolution and State Culture: The Circle of Justice and Constitutionalism in 1906 Iran," in *State/Culture: State-Formation After the Cultural Turn*, ed. G. Steinmetz (Ithaca, NY: Cornell University Press, 1999), 253–88.

6. Saïd Amir Arjomand, "Islam and the Making of the Iranian Constitution of 1906–7," in *Islam and Constitutionalism*, ed. H. Chehabi and S. Hashmi (Cambridge, MA: Harvard University Press, forthcoming).

7. There was considerable rhetorical confusion of the two notions, however. For example, the oath administered to the Majlis deputies in March 1907 was a pledge of allegiance to "the principles of constitutional monarchy and the rights of the nation" and the observance of the "interests of the Iranian nation and state according to the laws of the Muhammadan Shari'a" (*qawānīn-i sharʿ-i Muḥammadī*). *Mudhākirāt-i Majlis-i Shūrā-yi Millī* (Tehran: Rūznāme-yi Rasmī-yi Kishwar, 1325/1946–47), 1:103.

8. "In such matters the decision of this committee of *ʿulamā'* shall be followed and obeyed, and this article shall continue unchanged until the appearance of His Holiness the Proof of the Age [i.e., the Hidden Imam]."

9. Saïd Amir Arjomand, "Shi'ite Jurisprudence and Constitution Making in the Islamic Republic of Iran," in *Fundamentalisms and the State: Remaking Polities, Economies, and Militance*, ed. M. Marty and R. S. Appleby (Chicago: University of Chicago Press, 1993), 88–109.

10. Arjomand, "Islam and the Making of the Iranian Constitution of 1906–7."

11. Perhaps only one traditionalist cleric, ʿAbd al-Ḥusayn Lārī, can be said to have anticipated the Shari'ā-based constitution of 1979 in a vituperative pamphlet written in 1907–8 (1325) with the title *The Law of Shari'a-Based Constitutional Government* (*Qānūn-i mashrūṭa-yi mashrūʿa*), which he contrasted to "the national law (*qānūn-i millī*)

of the devils" (Gh.-H. Zargarinijād, *Rasā'il-i mashrūṭiyyāt: Hijdah risālah wa-lāyiha dar bāra-yi mashrūṭiyyāt* [Tehran: Kavir, 1377/1998], 388), and a second on jurisprudence. In the latter work Lārī differentiated among the exclusive authority of the hierocratic judge (*ḥākim-i sharʿ*) in the execution of the punishments and obligations of Shari'a, the authority of the imam and his deputy (*nā'ib*) in such matters as *kharāj* and agricultural rent, the general authority (*wilāyat*) of the *ʿulamā'* in matters that affect the interests of the Muslim, and last, the authority of the "just Muslims" by default (ibid., 406–14). Lārī's handwritten commentaries on the margin of the *Maqāsib* of Shaykh Murtaḍā Anṣāri have recently been published by Sayyid ʿAli Mīr-Shārifī under the misleading title *Wilā-yat al-faqīh*. Even there Lārī, who repeatedly uses the terms *sulṭanat al-faqīh* and *khilāfat al-faqīh*, does not include the right to rule under *ḥukūma* because Khomeini had not yet conflated the juridical meaning of that term with its Persian common usage for "government." ʿAbd al-Ḥusayn Lārī, "Shish risāla-yi siyāsī wa-ijtimāʿī," ed. S.ʿA. Mīr-Shārifī, in *Mirāth-i Islāmī-yi Īrān*, ed. R. Jaʿfariyān (Qom: Mariyashī Library, 1377/1998), 9:199–273, 209.

12. The model, which I have called the "ideological constitution," is designed not for the limitation of government but for the transformation of the social order according to a revolutionary ideology. Limited government and civil liberties have to give way because the constitution itself is now an instrument of social transformation. Saïd Amir Arjomand, "Constitutions and the Struggle for Political Order: A Study in the Modernization of Political Traditions," *European Journal of Sociology* 33, no. 4 (1992): 39–82, 46.

13. Saïd Amir Arjomand, "Authority in Shi'ism and Constitutional Developments in the Islamic Republic of Iran," in *The Twelver Shia in Modern Times: Religious Culture and Political History*, ed. R. Brunner and W. Ende (Leiden: Brill, 2000), 301–32.

14. Markaz-i Taḥqīqāt-i Fiqhī-yi Quwwa-yi Qazā'iyya, *Majmūʿah-yi Naẓariyyāt-i Mushawaratī-yi Fiqhī dar Umūr-i Kayfarī* (Qom, 1381/2002); and *Majmūʿah-yi Naẓariyyāt-i Mushwaratī-yi Fiqhī dar Umūr-i Qazā'ī* (Qom, 1381/2002).

15. Markaz-i Taḥqīqāt-i Fiqhī-yi Quwwa-yi Qazā'iyya, *Majmūʿah-yi Ārā-yi Fiqhī-yi Qazā'ī dar Umūr-i Ḥuqūqī* (Qom, 1381/2002), 209–11.

16. Markaz-i Taḥqīqāt-i Fiqhī-yi Quwwa-yi Qazā'iyya, *Majmūʿah-yi Ārā-yi Fiqhī-yi Qazā'ī dar Umūr-i Ḥuqūqī* and *Majmūʿah-yi Nazariyyāt-i Mushawaratī-yi Fiqhī dar Umūr-i Qazā'ī*.

17. The law of compensation was approved "experimentally" for five years, but has remained in force.

18. Markaz-i Taḥqīqāt-i Fiqhī-yi Quwwa-yi Qazā'iyya, *Majmūʿah-yi Naẓariyyāt-i Mushwaratī-yi Fiqhī dar Umūr-i Kayfarī*.

19. Ibid., 243–45.

20. Bahman Kishāvarz, *Majmūʿah-yi Mohshā-yi Qānūn-i Taʿzīrāt-i Musawwab-i 1375* (Tehran: Ganj-i Dānish, 1375/1996).

21. Markaz-i Taḥqīqāt-i Fiqhī-yi Quwwa-yi Qazā'iyya, *Majmūʿah-yi Ārā-yi Fiqhī-yi Qazā'ī dar Umūr-i Kayfarī*, 108–9. The disregard of the entire system of judiciary authority based on the *wilāyat-i faqīh* by Ayatollah Sayyid ʿAlī Sīstānī, who inherited most of the large global following of the late Grand Ayatollah Abū l-Qāsim Khū'ī, is less surprising. In response to the question concerning the right of a judge appointed by the supreme jurist as the *wālī-yi amr*, Sīstāni simply reaffirms that judgeship is the exclusive right of the fully qualified *mujtahid*, who requires no one else's permission (ibid., 29).

22. Cf. Clifford Geertz, *Local Knowledge: Further Essays in Interpretive Anthropology* (New York: Basic Books, 1983).

23. Markaz-i Taḥqīqāt-i Fiqhī-yi Quwwa-yi Qazā'iyya, *Majmūʿah-yi Ārā-yi Fiqhī-yi Qazā'ī dar Umūr-i Kayfarī* (Qom, 1381/2002), 7–16.

24. Saïd Amir Arjomand, "Democratization and the Constitutional Politics of Iran Since 1997," *Polish Sociological Review* 136, no. 4 (2001): 349–63.

25. Interview with the commission's chairman, Ayatollah Amīnī, on May 4, 1997 (13/2/1376).

26. Markaz-i Taḥqīqāt-i Fiqhī-yi Quwwa-yi Qazā'iyya, *Majmūʿah-yi Naẓariyyāt-i Mushawaratī-yi Fiqhī dar Umūr-i Qazā'ī*, 109–11.

27. *Iṭṭilāʿāt*, January 11, 2002.

Chapter 10

1. This thesis has been most prominently advocated by Amira El-Azhary Sonbol, "Adults and Minors in Ottoman Shari'a Courts and Modern Law," in *Women, the Family, and Divorce Laws in Islamic History*, ed. Amira El Azhary-Sonbol (Syracuse, NY: Syracuse University Press, 1996), 277–89, 250–51; the title of her chapter conveys that modern legislation and Ottoman court practice are directly comparable.

2. Lawrence Rosen, *The Anthropology of Justice: Law as Culture in Islamic Society* (Cambridge: Cambridge University Press, 1989).

3. Ziba Mir-Hosseini, *Marriage on Trial: A Study of Islamic Family Law* (London: I. B. Tauris, 1993), 18. Her experience in Iran is analogous to my own in Yemen. A parallel attitude, supposing a "real" Shari'a, exists in Western academia, either by positing a dichotomy of theory versus practice in Islamic law or by using "Islamicity" and "deviation" as the main categories to analyze contemporary legislation and jurisprudence.

4. Because of difficulties in obtaining a large-enough sample, not many authors have chosen this path, but see, for example, Bettina Dennerlein, *Islamisches Recht und sozialer Wandel in Algerien: Zur Entwicklung des Personalstatus seit 1962* (Berlin: Klaus Schwarz, 1998); and Ron Shaham, *Family and the Courts in Modern Egypt: A Study Based on Decisions by the Sharī'a Courts, 1900–1955* (Leiden: Brill, 1997). Michael Peletz, *Islamic Modern: Religious Courts and Cultural Politics in Malaysia* (Princeton: Princeton University Press, 2002), uses a much more limited sample that appears not quite sufficient for his interesting but broad conclusions.

5. A penal code drafted around 1985–86 was never passed by any legislative body but was nevertheless used. Only in 1994 was a properly codified penal code issued by presidential decree.

6. A very different path was taken in Sudan. See Aharon Layish and Gabriel Warburg, *The Reinstatement of Islamic Law in Sudan under Numayrī: An Evaluation of a Legal Experiment in the Light of Its Historical Context, Methodology, and Repercussions* (Leiden: Brill, 2002).

7. Art. 3 of the 1994 constitution (as last amended in 2001) defines "the Shari'a as the source for all legislation."

8. Fieldwork was done in the South Sanaa court during 1993–95, observing trials daily and working through the archives and registers kept at court, which covered the period between 1983 and 1995. This chapter draws on my *Aš-Šarīʿa fī Bāb al-Yaman: Recht, Richter und Rechtspraxis an der familienrechtlichen Kammer des Gerichts Süd-Sanaa, (Republik Jemen), 1983–1995* (Berlin: Duncker & Humblot, 2000), 114–52; I am grateful to Don Reneau, who translated parts from German.

9. Today al-Ṣāfiya designates the area extending south from Bāb al-Yaman to roughly 45m Street, bounded on the west by Kulliyyat al-Shurṭa Street and by Zubayrī Street to the north. The origins of urban settlement can be traced back to the second Ottoman occupation (1872–1918) and the construction of a military installation; the complete urbanization of the neighborhood ensued only in the early 1970s as a result of processes set in motion by internal Yemeni migration. See Ḥusayn al-ʿAmrī, art. "al-Ṣā-fiya," in *al-Mawsūʿa al-yamaniyya*, vol. 2, ed. Mu'assasat al-ʿAfīf al-Thaqāfiyya (Beirut: Dār al-Fikr al-Muʿāṣir, 1992), 558; R. B. Serjeant, "Ṣanʿā' the 'Protected': Hijrah," in *Ṣanʿā': An Arabian Islamic City*, ed. R. B. Serjeant and R. Lewcock (London: World of Islam Festival Trust, 1983), 39–43, 39.

10. I use "family court" instead of a more literal translation ("chamber for personal status") for the Arabic *qism al-aḥwāl al-shakhṣiyya.*

11. In the mid-1990s the district embraced 46 percent of the overall area of the city and was home to one-third of the city's population, or about 325,000 people: data according to Franck Mermier, "Sanaa, métaphore de l'Etat Yéménite," in *Sanaa hors les murs: Une ville arabe contemporaine*, ed. Gilbert Grandguillaume Franck Mernier, and Jean-François Train (Tours: CNRS/URBAMA, 1995), 37–70, 43, 63–70; and *al-Qaḍā'iyya* (irregular issuance, Ministry of Justice, Sanaa), December 29, 1998.

12. Shakib al-Khameri, "Intraurban Residential Preferences in the City of Sanaa, the Republic of Yemen" (Ph.D. diss., University of Kentucky, 1992), 93–99, 202–10.

13. This social heterogeneity of the district, as well as its exceptional size, may have motivated the split of jurisdiction in mid-1415 / early 1995. The new southwestern court became responsible for the prosperous clientele inhabiting the villas in the suburban developments, while responsibility for the southeastern court was restricted to the area with a distinctly poor population.

14. The data set is taken from an analysis of the 415 rulings rendered and archived by the family court between 1983 and 1995 and relates information about male litigants and witnesses (n = 699).

15. The census of 1994 does not list the military and security services as an employer. *The Military Balance, 1997/1998*, ed. International Institute for Strategic Studies (Oxford: Oxford University Press, 1998), 144, estimates that 146,300 persons were employed by the military; the World Bank estimates 218,700 persons. World Bank, *Republic of Yemen: Poverty Assessment* (Washington, DC: World Bank, 1996), 56.

16. Most anthropological accounts of Yemen that focus on family life were written in the 1970s, and many focus on rural areas. In these accounts every woman appears to have an extended family to turn to. See Susan Dorsky, "Women's Lives in a North Yemeni Highlands Town" (Ph.D. diss., Case Western Reserve University, 1981), 159–60; Martha Mundy, *Domestic Government: Kinship, Community and Polity in North Yemen* (London: I. B. Tauris, 1995), 133, 141. For similar assumptions about families in Sanaa, see Carla Makhlouf, *Changing Veils: Women and Modernisation in North Yemen* (London: Croom Helm, 1979), 66; Gabriele Vom Bruck, "Re-defining Identity: Women in Sanʿā'," in *Yemen: 3000 Years of Art and Civilisation in Arabia Felix*, ed. Werner Daum (Innsbruck: Pinguin, 1997), 396–408, 400. Only more recent studies by Yemeni authors deal with urban communities, but rarely with family life; see, for example, Muḥammad ʿAbd al-Wāḥid al-Maytamī, "Baḥth istiṭlāʿī ʿan al-shabāb fī l-Jumhūriyya al-Yamaniyya," *Dirāsāt Yamaniyya* 22 (1992): 279–366.

17. Ninety-seven percent of all litigants and witnesses (n = 947) declare Sanaa not to be their "place of origin," even if they might have been born and raised in Sanaa. More than half the litigants and witnesses declare that their place of origin is the populous southern provinces of North Yemen, Dhamār, Taʿizz, and Ibb.

18. Whether and to what extent these economic conditions, the relation to state institutions, and the marital conflicts of the parties are representative of the neighborhood inhabitants in general, or merely of the poorer members, cannot be determined from court decisions.

19. Full body cover with the *sharshaf* and face veiling have become prominent in Yemen since the 1950s. For details, see Martha Mundy, "Ṣanʿā' Dress, 1920–1975," in *Ṣanʿā': An Arabian Islamic City*, ed. R. B. Serjeant and R. Lewcock (London: World of Islam Festival Trust, 1983), 529–41.

20. Putting down arms is a part of adjudication in more customary settings and a strong symbol of the (always-temporary) willingness to submit to somebody's ruling; see Paul Dresch, *Tribes, Government, and History in Yemen* (Oxford: Clarendon Press, 1989), 92, 95, 113–14n23.

21. Law on Judicial Fees 43/1991, arts. 5, 10(9), 12; "Qarār jumhūrī bi-l-qānūn raqm 43 li-sanat 1991 bi-sha'n al-rusūm al-qaḍā'iyya," *al-Jarīda al-rasmiyya* 7, no. 1 (April 15, 1991).

22. Code of Civil Procedure 28/1992, arts. 29, 32, 33; "Qarār jumhūrī bi-l-qānūn raqm 28 li-sanat 1992 bi-sha'n al-murāfaʿāt wa-l-tanfīdh al-madanī," *al-Jarīda al-rasmiyya* 7, no. 1 (April 15, 1992). This law was thoroughly amended in 2002, with more stringent provisions on enforcement of civil rulings, borrowed largely from Egypt.

23. Code of Civil Procedure 28/1992, arts. 35, 86.

24. It appears that similar suits in Egypt during the 1970s and 1990s, respectively, took much longer: Enid Hill, *Mahkama: Studies in the Egyptian Legal System* (London: Ithaca Press, 1979), 43; Nathan Brown, *The Rule of Law in the Arab World: Courts in Egypt and the Gulf* (Cambridge: Cambridge University Press, 1997), 200.

25. In Yemeni dialectal usage Shari'a refers not only to a body of norms but also to judicial proceedings; *dakhalnā fī l-sharīʿa* thus means "we have brought court action," and the verbal form (dialect: *nitshārʿa*) connotes the same.

26. Mir-Hosseini, *Marriage on Trial*, 112, points out that Moroccan legal proceedings are almost impossible to conduct without a lawyer.

27. The significant exception to this rule is custody battles.

28. The Ministry of Justice is responsible for issuing licenses to lawyers and Shari'a experts, but was rather dysfunctional during the early 1990s. Lawyers have been critical of the *wukalā' al-sharīʿa* since the 1970s; see Brinkley Messick, *The Calligraphic State: Textual Domination and History in a Muslim Society* (Berkeley: University of California Press, 1993), 224, 312n42. By the late 1990s the lawyers' union had succeeded in legally barring *wukalā' al-sharīʿa* from being recognized as attorneys; *al-Qaḍā'iyya* (irregular issuance, Ministry of Justice, Sanaa), May 18, 1999; *al-Qisṭās* (legal quarterly/monthly, Sanaa), February 1999.

29. Al-Jumhūriyya al-ʿArabiyya al-Yamaniyya, Wizārat al-ʿAdl, *Kitāb al-Iḥṣā' al-sanawī li-l-ʿām al-qaḍā'ī 1982* (Sanaa, 1983), 53; al-Jumhūriyya al-ʿArabiyya al-Yamaniyya, Wizārat al-ʿAdl, *Al-Majalla al-qaḍā'iyya* 2 (1983), Table 4; al-Jumhūriyya al-ʿArabiyya al-Yamaniyya, Wizārat al-ʿAdl, *al-Majalla al-qaḍā'iyya* 3 (1985), 79; al-Jumhūriyya al-Yamaniyya, Maḥkamat Isti'nāf Amānat al-ʿĀṣima, *Kitāb al-Iḥṣā' al-sanawī al-thānī li-l-ʿām 1417* (Sanaa, 1997), 3–5, 19. The high number of criminal—as compared with civil and personal-status—cases is interesting in the Yemeni setting, where Islamic law is not marginalized to personal status. Not surprisingly, then, legal populism that demanded the "application of Shari'a," increasing during the early 1990s, concentrated on criminal law, particularly faster implementation of *qiṣāṣ* sentences and the application of *ḥudūd* in the provinces that formerly constituted the People's Democratic Republic of Yemen (PDRY). At least on the level of legislation, populism got its way in the autumn of 1994, when Penal Code 12/1994 was passed by presidential decree. The law resembled the draft penal code formerly in use in the Arab Republic of Yemen (see note 5) and criminalized behavior and acts previously legal in the PDRY.

30. Court register at South Sanaa primary court ($n = 1{,}673$).

31. The latter category comprises about 5 percent in any given year. A ruling on non-jurisdiction is rendered by the court either on its own initiative or in response to a petition by one of the parties. As a rule, the issue is the court's geographic jurisdiction, which is determined by the defendant's residence.

32. As elsewhere, judges are to encourage the parties to settle; Law on Civil Procedure, art. 118. Any settlement, whether reached in or out of court, is treated like a first-instance ruling, that is, it can be appealed to the court of appeals. Law on Arbitration 22/1992, art. 8; "Qarār jumhūrī bi-l-qānūn raqm 22 li-sanat 1992 bi-sha'n al-taḥkīm," *al-Jarīda al-rasmiyya* 6, no. 4 (March 31, 1992).

33. Law on Arbitration 22/1992, art. 5(1); Law on Personal Status 20/1992, art. 45.

34. The scribes at the gates of the court are required to have rudimentary formal training, administered by the Higher Judicial Institute.

35. This appears to be different in Morocco and Egypt: Mir-Hosseini, *Marriage on Trial,* 73, 112; Shaham, *Family and the Courts,* 126–27.

36. The low percentage of inheritance cases is intriguing; Martha Mundy, "Land and Family in a Yemeni Community" (Ph.D. diss., University of Cambridge, 1981), 122, describes a rural court in the 1970s where most cases were inheritance cases. The low number of inheritance cases in this urban court may be due to the poverty of court users, or it may indicate that most inheritance cases are resolved out of court.

37. For a detailed breakdown of the cases registered and decided, see Würth, *Aš-Šarīʿa fī Bāb al-Yaman,* 143, 145–47.

38. Law on Personal Status 20/1992, arts. 58, 59, 60, 348(2), "Qarār jumhūrī bi-l-qānūn raqm 20 li-sanat 1992 bi-sha'n al-aḥwāl al-shakhṣiyya," *al-Jarīda al-rasmiyya* 6, no. 3 (March 31, 1992). This law was thoroughly amended in 1998 and 1999, but the features mentioned in the text remain in place.

39. In fact, returning a runaway wife is not all that easy in Yemen; there is no state-backed enforcement of a ruling on marital obedience. See for details Anna Würth, "Employing Islam and Custom Against Statutory Reform: *Bayt at-Ta'a* in Yemen," in *Le cheikh et le procureur: Systèmes coutumiers, centralisme étatique et pratiques juridiques au Yémen et en Egypte*, ed. Baudouin Dupret and François Burgat (Brussels: Complexe, forthcoming).

40. Rosen mentions a similarly high proportion of successful female plaintiffs in Morocco and assumes that this is due to changes in the judicial system. He fails to offer evidence for this correlation: Lawrence Rosen, "A la barre: Regard sur les archives d'un tribunal marocain (1965–1995)," in *Droits et sociétés dans le monde arabe: Perspectives socio-anthropologiques*, ed. Gilles Boëtsch, Baudouin Dupret, and Jean-Noël Ferrié (Aix-en-Provence: Presse de l'Université d'Aix-Marseille, 1997), 85–99, 93. Daniel Lev aptly describes Indonesian Islamic courts during the 1950s as "women's institutions" but does not analyze statistically how many women plaintiffs won their claims: Daniel Lev, *Islamic Courts in Indonesia: A Study in the Political Bases of Legal Institutions* (Berkeley: University of California Press, 1972), 150.

41. See Würth, *Aš-Šarīʿa fī Bāb al-Yaman,* 234–43.

42. A court verdict in these cases establishes that the wife's utterance "I hereby dissolve my marriage to my husband for the reasons mentioned in the claim" (*infasakhtu ʿaqd nikāḥī min zawjī fulān ibn fulān li-l-asbāb al-madhkūra fī l-daʿwa*) is legally valid. The court's verdict is thus on the validity of dissolution (*siḥḥat al-faskh*) and does not constitute the dissolution.

43. Law on Personal Status 20/1992, art. 41(5).

44. I do not have reliable data on the percentage of rulings appealed because this is not recorded in any systematic fashion in the primary courts; my observations and the review of a number of appeals and Supreme Court decisions lead me to believe that almost all contentious divorces and all child custody cases tend to be appealed. The personal-status cases reviewed by the Supreme Court, on the other hand, appear to be largely confined to issues of the validity of repudiation and self-redemption, which are the most intricate personal-status issues.

45. Law on Personal Status 20/1992, arts. 50, 51, 52(1), 156. Marital support is considered a debt incumbent on the husband, but the law of 1992 limits the payment of owed support to one year before raising the claim.

46. On Egypt, see Oussama Arabi, *Studies in Modern Islamic Law and Jurisprudence* (The Hague: Kluwer Law International, 2001), 169–88. Egyptian legislation, however, spells out that a judicially supervised *khulʿ* will entail the loss of all financial rights, whereas Yemeni provisions on divorce for nonsupport do not.

47. According to the weekly of the armed forces, *26. Sibtimbir*, December 12, 1996.

48. It should be noted that even in a legal system that recognizes postmarital support for the divorcée, poverty often forced women to remarry; for Europe, see Jack Goody, "Dowry and the Rights of Women to Property," in *Property Relations: Renewing the Anthropological Tradition,* ed. C. M. Hann (Cambridge: Cambridge University Press, 1998), 201–13, 209.

Afterword

1. See Frank Stewart's article "Arab Customary Law" under the header "ʿUrf," in *The Encyclopaedia of Islam,* new ed., 11 vols. (London: Luzac & Co.; Leiden: Brill, 1956–2002), 10:888–92.

2. Marshall G. S. Hodgson, *The Venture of Islam: Conscience and History in a World Civilization,* 3 vols. (Chicago: University of Chicago Press, 1974), 1:59.

3. Jon E. Mandaville, "Usurious Piety: The Cash *waqf* Controversy in the Ottoman Empire," *International Journal of Middle East Studies* 10 (1979): 289–308.

4. See Hossein Modarressi, *An Introduction to Shīʿī Law: A Bibliographical Study* (London: Ithaca Press, 1984), 4n2.

ABOUT THE AUTHORS

Shahrough Akhavi is a professor in the Department of Political Science at the University of South Carolina in Columbia, South Carolina. He received his B.A. from Brown University (1962), M.A. from Harvard University (1964), and Ph.D. from Columbia University (1969). Akhavi has published *Religion and Politics in Contemporary Iran* (Albany: State University of New York Press, 1980) and numerous articles in academic journals. He conducted field research in the sociology of Islam in Iran and Egypt under grants from the Ford Foundation (1975), the National Endowment for the Humanities (1980–81), the Fulbright Senior Scholar Program (1991), and the Social Science Research Council (1998). He has served the profession in various capacities, such as president of the Society for Iranian Studies (2002–3), chairman of the Nominating Committee of the Society for Iranian Studies (1997–98), and a member of numerous nominating and program committees of the Middle East Studies Association (MESA) and the Biennial Conference of Iranian Studies. He is the editor of two book series for the State University of New York Press and for Routledge Publishers and has participated as section editor and senior consulting editor in the multivolume *Oxford Encyclopedia of the Modern Islamic World* (1995) and the forthcoming *Oxford Encyclopedia of Islam.*

Abbas Amanat is professor of history at Yale University. Among his publications are *Resurrection and Renewal: The Making of the Babi Movement in Iran, 1844–1850* (Ithaca, NY: Cornell University Press, 1989); *Pivot of the Universe: Nasir al-Din Shah Qajar and the Iranian Monarchy, 1831–1896* (Berkeley: University of California Press, 1997); "The Resurgence of Apocalyptic in Modern

Islam," in *The Encyclopedia of Apocalypticism* (New York: Continuum, 1999); and "Empowered Through Violence: The Reinventing of Islamic Extremism," in *The Age of Terror*, ed. Strobe Talbott and Nayan Chanda (New York: Basic Books, 2001). He coedited *Imaging the End: Visions of Apocalypse from the Ancient Middle East to Modern America* (London and New York: I. B. Tauris, 2002). His forthcoming book, *In Search of Modern Iran: Authority, Identity, and Nationhood,* will be published by Yale University Press.

Saïd Amir Arjomand (Ph.D., University of Chicago, 1980) is Distinguished Service Professor of Sociology at the State University of New York at Stony Brook. He was the inaugural Crane Fellow and visiting professor of public affairs at the Woodrow Wilson School of Princeton University (2004–5) and is visiting fellow at its Department of Near Eastern Studies (2006–8). He was the editor of *International Sociology* from 1998 to 2003 and is the founder and president (1996–2002, 2006–10) of the Association for the Study of Persianate Societies. He is the author of some eighty articles and book chapters, including "Constitutions and the Struggle for Political Order: A Study in the Modernization of Political Traditions," *European Journal of Sociology* 33 (1992), which won the American Sociological Association's award in 1993 for the Best Essay in Comparative and Historical Sociology. His books include *The Turban for the Crown: The Islamic Revolution in Iran* (New York: Oxford University Press, 1988) and, coedited with Edward A. Tiryakian, *Rethinking Civilizational Analysis* (London: Sage Publications, 2004). Arjomand is a Carnegie Scholar for 2006–8 and currently working on a constitutional history of the Islamic Middle East.

Noah Feldman is the Cecelia Goetz Professor of Law at New York University School of Law. He specializes in constitutional studies, with particular emphasis on the relationship between law and religion, constitutional design, and the history of legal theory. Feldman received his A.B. summa cum laude in Near Eastern Languages and Civilizations from Harvard University and his D.Phil. in Islamic thought from Oxford University. He received his J.D. from Yale Law School. He was a junior fellow of the Society of Fellows at Harvard University. Feldman is the author of *Divided by God: America's Church-State Problem and What We Should Do About It* (New York: Farrar, Straus & Giroux, 2005); *What We Owe Iraq: War and the Ethics of Nation Building* (Princeton: Princeton University Press, 2004); and *After Jihad: America and the Struggle for Islamic Democracy* (New York: Farrar, Straus & Giroux, 2003). He is a contributing writer for the *New York Times Magazine* and an adjunct senior fellow at the Council on Foreign Relations.

Frank Griffel is associate professor of Islamic studies at Yale University. He studied philosophy, Arabic literature, and Islamic studies at Göttingen and Damascus universities and at the Free University of Berlin. He received his Ph.D. in 1999 in Berlin. After working as a research fellow at the Orient Institute of the Deutsche Morgenländische Gesellschaft in Beirut (Lebanon), he came to Yale in 2000. In 2003–4 he was Andrew Mellon Fellow at the Institute for Advanced Study in Princeton. He has published in the fields of Islamic law, Muslim theology, and Muslim intellectual history. In his book *Apostasie und Toleranz im Islam* [Apostasy and Tolerance in Islam] (Leiden: Brill, 2000) he analyzes the development of the judgment of apostasy up to the twelfth century. More recent publications include articles on al-Ghazālī (d. 1111), Ibn Tūmart (d. 1130), Fakhr al-Dīn al-Rāzī (d. 1210), and other Muslim thinkers in the *Journal of Islamic Studies*, the *Journal of the American Oriental Society*, *Arabic Sciences and Philosophy*, and a number of collective volumes. Griffel is a Carnegie Scholar for 2007–9. His forthcoming book, *The Philosophical Theology of al-Ghazālī: An Introduction to the Study of His Life and Thought*, will be published by Oxford University Press.

David L. Johnston worked as a pastor and a teacher in Algeria, Egypt, and the Palestinian West Bank between 1978 and 1996. He subsequently completed a Ph.D. in Islamic studies at Fuller Theological Seminary in Pasadena, California, and spent five years as a postdoctoral fellow, part-time lecturer, and research associate at the Religious Studies Department of Yale University. Johnston is currently a visiting scholar at the Department of Near Eastern Languages and Civilizations of the University of Pennsylvania. His articles have appeared in *Islamic Law and Society*, *Islamochristiana*, and *Maghreb Review*. He contributed to *Encyclopaedia of the Qur'an* and *Encyclopedia of Islam and the Muslim World*. His book *Earth, Empire and Sacred Text: Muslims and Christians as Trustees of Creation* will be published in 2007 by Equinox in London.

Gudrun Krämer is professor of Islamic studies at the Free University of Berlin and a member of the Berlin-Brandenburg Academy of Sciences. She studied history, political science, English literature, and Islamic studies at Heidelberg, Bonn, and Sussex universities and obtained a Ph.D. in Islamic studies from

Hamburg University in 1982. In 1982–94 she was senior research fellow at the Stiftung Wissenschaft und Politik at Ebenhausen, Germany. She was appointed professor of Islamic studies at Bonn University in 1994 and moved to the Free University of Berlin in 1996. She has been a visiting scholar at the Centre d'Études et de Documentation Économique, Juridique et Sociale (CEDEJ) in Cairo; the School of Advanced International Studies of Johns Hopkins University, Bologna Center; the Institut d'Études Politiques (Sciences Po) and the École des Hautes Etudes en Sciences Sociales, both in Paris; the Islamic University in Jakarta, Indonesia; and the Max Weber Kolleg in Erfurt, Germany. She is a member of the academic boards of the Goethe Institut, the German Ministry of Economic Cooperation, and the French Ministère d'Affaires Étrangères, Pole Proche-Orient. She has published extensively on the modern history of the Arab world, Islamist movements, and Islamic political thought and is one of the executive editors of the forthcoming third edition of *The Encyclopaedia of Islam*.

Roy P. Mottahedeh is the Gurney Professor of History at Harvard University. He was educated at Harvard (A.B., 1960; Ph.D., 1970) and at Cambridge University (B.A., 1962) and has received numerous academic awards, including a Guggenheim Fellowship and a MacArthur Prize Fellowship. His major work is on the premodern social and intellectual history of the Islamic Middle East. His publications include *Loyalty and Leadership in an Early Islamic Society* (Princeton: Princeton University Press, 1980), *The Mantle of the Prophet: Religion and Politics in Iran* (New York: Simon and Schuster, 1985), and his translation of Muḥammad Bāqir al-Ṣadr, *Lessons in Islamic Jurisprudence* (Oxford: Oneworld, 2003). He is presently working on a history of the Iraqi Shiite *ʿulamāʾ* in the period 1958–2003.

Felicitas Opwis is assistant professor of Arabic and Islamic studies at Georgetown University in Washington, D.C. Earlier she worked as an adjunct professor of religion at Wake Forest University and a visiting lecturer on Islamic law at Yale School of Law. She graduated with an M.A. in Islamic studies from the University of Freiburg, Germany, and received her Ph.D. in Arabic and Islamic studies in 2001 from Yale University. Her main research interests are the development of legal theory in its historical context and the relationship between religious law and political authority. Recent publications include an article on the development of the concept of *maṣlaḥa* in the classical and contemporary period in *Islamic Law and Society* and a chapter on Islamic law in the modern world in the collective volume *An Islamic Reformation?* edited by M. Browers and C. Kurzman (Lanham, MD: Lexington Books, 2004).

Anna Würth holds a Ph.D. in Islamic studies from the Free University of Berlin. She taught at the University of Richmond (Virginia) and at the Free University of Berlin. She is the author of *Aš-Šarīʿa fī Bāāb al-Yaman: Recht, Richter und Rechtspraxis an der familienrechtlichen Kammer des Gerichts Süd-Sanaa, (Republik Jemen), 1983–1995* [Judges, the Law, and the Application of Law in the Personal Status Division of the South-Sanaa Court, 1985–1993] (Berlin: Duncker & Humblot, 2000), for which she did fieldwork in Yemen. Her research focuses on contemporary applications of Islamic law in Yemen and Egypt. Currently Würth is a researcher at the German Institute of Human Rights in Berlin, covering human rights in development cooperation. Recent publications include, together with Frauke Seidensticker, *Indices, Benchmarks, and Indicators: Planning and Evaluating Human Rights Dialogues* (Berlin: Deutsches Institut für Menschenrechte, 2005); and the forthcoming "Investigating and Prosecuting Police Abuse in Egypt," in the journal *Égypte/Monde Arabe* of the Centre d'Etudes et de Documentation Economique, Juridique et Sociale in Cairo.

INDEX